"I have no doubt that this companion is an unprecedented contribution to comprehending the 'business' of orchestra management, an essential foundation for supporting these remarkable institutions in navigating the present and preparing for the future."

Christopher Brenner, *University of Music &*
Conservatorio della Svizzera italiana, Switzerland

Orchestra Management in Practice

Introducing the business models, organisational structures, and fundamentals of orchestras, this book takes readers on a journey through the evolution of orchestra management.

The author explores the dynamics between artistic excellence and financial sustainability. Key aspects of orchestra management are examined in detail, including artistic programming, strategic planning, financial and compliance/legal matters, audience development, resilience and adaptability, governance and board relations, diversity and inclusion, partnerships, and the role of technology and innovation.

With actionable resources, such as checklists, templates, and frameworks, for current and future orchestra leaders and managers, this comprehensive guide empowers readers in education and practice to navigate the complexities of orchestra management confidently and effectively.

Salvino A. Salvaggio, PhD, is a Consultant to the Qatar Foundation. Among other positions, he has previously served as Executive Director (Chief of Staff) of the VP office for Research Development and Innovation at Qatar Foundation, and as an Expert Consultant at McKinsey & Co. In 2007, he was appointed Knight Commander by the President of the Italian Republic.

Discovering the Creative Industries

Series Editor: Ruth Rentschler

The creative and cultural industries account for a significant share of the global economy. Gaining and maintaining employment and work in this sector is a challenge and chances of success are enhanced by ongoing professional development.

This series provides a range of relatively short, student-centred books which blend industry and educational expertise with cultural sector practice. Books in the series provide applied introductions to the core elements of the creative industries. In sum, the series provides essential reading for those studying to enter the creative industries as well as those seeking to enhance their career via executive education.

Fundraising for the Creative and Cultural Industries
Leading Effective Fundraising Strategies
Michelle Wright, Ben Walmsley and Emilee Simmons

Managing the Arts and Culture
Cultivating a Practice
Edited by Constance DeVereaux

Managing Organizations in the Creative Economy
Organizational Behaviour for the Cultural Sector
Paul Saintilan and David Schreiber

Transformational Innovation in the Creative and Cultural Industries
Alison Rieple, Robert DeFillippi and David Schreiber

The Art Business
Art World, Art Market
Jeffrey Taylor

Funding the Arts
Politics, Economics and Their Interplay in Public Policy
Andrew Pinnock

Orchestra Management in Practice
Salvino A. Salvaggio

For more information about this series, please visit: www.routledge.com/ Discovering-the-Creative-Industries/book-series/DCI.

Orchestra Management in Practice

Salvino A. Salvaggio

Routledge
Taylor & Francis Group

LONDON AND NEW YORK

Designed cover image: © idil toffolo / Getty Images

First published 2024
by Routledge
4 Park Square, Milton Park, Abingdon, Oxon OX14 4RN

and by Routledge
605 Third Avenue, New York, NY 10158

Routledge is an imprint of the Taylor & Francis Group, an informa business

British Library Cataloguing-in-Publication Data
A catalogue record for this book is available from the British Library

Library of Congress Cataloging-in-Publication Data
Names: Salvaggio, Salvino A., 1963- author.
Title: Orchestra management in practice / Salvino A. Salvaggio.
Description: [1.] | Abingdon, Oxon ; New York : Routledge, 2024. | Series:
   Discovering the creative industries | Includes bibliographical references
   and index.
Identifiers: LCCN 2023035872 (print) | LCCN 2023035873 (ebook) |
   ISBN 9781032629612 (hardback) | ISBN 9781032626017 (paperback) |
   ISBN 9781032629636 (ebook)
Subjects: LCSH: Orchestra--Management.
Classification: LCC ML3790 .S2347 2024 (print) | LCC ML3790 (ebook) |
   DDC 784.2068/1--dc23/eng/20230809
LC record available at https://lccn.loc.gov/2023035872
LC ebook record available at https://lccn.loc.gov/2023035873

ISBN: 978-1-032-62961-2 (hbk)
ISBN: 978-1-032-62601-7 (pbk)
ISBN: 978-1-032-62963-6 (ebk)

DOI: 10.4324/9781032629636

Typeset in Berling
by Apex CoVantage, LLC

To Julia and Sami, for
providing the soundtrack of
my life.

Contents

Figures

Case Studies

Boxes

Keywords

Orchestra management
Management of arts and culture institutions
Classical music
Orchestra business models
Technology innovation
Audience development
Community engagement
Globalisation

Statements

A. CONFLICT OF INTEREST

The author confirms that he has no financial or non-financial interests or affiliations with any orchestra, opera, or arts and culture institution related to the subject matter of this book.

B. ARTIFICIAL INTELLIGENCE (AI)

The author declares that, not being a native English speaker, he relied on Large Language Models (LLMs) as editing tools ("copywriter companions") throughout the writing process of this whole book. These models were utilised to (i) identify and correct grammatical, syntax, and spelling errors; (ii) rephrase sentences, paragraphs, or sections of the draft that lacked fluency in order to ensure linguistic consistency and readability; (iii) translate paragraphs or sections that the author originally wrote in his mother tongues; (iv) improve the wording of the case studies; and (v) standardise the format of key learnings tables and end-of-chapter questions.[1] Also, from an academic standpoint, LLMs were utilised to peer-review the draft, identify gaps and weaknesses, and suggest improvements.

The author asserts that no content within this book has been created or generated by an LLM.

To ensure that the LLMs did not introduce plagiarised content when rephrasing text, correcting grammatical mistakes and linguistic inconsistencies, the manuscript has been repeatedly submitted to different plagiarism checkers that did not identify similarities with published documents.

The LLMs used for editing, copywriting, rephrasing, translating, and peer-reviewing the manuscript are GPT-3.5 and GPT-4 (via OpenAI ChatGPT Plus) and PaLM-2 (via Google Bard). Specific editing apps used are Hyper-WriteAI and Paperpal.

C. NON-PROMOTIONAL CONTENT

The mention of brands, programs, projects, initiatives, or legal entities, whether for-profit or not-for-profit, including orchestras, education institutions, community programs, or digital platforms, is solely for scholarly reference and not for business or marketing purposes. The information about these organisations is obtained from publicly available materials. Although efforts have been made to ensure accuracy, discrepancies may arise due to the lack of direct access to resources such as financial records or internal documents.

D. DISCLAIMER

This book reflects the author's personal views and positions and does not commit his present or past employers.

NOTE

1 As AI text classifiers are poorly capable of identifying a difference between text generated by AI and text corrected or rephrased by AI, the risk of misclassification is likely higher.

Foreword

Orchestras are indeed peculiar – if not paradoxical – entities, as they are *collective* bodies comprising highly trained musicians, each with *soloistic* education and, at times, ambitions as well. They are often perceived, sometimes mistakenly yet occasionally accurately, by those less familiar with the field as being steered by conductors whose roles appear to oscillate between those of an atavistic tribal leader and a 21st-century dictator. In order to create a compelling and cohesive performance on stage, all members must relinquish a portion of their egos. Laden with traditions and antiquated customs – as Gustav Mahler once criticised – modern orchestras are simultaneously resistant to change and aware of the need to evolve with their times.

Managing such a highly complex organism, while taking into account "secular" factors such as finance, policy, building maintenance, and social changes, may seem like an insurmountable task. The challenges faced by orchestras today are manifold, as the world evolves rapidly and people's behaviour follows suit. Disruptions of varying magnitudes occur at increasingly shorter intervals. The Covid-19 pandemic, for instance, posed a significant challenge for every manager, while the proliferation of social media and smartphones has drastically altered human habits of music consumption, leisure time, and beyond, impacting any and every aspect of our life.

Let's be clear: this is not new, for disruptions have always been part of the history of orchestras and the cultural industry in general. Almost a century ago, around 1930, the world economic crisis diminished funding and heightened competition, even among economic refugees and amateurs, resulting in large-scale salary dumping. The transition from silent to sound films led to the quite immediate decline of highly paid cinema orchestras, and the rise of "modern music" or jazz profoundly impacted consumption habits, thereby affecting the demand for classically trained musicians. But from tough times new opportunities emerged, such as the establishment of radio stations and radio orchestras. Over the past 25 years, the music industry has evolved at an extraordinary pace, witnessing changes almost daily. The advent of Napster, Spotify, medici, and a multitude of other streaming platforms blindsided the music industry, profoundly impacting classical music as well. Concurrently, whilst the number of orchestras, particularly those resident in radio stations, has been on the decline, we have observed a growth in specialised ensembles focusing on ancient or contemporary repertoire. Operational methods have also changed, with a shift towards weaker security and greater flexibility in work arrangements, significantly affecting the status of freelancers. The Covid-19 pandemic, a more recent occurrence, has had a considerable impact on musical activities as well, spanning performance and pedagogy. However, it still is too early to understand precisely whether the pandemic represents a true disruption and whether the changes it has triggered will last. Nevertheless, it is certain that new, authentic disruptions will emerge, again and again, necessitating that musicians adapt, as they have always done.

Changes are an integral part of the evolution of orchestras. While some disruptions can be forestalled, others are inevitable. Some changes are gradual, while others are swift and carry significant and perhaps abrupt consequences. Certain disruptions are systemic, such as the concern that symphonic concert audiences are ageing, while others affect specific aspects of performance only, such as the current usage of augmented reality technologies.

In the setting of the *University of Music* that I have the honour to lead, this book can clearly serve as an invaluable resource. For students, it lays a robust and quite comprehensive foundation in orchestra management, offering insights into the often overlooked aspects that occur behind the scenes, beyond the artistic performance. The book actually provides students with a thorough understanding of the challenges and complexities of running an orchestra, preparing them to contribute effectively to the field upon graduation. Teaching faculty may also benefit from this comprehensive work, as it presents a different perspective on music, emphasising that the administration of an orchestra is no less important than its artistic scope and values. By keeping the concepts and strategies presented in this book in the back of their mind, educators can better prepare their students to traverse the dynamic landscape of orchestras and adapt to the changing demands of the profession.

Salvino A. Salvaggio's *Orchestra Management in Practice* offers a deep dive into the business models, organisational structure, key roles, functions, challenges, and the impact of technology. From exploring the long and fluctuating history of orchestra management to the ideal profile of an executive director, the volume provides its readers (both students and professionals) a balanced approach, prioritising management abilities without compromising artistic vision. Experience shows that a skilled manager who is able to establish and nurture a harmonious and collaborative environment can better navigate the challenges of a rapidly changing world and secure – or, at least, facilitate – their organisation's continued growth and success.

The inclusion of key resources such as detailed checklists, templates, and frameworks, as well as a compilation of case studies and pertinent bibliography references, will help executive directors and managers of the future, as well as any student eager to develop their professional career in an arts and culture institution, to gain a deeper and clearer understanding of best practices, industry standards, and insightful research. These tools show students and professionals how to empower managers to face the complexities of management confidently and effectively, ensuring a higher likelihood of long-term success for their organisations.

Salvino A. Salvaggio's book may not offer a panacea, but it does provide a systematic description (and analysis) of the components and issues of management and the tools available for addressing them. Understanding the field and the resource at hand enables students and managers to better confront current realities and anticipate future developments. Ideally, this knowledge will also uncover new opportunities and possibilities. In this regard, I have no doubt that this companion is an unprecedented contribution to comprehending the "business" of orchestra management, an essential foundation for supporting these remarkable institutions in navigating the present and preparing for the future.

Christopher Brenner
General Director
University of Music & Conservatorio della Svizzera italiana
Switzerland

Author's Preface

In the early 2000s, as a consultant at McKinsey & Co, I found myself at the crossroads of two seemingly disparate worlds: the rapidly evolving domain of new digital technologies and the time-honoured tradition of orchestra management. While my primary professional focus in McKinsey centred on the impact of emerging technologies on large organisations, I was also serendipitously introduced to the field of orchestra management just as the internet began to make its presence heavily felt in the business world. With their rich cultural heritage and strong global presence, European orchestras were intrigued by the potential of the then-booming information and communication technologies. They sought ways to incorporate these technologies into their strategies, ensuring they could survive and compete in an increasingly digital environment. In addition to my more conventional business consulting projects in large telecoms, banks, high-tech companies, media, and the public sector, McKinsey also gave me the opportunity to contribute to consulting engagements focused on the comprehensive strategic restructuring of orchestras throughout Europe. In these endeavours, the business and strategic consulting skills acquired within the industry were tailored to the distinctive not-for-profit ecosystem of arts and culture, enabling orchestras to better adapt to the new management challenges arising from the rapidly transforming world of the late 1990s and early 2000s.

At that time, I also had the privilege of teaching one of the first courses on the "anthropology of the digital society" at the ICHEC ISC Saint Louis business school in Brussels (Belgium). Alongside my master's students – and, in particular, with the remarkable dedication, commitment, and support of Mr. Luc Calis, who owned a unique network of underground music record shops in Brussels, and Ms. Alexandra Fernandez, who later became a well-known senior manager in the audio and video streaming industry – we explored the ways digital technologies were starting to disrupt the music industry. Our investigations shed light on the necessity for all players of the live music spectrum (from rock, electro, or underground bands to chamber music ensembles, symphony orchestras, and operas) to integrate the then-novel tools of websites, ecommerce, blogs, streaming etc. into their development strategies, thereby setting the stage for my ongoing passion for orchestra management. This course eventually led to the publication of a book, now out of print, in two volumes titled *Anthropologie de la société digitale*, published by ICHEC ISC Saint Louis (Salvaggio and Bauwens 2000).[1]

My passion for music was not unfounded, as my father, who worked as a self-employed bespoke shoemaker, also had a deep love for music. He played the trumpet, sang tenor, and even dabbled in conducting local ensembles as an amateur. I vividly recall an anecdote where my parents and some of their close friends took me – aged eight or so – to an opera performance. My father and his friend were so dissatisfied with and outraged at the two lead singers that they began shouting in the middle of the performance, taking to the stage themselves to sing the aria instead of the professional opera singers. While the audience seemed confused by the uproar (to say the least), the musicians and, even more surprisingly, the conductor applauded my father and his friend for their improvised performance. My mum, however, was so embarrassed by the "incident" that she refused to speak to my dad for a week . . . and for years after that, my father had to promise he would behave himself before taking her to a concert!

During my childhood and into my early teenage years, I used to spend a lot of time with my uncle, who was a classical music enthusiast and an absolute geek for high-fidelity sound. He would listen to collector vinyl records of the greatest orchestras and operas on his unique valve amplifiers and speakers that he handmade out of vintage electronic parts and precious wood to preserve the warmth of the original sound that he was perhaps the only one able to hear. I was never sure if his neighbours appreciated the loud outcome of his electronic and DIY skills, but it was clear that his passion for music and technology had a profound impact on me as well.

Throughout the years, my interest in the field only grew stronger. After leaving McKinsey, my professional journey took me to other shores, to Ooredoo, a large international telecom company, where I managed digital strategies, data business plans, and implementation roadmaps. I subsequently joined Qatar Foundation, one of the world's largest private foundations, where I covered several roles in their remarkable Science & Technology Park and ultimately served as executive director of the VP office for research, development, and innovation. Eventually, I found myself in the dynamic nexus of applied research commercialisation, where I work on yet another advanced tech initiative in the exciting field of climate tech business acceleration. Over all these years, I have raised a violinist daughter and a drummer-biker son, who constantly kept the house filled with any genre of chord progressions and beats, from Baroque to rap, while I was trying to peacefully listen to Corelli, 'Kingfish' Ingram or Chrissie Hynde.

Over all these years, I have also used my evenings, weekends, and vacation time to nurture my passion for music and management and how they coalesce in the administration of an orchestra, observing management practices around the globe and, above all, talking to dozens of managers, conductors, musicians, patrons, scholars, and enthusiasts. More precisely, the genesis of this book dates back to approximately 15 years ago, around 2005–2007, when the first seeds of thought were sown in my mind. It was a time when my fascination for the confluence of music and management began to take a more concrete shape. A couple of years later, I found myself delving deeper into this exciting inter-section, dedicating my time and energy to collecting information, immersing myself in relevant readings, and initiating the foundational research work. Far from being a sporadic endeavour, it was a consistent and serious commitment that spanned over years. Each piece of information, each conversation, each observation, and each insight served as data points in a meticulous research project. Over the years, these elements fused into the detailed analysis that forms the basis of this book.

As an observer, I have witnessed first-hand how the confluence of man-agement and music, coupled with the transformative power of digital tech-nologies in the last two decades, has reshaped the landscape of orchestra management. This experience has provided me with a unique vantage point, enabling me to examine the intricate challenges faced by managers, as well as the opportunities that lie ahead in our global fast-paced and ever-changing world. My original background in sociology and anthropology has further enriched this perspective, providing me with the tools to observe the life of an orchestra and the managers' decisions through a different lens, focusing on actual practice rather than relying solely on formal interviews or surveys to gather individual perceptions of the matter.

While I may not have directly occupied the role of an orchestra manager, my consulting background in management and orchestra management, blended with a keen interest in music and music industry in a high-tech environment, have equipped me with the insight and expertise required to author a book on this fascinating subject. And with my extensive experience in the private sec-tor, rather than academic research, I approach analysis and decision-making in a practical and actionable manner, placing equal importance on tangible and pragmatic outcomes alongside analytical abstraction and theories. My journey across various sectors and industries has allowed me to witness the transformative effects of digital technologies on the music industry at large and, more specifically, on the world of orchestras and operas. Also, as I have been living in the Arabic-Persian Gulf for the last two decades, since 2003, I had the chance to notice that the ever-growing number of orchestras in countries without a long tradition of Western classical music is slowly but clearly shifting the ecosystem's centre of mass, presenting a new set of challenges and opportunities. It, therefore, is more crucial than ever before to provide a 360-degree, holistic approach to orchestra management that can assist students and professionals in this field *globally*.

During a recent weekend in early 2023, while I was having breakfast in an international patisserie, I bumped into a small delegation of orchestra managers (middle and senior management) from Europe, who were visiting the Gulf region for business meetings. They kindly invited me to share a coffee, and we had a long and informal chat about new, post-Covid trends in artistic planning. To my surprise, as their trip came to an end, they all concluded with a hint of self-importance – and an undeniable dose of prejudice – that the Gulf is not relevant in the classical music industry. I couldn't help but respond with a touch of sarcasm, reminding them that just 25 years ago, reputable business analysts stated without a shadow of a doubt that the Gulf would be forever irrelevant in the football industry.[2] Yet, in just 20 years, the Gulf countries have become significantly involved and actively participate in the management of the very best European and UK football clubs (and looking at further expanding their portfolios). And Qatar has organised one of the most glorious and festive FIFA World Cups in modern history.[3] I then told the visiting managers that they are free to consider the Gulf irrelevant in the classical music industry . . . until the day the new ensembles in Malaysia, China, India, Mongolia, the Middle East, Indonesia, Latin America, and Africa offer them more job opportunities, perhaps better packages, and a greater artistic latitude than struggling Western orchestras and festivals can. They all stopped laughing in a fraction of a second! In other words, it is challenging to argue for the marginal relevance of Gulf countries in the classical music industry when considering, for instance, that the Qatar Philharmonic Orchestra has attracted highly skilled professional musicians from 30 different countries.

I am convinced that the Western classical music industry (and related scholarly research) is not yet fully aware that the traditional (i.e., Western) approach to managing challenges and opportunities, resource constraints and audience expectations, artistic planning and cultural diversity may not remain dominant in management forever. A striking example is undoubtedly the far greater propensity to test new and still experimental technologies in recently formed orchestras – with some exceptions – compared to the desire to preserve intact the tradition demonstrated by many long-established orchestras.

By acknowledging and addressing these emerging trends, we can ensure that the management strategies and practices presented in this manual are applicable and valuable to a wide range of cultural contexts and organisational environments.

As the author of this companion, my objective is to bring my unique perspective on the world of orchestra management. Through a combination of research, literature review, personal experiences, and a passion for the subject, I aim to illuminate how tradition and innovation intersect in classical music management. It is my sincere hope that readers will find value in these pages as they explore the complexities of management and discover the intricate dance of artistry, multidimensional business, and technology.

To borrow the words of the illustrious Greek historian and biographer Plutarch, "the mind is not a vessel to be filled, but a fire to be kindled." As we embark on this exploration together, let us ignite the flames of curiosity and examine the captivating ecosystem of management, where the past, present, and future coalesce (not always harmoniously, though).

So, join me as we journey through the complex land of orchestra management, exploring its many nuances and challenges along the way. I invite you to discover the fascinating intersection of arts and business, tradition, and innovation, and to gain new insights into the dynamic world of classical music.

NOTES

1 Throughout this book, bibliographical details reporting "l. x" refer to the location of the quote in the Kindle edition.
2 Soccer, for US readers.
3 Similarly, on 6 June 2023, news broke that Saudi Arabia has essentially taken control over the global professional golf industry through the multi-billion-dollar merger of the PGA and DP World Tours and LIV Golf, orchestrated by the Saudi Public Investment Fund.

Acknowledgements

Although I deeply appreciate their preference for discretion, I would like to express my heartfelt gratitude to all those – musicians, managers, students, researchers, experts, patrons, sponsors, aficionados, concertgoers, and many more – who have supported me throughout the past 15 years in bringing this book to fruition. It is thanks to their support that I have been able to attend countless classical concerts around the globe, engage in fecund discussions (sometimes, arguments), and continually refine my ideas. Their contribution has been instrumental to the realisation of this project. Even without mentioning names, I am confident that they will recognise themselves in this humble tribute.

Executive Summary

In this book, which leans more towards a practical manual than a research report, we explore the various dimensions of orchestra management,[1] with a focus on the business models, organisation's structure, key roles, functions and challenges, contemporary issues, and the impact of technology. The volume is divided into ten chapters, each offering a deep dive into the subject matter.

1. INTRODUCTION

This section introduces readers to the author's personal perspective on the world of orchestra management, lending it a distinct touch that sets it apart from the rest of the book. Through an illuminating overview, this introductory section aims to facilitate readers' exploration of the intricate dynamics inherent in management, particularly emphasising the interplay between tradition and innovation within the realm of classical music management. The introduction outlines the main themes, encompassing the foundational principles of management, the role of technological innovation, and the desired profile of a manager. By inviting readers to kindle their curiosity, the author encourages them to embark on an enlightening journey through the captivating landscape of management. The introduction also provides a concise summary of the anticipated insights and knowledge that readers can expect to gain from the book, while also identifying the specific target readership that will find it particularly valuable.

2. A CONCISE HISTORY OF ORCHESTRA MANAGEMENT

Chapter 2 delves into the evolution of orchestra management over time. The chapter covers the early years of court orchestras in Europe during the pre-Baroque and Baroque eras, the rise of public concerts and the subscription model in the 18th century, and the emergence of professional orchestras and managers in the 19th century. The chapter also examines the impact of recording technology and government support in the 20th century, as well as the growing emphasis on artistic partnerships. The chapter provides readers with a clear understanding of how orchestras transformed from ensembles playing for European nobility to professional institutions with managers who oversee daily operations and financial affairs. The chapter highlights the importance of adapting to the times and changing technologies to maintain the viability of the orchestra. Readers will gain insight into how the past has shaped the present, and how history informs the challenges faced in managing orchestras today.

3. A TYPICAL ORCHESTRA ORGANISATION AND FUNCTIONS

Chapter 3 examines a typical orchestra organisation, including their management and artistic side. The chapter also explores the role of volunteers in the organisation. It offers an in-depth overview of the importance of understanding the management focus areas, namely artistic, marketing, development, financial, and administrative management. The chapter details the responsibilities of each department and provides readers with a clear understanding of the importance of cooperation and communication among key players to ensure smooth operations and a harmonious environment. It also underlines the significance of a board and staff within the organisation and their functions. The chapter is crucial for professionals or students looking to pursue a career in orchestra management as it covers essential information required to run an organisation effectively.

4. THE BUSINESS MODELS OF CLASSICAL ORCHESTRAS

Chapter 4 explores the various financial models adopted over time, from aristocratic patronage to corporate sponsorships. The chapter provides readers with an overview of the economic, social, and technological factors that have influenced the evolution of business models over time, as well as the challenges they face in adapting to changing audience preferences and demographics. The chapter also highlights the importance of balancing financial sustainability with artistic excellence, with a focus on cost optimisation and finding new revenue sources. Through case studies, readers gain a deeper understanding of the complexities of managing finances. The chapter also underscores the significance of innovation and adaptation in ensuring the sustainability of orchestras in the modern era. Overall, Chapter 4 is a crucial read for anyone interested in the intersection of economics and the arts, and the changing landscape of orchestra management.

5. THE FUNDAMENTALS OF ORCHESTRA MANAGEMENT

Chapter 5 is a core section of this book and offers a broad overview of the essential elements of managing effectively. It examines the various roles involved, from the CEO to the musicians, and highlights the importance of effective communication and collaboration throughout the organisation. The chapter also delves into issues of artistic excellence and programming, audience engagement, education, and diversity, equity, and inclusion. Additionally, it explores the importance of well-functioning governance structures, decision-making processes, financial management, risk management, fundraising, and philanthropy. The chapter provides readers with a deep understanding of what it takes to manage successfully. It emphasises the need for strong leadership, a commitment to innovation and adaptability, and an unwavering dedication to delivering quality artistic performances that connect with audiences.

6. CONTEMPORARY ISSUES IN ORCHESTRA MANAGEMENT

Chapter 6 examines the challenges that orchestras have faced in recent years, which have added complexity to the fundamentals of orchestra management. These challenges include the need for revenue diversification, increased resilience and adaptability, sustainability, addressing issues of diversity, equity, and inclusion, as well as understanding the impact of technology. The chapter offers readers an in-depth analysis of these challenges and their implications for the future of classical music management. It provides practical solutions for the innovative revenue streams available for orchestras to diversify their income sources and maintain long-term sustainability, including renegotiating public funding, increasing fundraising efforts, and optimising financial positions. The chapter also emphasises the importance of diversity, equity, and inclusion in creating a vibrant and sustainable community that reflects the diverse audiences it serves. It examines the significance of crisis management and contingency planning in dealing with unexpected challenges. It also offers an insightful perspective on contemporary issues critical for any student or manager seeking to navigate the changing landscape of the classical music industry.

7. TECH INNOVATION IN MODERN ORCHESTRA MANAGEMENT

Chapter 7 delves into the role of technology innovation in classical music management. The chapter discusses the importance of technology and social media for marketing, audience engagement, and public relations. In addition, it touches on the potential impact of artificial intelligence, augmented reality, and virtual reality technologies on the classical music industry, while considering the artistic implications of these technologies. The chapter emphasises the importance of embracing innovation and experimentation with new approaches to programming, marketing, audience engagement, inclusion, diversity, and more. Technology plays a crucial role in the evolution of the classical music industry and management, and orchestras must be willing to adapt, experiment, and take risks to stay relevant and competitive. The chapter also highlights the importance of effective leadership in managing the intersection of technology and classical music, and the need for managers to be open to new ideas and collaborations with other organisations to succeed in this domain.

8. THE IDEAL PROFILE OF THE CEO

Chapter 8 discusses the ideal profile of an orchestra CEO. The chapter explores the advantages and disadvantages of having a former musician or a skilled business manager as a CEO. It considers factors such as credibility with musicians and the public, adaptability, artistic understanding, and strong organisational and strategic skills. The chapter provides a comprehensive analysis of each profile, weighing their pros and cons, and offers insights into what makes an ideal top manager. It suggests that successful CEOs have a multifaceted approach with a strong emphasis on management skills and an appreciation for the creative process. They foster a collaborative environment that better navigates the challenges of a rapidly changing world and ensures their organisation's continued growth and success. The chapter highlights the importance of a balanced approach to orchestra management, prioritising management abilities without compromising artistic vision.

9. CONCLUSION

The final chapter emphasises the critical role of orchestra management as a dynamic and complex ecosystem. It underscores the importance of understanding the evolution of the management model in the context of the many challenges faced in today's world, such as competition for audiences, dwindling funding sources, technology disruption, and shifting demographics. The conclusion draws attention to the need to embrace innovations and change, and adopt a multifaceted approach to balance concerns of the artistic process and business operations. A strong leadership, collaboration, audience engagement, and diversity, equity, and inclusion are key ingredients in achieving organisational goals and success. The conclusion invites readers to reflect on the many nuances and complexities of the orchestral landscape and showcases the impact of management excellence in shaping and driving the art form into the future. It serves as an authoritative reference point for individuals interested in exploring and expanding the field of orchestra management.

10. KEY RESOURCES

Chapter 10 provides useful and actionable resources for students interested in a career in orchestra management as well as for current professionals and managers. It includes checklists and comprehensive templates to guide them through their weekly, monthly, quarterly, and annual tasks and milestones. These resources prioritise effective time management and ensuring that critical tasks are completed on time, while maintaining a strategic focus on the organisation's goals and objectives. The templates are meant to be adapted to each manager's specific background, context, and needs. Overall, this chapter serves as a comprehensive resource that empowers both students and professionals to navigate the challenges of management successfully.

NOTE

1 Although not perfectly precise, in this work we use the terms CEO and executive director interchangeably as synonyms.

BIBLIOGRAPHY

Salvaggio, Salvino, and Michel Bauwens. 2000. *Anthropologie de La Société Digitale*. Bruxelles: ICHEC ISC Saint Louis.

CHAPTER 1

Introduction

The world of large professional orchestras is an unstable blend of artistic vision, intricate operations, tough business decisions, and challenging implementation. The perennial struggle between financial pressures and the pursuit of artistic excellence leads to a crisis of survival that pervades most orchestras. Philosopher Immanuel Kant once remarked that "music is the language of emotions" (Kant 1952); however, almost three centuries later, serial entrepreneur Sean Rad championed the opposite idea that "data beats emotions."[1] What makes the field of orchestra management so complex is that both Kant and Rad would be right if they had to sit in an orchestra's driver seat! In this field of polarising contrasts between artistic emotions and business constraints, the executive director strives to create a cohesive, and possibly harmonious, experience. Behind the scenes, the senior managers serve as the linchpins, ensuring that all these elements come together to create a memorable experience for audiences, a transparent and effective framework for shareholders and donors, an affirmative and enthusiastic image for local and national authorities, a positive impact for stakeholders overall, and a fair and enjoyable workplace for all the staff and musicians. With a role as unique as their musical counterparts, CEOs and managers navigate the challenges of the artistic, business, and community aspects of classical music. In this broad exploration, we will delve into the world of management, examining the specific challenges CEOs face and how they adapt to the ever-changing – but always demanding – landscape of the classical music industry, particularly in the digital age, including the potential impact of the recent boom in artificial intelligence and its influence on the variety of components that make up the fabric of an orchestra.

Orchestra management has always been a multifaceted and multitasking endeavour involving, amongst others, artistic vision, financial oversight, operations pragmatism, and community interactions, to name a few. Novelist Chester Himes aptly captured this intricate balance when he wrote, "all the

DOI: 10.4324/9781032629636-1

harmony of the world, composed in one orchestra" (Himes 2000). In the last decades, profound changes in the funding models, abrupt modifications of audiences' tastes and behaviours, and the rapid succession of new and sometimes disruptive technologies have further contributed to the evolution of the management models, reshaping them more rapidly than ever before. In light of these developments, this exploration will also look at the core aspects of management from the perspective of the importance of social media platforms in attracting (and retaining) audiences and generating revenue, and the potential impact of artificial intelligence on the classical music landscape. We will examine both the opportunities and risks presented by these changes as we seek to understand how orchestras navigate and flourish in a dynamic environment.

BIS REPETITA

As readers progress through this book – which leans more towards a practical manual than a research report – they may notice that certain concepts and ideas – such as diversification of revenue streams, new technology adoption, audience education, board relations, artistic programming, community engagement, diversity, equity, and inclusion, and many more – are reiterated throughout the various chapters. Besides the usual *bis repetita placent* at the heart of pedagogy, this repetition is intentional, as it serves to underscore the importance of key themes in the fragmented field of orchestra management. Each time these concepts are revisited, they are examined from a slightly different angle, offering additional fresh insights and perspectives on their relevance and application to the orchestral landscape.

This approach of revisiting and re-examining vital themes allows for a more comprehensive understanding of their impact on the different aspects of management, such as history, business models, organisational structures, and day-to-day operations. Exploring these ideas from multiple vantage points encourages readers to consider the interconnections and complexity of the challenges and opportunities that orchestras face in today's cultural and economic environment.

As the book unfolds, readers are invited to reflect on these recurring themes and consider how they intertwine and complement one another, ultimately contributing to a broader understanding of management. This layered approach not only reinforces the importance of these concepts but also enables the reader to appreciate the nuanced and dynamic nature of managing a classical ensemble in the 21st century. We strongly believe that this perspective better equips readers in navigating the practicalities of management, ensuring the long-term success and sustainability of these treasured cultural institutions.

The book also features numerous text boxes, typically brief in nature. These boxes aim to provide examples or further insights that are tangentially related to the main subject or present arguments that, while not directly relevant, offer a different and complementary perspective.

QUALITATIVE AND QUANTITATIVE APPROACHES

Despite our professional and intellectual proximity, as well as familiarity with the world of data analysis, this book intentionally avoids presenting specific quantitative data on financial situations, as the figures vary significantly from one ensemble to another due to a multitude of factors, primarily the public and government subsidy policies, the overall regulatory bodies, the size of the ensemble, and its status (amateur vs professional). What value does it add to state nothing but excessively wide ranges only and say that ticket sales, for example, represent between 10% and 70% of the revenue depending on a variety of factors? It would carry little meaning and ultimately serve to bury, under a deceptive veil of precision, information related to a broad spectrum of observations that are not always compatible with each other. Instead, this book will provide macro models as high-level examples and quantitative averages or trends only, and should be perceived as an exploration of management frameworks and practices that investigates the qualitative aspects of management, offering a more meaningful and insightful understanding of the field. Focusing on the qualitative dimensions of management – without ignoring or underestimating the importance of quantitative management at a single orchestra's level – provides readers with a more context-driven analysis of the issues, challenges, and opportunities faced by orchestras in today's cultural landscape.

While we fully appreciate the need to study or research every single orchestra (or a cluster within the same context) from a quantitative standpoint, by refraining from a sole figure-based analysis of each possible situation, we allow for a more nuanced exploration of the key themes and concepts in management, emphasising the factors (rather than their magnitude) that influence these institutions. In different words, we have chosen to focus on analytical categories and archetypes rather than diving into the specific statistics. We have summarised the quantitative facts using generic models that provide averages instead of drawing myriad specific conclusions based on the financial statements (sometimes) published by organisations.

As we conclude this introductory chapter, it is essential to provide further clarity on the scope and intended audience.

WHAT CAN YOU EXPECT TO LEARN?

While we endeavour to cover the key components of orchestra management, we also want to acknowledge that this book does not claim to provide an exhaustive exploration of any and every aspect in the field. Nevertheless, the core aim of this work is to offer a solid foundation by examining the most critical elements of managing an orchestra effectively.

Orchestra management is a minefield that requires a deep understanding of business models, organisational structures, key roles and functions, the impact of technology, the evolution of society and the world of classical music – all within an industry shaped by passionate emotions, heightened sensitivities, and fervent sentiments that may not easily align with rational thinking, logical analysis, legal constraints, or accounting and tax regulations. In this guide, we explore most of these dimensions of management, providing insights into the challenges facing orchestras today and how they are addressed.

One of the key themes that emerges from the book is the importance of innovation. As the classical music industry continues to evolve in response to changing audience preferences and technological revolutions, orchestras must be willing to adapt and experiment with new approaches to programming, marketing, recruiting, audience engagement, inclusion, diversity, etc. This requires a willingness to take risks, venture into unexplored and often steep paths, experiment with new approaches and technologies, collaborate with other organisations, partner with the community, establish connections with segments of society that have often been overlooked by classical music elites in the past and, above all, accept the possibility of being wrong more than is reasonable in order to stay relevant and competitive. Another important theme that emerges is the need for effective leadership in management. Whether it is the CEO, artistic director, resident conductor, or other key stakeholders within an organisation, inspiring leadership is essential for creating a clear vision for the future and inspiring others to work towards that vision. This requires not only strong communication skills but also a deep understanding of the unique challenges facing orchestras today and how they are overcome through collaboration, innovation, inclusiveness, and strategic planning.

Overall, this work provides an overview of orchestra management that will be useful for anyone interested in pursuing a career in this field or seeking to improve their knowledge of classical music industry trends.

In addition to its broad perspective that scrutinises the fundamentals of management, another unique aspect of this work is its practical and actionable approach to the subject matter. To accomplish this, we have included a wealth of concrete resources such as case studies, review questions, management checklists, templates and frameworks, and comprehensive sets of key performance indicators (KPIs), which will serve as valuable – and, above all, actionable – tools for students, managers, and other stakeholders. Almost a fifth of this volume is taken up by the practical toolbox. These resources have been designed to enable readers to apply the knowledge gained from the book directly to their case analysis, problem-solving sessions, or management roles within the sector, thus bridging the gap between theory and practice.

The focus on providing actionable guidance and practical tools sets this volume apart from other resources on orchestra management.[2] As it offers both theoretical knowledge and tangible frameworks for solutions and processes, the book empowers readers to master the subject matter more effectively and make well-informed decisions that drive positive change within their organisations.

WHO IS THIS BOOK FOR?

To provide an overview, the intended readership prioritises the following categories: (i) students interested in the management of arts and culture institutions; (ii) executive directors, managers, and seasoned professionals confronting the hurly-burly of performing arts; (iii) academics and researchers exploring the intersection of management and arts and culture; (iv) board members, music enthusiasts, and stakeholders; (v) professionals in other arts and culture sectors; (vi) experienced musicians including concertmasters and section leaders; and (vii) any individual passionate about classical music.

Let us now explore each of these categories in greater detail, carefully examining their specific needs, interests, and involvement within the field of management. These categories have been outlined in an order reflecting the perceived priority of their potential interest. Thus, we aim to answer the pivotal question: who is this book for and how can it best serve their needs?

1 **Students** eager to pursue a career in the field of management of arts and culture institutions will find this manual an invaluable resource, as it provides an overview of the crucial components involved in managing an orchestra. The various aspects explored within these pages include business models, organisation, roles, and functions, as well as contemporary challenges and

emerging perspectives, acting as a springboard for further learning and a catalyst for deeper analysis. Each chapter starts with a brief overview of the main insights and ends with a set of engaging questions that aim to expand the perspective, support and inspire deeper discussions, going beyond the dry dissemination of knowledge that a research report may offer.

BOX 1.1 ABOUT REVIEW QUESTIONS

The questions presented at the end of each chapter are not devised as an examination or assessment with defined right or wrong answers. Rather, they serve as catalysts for constructive discussions and encourage the examination of issues or historical periods from an array of perspectives. It would be beneficial for both students and professionals to contemplate these scenarios within the context of varying cultural and geographical backgrounds. Such consideration may prompt the questioning of assumptions that may seem self-evident in one context but not in another.

2 **Orchestra professionals and managers**, with their wealth of hands-on experience and deep-rooted expertise, may initially view this work as superficial or missing the full complexity of their craft. However, it serves a crucial purpose: not merely to replicate the vastness of management, but to act as a prompt, stimulating reflection and deeper understanding of established principles. This volume provides an opportunity to revisit and consolidate knowledge acquired from higher education, professional training, and day-to-day experience. It encourages a refocusing on fundamental aspects of orchestra management, which, at times, are obscured by the urgency and immediacy of an endless flow of issues to deal with and problems to solve in the tumult of daily professional life. This book also places a particular emphasis on young professionals and mid-level managers, recognising them as privileged targets for the insights it offers.

3 Although not a primary target, **academics and business school educators and researchers** can find value in this manual too, as it probes into a domain of the music industry that is not often covered in traditional management and business administration teaching materials. The unique challenges and opportunities presented in management offer fresh perspectives on key concepts, and by incorporating these insights into their curricula, educators

develop critical thinking and innovative approaches amongst students. This book broadens the understanding of an often-overlooked sector and also expands educators' teaching repertoire, preparing future business leaders for diverse industries.

4   In addition to the aforementioned audiences, this work, to a certain extent, is also a resource for **board members, stakeholders, and other individuals involved in the governance and oversight** of orchestras. Individuals who familiarise themselves with the fundamental aspects of management make more informed decisions and contribute more effectively to the strategic direction of the organisation.

5   **Arts administrators and professionals from other sectors of the creative industries** will find this book informative and insightful. Having a greater understanding of the unique challenges and opportunities allows for improved collaboration, support, and learning from these organisations. This, in turn, leads to the development of strong cross-disciplinary alliances and initiatives that enrich the overall cultural landscape.

6   **Senior musicians** also benefit from this companion by gaining an insight into the non-artistic aspects of an orchestra's life. While their primary contribution is undoubtedly artistic, this work introduces concertmasters and section principals to a multitude of other elements that contribute to the overall functioning and success of an orchestra. By broadening their understanding, musicians will be able to better appreciate the complexities of management and the symbiotic relationship between artistic and administrative components. Also, it is worth underlining that in several countries, regulations impose the presence of musicians' representatives into the board and management committees whether they do or do not have some level of expertise in management. For them, this manual could quickly become a significant asset to acquire a more formal understanding in a domain with which they are required to engage. It offers clear and concise insights, suggestions, or recommendations, enhancing their ability to contribute effectively within the board or management committee.

7   Lastly, this practical guide will also appeal to **classical music enthusiasts and patrons** who wish to deepen their understanding of the behind-the-scenes workings of an orchestra. Gaining insights into the complexities of management allows them to better appreciate the efforts required to bring high-quality performances to the stage and support the continued vitality and evolution of the art form.

***

In summary, this companion aims to provide a strong foundation in the key components of orchestra management, with a diverse range of potential readers who could benefit from its contents. The unique focus on actionable guidance and practical resources further increases the value of this book, allowing readers to translate their understanding of the subject into real-world applications. The insights and perspectives shared within these pages will hopefully contribute to the continued growth, innovation, and success of orchestras in the ever-changing landscape of the arts world.[3]

NOTES

1 The exact date and context of Rad's utterance of this particular aphorism have not been meticulously documented in public records.
2 Two notable exceptions are Radbourne and Fraser (1996) and Heyman and Brenner (2019), which also follow a practical and actionable path.
3 A definition of the concept of art lies beyond the scope of this book. Readers wishing to explore this further may look at the pillar contribution given by Luhmann (2000) and Rampley (2009).

BIBLIOGRAPHY

Heyman, Darian Rodriguez, and Laila Brenner. 2019. *Nonprofit Management 101: A Complete and Practical Guide for Leaders and Professionals*. NJ: John Wiley & Sons.
Himes, Chester B. 2000. *The Collected Stories of Chester Himes*, 1st U.S. ed. New York: Thunder's Mouth Press.
Kant, Immanuel. 1952. *The Critique of Judgement*. Oxford: Clarendon Press.
Luhmann, Niklas. 2000. *Art as a Social System*. Meridian, Crossing Aesthetics. Stanford, CA: Stanford University Press.
Radbourne, Jennifer, and Margaret Fraser. 1996. *Arts Management: A Practical Guide*. St. Leonards, N.S.W.: Allen & Unwin.
Rampley, Matthew. 2009. "Art as a Social System: The Sociological Aesthetics of Niklas Luhmann." *Telos* 2009 (148): 111–140. https://doi.org/10.3817/0909148111.

CHAPTER 2

A Concise History of Orchestra Management

Throughout history, the management of orchestras has undergone a deep and extensive transformation, driven by an array of factors. While changing political backgrounds, macro-economic evolutions, new social expectations, and a remodelled wealth distribution may seem more obvious levers, other facets of social evolution are no less important ingredients of the transformation, including cultural and behavioural shifts, technological innovations, demographic mutations, leisure transformations, and shifting artistic landscapes. This chapter examines and highlights the key milestones and developments in the history of orchestra management, offering a broader understanding of how orchestras have adapted to maintain their relevance and impact over time.[1]

WHAT YOU WILL LEARN IN THIS CHAPTER

Section	Key Learning Points
A. The Early Years: Patronage and Court Orchestras	In the pre-Baroque and Baroque eras, court orchestras emerged as small ensembles playing for European nobility, with distinctive styles developing in Italy, Germany, France, and Austria under the patronage system. Prominent patrons such as Ferdinando de' Medici and the Margrave of Brandenburg enabled the flourishing of classical music through their support of composers and musicians.
B. The Rise of Public Concerts and the Subscription Model	The rise of public concerts and the subscription model in the 18th century signalled a shift in management, with orchestras moving from exclusive court settings to more accessible public venues. This change allowed orchestras to connect with wider audiences and helped establish a steady income through subscription concerts pioneered by composers such as Franz Joseph Haydn.

DOI: 10.4324/9781032629636-2

Section	Key Learning Points
C. The Emergence of Professional Orchestras and Managers	The 19th century saw the emergence of professional orchestras and managers, who oversaw daily operations and financial affairs, ensuring the ensemble's artistic success and stability. The role of managers continued to evolve in the 20th century, with organisations such as the *League of American Orchestras* supporting the growing importance of professional management.
D. The Impact of Technology and Recording	The advent of recording technology and radio broadcasting revolutionised the way orchestras reached audiences, enabling them to share their performances beyond concert halls and inaugurate new revenue streams. This required a deep transformation of the managerial approach, forming relationships with recording companies and broadcasters and bonding with listeners in innovative ways.
E. The Role of Government Support and Arts Funding	Government support and arts funding in the 20th century significantly influenced the financial landscape of management, allowing for high artistic standards and a diverse musical ecosystem. However, reliance on public funding presented challenges, as orchestras had to navigate funding complexities and adapt to changing priorities and policies.
F. The Shift Towards Community and Education	The shift towards community and education prompted orchestras to create innovative programmes to connect with diverse and underserved populations. Management played a key role in building partnerships and developing initiatives aimed at a more inclusive and vibrant cultural landscape for future generations.
G. The Emergence of Artistic Partnerships and Collaborations	Artistic alliances and collaborations have revolutionised artistic programming, with ensembles more open to interdisciplinary projects that challenge traditional performance boundaries. Orchestras expand the reservoir of artists and organisations they work with to offer more inclusive experiences, attract broader audiences, and drive the art form's evolution.
H. The Challenges of the 21st Century	Challenges of the 21st century include rapid digital transformation and a growing emphasis on sustainability, diversity, equity, and inclusion. Adapting to online music consumption, championing underrepresented composers, and leveraging social media help orchestras stay relevant and enrich society's cultural fabric.
I. Global Perspectives: A Comparative Analysis	Management practices differ worldwide, reflecting unique cultural, historical, and socioeconomic contexts. As ensembles adapt strategies to suit specific contexts, they address regional challenges, as well as collaboration and innovation, to ensure the ongoing vitality of the global classical music community.

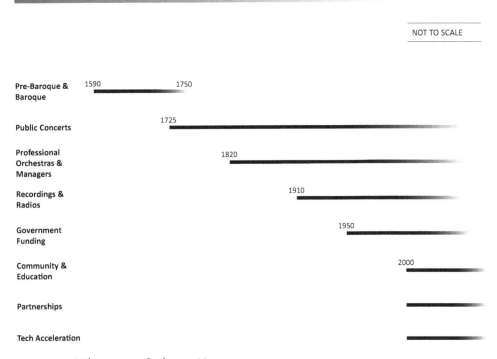

FIGURE 2.1 Milestones in Orchestra Management

A. THE EARLY YEARS: PATRONAGE AND COURT ORCHESTRAS

The birth of orchestras can be traced back to the Baroque period in the 17th century when small ensembles performed in the courts of European nobility (Spitzer and Zaslaw 2004). The tradition of court orchestras was well-established in several European countries, such as Italy, Germany, France, and Austria, each developing its distinct style and repertoire.

One of the earliest examples of a court orchestra was established by Grand Duke Ferdinando de' Medici in Florence, Italy, in the late 16th century. As a passionate fine arts and music lover (Spinelli 2013), he supported the work of numerous composers and musicians, including the Italian composer Claudio Monteverdi, a crucial figure in the transition from the Renaissance to the Baroque period in music (Tomlinson 1987), and Francesca Caccini, a dominant female figure of the musical scene of her time (Cusick 2009; Drinker and Solie 1995).

BOX 2.1 PIONEERING FEMALE ARTISTS

The narratives of Francesca Caccini and Artemisia Gentileschi, two pioneering female artists of the Baroque era, run strikingly parallel. Both women, talented beyond measure, made significant contributions in their respective fields, often overshadowed by the male-dominated narratives of their time.

Francesca Caccini, born in Florence in 1587, was an accomplished composer, singer, lutenist, poet, and music teacher. Her opera, *La liberazione di Ruggiero*, is considered the earliest known work of its kind by a woman. Despite the societal constraints of her era, Caccini pursued her artistic passion with relentless dedication, even serving by 1614 as the most highly paid musician in the Medici court, where she served in various roles including teacher, chamber singer, rehearsal coach, and composer of both chamber and stage music. Her journey was marked by personal challenges (including the death of her first husband) and societal pressures to align with the archetype of woman that was common to her time, but her commitment to music remained resolute.

In parallel, Artemisia Gentileschi, a prominent Italian Baroque painter, navigated a similar path. Known for her skill in capturing the female experience and perspective in a time when women were rarely acknowledged in the arts, Gentileschi emerged as one of the most progressive and expressive painters of her generation. Like Caccini, Gentileschi's personal life was fraught with challenges, including being a victim of sexual assault. Yet, she used these experiences to fuel her work, painting powerful depictions of women from myths, allegories, and the Bible.

Both Caccini and Gentileschi exemplify the often-overlooked contributions of women artists in the Baroque era, and afterwards. Their stories illuminate the struggles and triumphs of women in the arts, challenging the male-centric narratives of their time.

In Germany, the rise of the court orchestra was exemplified by the patronage of the Margrave of Brandenburg, who commissioned Johann Sebastian Bach to write the Brandenburg Concertos in 1721. These concertos were a testament to the rich musical culture under the patronage system and remain iconic pieces of the Baroque aesthetics (Leonard 2015; Marissen 1999).

During the reign of Louis XIV in France (1643–1715), the royal court at Versailles became a hub of artistic activity. Louis XIV established academies under royal patronage with the aim of influencing and politicising cultural pursuits, aligning them with the interests of the state (Morrill 1978). These academies encompassed various disciplines such as music, dance, and inscriptions.[2] In 1669, the "Sun King" established the Royal Academy of Music – the orchestra of the Academy, known as the *Vingt-quatre Violons du Roi* (Twenty-four Violins of the King), was instrumental in the development of French Baroque music, propelling the careers of influential composers such as Jean-Baptiste Lully (Gétreau 2011; Gétreau and Duron 2015; Geay 2008; Charles-Dominique 2019).

The Habsburg court in Vienna, Austria, provided patronage to eminent composers such as Mozart, Beethoven, and Haydn (Reisinger 2019), who served as the court composers for the Esterházy family from 1761 to 1790 (Vásquez Rocha 2011; Somfai 1989). Under their patronage, Haydn contributed to transitioning music out from Baroque aesthetics, composing chamber music, symphonies, string quartets, and other works that would become cornerstones of the early classical music repertoire.

During this time, orchestras were primarily financed by royal or aristocratic patrons, who provided the necessary resources for musicians, composers, and conductors to create and perform music. This patronage system allowed for a close relationship between the artists and their benefactors, with patrons often taking an active role in shaping the artistic vision and direction of the ensemble (sometimes with, but sometimes without, the full assent of the composer that could feel trapped in a relationship of complete dependence and subordination vis-à-vis the prestigious but potent patron).

B. THE RISE OF PUBLIC CONCERTS AND THE SUBSCRIPTION MODEL

Following the profound mutations of the sociopolitical landscape across Europe over the 18th century, the musical landscape also shifted towards new territories. The notion of public concerts gained popularity, moving orchestras away from exclusive court settings and towards more accessible public venues. This transition, coupled with the nascent professionalisation of music ensembles, marked a crucial development in the history of management, as it necessitated the establishment of new structures and proto-revenue models to support the costs associated with performances.

One of the earliest examples of public concert series was the *Concert Spirituel* in Paris, founded in 1725 by Anne Danican Philidor and ran until 1790 (Rushton 2001; Pesic 2021). Initially intended as an alternative to the opera during the religious season of Lent, these concerts soon became popular and were held throughout the year, offering a diverse range of sacred and secular music.

London emerged as a pioneering hub for the early adoption and rapid expansion of the subscription model, with key musical institutions and composers leading the way (McVeigh 1989; Sadie 1958). The Hanover Square Rooms became the centre of public concerts during the second half of the 18th century, hosting performances by the likes of Johann Christian Bach, George Frideric Handel, and Joseph Haydn. The establishment of the Professional Concerts series in 1783 further expanded the concert-going experience for the public.

One such revenue model was the subscription system, which allowed patrons to purchase tickets in advance for a series of concerts, securing *ex ante* revenue as a result. This provided a steady – and slightly more predictable – source of income, enabling a more accurate and effective planning of the budget. The concept of subscription concerts was pioneered by Franz Joseph Haydn, who organised a series in Vienna in the 1770s. These concerts not only showcased Haydn's latest compositions but also featured works by other composers.

Subscription concerts also contributed to the rise of what we now call the middle-class concert-going audience, as they offered a more affordable and predictable way for music lovers to experience live performances. The *Philharmonic Society of London*, founded in 1813, was another notable example that opted for the subscription model (Foster 1912; Hogarth 2009). The society aimed to stimulate the performance of instrumental music, with a particular focus on new compositions, and its concert series quickly became an important fixture in London's musical calendar.

In the United States, the New York Philharmonic, established in 1842, embarked on a series of financial strategies to secure its longevity. This journey began in 1877 with the appointment of Theodore Thomas as conductor, who focused on both artistic and financial excellence. The financial journey advanced in 1909 through the formation of the Guarantors Committee, and was further strengthened by the 1928 merger with the New York Symphony Society. Integral to these measures was the early adoption of the subscription model. The model soon spread to other ensembles across the country, laying the groundwork for the growth and development of the American orchestral scene.

The rise of public concerts and the subscription model marked a significant shift in the history of orchestra management. Through the development of new organisational structures and revenue models alongside the move away from court patronage, orchestras were able to broaden their reach and embrace a wider audience. The subscription system, in particular, provided a more reliable source of income, allowing them to plan and budget more effectively while also making live performances more accessible to the growing middle-class[3] audience.

C. THE EMERGENCE OF PROFESSIONAL ORCHESTRAS AND MANAGERS

The 19th century witnessed the establishment of professional orchestras,[4] with musicians being employed on a full-time basis rather than relying solely on patronage or freelance work. This change required the development of a more formalised management structure, including the introduction of dedicated managers to oversee the day-to-day operations and financial affairs of the ensemble.

One of the earliest examples of a professional orchestra was the *Leipzig Gewandhaus Orchestra*, founded in 1781.[5] Initially a group of amateur musicians, they eventually transitioned to a professional ensemble, with musicians receiving regular salaries. This shift was instrumental in attracting top talent, including its famous conductor, Felix Mendelssohn, who led the *Leipzig Gewandhaus* from 1835 to 1847.

Similarly, the *Vienna Philharmonic* was founded in 1842, primarily composed of professional musicians from the court of the Habsburg monarchy. Over time, it developed a distinctive management structure, with decision-making power shared among the musicians, while a manager handled administrative and financial matters.

Managers were responsible for various aspects of the orchestra's functioning, from securing performance venues and negotiating contracts to administering budgets and publicising concerts. One notable example of an early manager is Henry Lee Higginson, the founder and first manager of the *Boston Symphony Orchestra*. Higginson, a wealthy businessman and music lover, established the orchestra in 1881 and played a crucial role in shaping its artistic vision and ensuring its financial stability.

In Britain, the formation of professional orchestras such as the *Hallé Orchestra* in Manchester (1858), led by Sir Charles Hallé, and the *London Symphony*

Orchestra (1904) (Morrison 2004) signalled the growing importance of professional ensembles and the need for dedicated management. Both orchestras were set up with the assistance of prominent figures on the music scene who took on managerial responsibilities to support the artistic endeavours of the musicians.

The role of managers continued to evolve in the 20th century, with the increasing complexity of the orchestral landscape and the growing demands of audiences and musicians alike. The establishment of the *American Symphony Orchestra League* (now the *League of American Orchestras*) in 1942 demonstrated the increasing recognition of the importance of professional management. The league aimed to support orchestras and their managers by providing resources, networking opportunities, and advocacy on behalf of the orchestral community.

In summary, the emergence of professional orchestras and managers in the 19th century marked a significant milestone in the history of management. From securing performance venues to administering budgets and publicising concerts, the evolution of the manager's role played a vital part in ensuring the financial stability and artistic success of the ensemble. As the soundscape landscape continued to develop, the importance of professional management only grew, shaping the way orchestras function today.

D. THE IMPACT OF TECHNOLOGY AND RECORDING

The advent of recording technology during the late 19th and early 20th centuries, swiftly followed by the more widespread dissemination of radio broadcasting in the 1920s, brought about a seismic shift in the way orchestras and musicians reached their audiences (Gronow 2021). As the accessibility of recorded music ascended, orchestras began to surmount the physical limitations of the concert hall, thereby disseminating their performances to an increasingly expansive and diverse listener base. This advancement served to unlock new sources of income, with orchestras reaping financial benefits from the royalties engendered by their recording sales.

For instance, the *London Symphony Orchestra* (LSO) made its first recording in 1913, performing Beethoven's Symphony No. 8.[6] Over time, the LSO has compiled an extensive portfolio of recordings, and in 1999, it inaugurated its proprietary label, LSO Live. This venture has enabled greater control over its recordings and enhanced the financial returns on its performances.

BOX 2.2 THE JOURNEY OF RECORDING

The historical journey of recordings is a tale of ceaseless evolution, shaped by technological advancements and artistic vision. In the early 20th century, the cumbersome process of acoustic recording presented challenges, with orchestras arranged around a single horn that captured the sound on wax cylinders. The advent of electrical recording in the 1920s, with microphones and amplifiers, greatly enhanced sound fidelity. This innovation allowed for more nuanced capturing of the dynamic range, and the recording process became more sophisticated.

The journey of recordings was further revolutionised by the introduction of multitrack tape recorders in the mid-20th century that allowed for each instrumental section to be recorded separately, providing the opportunity for a detailed post-production process, and refining the balance and blend of the ensemble. The evolution of digital technologies in the late 20th century further refined the recording process, introducing new possibilities for sound editing and manipulation.

Yet, amid these technological evolutions, the art and science of capturing the essence of an orchestra in a recording remained a delicate balancing act: the orchestral sound is defined by the complex mix of different sections, the resonant acoustics of the concert hall, and the interpretive vision of the conductor. The challenge for recording engineers was to capture this elusive quality, often referred to as the 'magic' of live performance – this required not just technical expertise, but also a deep understanding of the music, the performing ensemble, and the acoustic environment.

Alongside recorded music, the rise of broadcasting technology and its widespread acceptance have catalysed the development of radio orchestras, affording them the opportunity to deliver live performances to a tremendous regional and national audience. The BBC Symphony Orchestra, established in 1930, stands as a prominent example, having evolved into an indispensable pillar of British classical music. It frequently performs on BBC Radio 3 and at the annual BBC Proms.

Such technological innovations significantly impacted the managerial strategies, necessitating adaptability to emergent markets, and establishing fresh alliances with recording companies, broadcasters, and audiences. The Philadelphia Orchestra, guided by Leopold Stokowski, was amongst the pioneering organisations that embraced electrical recording technology during the 1920s. The orchestra further marked its historical importance by conducting the first live radio broadcast of a symphony orchestra in the United States in 1933.

In reaction to these evolutions, senior management was impelled to formulate strategies for negotiating recording contracts, advocating for fair remuneration for musicians, and striking a balance between recording and live performance schedules. They also were tasked with inventing novel methods of marketing their recordings and capitalising on their radio presence to bolster their reputation and audience engagement.

Overall, the impact of technology and recording during the early decades of the 20th century profoundly reshaped the ways in which these institutions engaged with audiences, generated revenue, and governed their operations. Innovation and adaptability to the changing landscape empowered orchestras to broaden their outreach, establish new alliances, and position themselves as crucial cultural entities in an embryonic interconnected world.

E. THE ROLE OF GOVERNMENT FUNDING

The 20th century saw a growing awareness of the essential role of governmental and local authority support for the arts. Many nations established public funding bodies intended to cultivate and sustain their cultural institutions, especially in the wake of World War II. This development initiated a profound alteration in the financial dynamics of management, as it provided a major source of revenue and support. However, it also ushered in the era of political influence on the managerial practices of these cultural entities.

In the United Kingdom, the establishment of the Arts Council of Great Britain in 1946 marked a crucial step towards the institutionalisation of public support for the arts. The Arts Council, later divided into Arts Council England, Creative Scotland, and the Arts Councils of Wales and Northern Ireland, assumed a fundamental role in funding and promoting cultural institutions. Such governmental backing enabled orchestras, such as the *Royal Liverpool Philharmonic* and the *City of Birmingham Symphony Orchestra*, to uphold high artistic standards, whilst ensuring affordability and accessibility for their audiences.

Similarly, in the United States, the National Endowment for the Arts (NEA) was established in 1965 to support and strengthen the creative vigour of communities by offering diverse artistic prospects. Through its various funding initiatives, the NEA has significantly contributed to the growth and sustainability of numerous American orchestras, including regional and youth ensembles.

Parallel practices are evident in nations such as Germany and France, where public funding for the arts has entrenched roots, and state and regional governments offer considerable support to cultural institutions, effectively rendering them public services (Oki 2000). For instance, in Germany, cultural funding is primarily distributed via the Länder, or federal states, which possess considerable autonomy in delineating cultural priorities. This system has facilitated the flourishing of a vibrant network of state-supported orchestras, including, amongst many others, the *Berliner Philharmoniker* and the *Munich Philharmonic*.

While government funding allowed orchestras to maintain high artistic standards and facilitated accessibility and affordability for audiences,[7] it also encouraged the growth of regional and youth orchestras. Overall, this created the prerequisite for a rich and diverse musical ecosystem as we know it. However, dependency on governmental support has also presented challenges, requiring orchestras to negotiate public funding and sometimes align their objectives with the priorities and policies of funding bodies, if not the agendas of the respective politicians at the helm.

For instance, political volatility and financial constraints in numerous countries have resulted in reductions in arts funding over the last 30 years, compelling orchestras to seek alternative revenue streams, such as private contributions, corporate sponsorships, and income generated from other activities. Moreover, public funding often carries specific obligations and expectations, such as educational outreach programmes or the promotion of novel and diverse music. Orchestras must strike a balance between these objectives and their artistic vision and financial viability.

The Australian context provides yet another compelling case study to illustrate a distinct approach to governmental funding or, more specifically, the transition from government financial support to a corporatised structure (Boyle 2022). Established in 1932, the Australian Broadcasting Commission (ABC) was birthed by an Act of Federal Parliament to provide free-to-air radio broadcasting nationally. To furnish musical content for its broadcasts, the ABC assembled several ensembles, eventually leading to the establishment of a network of six full-time professional symphony orchestras. Between 1950 and 1996, they functioned as a governmental department, but each was restructured as a distinct corporate entity responsible for its own Profit and Loss statement between 1997 and 2000.[8]

Governmental support and funding to the arts and culture industry in the 20th century had in return an indelible impact on the financial landscape of management. While this support has been instrumental in sustaining high artistic standards and a prosperous musical environment, it has also introduced challenges to navigate the complexities of public funding and adapt to ever-changing political priorities and national policies.

F. THE SHIFT TOWARDS COMMUNITY AND EDUCATION

As orchestras transitioned through the later quarter of the 20th century and into the new millennium, the emphasis on deepening their engagement with communities, widening their appeal, and onboarding more diversity and sustainability became increasingly pronounced. This resulted in novel paradigms of interaction with the local communities and a burgeoning interest in educational initiatives intended to cultivate a love of music and the arts among diverse and underserved populations.

For instance, the *Los Angeles Philharmonic* (LA Phil) initiated its *Youth Orchestra Los Angeles* (YOLA) programme in 2007, taking inspiration from Venezuela's renowned *El Sistema* initiative. YOLA provides free instruments, music training, and academic support to more than 1,200 young people from underserved communities, helping them develop their musical abilities while instilling values of teamwork, discipline, and perseverance. In 2019, the LA Phil's YOLA became a national programme (Los Angeles Philharmonic Orchestra 2019).

In a parallel vein, the *Orchestra of the Age of Enlightenment* (OAE), based in London, inaugurated its OAE TOTS initiative, aiming to introduce children aged between 2 and 5 years old to classical music via interactive workshops and concerts. This initiative seeks to plant the seed of an early love for music and spark curiosity in young minds with the hope that it ignites a long-lasting passion for the arts.

Senior management teams played a crucial role in this process, as they sought partnerships with schools, community organisations, and local businesses to support their education and outreach initiatives. For instance, the New York Philharmonic's *Very Young Composers* programme, founded in 1995, works closely with local schools to help students develop their compositional skills and have their works performed by professional musicians.

Orchestras also offer a strong contribution in creating opportunities for young people and community members. They allowed the young to experience live classical music and participate in music-making activities, building lasting connections and densifying the cultural fabric of the community. In 1991, the

Baltimore Symphony Orchestra launched its *OrchKids* programme, which has since offered music education, mentorship, and performance opportunities to thousands of children in Baltimore City Public Schools, thereby contributing to life transformation and community enhancement.

The redirection towards community and education within the orchestral sphere has been integral in broadening the reach and influence of these organisations. Management teams have played a pivotal role in forging alliances and developing innovative programmes that not only bring the joy of music to diverse audiences but also pave the way to a more inclusive and vibrant cultural landscape for future generations.

G. THE EMERGENCE OF ARTISTIC PARTNERSHIPS AND COLLABORATIONS

In recent decades, orchestras have sought to diversify their programming and expand their creative horizons. To this end, they worked with artists from various disciplines and cultural backgrounds. This trend emerged notably in the late 20th and early 21st centuries, with artistic partnerships and collaborations becoming increasingly important aspects of management.

One example of this collaborative approach is the partnership between the *Berlin Philharmonic* and Sir Simon Rattle, which began in 2002. Under Rattle's leadership, the orchestra embarked on a series of innovative external collaborations, including projects with visual artists, dancers, and even film directors that enriched the artistic offerings and challenged conventional ideas about what a performance should be.

The *Los Angeles Philharmonic*, under the direction of Gustavo Dudamel since 2009, has also become known for its ground-breaking collaborations with artists from diverse backgrounds. The partnership with the *Youth Orchestra Los Angeles* (YOLA) programme has brought new perspectives to the concert-going experience while developing social responsibility in the community.

Management teams play a crucial role in forging alliances. They liaise with other arts organisations and artists to develop innovative projects that push boundaries and offer fresh interpretations of the traditional repertoire or the introduction of new components (music or composers) into the repertoire.[9] Collaboration allows for the creation of a variety of concert experiences, appealing to a broader range of audiences and contributing to the ongoing evolution of the art form.

The history of orchestra management has been marked by a sequence of evolutions and innovations that have shaped the way ensembles operate and engage with their audiences. From the early days of patronage and court orchestras to the rise of professional orchestras and government support for the arts, these changes have had a profound impact on the financial, organisational, and artistic aspects of management.[10] As orchestras continue to adapt to the challenges and opportunities of the 21st century, accepting artistic partnerships and collaborations and adapting to new technologies (Wlömert and Papies 2016) is essential in ensuring their ongoing relevance and success.

H. THE CHALLENGES OF THE 21ST CENTURY

The 21st century has brought new challenges to cultural institutions that impact management and artistic endeavours. From the rise of digital technology and streaming services to the growing emphasis on community development and diversity, equity, and inclusion, as well as the need for environmental protection, management adapts to ensure organisations remain relevant, sustainable, and aligned with their audiences.

BOX 2.3 THE NEED TO ADAPT

A useful perspective on the need to adapt to different conditions is given by M. A. Glynn (Glynn 2000; Glynn 2002). Across her works, she examines the connections between organisational crisis and institutional shifts in the world of symphony orchestras, focusing on the impact these factors have on the musical canon. Glynn discusses the relationships and interactions connecting symphony orchestras, musicians, composers, and audiences (that she calls the "Symphonyweb"). She investigates how this network is shaped by and responds to various crises, such as financial difficulties, audience decline, and shifts in cultural preferences, and the role of institutional shifts, including changes in funding models, audience expectations, and cultural norms, in shaping the musical canon. She asserts that the tension between the need for adaptation and the preservation of tradition is a central dynamic driving the evolution of the Symphonyweb.

One significant challenge in the 21st century is the rapid evolution of digital technology and streaming services. With music consumption increasingly shifting towards online platforms, orchestras have had to explore new ways of reaching their audiences and staying relevant whilst protecting their assets from fraudulent distribution.

For example, the *Berlin Philharmonic* launched the *Digital Concert Hall* in 2009. A pioneering online platform, it offered livestreams and an extensive archive of past performances, providing access to their concerts to a global audience. Similarly, the *London Symphony Orchestra* has embraced digital technology through its LSO Play initiative, which allows viewers to watch performances from multiple camera angles and access interactive content.

Another crucial challenge in the 21st century is the growing importance of the role orchestras play in civil society overall (Ramnarine 2011). This is particularly evident in the expanding commitment to confront issues of diversity, equity, and inclusion within the arts sector. Management has had to address historical imbalances in representation, both in terms of personnel and programming, to ensure that their ensembles reflect the rich diversity of contemporary society. In a similar vein, the heightened recognition of the underrepresentation of certain societal sectors within the audience has propelled the issue to the forefront with compelling immediacy. This emergent consciousness is reshaping the dynamics of audience interaction, including the structure and substance of the dialogue between an orchestra and the community to which it belongs.

One notable example is the *Chineke! Orchestra*. Founded in 2015 by Chi-chi Nwanoku, it aims to provide career opportunities to young musicians from all and any ethnic backgrounds in the UK and Europe (Nwanoku 2023). The *Chineke!* has made significant strides towards greater inclusivity within the classical music sector as it expanded its focus to diverse musicians and composers.

In addition to these initiatives, orchestras have also sought to diversify their programmed performances by featuring works from underrepresented composers or different musical traditions. For instance, the *Los Angeles Philharmonic*'s Green Umbrella series showcases contemporary music from around the world, including works by female composers and composers from diverse cultural backgrounds.

Responding to the changing landscape of music consumption and audience tastes (Mueller 2018), orchestras developed innovative communication strategies to reach and connect with their audiences. The use of social media and digital platforms has become increasingly important in advertising concerts, sharing behind-the-scenes content, and ultimately fertilising a sense of community among fans. The *New York Philharmonic* regularly shares videos of rehearsals, interviews with musicians, and other exclusive content on its YouTube channel. The *San Francisco Symphony* utilises its Instagram account to showcase stunning photography and offer a glimpse into its daily life.

The challenges of the 21st century have triggered a continuous evolution in management, from digital technology and streaming services to diversity and inclusion within the organisation. Orchestras continue to enrich the cultural fabric of society as long as they adapt to shifting landscapes and stay attuned to the needs and interests of their audiences.

I. GLOBAL PERSPECTIVES: A COMPARATIVE ANALYSIS

Orchestras worldwide have been profoundly influenced by the diverse cultural, historical, and socioeconomic contexts in which they have evolved. As a result, their management practices often differ, sometimes even significantly, reflecting the distinct dynamics they encounter in their respective environments. This brief comparative overview reveals some of the most notable variations in management practices across various regions.

With a rich history of patronage, public support, and artistic excellence, Europe has a long-standing tradition of classical music. In many European countries, arts and culture institutions receive substantial public funding, enabling them to concentrate on a strong identity and upholding high artistic standards. For instance, in Germany, the extensive public funding system has contributed to the proliferation of professional orchestras, boasting more than 130 full-time ensembles,[11] while facilitating the experimentation of innovative management tools, frameworks, and technologies (Teohari, Bibu, and Brancu 2020). However, this relative financial comfort eroded the entrepreneurial spirit, transforming management into more of an administrative function. Scandinavian countries such as Sweden and Finland also benefit from significant government support, resulting in robust infrastructures that prioritise artistic innovation, education, and audience. However, despite these advantages, European orchestras face challenges in maintaining financial sustainability and diversifying their audiences in an increasingly competitive cultural landscape. Balancing traditional repertoire with contemporary compositions to intercept younger, more diverse audiences has become a crucial aspect of management in Europe.

In contrast, American orchestras rely more heavily on private funding, with support from individual donors, corporate sponsorships, and endowments. This necessitates a more entrepreneurial approach to management, with an emphasis on marketing, audience development, and programming to attract and retain patrons. As such, American orchestras typically invest considerable resources in community outreach initiatives, aiming to broaden their appeal and strengthen their connections with local audiences. This approach brings its own challenges, such as the necessity to balance artistic integrity with the financial imperative to generate revenue, sometimes leading to tensions between artistic and administrative stakeholders. The need to innovate and utilise technology for audience engagement is also a significant concern for American orchestras, requiring effective strategies for leveraging digital platforms and online content.

In the Asia-Pacific region, orchestras have experienced rapid growth and development in recent decades, reflecting the region's increasing economic influence and cultural aspirations. Countries such as China, Japan, and South Korea[12] have followed Western classical music standards as a symbol of modernisation and globalisation, investing heavily in establishing and expanding professional ensembles. Management practices in this region tend to combine elements from both European and American models, with a mix of public and private funding sources and a strong focus on education and audience development. However, orchestras in the Asia-Pacific region also face unique challenges, such as navigating cultural differences, scouting local talent, and establishing a distinct artistic identity amid the dominance of Western classical music traditions. Building a strong connection between Western classical music and local cultures is an essential aspect of management in this region.

Latin America presents a different picture, with many orchestras facing significant financial constraints and limited public support. Management in this region often necessitates resourcefulness and adaptability, with ensembles exploring alternative funding models and partnerships to ensure survival. One notable success story is the Venezuelan *El Sistema* programme (Puromies and Juvonen 2020; Bolden, Corcoran, and Butler 2021), which has gained international acclaim for its innovative approach to music education and social change. Through government support and a network of local and international partners, *El Sistema* has provided thousands of disadvantaged children with access to music education, nurturing a new generation of musicians and inspiring similar initiatives across the region. Latin American orchestras also place a strong emphasis on incorporating traditional and regional music into their repertoire, creating a unique blend of classical and local musical expressions.

In the Middle East, particularly the Gulf Cooperation Council (GCC) countries, arts and culture institutions, including museums, orchestras, and operas, are a relatively recent phenomenon, reflecting the region's burgeoning interest in cultural development and international artistic exchange (Mikdadi 2008; Tobelem 2013; Litova 2020). As governments in the Gulf region invest heavily in the arts and culture sector, orchestras have emerged as symbols of progress and cultural sophistication and, above all, a means to build bridges between different cultures of the world, a potent tool of cultural diplomacy and integration into the large international community. The recent establishment of orchestras and large musical ensembles in Qatar, the Arab United Emirates, and Oman, and prestigious venues, such as the Dubai Opera, the Royal Opera House Muscat, the Opera House, part of the larger Katara Cultural Village in Doha, or the Sheikh Jaber Al-Ahmad Cultural Centre, better known as the Kuwait Opera House, have attracted internationally renowned artists, fostering an environment of artistic excellence and global collaboration. Management practices in the GCC countries often draw inspiration from European and American models, with strong financial support from local governments and more recent attempts to access private funding, sponsorships, and partnerships.

However, the unique sociocultural context of the Middle East presents distinct challenges for management, such as navigating cultural sensitivities, building a pool of local talents, and laying the foundation of an appreciation for classical music among local audiences. To address these challenges, orchestras in the region often undertake extensive educational and outreach efforts, aiming at a better understanding of classical music and bridging cultural divides. Additionally, many orchestras in the Middle East collaborate with local or regional composers and musicians, incorporating traditional musical elements into their repertoire to create a distinctive fusion of Western and regional musical styles. Last but not least, they also introduce non-Western audiences to classical music through special concerts that are more inclined to ignite enthusiasm, such as events featuring film soundtracks or orchestral renditions of pop music standards.

Yet, countries within the GCC grapple with the considerable task of cultivating and identifying local talents to occupy both artistic and administrative roles. This issue is tackled via a twofold strategy: on the one hand, the shortfall of local talents is managed by attracting international specialists, thereby nurturing the genesis of a global network of connections. On the other hand, GCC nations have undertaken initiatives to create music academies and schools, a notable example being the Qatar Music Academy. Remarkably, in a span of less than a decade since its inception, the Academy has successfully propelled its most distinguished alumni into the echelons of renowned international music conservatories and universities, preparing the next generation of talents.

BOX 2.4 UNIQUE CHALLENGES OF ORCHESTRAS IN THE GCC

Orchestras in the GCC countries face some unique challenges due to the local demographic composition of their population. The region's oil and gas wealth, which has enabled high-income economies, fuelled a substantial demand for foreign labour. The GCC demography is therefore skewed towards a younger male population. The expatriate populations in some of these nations, particularly in the UAE and Qatar, exceed the number of citizens. Additionally, the expatriate population, primarily from Asia and other Arab nations, shares limited cultural background with Western classical music, and typically leaves the region before reaching the age of 60–65. As a result, unlike their Western counterparts, where research often shows that the primary demographic for classical music attendance comprises older individuals (Knight Foundation 2002; Onditi 2020), orchestras in the GCC countries have to grapple with the challenge of catering to a demographic that significantly deviates from the typical audience profile for classical music. This unique demographic structure requires innovative strategies for audience development in order to establish a sustainable classical music scene in the region.

This comparative analysis highlights the diverse approaches to management around the world, demonstrating the profound impact of cultural, historical, and socioeconomic factors on the evolution of orchestras. It is crucial for managers and stakeholders to remain aware of these differences, adapting their strategies and practices to suit their specific contexts and address the challenges they face. By learning from and collaborating with their counterparts in other regions, orchestras worldwide continue to innovate, adapt, and thrive in the ever-changing landscape of the arts world.

***

The history of orchestra management has been marked by significant developments and milestones, each shaping the ways in which orchestras have been organised, financed, and related to their communities. From the early days of court patronage to the advent of recording technology and the rise of public funding, the evolution of management has been a story of adaptation, resilience, and extraordinary creative thinking. As orchestras continue to navigate the 21st century, the role of management will remain integral to their success, ensuring that these vital cultural institutions continue to flourish and contribute to the rich tapestry of our musical heritage.

Box 2.5 Expanding Perspectives: Review Questions

1 How did the transition from court patronage to public concerts and the subscription model shape the evolution of management, both financially and in terms of audience engagement? How have contemporary orchestras incorporated or moved beyond this model to ensure sustainability and reach?

2 The role of a manager has evolved significantly since the 19th century. Consider the impact of technological innovation, an emphasis on diversity, equity, and inclusion, and the shift towards community and education. How have these influences transformed the responsibilities and skills required for successful orchestra management in the 21st century?

3 Discuss how orchestras have negotiated the opportunities and challenges presented by the advent of recording technology and radio broadcasting. How have these developments forced us to rethink traditional managerial approaches and redefine relationships with audiences?

4 Reflecting on the complexities and implications of government support and arts funding, discuss how orchestras have adapted their strategies to secure funding and navigate changing policies. In this context, how do orchestras maintain high artistic standards and promote a diverse musical ecosystem?

NOTES

1 Useful readings on the history of orchestra are Spitzer and Zaslaw (2004) and Mueller (2018).
2 In this context, the term "inscriptions" relates to one of the academies established by the monarch, namely the *Académie des Inscriptions et Belles-Lettres*. Initially conceived to compose inscriptions for medals, a practice of producing commemorative pieces to mark significant events of Louis XIV's reign, this academy gradually evolved to undertake a wider scholarly activity. The *Académie des Inscriptions et Belles-Lettres* became renowned for its focus on the study and interpretation of historical documents and texts, with particular emphasis on those of significant archaeological interest.
3 It is interesting to underline that the term "middle class" initially appeared in the late 18th century in the United Kingdom. However, its widespread use and prominence

grew during the 19th century, coinciding with the Industrial Revolution in Europe (Earle 1989). The evolution of the middle class concept was closely linked to the significant social, political, and economic changes of the time, which also led to the new orchestra landscape.

4 An interesting approach is found in Ponchione-Bailey and Clarke (2021a, 2021b), who used digital methods to study changes in European musical culture, including changes in the size and nature of the orchestra and the rise of the modern conductor.

5 The beginnings of the Leipzig Gewandhaus Orchestra can be traced back to the year 1743. At this time, a collective known as the Grosses Concert initiated their musical performances, which originally took place within the confines of private residences. A year later, in 1744, this group of musicians transitioned their performances to a local tavern, the "Three Swans." This venue served as their concert location for a substantial period of 36 years, until 1781.

6 The history of recording is a complex one given the variety of early technological approaches utilised to carry out the recordings (acoustic, electric, etc.). Therefore, several orchestras (rightfully) claim to be the first. See Paris (2020).

7 Despite the government's efforts to increase accessibility and affordability, the sociological composition of classical concert audiences remained largely unchanged in the late 20th century. In Belgium, this situation was seen by left-wing unions and political parties as a prime example of poor governance, as they criticised the use of tax money from the "working class" to provide discounted concert tickets to the "bourgeoisie."

8 While this decision of making the six orchestras independent from ABC to an optimisation of their managerial structures, limited-to-no technical efficiency was gained (Boyle and Throsby 2012).

9 For a remarkable study on the factors that trigger and support the introduction of new composers into orchestral repertoire, see Dowd et al. (2002). The actual impact of the repertoire programming on the attendance is well-known too and supported by empirical and quantitative data (Pompe, Tamburri, and Munn 2013).

10 A crisp contribution to this matter is the concise yet insightful overview of the history, structure, and function of orchestras, as well as their impact on music and society, developed by Holoman (2012), who provides a detailed exploration of the evolution of orchestras and their role in shaping the world of classical music.

11 While still prominent, continuity in high levels of public funding in Germany should not be taken for granted; see Hausmann (2007).

12 For China: Mellor (2019). For Japan: Association of Japanese Symphony Orchestras (2022) and Walnutcreekband (2023). For South Korea: Park (2012).

BIBLIOGRAPHY

Association of Japanese Symphony Orchestras. 2022. *Japanese Professional Orchestras Yearbook 2022*. www.orchestra.or.jp/eng/.

Bolden, Benjamin, Sean Corcoran, and Alana Butler. 2021. "A Scoping Review of Research That Examines El Sistema and Sistema-inspired Music Education Programmes." *Review of Education* 9 (3). https://doi.org/10.1002/rev3.3267.

Boyle, Stephen, and David Throsby. 2012. "Corporatisation, Economic Efficiency and the Australian Symphony Orchestras." *Economic Papers a Journal of Applied Economics and Policy* 31 (1): 36–49. https://doi.org/10.1111/j.1759-3441.2011.00150.x.

Boyle, Stephen John. 2022. "Ownership, Efficiency and Identity: The Transition of Australia's Symphony Orchestras from Government Departments to Corporate Entities." Thesis PhD. Macquarie University.

Charles-Dominique, Luc. 2019. "L'orchestre à Cordes Sous Louis XIV. Instruments, Répertoires, Singularités." *Revue de Musicologie* 105 (1): 193–197.

Cusick, Suzanne G. 2009. *Francesca Caccini at the Medici Court: Music and the Circulation of Power.* University of Chicago Press. https://doi.org/10.7208/chicago/9780226338101. 001.0001.

Dowd, Timothy J., Kathleen Liddle, Kim Lupo, and Anne Borden. 2002. "Organizing the Musical Canon." *Poetics* 30 (1–2): 35–61. https://doi.org/10.1016/s0304-422x(02) 00007-4.

Drinker, Sophie, and Ruth A. Solie. 1995. *Music and Women: The Story of Women in Their Relation to Music.* New York: Feminist Press at CUNY.

Earle, Peter. 1989. *The Making of the English Middle Class: Business, Society, and Family Life in London, 1660–1730.* Berkeley: University of California Press.

Foster, Myles Birket. 1912. *History of the Philharmonic Society of London 1813–1912: A Record of a Hundred Years' Work in the Cause of Music.* London: John Lane.

Geay, Gérard. 2008. "Le style des vingt-quatre violons et les premières compositions du jeune Lully." In *La naissance du style français (1650–1673)*, 115–134. Brussels: Mardaga.

Gétreau, Florence. 2011. "Les ensembles de violons en France à travers les sources visuelles (1650–1715)." In *Les cordes de l'orchestre français sous le règne de Louis XIV: instruments, répertoires et singularités.* Paris: Vrin.

Gétreau, Florence, and Jean Duron. 2015. "L'orchestre à cordes sous Louis XIV." In *Les cordes de l'orchestre français sous le règne de Louis XIV: instruments, répertoires et singularités.* Vol. 21. Paris: Vrin.

Glynn, Mary Ann. 2000. "When Cymbals Become Symbols: Conflict Over Organizational Identity Within a Symphony Orchestra." *Organization Science* 11 (3): 285–298. https://doi.org/10.1287/orsc.11.3.285.12496.

Glynn, Mary Ann. 2002. "Chord and Discord: Organizational Crisis, Institutional Shifts, and the Musical Canon of the Symphony." *Poetics* 30 (1–2): 63–85. https://doi. org/10.1016/S0304-422X(02)00004-9.

Gronow, Pekka. 2021. "Music Recording and the Recording Industry." In *The Oxford Handbook of Global Popular Music*, edited by Simone Krüger Bridge. Oxford: Oxford University Press. https://doi.org/10.1093/oxfordhb/9780190081379.013.59.

Hausmann, Andrea. 2007. "Visitor Orientation and Its Impact on the Financial Situation of Cultural Institutions in Germany." *International Journal of Nonprofit and Voluntary Sector Marketing* 12 (3): 205–215. https://doi.org/10.1002/nvsm.302.

Hogarth, George. 2009. *The Philharmonic Society of London: From Its Foundation, 1813, to Its Fiftieth Year, 1862.* Cambridge: Cambridge University Press. https://doi.org/10.1017/ CBO9780511701344.

Holoman, D. Kern. 2012. *The Orchestra: A Very Short Introduction.* New York: Oxford University Press.

Knight Foundation. 2002. *Classical Music Consumer Segmentation Study. How Americans Relate to Classical Music and Their Local Orchestras*. Miami: Knight Foundation.

Leonard, Michael F. 2015. "Bach as Humanist: The Influences of the Classics and Court Aesthetics on the Design of the Six Brandenburg Concertos, BWV 1046–1051." Urbana: University of Illinois at Urbana-Champaign.

Litova, D. S. 2020. "Louvre Abu-Dhabi or the Myth of Westernalism." *Concept: Philosophy, Religion, Culture* 1 (July): 194–200. https://doi.org/10.24833/2541-8831-2020-1-13-194-200.

Los Angeles Philharmonic Orchestra. 2019. "LA Phil Introduces YOLA National Programs." *Hollywood Bowl*. www.hollywoodbowl.com/press/releases/1846.

Marissen, Michael. 1999. *The Social and Religious Designs of J. S. Bach's Brandenburg Concertos*. Princeton, NJ: Princeton University Press.

McVeigh, Simon. 1989. "The Professional Concert and Rival Subscription Series in London, 1783–1793." *Royal Musical Association Research Chronicle* 22: 1–135. https://doi.org/10.1080/14723808.1989.10540933.

Mellor, Andrew. 2019. "China and Classical Music: An Extraordinary Story of Growth." *Gramophone*. www.gramophone.co.uk/features/article/china-and-classical-music-an-extraordinary-story-of-growth.

Mikdadi, Salwa. 2008. "Arab Art Institutions and Their Audiences." *Review of Middle East Studies* 42 (1–2): 55–61. https://doi.org/10.1017/S002631840005152X.

Morrill, John Stephen. 1978. "French Absolutism as Limited Monarchy." *The Historical Journal* 21 (4): 961–972. https://doi.org/10.1017/S0018246X00000777.

Morrison, Richard. 2004. *Orchestra: The LSO: A Century of Triumphs and Turbulence*. London: Faber & Faber.

Mueller, John H. 2018. *The American Symphony Orchestra: A Social History of Musical Taste*. Bloomington, IN: Indiana University Press (reprint).

Nwanoku, Chi-Chi. 2023. *Changing Classical Music from the Inside: An Interview with Chi-Chi Nwanoku*. Oxford: Oxford University Press. https://doi.org/10.1093/oso/9780197601211.003.0023.

Oki, Yuto. 2000. "New Directions in French Orchestra Management." *Journal of Cultural Economics* 2 (2): 117–126. https://doi.org/10.11195/jace1998.2.2_117.

Onditi, David. 2020. *Symphony Orchestra Challenge*. 1. Auflage, digitale Originalausgabe. München: GRIN Verlag.

Paris, Olajide. 2020. "Recording the Orchestra." *Sound on Sound*. www.soundonsound.com/techniques/recording-orchestra.

Park, Mikyung. 2012. "Modern Orchestra of Korean Instruments from Its Birth to the Present: A Critical Survey." *The World of Music* 1 (1): 59–80.

Pesic, Andrei. 2021. "Concerts and Inadvertent Secularization: Religious Music in the Entertainment Market of Eighteenth-Century Paris." *Past & Present* 250 (1): 135–169. https://doi.org/10.1093/pastj/gtaa011.

Pompe, Jeffrey, Lawrence Tamburri, and Johnathan Munn. 2013. "Symphony Concert Demand: Does Programming Matter?" *The Journal of Arts Management, Law, and Society* 43 (4): 215–228. https://doi.org/10.1080/10632921.2013.818085.

Ponchione-Bailey, Cayenna, and Eric F. Clarke. 2021a. "Digital Methods for the Study of the Nineteenth-Century Orchestra." *Nineteenth-Century Music Review* 18 (1): 19–50. https://doi.org/10.1017/S1479409819000661.

Ponchione-Bailey, Cayenna, and Eric F. Clarke. 2021b. "Technologies for Investigating Large Ensemble Performance." In *Together in Music*, 119–128. Oxford: Oxford University Press.

Puromies, Maija, and Antti Juvonen. 2020. "Systematized Literature Review of El Sistema, the Venezuelan Social Music Education Method." *Problems in Music Pedagogy* 19 (2): 35–63.

Ramnarine, Tina K. 2011. "The Orchestration of Civil Society: Community and Conscience in Symphony Orchestras." *Ethnomusicology Forum* 20 (3): 327–351. https://doi.org/10.1080/17411912.2011.638515.

Reisinger, Elisabeth. 2019. "The Prince and the Prodigies: On the Relations of Archduke and Elector Maximilian Franz with Mozart, Beethoven, and Haydn." *Acta Musicologica* 91 (1): 48–70.

Rushton, Julian. 2001. "Philidor, Anne Danican." In *Oxford Music Online*, edited by Rebecca Harris-Warrick. Oxford: Oxford University Press. https://doi.org/10.1093/omo/9781561592630.013.90000380336.

Sadie, Stanley. 1958. "Concert Life in Eighteenth Century England." *Proceedings of the Royal Musical Association* 85: 17–30. https://doi.org/10.1093/jrma/85.1.17.

Somfai, László. 1989. "Haydn at the Esterházy Court." In *The Classical Era: From the 1740s to the End of the 18th Century*, edited by Neal Zaslaw, 268–292. London: Palgrave Macmillan. https://doi.org/10.1007/978-1-349-20628-5_10.

Spinelli, Riccardo. 2013. *Il gran principe Ferdinando de' Medici (1663–1713): collezionista e mecenate*. Firenze: Giunti.

Spitzer, John, and Neal Zaslaw. 2004. *The Birth of the Orchestra: History of an Institution, 1650–1815*. New York and Oxford: Oxford University Press.

Teohari, Georgiana Alina, Nicolae Aurelian Bibu, and Laura Brancu. 2020. "Innovative Aspects in Managing Classic Professional Orchestras, as Multiple Stakeholder Organizations." In *Innovation in Sustainable Management and Entrepreneurship*, 507–525. Springer International Publishing. https://doi.org/10.1007/978-3-030-44711-3_38.

Tobelem, Jean-Michel. 2013. "Stratégie Culturelle à Abou Dhabi et Au Qatar: éléments de Convergence et de Singularité." *Bulletin de l'Association de Geographes Francais* 90 (2): 142–152. https://doi.org/10.4000/bagf.2277.

Tomlinson, Gary. 1987. *Monteverdi and the End of the Renaissance*. Berkeley, CA: University of California Press.

Vásquez Rocha, H. 2011. "La Música Como Asunto de Estado: La Relación Esterházy-Haydn." *Punto Cero* 16 (22): 9–17.

Walnutcreekband. 2023. "Classical Music in Japan: A Comprehensive Guide." *Walnutcreekband.org*. Walnut Creek Band. https://walnutcreekband.org/classical-music-in-japanese/.

Wlömert, Nils, and Dominik Papies. 2016. "On-Demand Streaming Services and Music Industry Revenues – Insights from Spotify's Market Entry." *International Journal of Research in Marketing* 33 (2): 314–327. https://doi.org/10.1016/j.ijresmar.2015.11.002.
Cited content from websites was last accessed on 01 July 2023.

CHAPTER 3

A Typical Orchestra Organisation and Functions

Orchestras are complex entities that rely on effective collaboration among diverse departments and roles, which often have diametrically opposed functions and seemingly contradictory scopes (Faulkner 1973; Otis 1924; Glynn 2000; Poulios and Kamperou 2022; Teohari, Bibu, and Brancu 2020). This chapter offers an overview of the standard structure and functions within an orchestra. The way these functions are integrated into specific roles and positions, distributed across departments, or arranged into work groups or project-related task forces considerably vary. However, even when these roles are not formally embodied in specific positions, the functions that they reflect are inherently present in the daily activities of the management team.

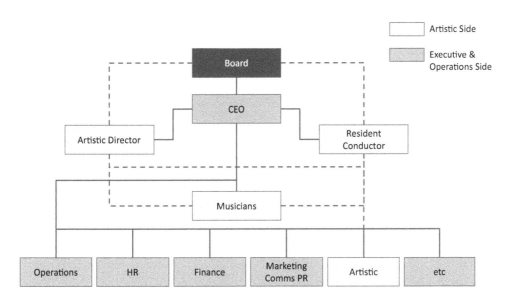

FIGURE 3.1 Example of Organisation Chart

DOI: 10.4324/9781032629636-3

WHAT YOU WILL LEARN IN THIS CHAPTER

Section	Key Learning Points
A. Management Structure	The CEO's role includes facilitating collaboration, providing clear direction, supporting the artistic team in achieving their goals, and overseeing operations. The top manager also ensures that the entire organisation shares a common vision and understanding of their respective roles. The roles of the artistic director and conductor should be clearly defined to prevent conflicts. The CEO actively addresses potential conflicts of authority and fosters a positive and inclusive organisational culture that values collaboration, respect, and open dialogue, while always paying attention to smooth execution of day-to-day activities.
B. Volunteers	Volunteers are vital to the operations, involved in everything from fundraising to community programmes. They should be recognised for their efforts and work closely with staff to achieve the collective goals. Volunteers usually raise between 5–10% of the budget. Balancing the expectations of volunteers, who are not financially compensated, with the professional rights of the musicians and other staff is crucial.
C. Understanding the Governance Structure	Understanding the management structure is essential for its efficient functioning. The executive team and artistic team need to maintain a strong and transparent relationship to balance artistic goals with financial sustainability. The administrative department supports several functions such as operations, finance, public relations, marketing, and fundraising. Effective communication and collaboration among various departments are required to meet artistic and financial goals.
D. The Roles of the Board and Staff	Board members contribute their expertise, time, and financial resources to the organisation's mission. They provide guidance to the staff, oversee ongoing responsibilities, and form ad hoc committees for specific purposes. Musicians' involvement on the board contributes to shared responsibility. The staff work closely with the Music Director and the CEO to implement the strategic plan, execute day-to-day operations, and participate in donor cultivation events and educational outreach programs. The board members also have key responsibilities that range from maintaining the financial stability to acting as ambassadors in the community.

A. MANAGEMENT STRUCTURE

Executive Leadership

CEO

In addition to the usual admin responsibilities common to any company or organisation, the orchestra Chief Executive Officer (or executive director) has different roles depending on the organisation type, its focus, its scope, or its level of maturity. In some cases, the CEO is tasked with harmonising artistic, financial, and operational elements of the ensemble, frequently referred to as the "three-legged stool" model.[1] Musicians are sometimes viewed as the "fourth leg" in this model, participating in decision-making and shaping the organisation's direction. An exemplary CEO embodies a blend of artistic insight, strategic acumen, business management capabilities, and compelling leadership abilities. Drawing from key concepts in relevant literature (Byrnes 2022; DeVereaux 2019; DiMaggio 1987), the ideal CEO is proficient in navigating the organisational governance framework, advocating for the mission, overseeing and guiding the day-to-day operations, and nurturing a culture of innovation, inclusivity, and excellence.

The CEO is expected to favour effective communication, diversity, collaboration, equity, and trust among various stakeholders, including the board, musicians, staff, and community partners. They should also be skilled in long-range planning and identifying opportunities for growth and improvement within the organisation. To effectively lead, they require versatility in their approach, displaying a breadth of knowledge across the various facets of management. This adaptability enables the CEO to grasp the essentials of each component while relying on the sectorial and functional experts within their team to handle the technicalities and details. This balance empowers the CEO to be well-informed and maintain a holistic view of the organisation, ensuring – or, at least, facilitating – its harmonious operations and overall success.

Operations

The operations department is accountable for all logistics. This includes, amongst others, stagehand management and coordination, set-up, touring, and IT and audio equipment performance. In direct alignment with the Human Resources department, operations may manage the staff and musician labour contracts and maintain the closest relationship with musicians. The operations department also supervises the library, facility management and maintenance, safety and security, and logistics for ancillary concerts, amplified concerts, and chamber and community programmes. The artistic and operations departments may be combined in smaller orchestras, or a general manager may oversee both departments. Effective operational management involves coordinating rehearsal schedules, maintaining clear communication with musicians and staff, and ensuring a seamless concert experience for performers and audience members. The operations department should be skilled in risk management, contingency planning, and addressing any challenges or concerns that may arise during performances.

Communications, Public Relations, and Marketing

The communications, PR, and marketing department is responsible for earned revenue (ticket sales being one of the possible revenue streams), the organisation's public image, and audience development. This department designs and oversees printed and online materials, social and digital media, advertising, internal publications, newsletters, and press releases. It maintains relationships with the press and manages artist interviews; advises the board and management on potential press and public reactions to statements or ideas; and offers visibility to the music director and conductor. A successful PR and marketing strategy comprises traditional and digital media, targets diverse audiences within and outside the reference community, and pushes towards building long-term audience loyalty. Over the last decade, the department has had to become well-versed in the use of social media, digital content creation, and data-driven marketing techniques to maximise and optimise reach. It also plays a vital role in crisis management.[2]

Development

When focusing on fundraising through individual, foundation, and corporate donations, the (business) development department oversees donors, works with volunteer chairs on special events, and motivates the board to raise funds. The department is also responsible for special project fundraising (e.g., tours, radio broadcasts, one-time events), government relationships, endowment drives, and planned givings. Effective business development strategies involve understanding donor motivations and preferences, building strong relationships with supporters, and demonstrating the impact of donor contributions on the mission and programmes. Frequently, this function is performed by a diverse team of staff members rather than being centralised in a specific department. It usually relies directly on the CEO's guidance and works in close coordination with the Communications, PR, and Marketing team.

Finance

Overseeing the operating budget, payroll, benefits, and human resources, the finance department plays a crucial role in the organisation's overall health and stability. It supervises cash flow, investment management, and endowment oversight. The department also handles accounts payable and receivable, transactions execution, and legal and corporate issues involving finance (e.g., insurance, attorney relations, government licensing requirements, and taxes). Effective financial management requires the implementation of robust budgeting, forecasting, and reporting processes to inform decision-making and ensure long-term sustainability. The finance department collaborates closely with other departments to identify potential cost-saving measures and opportunities for increased efficiency while maintaining a commitment to the artistic and community goals. It also falls under the finance department's responsibility to ensure compliance with relevant laws and regulations and maintain a high degree of transparency and accountability in its financial reporting.

HR

The Human Resources department is an orchestra's cornerstone, fostering a balanced work atmosphere. Their responsibilities typically span an array of areas. They handle the recruitment and selection processes, which entails recognising staffing requirements, facilitating auditions and interviews for potential musicians, and confirming that the selected individuals possess the necessary talents, administrative qualifications, and align well with the overall corporate culture. HR also looks after employee relations, acting as an intermediary between management and musicians, addressing grievances, and promoting a climate of reciprocal respect and understanding. They play a significant role in conducting the performance evaluation process, encouraging talents, and contributing to their career growth. The HR department is also vital in endorsing, promoting, and executing diversity, equity, and inclusion policies. They supervise contractual aspects, ensuring compliance with the agreements established among the musicians, management, and any relevant unions. The significance of health and safety policies is of utmost importance too, and it is within the HR's remit, in close coordination with the operations department, to enforce these provisions. Thus, the HR department forms an integral foundation of any orchestra, ensuring its seamless operations whilst also safeguarding the well-being and advancement of its musicians.

Artistic Side of the Organisation

Artistic Director

The artistic director's role covers various responsibilities, including maintaining relationships with musicians, the CEO, and the board. They are generally responsible for the overall artistic vision and have (sometimes full or, frequently, partial) authority over auditions and terminations of musicians. The artistic director collaborates with the conductor and its staff (if any) and guest artists, and the degree of authority and residence within the community vary depending on the organisation setup, values, scope, or model.

In the absence of a dedicated full- or part-time artistic director, a committee comprising a number of principal and co-principal musicians (i.e., chiefs of instrumental sections) can step in to fill in the gap. This alternative approach allows for a more collaborative decision-making process and ensures that the artistic direction is shaped by the collective wisdom and expertise of the orchestra's key musicians. The organisation effectively harnesses the unique insights and experiences of senior musicians by involving them in this capacity, thus fostering an inclusive artistic environment conducive to creativity and excellence. Additionally, assigning the artistic direction responsibilities to a committee of section (co-)principals may lead to financial savings, as there is no need to recruit a high-calibre artistic director. This cost-saving measure is particularly crucial for smaller orchestras or those with limited resources, helping them to allocate the savings more effectively and ensure the sustainability of their artistic endeavours. However, it is essential to bear in mind that while this approach may yield financial benefits, it also requires careful management and clear communication to prevent potential conflicts arising from a shared responsibility. The CEO plays a critical role in ensuring a collaborative, positive, and constructive spirit within the team, as well as in clearly allocating tasks and responsibilities to prevent any possible overlap from turning into an internal power struggle.

Artistic Department

Under the guidance of the artistic director, the artistic department assumes a vital role in programme planning, artist booking, artist care, and musician coordination. The artistic director's involvement (who may or may not be a single individual or a team holding shared responsibilities) vary depending on the specific organisation. This department maintains close ties with the (resident) conductor and supervises the integration of soloists, conductors, and repertoire. Additionally, the artistic department oversees staff conductors and manages educational and community programmes, including the chorus and youth orchestra. Commissioning new works, curating innovative and diverse performances, and collaborating with other artistic organisations are also key responsibilities of the artistic department. The artistic director should possess a keen understanding of artistic trends and audience preferences, enabling them to develop programming that is both captivating and relevant to the community. Although being a musician is not a mandatory requirement for the CEO, it is recommended for the artistic director to have a strong background in music. It is worth noting that for its operations, the Artistic Department depends on or reports to the operations manager. This may create management tensions and potential authority overlaps or inefficiencies that need to be closely and regularly collegially monitored by the CEO, the operations manager, and the artistic director.

Conductor

The conductor holds a special position within the artistic side of the organisation, leading the ensemble in performances and rehearsals.[3] Depending on the orchestra's structure and requirements, they may or may not be a resident conductor, but they work closely with the artistic director, musicians, and staff conductors to execute the artistic vision and maintain high-quality performances. Their responsibilities include interpreting the musical scores (making decisions on tempo, phrasing, dynamics, and a myriad of other technical or theoretical details related to music interpretation and execution) and ensuring that the musicians perform cohesively as a unit and at their best as part of an interactive process (Atik 1994; Koivunen and Wennes 2011). The conductor collaborates with the artistic director in selecting repertoire and guest artists while also offering input on auditions, promotions, and musician evaluations. They work with the CEO and management team to ensure alignment between the artistic and organisational goals and may participate in community-oriented activities, fundraising, and public relations. An effective conductor capable of adopting a transformational leadership style (Boerner and Freiherr Von Streit 2005; Boerner, Krause, and Gebert 2004) creates a supportive and collaborative environment that encourages artistic growth and development among musicians. They maintain open lines of communication with the musicians, staff conductors, and other members of the artistic team to address any concerns or suggestions. Their leadership style is a key factor to achieve excellent outcomes but also create a positive and collaborative work climate and vision for the performance (Lanaro et al. 2023; Krause 2015; Boerner and Freiherr Von Streit 2005). Moreover, they strive to establish strong relationships with the CEO, board, and stakeholders, contributing to the overall success and sustainability of the organisation. At the crossroads of artistic and leadership responsibilities, the conductor plays a vital role in shaping the orchestra's identity, enhancing its reputation, impacting the quality of the ensemble, and promoting artistic quality (Boerner, Krause, and Gebert 2004).

Staff Conductors

Staff conductors, including assistant, associate, apprentice, and resident conductors, as well as chorus directors and youth orchestra conductors, support the artistic director in fulfilling the artistic mission. They are responsible for leading various performances, rehearsals, and educational programmes, as well as collaborating with guest artists and conductors. It is worth noting that a handful of orchestras only have staff conductors, and even amongst the large symphonic orchestras, this function is not always carried out by a devoted separate department.

Musicians

Musicians form the backbone of the organisation and interact with the conductor, artistic director, management, and fellow musicians. Relationships between section leaders and other members are essential for maintaining a harmonious performance environment. Musicians often have a committee that represents their interests and collaborates with the HR manager. The management team should strive for open communication with the entire orchestra, not just the committee. Board interaction, musicians' involvement in community and education programmes, and participation in governance structures (e.g., boards and committees) help strengthen the relationship between musicians and the organisation.

***

Although Flanagan's remarks were focused on the cost structure (Flanagan 2012, 1. 1068), he is correct when he underlines that "most people who attend a symphony orchestra concert do not realise that the musicians, guest soloists, and conductors who deliver the performance account for little more than half of the orchestra's expenses." In other words, despite musicians being the lion's share of visibility and reputation (and employment), the overall organisation is broader and more complex. However, musicians are part of a complex sub-organisation on their own. A *full-size* modern orchestra comprises between 90 and 115 musicians across no less than 20 different instrumental sections (Hafzoglu and Öztürk 2009). Professional music ensembles manifest

TABLE 3.1 Size Comparison (Indicative)		
	Full-Scale	Chamber
I. Strings		
1. Violins		
a. First violins	22	10
b. Second violins	16	7
2. Violas	12	5
3. Cellos	12	5
4. Double basses	10	3
II. Woodwinds		
1. Flutes and piccolo	4	2
2. Oboes and English horn	4	2
3. Clarinets and bass clarinet	4	2
4. Bassoons and contrabassoon	4	2
III. Brass		
1. French horns	6	3
2. Trumpets	5	3
3. Trombones and bass trombone	4	2
4. Tubas	2	1
IV. Percussions		
1. Timpani	2	1
2. Other percussion instruments	3	1
TOTAL	**110**	**49**

in various forms and dimensions; however, orchestras rooted in the Western classical tradition typically fall into two primary categories: full-scale or compact. A compact orchestra, often referred to as a chamber orchestra, generally comprises up to 50–60 members – about half the size of a full-scale symphony orchestra. Both smaller chamber and larger philharmonic orchestras have the capacity to augment their numbers when necessary. The composition of amateur orchestras, such as school, youth, and community orchestras, displays even greater diversity in form and type. Nevertheless, the determining factor of the size is the genre of music performed: for example, smaller orchestras are sufficient for Baroque music whereas full-scale orchestras are required for the 19th-century symphonies (Sigurjónsson 2022).

The following table, although not comprehensive and merely illustrative, provides an overview of the key roles in a typical org chart and outlines their do's and don'ts, serving as a reference for students and managers. It highlights the essential responsibilities and actions to be taken by each role, as well as the pitfalls to avoid.

	Do's	Don'ts
CEO	• Harmonise artistic, financial, and operational elements; advocate for the mission • Nurture a culture of innovation, inclusivity, and excellence • Foster effective communication, collaboration, and trust • Balance financial operations constraints or limitations and aspirations to artistic excellence • Coordinate and expand revenue sources • Allocate resources	• Neglect any aspect of management • Disregard stakeholder input • Ignore long-term planning and growth opportunities • Underestimate potential conflicts from overlapping responsibilities
Operations	• Coordinate rehearsal schedules • Maintain clear communication with musicians and staff • Ensure seamless concert experiences • Address challenges promptly • Manage logistics, venue, equipment	• Overlook risk management • Neglect contingency planning • Fail to collaborate with other departments

	Do's	Don'ts
PR, Communication, Marketing	• Incorporate digital and traditional media • Target diverse audiences • Build long-term audience loyalty • Utilise data-driven marketing techniques • Manage crisis effectively • Explore new technologies	• Ignore social media opportunities • Disregard audience preferences • Neglect press and sponsors relations
(Business) Development	• Understand donor motivations and preferences • Build strong relationships with supporters • Demonstrate the impact of donor contributions • Explore new revenue sources	• Overlook potential fundraising and revenue opportunities • Neglect donor stewardship • Underestimate the importance of government relationships
Finance	• Implement robust budgeting, forecasting, and reporting processes • Collaborate with other departments for cost-saving measures and increased efficiency • Maintain transparency and accountability • Ensure compliance with laws and regulations	• Disregard long-term sustainability • Underestimate financial risks • Ignore potential inefficiencies
Artistic Director	• Develop moving and relevant programming • Maintain relationships with musicians, the Executive Director, and the Board Chair • Involve principal musicians in decision-making processes • Ensure clear task allocation and communication	• Ignore artistic trends and audience preferences • Overlook collaborative decision-making • Fail to establish a positive and constructive team environment
Artistic Dept.	• Coordinate artist booking, care, and musicians • Oversee educational and community programmes • Collaborate with other artistic organisations	• Neglect the integration of soloists, conductors, and repertoire • Disregard the importance of innovation and diversity in performances

	Do's	Don'ts
Conductor	• Execute the artistic vision • Maintain high-quality performances • Promote a supportive and collaborative environment • Establish strong relationships with stakeholders	• Overlook musician development and growth • Disregard input from musicians, staff conductors, and artistic team • Neglect the alignment of artistic and organisational goals
Staff Conductor	• Support the artistic director in fulfilling the artistic mission • Lead various performances, rehearsals, and educational programmes • Collaborate with guest artists and conductors	• Underestimate their role in the organisation • Neglect opportunities for collaboration and growth
Musicians	• Maintain harmonious performance environment • Participate in governance structures (e.g., boards, committees) • Develop and deliver community and education programmes	• Fail to communicate with the Committee • Disregard input from fellow musicians • Overlook the importance of maintaining relationships with the organisation

Authority and Remit Conflicts Between Artistic Director and Conductor: A CEO's Role in Forging Collaboration

We have already seen that in the environment of an orchestra organisation, the relationship between the artistic director and conductor plays a crucial role in shaping the ensemble's artistic success. As both individuals possess significant authority and expertise within their respective domains, it is natural for some overlaps or mild conflicts to arise concerning their roles and responsibilities. The CEO must be vigilant in recognising these potential conflicts and proactively address them to maintain a collegial and productive work environment.[4]

Although not often paroxysmal (despite the disproportionate visibility offered by media to some cases, especially if they involve known players in the industry), this form of conflict is not uncommon, as illustrated in the following table.[5]

Teatro Regio di Torino (Italy)	In 2018, the Teatro Regio Torino, a celebrated Italian opera house, encountered a transformative event when its conductor, Gianandrea Noseda, opted to leave his position. This decision was precipitated by a series of institutional disputes, including administrative upheaval and disagreements on the artistic vision. Noseda's departure underscored the potential fragility of cultural institutions, demonstrating how discord between artistic and administrative leadership engenders critical turning points that shape an organisation's trajectory (Midgette 2018; Cooper 2018; Lebrecht 2018).
Minnesota Orchestra (USA)	In 2012, the Minnesota Orchestra faced a lockout that lasted for 15 months due to a labour dispute between management and the musicians. During this time, a conflict arose between music director Osmo Vänskä and then-President and CEO Michael Henson. Vänskä publicly expressed his support for the musicians and criticised the management's handling of the situation, leading to tensions between him and Henson. In 2013, Vänskä resigned from his position in protest, but after Henson stepped down in 2014, Vänskä was reappointed as the Music Director of the Minnesota Orchestra (Gabler 2014; Kerr 2012; Allen 2016).
Teatro La Scala di Milano (Italy)	Against the backdrop of simmering tensions and longstanding disagreements between, on the one hand, maestro Riccardo Muti, "who is widely considered one of the most talented but tempestuous personalities in Italian music" (New York Times 2005), and, on the other hand, the musicians and management of Teatro La Scala, the maestro's resounding resignation in April 2005 revealed a profound rupture within the organisation, shedding light on the critical role of effective collaboration and harmonious dynamics between conductors and the rest of the staff in classical music.
Seattle Symphony Orchestra (USA)	In 2006, the Seattle Symphony Orchestra's significant deficit unfolded against a backdrop of internal discord, as a controversial survey of the musicians was seen by some as a vote of no confidence in Gerard Schwarz, the music director for more than two decades. This tension, simmering beneath the surface, was arguably exacerbated by the sudden resignation of the symphony's executive director, Paul Meecham. This sequence of events underscores the potential for internal conflict to precipitate a financial crisis, particularly when leadership roles are left in flux. The dynamic interplay among artistic direction, administrative management, and the sentiments of the musicians themselves significantly influences the orchestra's financial stability and overall success (Campbell 2006; Bargreen 2006).

A proactive approach to delineating tasks and responsibilities is essential to mitigate the risk of misunderstandings or friction between the artistic director and conductor (and, sometimes, other members of the senior management team). The CEO facilitates open and transparent communication from the outset, ensuring that each party understands their respective duties and areas of authority. Clear expectations and guidelines established by the CEO help minimise the likelihood of acute disputes and set the ground for a collaborative and constructive atmosphere within the team. However, this is not an easy task, considering the grey areas in the table of delegated authorities and the reporting lines amongst the senior leaders of an orchestral organisation, which often leave room for ambiguity and confusion.

Conflict resolution must therefore be viewed as a critical skill for the CEO when differences of opinion or approach inevitably arise, especially in the highly sensitive domain of artistic programming and execution, where the expressive power of emotions plays a significant role alongside more rational or rationalisable considerations. Active listening to both parties, understanding their perspectives, and identifying common ground or mutually acceptable solutions are crucial steps that must be undertaken. Demonstrating empathy and a genuine commitment to resolving conflicts helps build trust and encourages the artistic director and conductor to work more effectively together.

Ideally, the CEO also leads by example, adopting a positive and inclusive organisational culture that values collaboration, respect, equity, and open dialogue. Encouraging regular communication and feedback between the artistic director, conductor, and other team members helps prevent issues from escalating. Moreover, providing opportunities for professional development, team-building activities, and social interactions further strengthens relationships and offers unity among the artistic team.

In addition to managing the dynamics between the artistic director and conductor, the CEO also ensures that the entire organisation, including the board, staff, and musicians, shares a common vision and understanding of their respective roles. Offering regular updates, inviting input, and involving all stakeholders in strategic planning and decision-making processes contribute to a more cohesive and supportive organisational culture.

Ultimately, the CEO's role is to facilitate collaboration, provide clear direction, and support the artistic team in achieving their goals. The CEO primarily creates a harmonious and efficient working environment that enables the orchestra to thrive artistically and organisationally by actively addressing potential conflicts of authority and remit between the artistic director and conductor. With a proactive and empathetic leadership approach, the CEO nurtures creativity, innovation, and excellence, ensuring a lasting impact on the community.

	Do's	Don'ts
CEO	• Facilitate open communication between artistic director and conductor • Set clear expectations and guidelines for roles and responsibilities • Grow a positive organisational culture that values collaboration and respect	• Avoid taking sides in conflicts • Overlook the importance of regular feedback and communication • Neglect to involve all stakeholders in strategic planning and decision-making
Artistic Director	• Actively work with the conductor in planning and decision-making • Communicate any concerns or challenges openly with the CEO and conductor • Be open to feedback and collaboration with the conductor	• Make unilateral decisions without consulting the conductor • Allow personal differences to impact the artistic direction • Disregard the conductor's expertise and input
Conductor	• Collaborate closely with the artistic director in selecting repertoire, guest artists, and other artistic decisions • Maintain open lines of communication with the artistic director and CEO • Actively participate in team-building activities, professional development, and social interactions with the artistic director and other team members	• Disregard the artistic director's authority and vision • Avoid discussing potential conflicts or concerns with the artistic director or CEO • Isolate oneself from the artistic team and organisational culture

BOX 3.1 INSIGHTS FROM EXPERIENCED CEOs

Senior managers have a wealth of knowledge to share, providing invaluable insights into the inner workings of orchestras and the challenges they face. Their perspectives shed light on the traditional structure of an orchestra, which has remained relatively unchanged for decades. In this structure, volunteer board members are responsible for hiring professional managers and conductors, while musicians report to both the artistic director and the conductor, and staff report to the manager.

1   One critical issue experienced CEOs often discuss is the matter of term limits for conductors and board chairs. While some argue that term limits bring fresh perspectives and prevent stagnation, others maintain that exceptional conductors and board chairs should remain in their positions (or should be given a choice to remain in their positions) for as long as they continue to excel in their roles.

2   Another point raised by these CEOs is the varying degree of musicians' involvement in decision-making processes. In some orchestras, musicians prefer not to be involved in management decisions (or are not allowed to), while in others, musicians request a consultation and participate actively in the direction (Schmitz 1996). And in some countries or regions, it is even a regulatory obligation to have musicians elected by their peers sitting on the board or management committee.

3   Accountability and evaluations are important components of success too. While staff members are evaluated regularly, musicians' evaluations are often limited to the conductor's judgement, with little input from management and no structured approach. Concert reviews are the primary method for evaluating conductors and managers, but experienced CEOs stress the importance of comprehensive evaluations from the board to improve accountability and overall performance.

4   Managing small and large orchestras may seem different, but the underlying principles remain the same. Leading a small ensemble teaches board relations, budgeting, negotiations, and long-term planning. Larger orchestras may be more forgiving, and spotting incompetence could take longer due to the size and complexity of the organisation.

5   Most CEOs also agree that the composition of a board plays a significant role in the organisation's success. Society boards, typically made up of members with long-standing connections and backgrounds, differ from business boards, which are primarily dominated by corporate members. Experienced CEOs find that managing society boards is more challenging due to a lack of experience in operations as well as in delegating tasks and supervising people among members.

6   Leadership is another pillar factor in turning around a struggling orchestra. A strong leader revitalises the board, hires better managers and staff, and implements necessary changes to enhance the performance. When hiring a manager, experienced CEOs recommend selecting a

professional with a proven track record and relevant experience in areas such as ticket sales and non-profit management.[6] The search committee should consist of individuals with sound judgement and influential positions on the board and in the community to ensure their investment in the manager's success.

These insights highlight the value of understanding the subtleties of management. Taking into account the perspectives and wisdom of others allows leaders to navigate the challenges of the industry and ultimately guide their organisations to success.

B. VOLUNTEERS

To be clear, volunteers are vital in supporting the operation and contributing to its success in various ways. Expectations of volunteers include:

- **Involvement in more than just fundraising activities:** Volunteers are or should be given roles of importance within the institution, such as participating in education and community programs or serving as docents.
- **Recognition and reinforcement:** Volunteers should receive positive reinforcement for their contributions, as they are not financially compensated.
- **Collaboration with the staff:** Volunteers should work closely with staff members to ensure a unified approach to the goals.

In addition to contributing to the operations, volunteers raise between 5–10% of the organisation's budget (especially in the US). While their contributions are invaluable, the management team balances volunteers' expectations with musicians' rights, as it could be challenging to explain why musicians cannot perform for free.

***

A thorough understanding of the various roles and functions is crucial for effective management to coordinate efforts, streamline operations, and create an environment where all stakeholders contribute to the artistic and financial success.

C. UNDERSTANDING THE GOVERNANCE STRUCTURE

An in-depth comprehension of the governance structure is vital for the efficient functioning and the harmonious collaboration of all the components. Orchestras are typically composed of several departments, including executive, artistic, and administrative, that work together to support the organisation's operations while championing values and objectives that are hardly compatible, such as artistic excellence on the one hand, and operational efficiency and financial sustainability on the other hand.

Executive and artistic departments determine the direction and programming. The executive team, led by the CEO, oversees the organisation's administration, financial management, and strategic planning. Meanwhile, the artistic team, headed by the artistic director or conductor, and sometimes with the input of the musicians, shapes the artistic vision and repertoire. A strong and transparent relationship between the music director and the CEO is essential for striking a balance between artistic aspirations and operational and financial sustainability.

The administrative department encompasses several functions, such as operations, finance, public relations, marketing, and fundraising. The operations team manages day-to-day logistics, including concert production, scheduling, and coordination among musicians, conductors, and guest artists. The finance team oversees the budget, financial reporting and key performance indicators (KPIs), and compliance with regulatory requirements.

Communications, marketing, and public relations work on strengthening the brand, reaching out to the audience, and attracting new patrons. While these functions are sometimes merged due to budget constraints, they serve distinct purposes: broadly speaking, public relations focuses on media relations and reputation management, while marketing is concerned with advertising, ticket sales, and audience development.

Regardless of the magnitude of government subsidies, fundraising is always a crucial aspect of the management structure, as it helps secure the financial resources necessary to support artistic endeavours and community outreach initiatives. Fundraisers are responsible for building relationships with donors, securing grants, and organising special events, often with the help of volunteers.

The overall size significantly impacts the staff structure. Smaller ensembles might have a more condensed organisation, whereas larger ones employ up to a hundred staff members, depending on factors such as hall ownership and groundskeeping needs. Regardless of size, a well-functioning orchestra requires effective communication and collaboration among its various departments to realise its artistic and business goals.

D. THE ROLES OF THE BOARD AND STAFF

An active board is a valuable asset for governance, advocacy, fundraising efforts, and definition of overall mission and vision. Typically composed of community leaders, philanthropists, experts, and musician representatives, board members contribute their expertise, time, and financial resources to support the organisation's mission.[7]

Board committees provide guidance to the professional staff, with standing committees overseeing ongoing responsibilities and ad hoc committees formed for specific purposes. The involvement of musicians on the board has become more common in recent years, and it is generally seen as a positive development, as it contributes to ownership and shared responsibility among the stakeholders.

In addition to the board, staff also play a vital role in implementing the strategic plan and executing the day-to-day operations. They work closely with the artistic director and the CEO to ensure the organisation's artistic and financial success as well as contributing to the fundraising and community efforts, participating in donor cultivation events and educational outreach programs.

However, things are much less simple than they may appear when compared to most other professional backgrounds and contexts. As Newton rightly pointed out (Newton 2022, 1. 1327):

> the relationship between the board of directors, as the governing body, and the musicians of the orchestra, as the resident artists, is not as simple as the organisational chart might suggest. In a typical orchestra, musicians are accountable to the music director and the orchestra manager, both of whom report to the board.

In conclusion, success hinges on the effective collaboration and communication among various components, including the board, staff, musicians, and volunteers. A spirit of teamwork and shared responsibility enables the achievement of artistic, financial, and community objectives. Following Hirzy (1997), the board members have ten key responsibilities:

1 Board members have the ultimate responsibility for the organisation's success.
2 They ensure financial stability by establishing a realistic budget and providing sufficient funds for operations.
3 Board members work to maintain and increase the public profile through effective marketing and fundraising efforts.

4 They are responsible for hiring and evaluating the performance of the executive director, who oversees the day-to-day operations.

5 Board members oversee the development and implementation of policies and procedures to ensure ethical and legal operations.

6 They work to develop and maintain relationships with donors, sponsors, and other stakeholders.

7 Board members ensure that the orchestra maintains a high level of artistic quality by hiring and evaluating conductors and musicians.

8 They work to develop and implement strategic plans to guide the future direction and growth.

9 Board members oversee the management of the facilities and equipment to ensure that they are maintained in good condition.

10 They act as ambassadors, representing the orchestra in the community and advocating for its interests.

Last but not least, management research tends to demonstrate a correlation between diversity in the boardroom and organisational performance (Kusumastati et al. 2022). Diverse boards bring a broader range of perspectives, experiences, and expertise, fostering more informed decision-making, innovative problem-solving, and ultimately driving better overall performance.

CASE STUDY 3.1

Reorganising for Efficiency and Evolving Audiences

The classical music landscape undergoes constant changes, necessitating orchestras to adapt and cater to the needs of both in-person and online audiences. This case study delves into the quantitative restructuring of a full-size orchestra to bolster efficiency and better align with the shifting expectations of audiences in the digital era, whilst addressing staff reallocation, termination, and recruitment.

The management team took the following actions:

1. ASSESSING THE CURRENT SITUATION

- Identifying inefficiencies: A comprehensive audit revealed that 30% of the resources were underutilised or misallocated.

- Evaluating the digital impact: Audience surveys showed that 65% of respondents would prefer more digital engagement opportunities and 45% requested diversified concert experiences.
- Conducting stakeholder consultations: 120 musicians, staff, board members, and audience members participated in in-depth interviews and focus groups.
- Assessing staff skill sets: 20% of the staff were found to possess skills misaligned with the strategic objectives.

2. ESTABLISHING REORGANISATION OBJECTIVES

- Increasing operational efficiency: Aim to reduce operational costs by 15%.
- Improving audience participation and experience: Target a 20% increase in audience engagement metrics.
- Expanding digital and online presence: Boost online audience by 30% within two years.
- Addressing skill gaps and optimising staff allocation: Ensure 95% of staff hold roles that align with their skill sets and the objectives.

3. REDESIGNING THE ORGANISATIONAL STRUCTURE

- Streamlining management: Reduce the number of hierarchical levels by 25%.
- Stimulating collaboration: Implement three cross-functional teams to promote interdepartmental cooperation.
- Appointing dedicated staff: Allocate six full-time staff members to manage digital initiatives and audience engagement.
- Identifying staff reallocation, termination, and recruitment opportunities: Reallocate 10% of current staff, terminate 5% with transition support, and recruit 8% new staff members with required skills.

4. IMPLEMENTING NEW TECHNOLOGY AND PROCESSES

- Deploying CRM systems: Integrate audience segmentation and personalised communication capabilities.
- Utilising streaming and virtual performance platforms: Increase online concert offerings by 50%.
- Leveraging social media: Achieve a 40% increase in social media interactions.
- Streamlining ticketing and booking systems: Reduce booking friction by 20%.

5. ENRICHING THE CONCERT EXPERIENCE

- Offering pre-concert events: Schedule 15 pre-concert talks, master-classes, and educational events per season.
- Encouraging audience interaction: Host Q&A sessions and post-concert discussions for 50% of performances.
- Showcasing behind-the-scenes content: Share musician profiles and exclusive content on digital platforms, targeting a 30% increase in engagement.

6. PROMOTING A CULTURE OF INNOVATION AND ADAPTABILITY

- Encouraging experimentation: Introduce three new concert formats and programming initiatives per season.
- Offering professional development opportunities: Allocate resources for the development of 25% of staff and musicians.
- Establishing a feedback loop: Conduct bi-annual reviews to evaluate and refine reorganisation efforts.

7. MEASURING THE IMPACT AND SUCCESS OF THE REORGANISATION

- Tracking KPIs: Monitor audience size, ticket sales, and online presence growth rates.
- Conducting regular reviews: Perform quarterly evaluations and adjust strategies as necessary.
- Collecting feedback: Survey 10% of stakeholders bi-annually to inform future improvements.

The reorganisation led to augmented efficiency, heightened audience engagement, and a more vibrant online presence. By embracing new technologies, adopting an audience-centric approach, and addressing staff reallocation, termination, and recruitment, the orchestra successfully adapted to the changing expectations of both in-person and online audiences. Key lessons learned from this case study include the importance of continuously assessing and adapting to the evolving landscape, promoting a culture of innovation, maintaining open communication with stakeholders, and effectively managing human resources to ensure the success of the reorganisation. The restructuring serves as a valuable example for other organisations looking to navigate the challenges presented by the digital era and the ever-changing expectations of audiences.

QUESTIONS:

1   Considering the reorganisation strategy, to what extent do you believe the decision to reduce the hierarchical levels by 25% influenced the success of their operations? Are there alternative organisational structures that could have been more effective?

2   Given that the objective was to boost online audience by 30% within two years, how do you think the implementation of streaming and virtual performance platforms, along with dedicated staff for digital initiatives, affected this outcome? What other strategies might have been employed to increase the digital audience?

3   The reorganisation led to an augmented efficiency and heightened audience engagement, but how would you navigate the potential conflicts and resistance that often come with change, such as staff reallocation, termination, and recruitment?

4   Reflecting on the notion of an 'audience-centric' approach, what do you believe are the most effective methods of measuring audience engagement and satisfaction? How can such feedback be utilised to continuously adapt and enhance the concert experience?

5   The case study emphasises a culture of innovation and adaptability, introducing new concert formats and providing professional development opportunities. In your view, how vital is such a culture in the digital age? Can you identify any risks associated with this approach, and how might they be mitigated?

Box 3.2 Expanding Perspectives: Review Questions

1   How do the various components of a management structure, including the roles of the CEO, artistic director, conductor, and volunteers, interact to maintain harmony and efficiency within the organisation? How can potential conflicts of authority be managed effectively, and how does a positive and inclusive organisational culture contribute to the success?

2 Volunteers play a significant role in the operations, including fundraising and community programmes. Considering their essential contributions but lack of financial compensation, how can an orchestra effectively balance the expectations of volunteers with the professional rights of its musicians?

3 Delving into the dynamics of the management structure, explore how the relationship between the executive team and the artistic team can be maintained to balance artistic goals with financial sustainability. In this context, discuss the critical roles that effective communication and collaboration play across different departments.

4 The board and staff fulfil a multitude of roles, from guiding the staff and overseeing ongoing responsibilities to implementing the strategic plan and participating in community outreach. Discuss the potential challenges and rewards of musicians' involvement on the board and how their participation contributes to a shared sense of responsibility. What are some ways board members can effectively execute their ten key responsibilities, including maintaining financial stability and serving as ambassadors in the community?

NOTES

1 Peter Pastreich, the former executive director of the San Francisco Symphony, is often credited with the "three-legged stool" model. This model illustrates the need for a balanced and collaborative relationship among the music director, the executive director, and the board chair. Each "leg" of the stool represents one of these key stakeholders, and together they form a stable foundation. See Fogel (2000).

2 While traditional management of arts and cultural institutions seems to have fundamentally misunderstood arts marketing and audience development, in his remarkable book, Hadley (2021) profoundly changes the idea of audience development, highlighting its relationship to cultural policies.

3 Although some orchestras do not have a resident conductor, examples of completely conductorless large ensembles are extremely rare, such as the Orpheus Chamber Orchestra, already explored by Vredenburgh and Yunxia He (2003) or Lubans (2009).

4 An excellent analysis of interpersonal relationships, power dynamics, and organisational structures that underpin a symphony orchestra's inner workings is provided by Allmendinger, Hackman, and Lehman (1996).

5 This same form of conflict is not unusual in other performing arts as well; see Fraissard (2023).

6 For more details and accurate analysis of managing non-profit organisations, see Tschir-hart and Bielefeld (2012) and Worth (2021).
7 In her outstanding book on Arts Governance, Rentschler (2014, Part II) provides a sharp analysis of the typical profiles and roles of board members in cultural industries.

BIBLIOGRAPHY

Allen, David. 2016. "The Minnesota Orchestra Rebounds from a 'Near Death Experi-ence'." *The New York Times*, February 25. www.nytimes.com/2016/02/28/arts/music/the-minnesota-orchestra-rebounds-from-a-near-death-experience.html.

Allmendinger, Jutta, J. Richard Hackman, and Erin V. Lehman. 1996. "Life and Work in Symphony Orchestras." *The Musical Quarterly* 80 (2): 194–219. https://doi.org/10.1093/mq/80.2.194.

Atik, Yaakov. 1994. "The Conductor and the Orchestra: Interactive Aspects of the Leader-shipProcess." *Leadership & Organization Development Journal* 15 (1): 22–28. https://doi.org/10.1108/01437739410050123.

Bargreen, Melinda. 2006. "Seattle Symphony Orchestra Musicians' Survey Creates Discord with Board of Trustees." https://archive.seattletimes.com/archive/?date=20060703&slug=symphony03.

Boerner, Sabine, Diana Krause, and Diether Gebert. 2004. "Leadership and Co-Operation in Orchestras." *Human Resource Development International* 7 (4): 465–479. https://doi.org/10.1080/1367886042000246030.

Boerner, Sabine, and Christian Freiherr Von Streit. 2005. "Transformational Leadership and Group Climate-Empirical Results from Symphony Orchestras." *Journal of Leadership & Organizational Studies* 12 (2): 31–41. https://doi.org/10.1177/107179190501200203.

Byrnes, William J. 2022. *Management and the Arts*, 6th ed. New York: Routledge.

Campbell, R. M. 2006. "Orchestra Deficit Exceeds $3 Million." *Seattle Post-Intelligencer*. www.seattlepi.com/news/article/Orchestra-deficit-exceeds-3-million-1214871.php.

Cooper, Michael. 2018. "Tumult at an Italian Opera House: A Major Conductor Leaves Turin." *The New York Times*, April 26. www.nytimes.com/2018/04/26/arts/music/giandrea-noseda-teatro-regio-torino.html.

DeVereaux, Constance, ed. 2019. *Arts and Cultural Management: Sense and Sensibilities in the State of the Field*. New York: Routledge.

DiMaggio, Paul. 1987. *Managers of the Arts: Careers and Opinions of Senior Administrators of U.S. Art Museums, Symphony Orchestras, Resident Theatres, and Local Arts Agencies*, 1st ed. Research Division Report/National Endowment for the Arts, no. 20. Washington, DC: Seven Locks Press.

Faulkner, Robert R. 1973. "Orchestra Interaction: Some Features of Communication and Authority in an Artistic Organization." *The Sociological Quarterly* 14 (2): 147–157. https://doi.org/10.1111/j.1533-8525.1973.tb00850.x.

Flanagan, Robert J. 2012. *The Perilous Life of Symphony Orchestras: Artistic Triumphs and Economic Challenges*. New Haven: Yale University Press.

Fogel, Henry. 2000. "Are Three Legs Appropriate? Or Even Sufficient?" *Harmony. Forum of the Symphony Orchestra Institute* 10 (April): 11–34.

Fraissard, Guillaume. 2023. "Le conflit entre le metteur en scène Krystian Lupa et l'équipe technique de la Comédie de Genève illustre un changement d'époque pour les créateurs." *Le Monde*, June 23. www.lemonde.fr/idees/article/2023/06/23/le-conflit-entre-le-metteur-en-scene-krystian-lupa-et-l-equipe-technique-de-la-comedie-de-geneve-illustre-un-changement-d-epoque-pour-les-createurs_6178967_3232.html.

Gabler, Jay. 2014. "Minnesota Orchestra Lockout: What Have We Learned?" *Minnesota Public Radio*. www.yourclassical.org/story/2014/01/15/minnesota-orchestra-lockout-what-have-we-learned.

Glynn, Mary Ann. 2000. "When Cymbals Become Symbols: Conflict Over Organizational Identity Within a Symphony Orchestra." *Organization Science* 11 (3): 285–298. https://doi.org/10.1287/orsc.11.3.285.12496.

Hadley, Steven. 2021. *Audience Development and Cultural Policy*. New York: Springer Nature.

Hafzoglu, Mustafa, and Mustafa Cumhur Öztürk. 2009. "What Does an Orchestra Conductor Actually Do? – Project Managers." www.pmi.org/learning/library/2019/04/07/15/29/what-orchestra-conductor-actually-do-6882.

Hirzy, Ellen Cochran. 1997. *Guide to Orchestra Governance*, revised ed. New York: American Symphony Orchestra League.

Kerr, Euan. 2012. "Locked-out Minn Orch Musicians Take Cause to Streets." *MPR News*. www.mprnews.org/story/2012/10/01/locked-out-minn-orch-musicians-take-cause-to-streets.

Koivunen, Niina, and Grete Wennes. 2011. "Show Us the Sound! Aesthetic Leadership of Symphony Orchestra Conductors." *Leadership* 7 (1): 51–71. https://doi.org/10.1177/1742715010386865.

Krause, Diana E. 2015. "Four Types of Leadership and Orchestra Quality." *Nonprofit Management & Leadership* 25 (4): 431–447. https://doi.org/10.1002/nml.21132.

Kusumastati, Widyahayu Warmmeswara, Sylvia Veronica Siregar, Dwi Martani, and Desi Adhariani. 2022. "Board Diversity and Corporate Performance in a Two-Tier Governance Context." *Team Performance Management* 28 (3/4): 260–279. https://doi.org/10.1108/tpm-11-2021-0076.

Lanaro, Lucia, Andrea Bobbio, Michele Biasutti, and Evangelos Himonides. 2023. "Five Parameters for Studying Leadership Styles in Orchestra Conductors." In *Research Studies in Music Education*. SAGE Publications Ltd. https://doi.org/10.1177/1321103X221149940.

Lebrecht, Norman. 2018. "Gianandrea Noseda Quits Turin in Outrage." https://slippedisc.com/2018/04/breaking-gianandrea-noseda-quits-turin-in-outrage/.

Lubans, John. 2009. "Peer Coaching for the New Library." In *Strategies for Regenerating the Library and Information Profession*, edited by Jana Varlejs, Liz Lewis, and Graham Walton, 126–136. Berlin and New York: K. G. Saur. https://doi.org/10.1515/9783598441776.2.126.

Midgette, Anne. 2018. "Noseda Resigns Torino Post." *The Washington Post*, April 26. www.washingtonpost.com/news/style/wp/2018/04/26/noseda-resigns-torino-post/.

Newton, Travis. 2022. *Orchestra Management Handbook: Building Relationships in Turbulent Times*, 1st ed. New York: Oxford University Press.

New York Times. 2005. "Conductor of Italy's La Scala Opera Resigns." *The New York Times*, April 2. www.nytimes.com/2005/04/02/arts/music/conductor-of-italys-la-scala-opera-resigns.html.

Otis, Philo Adams. 1924. *The Chicago Symphony Orchestra: Its Organization Growth and Development, 1891–1924*. Chicago, IL: Books for Libraries.

Poulios, Ioannis, and Efrosini Kamperou. 2022. "Business Innovation in Orchestra Organizations Supported by Digital Technologies: The Orchestra Mobile Case Study." *Sustainability: Science Practice and Policy* 14 (7): 3715. https://doi.org/10.3390/su14073715.

Rentschler, Ruth. 2014. *Arts Governance: People, Passion, Performance*. London: Routledge.

Schmitz, Michael J. 1996. "Musician Participation in Symphony Orchestra Management: The Milwaukee Symphony Orchestra Experience." *Harmony. Forum of the Symphony Orchestra Institute* 3: 23–29. www.esm.rochester.edu/iml/prjc/poly/wp-content/uploads/2012/02/Musician_Part_Schmitz.pdf.

Sigurjónsson, Njörður. 2022. "Orchestra Leadership." In *Managing the Arts and Culture*, edited by Constance DeVereaux, 1st ed., 240–262. London: Routledge.

Teohari, Georgiana Alina, Nicolae Aurelian Bibu, and Laura Brancu. 2020. "Innovative Aspects in Managing Classic Professional Orchestras, as Multiple Stakeholder Organizations." In *Innovation in Sustainable Management and Entrepreneurship*, 507–525. Cham: Springer International Publishing. https://doi.org/10.1007/978-3-030-44711-3_38.

Tschirhart, Mary, and Wolfgang Bielefeld. 2012. *Managing Nonprofit Organizations*, 1st ed. San Francisco: Jossey-Bass.

Vredenburgh, Donald, and Irene Yunxia He. 2003. "Leadership Lessons from a Conductorless Orchestra." *Business Horizons* 46 (5): 19–24. https://doi.org/10.1016/S0007-6813(03)00067-3.

Worth, Michael J. 2021. *Nonprofit Management: Principles and Practice*, 5th ed. Thousand Oaks, CA: SAGE Publications.

Cited content from websites was last accessed on 01 July 2023.

CHAPTER 4

The Business Models of Classical Orchestras

With its rich history and enduring cultural significance, the classical music industry has long been a vital component of the global artistic landscape. Orchestras, as the centrepieces of classical music, have played an essential role in shaping the soundscape of the Western world. However, the challenges of the 21st century have compelled these organisations to reconsider their *modus operandi*. In this chapter, we review the business models of classical orchestras, and we examine the tension between (constantly growing) costs and (perennially insufficient) revenues and the challenges they face.

In recent years, orchestras have found themselves struggling with a myriad of obstacles. From shifts in socioeconomic and demographic structure of audiences to evolving preferences and tastes (Weber 2008), coupled with the pervasive influence of digital technologies, the industry has been compelled to evolve and adapt at a rapid pace. That does not even take into account the looming threat and disruptive scenarios of the most recent advancements in augmented reality and artificial intelligence, which could potentially upset the entire ecosystem. As a consequence, the traditional business models that once supported these institutions are under increased scrutiny, with a growing emphasis on the need to pivot towards change and still mysterious horizons. Within this context, this chapter aims to provide a holistic examination of the prevailing state of business models, pinpointing the pivotal elements that underpin their financial (un)stability and artistic vitality.

The chapter commences with an investigation into the metamorphosis of business models, tracing their development from historical beginnings to the contemporary versions that have surfaced in reaction to the exigencies of today's world. We will discuss the impact of various economic, social, and technological factors on the business models, shedding light on the drivers behind their evolution over time. Subsequently, we pivot our focus to the fundamental components of revenue and cost structure. By examining the

DOI: 10.4324/9781032629636-4

diverse revenue streams, such as ticket sales, corporate sponsorships, and fundraising initiatives, we will gain insights into the financial bedrocks of these institutions. Moreover, we will probe into the cost structures, identifying strategies for cost optimisation that could ensure their continued relevance. As we investigate further into business models, we will also consider the challenges and opportunities they face. Ranging from the intricate equilibrium between financial stability and artistic excellence to manoeuvring the intricate web of stakeholder relations, we will delve into the obstacles that orchestras surmount in their quest for success. We will discuss the significance of innovation and adaptation in this context, highlighting the importance of change while preserving the traditions that have come to define the classical music world.

To further enrich our understanding of these issues, the chapter will end with a case study of a leading classical ensemble that has successfully adapted its business model in the face of contemporary issues. Through a close examination of their revenue and cost strategies, as well as their approach to addressing the obstacles they face, we will glean insights that apply more broadly across the industry.

In providing a comprehensive dissection of the business models, this chapter aims to shed light on the critical factors that contribute to success and resilience in an increasingly unpredictable market. By doing so, we hope to offer guidance for those navigating the waters of management in the broader artistic landscape.

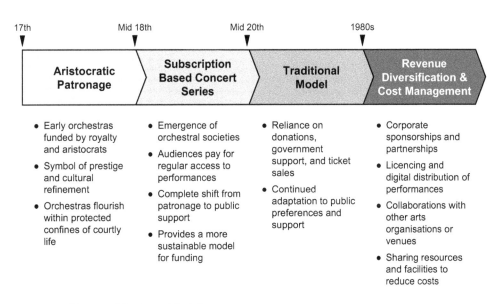

FIGURE 4.1 History of Business Models

WHAT YOU WILL LEARN IN THIS CHAPTER

Section	Key Learning Points
A. The Evolving Landscape of Business Models	Traditional reliance on government subsidies, ticket sales, and private donations have been challenged due to evolving audience preferences, technological innovations, and shifting economic landscapes. A variety of different revenue streams are now being considered, including corporate sponsorships, partnerships, fundraising campaigns, and digital platforms to reach a broader audience. Simultaneously, orchestras are striving to improve cost management and optimise resource allocation to ensure financial sustainability. Nonetheless, they also maintain a commitment to artistic excellence, as it is crucial to their identity and audience engagement.
B. Revenue Streams and Cost Structure	The revenue streams are becoming more diversified, going beyond traditional government funding and ticket sales. They are leveraging digital platforms for both performances and marketing to global audiences, partnering with corporations for sponsorships, and increasingly relying on philanthropy to supplement their income. This expanded revenue model calls for a more strategic approach to cost management, with a focus on balancing financial imperatives and artistic objectives. Optimised budgeting and resource allocation, such as investment in high-quality artists and innovative programming, are key to sustaining this balance and achieving long-term organisational resilience.
C. Adapting Business Models	Adapting to shifting audience demographics and preferences poses a significant challenge. To engage younger and more diverse listeners, orchestras employ strategies such as innovative programming that breaks away from traditional repertoire, using digital technology for enhanced connectivity and engagement, and improving the audience experience with initiatives such as pre-concert talks and sensory-friendly performances. On the financial side, the decline of traditional funding sources necessitates exploration of alternative funding models and building a culture of philanthropy. Balancing artistic and financial imperatives is a delicate task that requires strategic planning and resource allocation. Moreover, change and organisational resilience are critical to navigate these challenges and capitalise on new opportunities to foster a culture of innovation, strengthen leadership and governance structures, and maintain alignment with core values and mission.
D. Business Models and Management Mindset	The relationship between business models and management mindsets highlights the impact of funding sources on the prevailing management approaches, which ranges from administrative to entrepreneurial mindsets. The hybrid funding model, combining government and private funding, leads to a blended management approach. A two-dimensional graphical representation is proposed, demonstrating the prevailing operational models in different countries while acknowledging the temporal nature of these dynamics. However, further research in this area is needed.

A. THE EVOLVING LANDSCAPE OF BUSINESS MODELS

Traditional Business Models in the Classical Music Industry

As highlighted in Chapter 2, the history of classical orchestras dates back several centuries, with their organisational and financial structures evolving alongside broader societal and cultural changes. In their earliest forms, orchestras were often funded by the patronage of aristocrats and royalty, who supported the arts as a symbol of prestige and cultural refinement (Weber 2008). This patronage system, which allowed some security and prosperity within the protected confines of courtly life, gradually gave way to a more diverse range of funding sources in the 19th and 20th centuries. As orchestras expanded beyond the confines of aristocratic patronage, they began to rely increasingly on ticket sales, private donations, and government subsidies to support their activities. The establishment of orchestral societies and subscription-based concert series, such as the *Leipzig Gewandhaus* in 1781 and the *Vienna Philharmonic* in 1842, provided a more sustainable model for funding, with audiences paying for regular access to performances (Lebrecht 1997).

Despite these changes, the traditional business model has remained relatively stable, with a heavy reliance on donations, government support, and ticket sales. However, as we shall see, the landscape of business models has undergone a more rapid transformation in recent years, driven by an array of economic, social, and technological factors.

Current Trends and Emerging Models

Since the 1980s and the political swing towards a progressive government disengagement from arts and culture funding, classical orchestras have faced a variety of problems that have forced them to re-evaluate and adapt their business models. These challenges include, amongst many more issues, dwindling government subsidies, shifting audience preferences, and the impact of digital technology on the consumption and distribution of music.

One notable trend in the classical music industry has been the increasing emphasis on revenue diversification that translated into a thorough exploration of new sources of income beyond traditional reliance on ticket sales, donations, and government support. For instance, corporate sponsorships and partnerships have gradually stepped in to offset the decline in public funds and supplement the traditional income sources (Caves 2002, 2003). These alliances take various forms, from sponsoring individual concerts or seasons to providing ongoing support for specific artistic initiatives.

Another avenue for revenue diversification has been the licensing and (analog first, then digital) distribution of performances. With the rise of digital music stores in the 2000s and the growth of online streaming platforms in the early 2010s, a new avenue has opened to reach a global audience and generate income from recorded performances. These technological innovations expand audiences like never before but also tap into new revenue streams that bolster their financial sustainability. The advent of digital platforms[1] has profoundly transformed the dissemination of classical music. These platforms, with their global reach and ease of access, have significantly expanded the capability to engage audiences far beyond traditional physical limitations. However, Spotify data reveals a marked bias favouring well-established ensembles, perceived more as global brands than as local cultural institutions. This phenomenon foregrounds a new dynamic wherein the utility of digital distribution emerges as an instrument for fostering and sustaining a global brand identity.

BOX 4.1 MOST-STREAMED ORCHESTRAS

In 2016, the most-streamed orchestras by monthly listens on Spotify were (Wise 2016):

	Monthly Listens (2016)
London Symphony Orchestra	1,499,220
London Philharmonic Orchestra	1,384,370
Royal Philharmonic Orchestra	685,091
Vienna Philharmonic Orchestra	677,777
Academy of St. Martin in the Fields	490,937
Cleveland Orchestra	354,171
Philharmonia Orchestra	333,509
New York Philharmonic	304,499
Royal Scottish National Orchestra	233,412
Royal Concertgebouw Orchestra	213,116

In addition to diversifying their revenue sources, orchestras have also sought to refine and optimise their cost structures. This has led to a greater focus on cost management and efficiency, with various strategies for reducing expenses without compromising artistic quality. For example, some have entered into collaborations with other arts organisations or venues, sharing resources and facilities to reduce costs.

The Impact of Economic, Social, and Technological Factors on Business Models

The business models of classical orchestras have been significantly influenced by a range of economic, social, and technological factors.[2] The reduction in government funding for artistic activities has precipitated a search for alternative sources of income and a greater emphasis on financial independence among cultural institutions. This shift has led to a greater emphasis on revenue diversification and the need to define new cost management strategies to maximise the efficient use of limited resources. As highlighted by Giraud Voss (2020), who examined the economic, artistic, and structural landscape of 65 professional orchestras of varying sizes over a nine-year period, the economic recession that began in the late 2000s in the US, following the financial crisis, led to reductions in ticket sales, donations, and government support, forcing orchestras to adjust their operations and finances accordingly.

Shifting audience preferences and demographics have also played a role in shaping the business models. The evolving demographics of audiences revealed a decline in overall attendance, particularly among younger generations. This decline is attributed to various factors, such as changes in music education, shifting leisure patterns, and the growing popularity of alternative music genres.

B. REVENUE STREAMS AND COST STRUCTURE

Government Funding and Revenue Diversification

In the recent economic climate, revenue diversification has become increasingly important as a means of ensuring financial survival. As traditional sources of income, such as government subsidies and ticket sales, become less reliable, orchestras are compelled to explore alternative revenue streams.

Ticket sales and subscription models: Ticket sales remain a crucial source of income. Although its share of the total revenue considerably varies depending

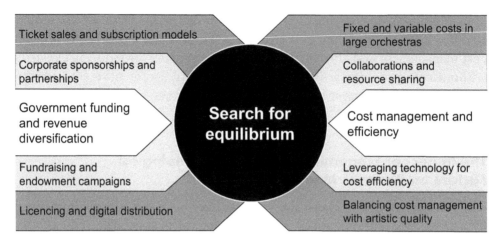

FIGURE 4.2 Revenue Streams and Cost Structure

on the predominant funding framework in the country, state, or region, various strategies have been employed to maximise income from this channel. These include offering a range of ticket prices to accommodate different budgets, providing discounts for group bookings or early bird purchases, and implementing dynamic pricing models that adjust ticket prices based on demand.

Subscription models also play an important role in generating revenue and forming long-term audience relationships. Subscribers often receive benefits such as priority seating, discounted ticket prices, and exclusive access to special events. This approach not only guarantees a certain level of income but also promotes audience loyalty and engagement.

Corporate sponsorships and partnerships: Following the decline of government funding for the arts, corporate sponsorships and partnerships have gained increasing prominence in the revenue mix. Such relationships are mutually beneficial, with the cultural institution receiving financial support and the corporate partner gaining exposure and positive brand association. Sponsorship deals vary greatly in scope and scale, from sponsoring individual concerts to supporting an entire season or specific artistic initiatives.

In addition to monetary contributions, corporate partners may also offer in-kind support, such as providing access to resources or expertise in areas such as marketing, logistics, or technology. Building long-term, strategic relationships with corporate sponsors is instrumental in enhancing financial sustainability.

Fundraising and endowment campaigns: Private donations from individuals or foundations are another key source of revenue. Fundraising campaigns take many forms (Loots et al. 2022), including annual appeals, capital campaigns for infrastructure projects, and planned giving programmes that encourage donors to include orchestras in their estate planning.

Endowment funds, which invest donated capital to generate income through interest and dividends, provide a stable and long-term source of revenue. Building a substantial endowment reduces the reliance on fluctuating income sources, such as ticket sales and government support, and secures their financial future.

Licensing and digital distribution of performances: The digital revolution has opened up new revenue channels through the licensing and distribution of performances. Streaming of existing recordings or live events on digital platforms touches a much larger audience and potentially generates additional income. This also helps expand the reach beyond the local classical music scene, allowing new listeners who might not otherwise to have access to these live performances.

In addition to distributing recorded performances, licensing performance recordings for use in films, shows, commercials, and other media has emerged as a new avenue of business opportunities. While this shift serves as another source of revenue, it is also a means of raising the orchestra's profile and attracting new audiences.

Cost Management and Efficiency

In light of the prevailing financial pressures, the significance of effective cost management has escalated. Arts and culture institutions now increasingly depend on a thorough examination of their cost structures and the development of cost optimisation strategies, instead of relying solely on public funding, to maintain a balanced budget. In this context, accurate financial analysis and cost-control measures are essential to ensure the sustainability of operations. Similarly, identifying the key characteristics of operational practices is crucial in pursuing financial efficiency (Cheung Leung 2013).

Fixed and variable costs: Any organisation typically faces a mix of fixed and variable costs. Fixed costs include items such as staff salaries, venue rental or maintenance, utilities and insurances, and administrative overheads. Variable costs may encompass expenses such as guest artist fees, production costs for specific performances, touring and travels, and marketing and advertising expenses.

Understanding the breakdown of fixed and variable costs, their levers and sensitivity is crucial for effective cost management. After areas where costs can be optimised have been identified and assessed, resource allocation and budgeting decisions gain substantial precision. For instance, negotiating better rental terms for performance venues decreases fixed costs while outsourcing marketing efforts related to special events mitigates variable costs, which free up financial resources to be invested in higher-return initiatives.

Collaborations and resource sharing: Collaboration and resource sharing offer significant cost-saving opportunities. Partnerships with other arts organisations or venues and sharing resources and facilities reduce individual expenses. For example, orchestras might collaborate with local theatre companies or dance ensembles to share performance spaces, rehearsal facilities, and administrative staff.

Collaborative projects also lead to cost savings by pooling resources for joint productions or artistic initiatives. Of course, alongside reducing costs, these alliances also foster creative synergies and opportunities for cross-disciplinary artistic exploration.

Leveraging technology for cost efficiency: Technology offers numerous cost-saving opportunities too. For example, digital marketing and social media platforms provide cost-effective ways to communicate with audiences and publicise performances. In recent years, cultural institutions have shown an increased capacity to master technologies for a more cost-effective reach of their desired audience, reducing the share of traditional marketing channels in their communication mix.

Technology also plays a role in streamlining administrative processes by reducing overhead costs and improving overall efficiency. Implementing software for tasks such as ticket sales management, donor tracking, customer relationship, and financial reporting saves time and resources and also provides valuable data to inform decision-making and strategy development. Although tools such as Large Language Models (and their derived specific or sectorial applications) are not commonly used at the time of writing this book, there is no doubt that several routines and time-consuming tasks can already benefit from an integration of artificial intelligence solutions in numerous processes of day-to-day administration (such as drafting communication materials, semi-automated replies to emails, simple marketing data analysis, copywriting, assessment of prospective initiatives, generating reports, brainstorming etc.).

Balancing cost management with artistic quality: While financial sustainability requires sound cost management, it is a common practice to strike a balance between cost efficiency and artistic quality of public performances. Observation shows that this balance often demands a nuanced approach to budgeting and resource allocation, ensuring investment continuity in areas that directly contribute to the quality of the artistic output, such as hiring skilled musicians, engaging top-tier guest artists, and developing innovative programming.

In conclusion, understanding and managing revenue streams and cost structures is a critical component of the business models of large ensembles. Revenue diversification, cost structure optimisation, and fast reaction to challenges and opportunities that arise in this complex environment increase the likelihood of achieving financial stability while continuing to deliver the highest level of artistic excellence to the audiences.

The tense situation experienced by many orchestras in recent years due to a constant imbalance in their cost and revenue structure is a striking counterexample of the necessity for sound financial management if they intend to continue excelling on the artistic side.

	Case Description
Danish National Chamber Orchestra (Denmark)	In 2014, the Danish National Chamber Orchestra faced closure due to severe budget cuts from the Danish Broadcasting Corporation. However, a crowdfunding campaign that raised US$145,000 from Kickstarter and approximately US$250,000 from private corporations[3] saved the orchestra. It then continued as a private ensemble under the name Danish Chamber Orchestra but faced ongoing financial challenges to maintain its activities (Wikipedia contributors 2023).
RTÉ National Symphony Orchestra (Ireland)	The RTÉ National Symphony Orchestra encountered financial difficulties in the 2010s due to budget cuts from its parent organisation, RTÉ. In 2018, an independent report commissioned by RTÉ recommended several options, including a transfer to the National Concert Hall to create a more sustainable funding model and secure its future. This operation was finalised between 2020 and 2022 thanks to an additional budget (€8m) provided by the Irish Government (Department of Tourism, Culture and Arts) (Wikipedia contributors 2022b; Dervan 2018; McGreevy 2018).
Orchestra Sinfonica di Roma (Italy)	The Orchestra Sinfonica di Roma, founded in 2002, went through a challenging period in 2014 when it faced severe financial issues due to reduced public funding and difficulties in obtaining private sponsorship. The orchestra was forced to cancel its 2014–2015 season and struggled to recover, ultimately ceasing operations despite its artistic success and reputation (Wikipedia contributors; Tempo 2014).
Greek National Opera Orchestra (Greece)	As a consequence of Greece's economic downturn in the 2010s, the overall arts and culture industry in the country faced a severe crisis. Due to austerity measures, the government significantly reduced funding for cultural institutions. Despite ongoing financial struggles, the orchestra managed to survive and continues to perform, albeit with a reduced budget and a leaner structure.

	Case Description
Southbank Sinfonia (United Kingdom)	Southbank Sinfonia, established in 2002, faced financial pressures in the late 2010s due to the evolving funding landscape for the arts in the United Kingdom. To mitigate the impact of these challenges, the ensemble diversified its income streams, focusing on engaging with a wider audience, offering a variety of concert formats, and establishing alliances with other cultural organisations. Additionally, the orchestra prioritised its role as an educational and training institution for young musicians, thereby attracting support from donors interested in nurturing emerging talent. Through these efforts, Southbank Sinfonia managed to navigate the financial difficulties and continue its mission of providing valuable opportunities for young musicians. Last but not least, in 2021, the Southbank Sinfonia merged with St John's Smith Square (SJSS) in order to provide a stable foundation on which to build a future (Redmond 2021; Charity Commission for England and Wales 2023).
Nashville Symphony (USA)	In 2013, the Nashville Symphony underwent a dire financial crisis, which brought it perilously close to foreclosure on its concert hall, the Schermerhorn Symphony Center. The costs associated with the building, coupled with the burden of high interest rates, forced the institution to consider defaulting on their mortgage. A confidential agreement with generous symphony supporters averted homelessness though. The following couple of years remained difficult as the organisation continued to grapple with significant deficits and an impending contract negotiation with its musicians (Wikipedia contributors 2022a; Kennicott 2013).
Seattle Symphony Orchestra (USA)	In the 2005–06 season, the Seattle Symphony Orchestra (SSO) reported a substantial deficit of $2.15 million, accumulating to a total of $3.2 million, a figure unprecedented in Seattle's arts scene. This increase in deficit was attributed to lower ticket sales due to oversaturation of holiday concerts and poorly received baseball-themed concerts (Campbell 2006; Schweitzer 2006).

C. ADAPTING BUSINESS MODELS

In the age of the knowledge revolution, businesses face new challenges as they strive to innovate and adapt. The competitive environment has undergone a fundamental shift, with the primary source of value creation transitioning from tangible assets to intangible ones, such as information, expertise, and intellectual property. To navigate this new terrain, organisations transform their business models, employing an evolutionary theory perspective to guide their approach (Downs and Velamuri 2018).

The knowledge revolution demands that companies leverage and exploit intangible assets to maintain their competitive edge. To achieve this goal, they

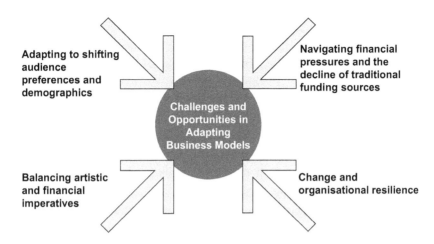

FIGURE 4.3 Adapting Business Models

engage in a process inspired by evolutionary theory, consisting of variation, selection, and retention:

- Variation involves generating innovative business model ideas through experimentation, learning from others, or external collaboration.
- Selection requires identifying and prioritising the most promising concepts based on their potential for value creation and alignment with the firm's strategic objectives.
- Retention entails the successful implementation and institutionalisation of the selected ideas, which may necessitate changes to the organisation's structure, culture, and processes.

This approach suggests that orchestras should adapt their business models to capitalise on the opportunities presented by the knowledge revolution. Possible strategies include adapting to shifting audience preferences and demographics, navigating financial pressures and the decline of traditional funding sources, balancing artistic and financial imperatives, and increasing the level of organisational resilience (in addition to embracing new technologies, promoting collaboration and knowledge-sharing, and diversifying revenue streams to reduce reliance on traditional funding sources).

Adapting to Shifting Audience Preferences and Demographics

One of the most significant obstacles is the need to adapt to the changing preferences and demographics of audiences. As the traditional audience for classical music ages, classical music struggles to find ways to engage with younger and more diverse listeners to ensure their long-term sustainability.

Developing innovative programming: To undertake a generational renewal of the audience, innovative programming strategies[4] that move beyond the traditional repertoire are explored. This involves commissioning new works, collaborating with artists from different genres or disciplines, and presenting concerts with unconventional formats or themes. Pushing the boundaries of "classical" music and adapting and arranging pop songs and movie soundtracks for large ensembles also draw in new audiences while stimulating creativity and artistic growth within the organisation.

Embracing digital technologies and social media: In the digital age, technology and social media cement a new type of bond with audiences. From streaming performances and hosting online events to creating shareable content on social media platforms, orchestras connect with a global audience and cultivate an online community of supporters in addition to making their past performances always available and visible. Digital technology and social media not only expand the reach but also enrich marketing strategies to better align with the preferences of younger generations (Rizkallah 2012).

Advancing audience experience: Creating a memorable audience experience is another key aspect of attracting new listeners and fostering loyalty among existing patrons. A variety of options, such as offering pre-concert talks, post-concert discussions, or interactive workshops, are available to provide context and deepen audience understanding of the music. Several orchestras have already explored ways to make the concert experience more accessible and enjoyable for diverse audiences, such as offering sensory-friendly performances for individuals with autism, providing audio descriptions for visually impaired patrons, offering translations in subtitles to overcome linguistic barriers in operas, or hosting relaxed performances designed for teenagers and families with children.

Navigating Financial Pressures and the Decline of Traditional Funding Sources

As previously discussed, the entire industry is under significant financial pressure due to the decline of traditional funding sources, such as government subsidies and private donations (especially in the years that followed the financial crisis of 2008). Adapting business models to survive these restrictions is essential.

Building a culture of philanthropy: Rather than just seizing one-shot philanthropic opportunities from time to time, developing a well-structured culture of philanthropy within the community helps both bolster recurrent private donations and establish a blanket funding base.[5] In the United States, cultural institutions have a broader and deeper experience in this domain, whereas in Europe they are being forced to rapidly gain philanthropic acquaintance due to the current financial stress. Main actions adopted are developing targeted fundraising campaigns, hosting special events, and implementing donor recognition programmes to acknowledge the contributions of supporters.

Additionally, strengthening relationships with major donors and associating them with the mission leads to longer-term financial partnerships and a greater sense of investment in the organisation's success.

Exploring alternative funding models: With the waning predictability and reliability of traditional funding sources, alternative budgetary paradigms emerge as imperative in supporting artistic activities. Seeking corporate sponsorships and partnerships, or investigating innovative funding mechanisms such as crowdfunding campaigns (Cicchiello, Gallo, and Monferrà 2022; Van Den Hoogen 2020) or social impact bonds usually increases the likelihood of bringing more fruitful outcomes in terms of both finance and loyalty. Overall, diversified sources of funding actively reduce reliance on any single point of potential financial failure and increase financial resilience in the face of economic uncertainty.

Balancing Artistic and Financial Imperatives

Properly managed orchestras face a continuous struggle to balance both their artistic and business objectives, and the shareholders' expectations to adopt a commercial approach while remaining anchored to a social good (and non-profit) attitude (Gałecka and Smolny 2017). They ensure that their pursuit of financial sustainability does not compromise their artistic quality and vice versa. Striking this delicate balance requires careful planning, smart financial management, and a deep commitment to artistic excellence.

Investing in artistic excellence: While cost management and efficiency are essential, underinvesting in artistic excellence would lead to a considerable erosion of the ensemble's appeal in the medium to long term. Hiring skilled musicians, engaging top-tier guest artists, and experimenting with innovative programming are just a few examples of measures that are frequently taken.

A strong commitment to continuous artistic quality underpins the high level of expressive performance over time, keeping an orchestra as remarkable as possible and worthy of audience support, even in the face of financial challenges.

Strategic planning and resource allocation: Effective strategic planning and resource allocation are common yet essential levers to balance artistic and financial imperatives. A comprehensive strategic plan that outlines their artistic vision, financial goals, and key performance indicators is often essential to obtaining accurate and consistent resource allocation, in a way that is aligned with artistic and financial objectives.

Regularly updating this plan also helps the organization to stay on track and adapt to changing circumstances, allowing it to remain responsive in a dynamic environment.

Increasing Organisational Resilience

In a rapidly evolving landscape, a willingness to embrace change and foster organisational resilience may well make the difference between a rigid, backward-looking approach and adaptive flexibility. It does not come as a surprise then that re-evaluating core values, mission, and vision and ensuring that these remain relevant and aligned with the needs and expectations of audiences, stakeholders, and the wider community, is a tactic frequently used to fuel flexibility.

Encouraging innovation and experimentation: A culture of innovation and experimentation within the organisation helps it adapt to change and stay ahead of the curve. When the staff and musicians feel supported to think creatively, take reasonable risks, and challenge the status quo, orchestras have a reservoir of new ideas and approaches to enhance their artistic and financial sustainability.

Building strong leadership and governance structures: Staff usually need to feel support from and rely on strong leadership and governance structures to navigate the challenges and opportunities that lie ahead. Recruiting board members and executive leaders with diverse skills, experiences, and perspectives gives the strategic guidance and oversight necessary to make informed decisions and adapt to changing circumstances.

The challenges and opportunities facing classical orchestras in adapting their business models are complex, to say the least. In some respects, orchestras are like major luxury brands, which also preserve tradition and history while taking into account changes in their customer base, evolving tastes and preferences, and the arrival of technology in management, administration, production, marketing and in bi-directional communication with customers (Kapferer and Bastien 2012; Light 2022).[6]

A constructive and pragmatic approach towards change, along with organisational resilience and a commitment to artistic excellence, serves as the foundation for not only ensuring the survival of cultural institutions but also nurturing their flourishing in this evolving landscape, continuing to enrich the lives of their audiences and contribute to the cultural fabric of their communities.

***

In summary, while the recipe for success varies significantly depending on background and situation, the key ingredients of a successful business model are well-known. What must be adapted are the proportions of each lever, the focus of the management team, and the priorities that guide both strategic and operational decision-making.

Ingredients of Modern Orchestra Business Models

1. Elements of Background

The Evolving Landscape of Business Models	• Traditional business models in the classical music industry • Current trends and emerging models • The impact of economic, social, cultural, and technological factors on business models	

2. Elements of Business

Revenue Streams and Cost Structures	• Government funding and revenue diversification	• Ticket sales and subscription models • Corporate sponsorships and partnerships • Fundraising and endowment campaigns • Licensing and digital distribution of performances
	• Cost management and efficiency	• Fixed and variable costs • Collaborations and resource sharing • Leveraging technology for cost efficiency • Balancing cost management with artistic quality
Adapting Business Models	• Adapting to shifting audience preferences and demographics	• Developing innovative programming • Espousing digital technology and social media • Advancing audience experience
	• Navigating financial pressures and the decline of traditional funding sources	• Building a culture of philanthropy • Exploring alternative funding models
	• Balancing artistic and financial imperatives	• Investing in artistic excellence • Strategic planning and resource allocation
	• Change and organisational resilience	• Encouraging innovation and experimentation • Building strong leadership and governance structures

In this section, we have explored the business models of classical orchestras, delving into the complexities of revenue streams, cost structures, and the myriad issues faced in today's rapidly evolving landscape. As traditional sources of income, such as government subsidies and, to a lesser extent, ticket sales, tend to decrease, go-to-market strategies need to be updated to ensure financial sustainability without harming artistic relevance.

To navigate these challenges, cultural institutions have embraced revenue diversification, exploring less traditional ways to generate income through corporate sponsorships, partnerships, fundraising campaigns, philanthropic activities, and digital distribution of their performances. Equally important is the need for effective cost management, which requires a nuanced approach to budgeting and resource allocation that balances financial stability with artistic excellence.

In addition to the financial constraints and artistic imperatives, shifting audience preferences and demographics significantly affect the state of the market too. Through the development of innovative programming, the adoption of digital solutions, and the enhancement of the audience experience, orchestras attract new and diverse listeners and foster loyalty among existing patrons.

Ultimately, the key to success lies in the ability to adapt, innovate, and remain agile in the face of change. This has, however, to happen without losing contact with the roots, profoundly anchored to a multi-century tradition. Fostering a culture of experimentation and encouraging creative risk-taking pushes orchestras ahead of the curve and keeps them relevant to their audiences, while building their future on the shoulders of their history keeps them relevant to the classical music industry that values its glorious past as much as its present perspectives. Strong leadership and governance structures, coupled with a commitment to artistic quality, is also crucial to navigate through these challenging times.

The business models of classical orchestras are complex, requiring a fragile equilibrium between artistic and financial objectives. With a proactive stance towards change, a strategic approach to diversifying revenue streams, and an unwavering commitment to artistic excellence, orchestras can indeed continue to thrive; they have the opportunity to enrich the lives of their audiences, contributing to the cultural fabric of their communities.

CASE STUDY 4.1

The Transformation of the London Symphony Orchestra[7]

INTRODUCTION

The London Symphony Orchestra (LSO), founded in 1904, is renowned for its artistic excellence, innovation, and commitment to education and community engagement. Over the past decade, the LSO has faced many of the same challenges as others in this industry, including shifting audience preferences, declining traditional revenue streams, and the need to adapt its business model to ensure long-term sustainability. This case study explores steps taken by the LSO to address these challenges, highlighting the strategies implemented and the lessons learned along the way.

RESOLUTION OF THE CASE

Innovative programming: The LSO has been proactive in exploring new programming strategies that move beyond the traditional classical music repertoire. These efforts have included commissioning new works, collaborating with artists from different genres, and hosting themed concerts that appeal to diverse audiences.

Digital presence: The LSO has made significant investments in digital technology to expand its reach and engage with audiences in new ways. This has involved livestreaming performances, creating high-quality digital content for online platforms, and utilising social media to build a global community of supporters.

Audience experience: The LSO has made concerted efforts to improve the overall audience experience by offering pre-concert talks, post-concert discussions, and interactive workshops. It has taken steps to make its performances more accessible to diverse audiences, including offering relaxed concerts and implementing sensory-friendly initiatives.

Revenue streams: The LSO has actively pursued alternative revenue sources, such as corporate sponsorships and partnerships, in addition to hosting targeted fundraising events and campaigns. It has also leveraged its digital presence to monetise online content, such as offering paid subscriptions to its digital concert series.

Cost structure: The LSO has implemented several cost-saving measures, including more efficient marketing strategies, resource sharing with other arts organisations, and leveraging technology to streamline administrative processes.

Culture of philanthropy: The LSO has worked to cultivate a strong culture of philanthropy within its community, focusing on building relationships with major donors, recognising their contributions, and engaging them in its mission.

Strong leadership and governance structures: The LSO has placed significant emphasis on recruiting board members and executive leaders with diverse skills and experiences, providing strategic guidance and oversight.

CONCLUSION AND LESSONS LEARNED

The transformation of the LSO serves as an inspiring example of how a classical orchestra adapts its business model to overcome the challenges of a rapidly evolving landscape. By embracing innovative programming, diversifying revenue streams, and enhancing the audience experience, the LSO has been able to attract new and diverse listeners and maintain its artistic relevance.

Key lessons learned from the LSO's transformation include:

- The importance of a proactive and forward-thinking approach to addressing challenges and seizing opportunities.
- The need to strike a balance between artistic and financial imperatives, ensuring that cost management does not come at the expense of artistic quality.
- The value of strong leadership and governance structures in guiding the organisation through periods of change and uncertainty.

Ultimately, the success of the LSO's transformation demonstrates the potential to adapt, innovate, and thrive in the face of an ever-changing environment. By learning from the LSO's example, other orchestras could find their own path to long-term sustainability and artistic excellence, ensuring that they continue to enrich their audiences' lives and contribute to the cultural fabric of their communities for generations to come.

D. BUSINESS MODELS AND MANAGEMENT MINDSET[8]

The intrinsic relationship between business and funding models and management mindset may seem obvious but still is quite an understudied aspect of cultural institution operations.[9] To put it in very simple words, the type of predominant funding form – mainly government, mainly private sector, or a mix of both – impacts the management approach, pushing towards an entrepreneurial or administrative mindset, or a combination of both. Substantial government backing seems more likely to lead to a more administrative mindset, where financial stability allows managers to focus primarily on orchestral operations, artistic excellence, and routine processes. Conversely, the unpredictability of private funding in a highly competitive framework often forces managers to develop an entrepreneurial mindset to actively secure the financial footing. Hybrid models display an amalgamation of both approaches.

This highly schematic funding-vs-mindset relationship is, however, not static. Management approach influences an orchestra's ability to attract certain types of funding. For instance, an entrepreneurial mindset is more adept than an administrative one at soliciting private sector funds.

Additionally, our preliminary research and discussions with experts suggest that risk propensity in specific domains may also be influenced by the type of funding and management mindset, although this aspect remains less precise at this early stage of investigation. Some experts argue that financial stability enables orchestra executive directors to experiment with innovative programming or technologies, while others contend that financial comfort tends to favour a routine approach and a hassle-free conservative attitude. These opposing yet plausible interpretations of the situation primarily indicate the need for further exploration in this area.

Aiming for a comprehensive overview, we also adopt a cross-national perspective: by placing countries in a two-dimensional figure – funding on one axis, mindset on the other – it is possible to visually encapsulate the dominant operational model in each context. Notably, these positions aren't fixed; shifts in funding models over time require or cause a change in the management approach.

To offer a more nuanced understanding of the varying management mindsets, it proves useful to delineate the distinct features characterising administrative and entrepreneurial approaches (seen as archetypal categories). These management mindsets manifest in distinct operational, strategic, and relational practices which profoundly shape the operations and engagement with various stakeholders. The key features distinguishing an administrative mindset from an entrepreneurial one within the context of orchestral management are summarised in the following table. While this comparative overview serves as a preliminary understanding, it is worth underlining that these distinctions represent an area of ongoing inquiry, warranting further refinement and validation through empirical research and practical experiences.

Administrative Management Mindset	Entrepreneurial Management Mindset
Operational Efficiency: Prioritises operations to ensure smooth and efficient performances and rehearsals.	**Innovation and Risk-taking:** Actively seeks new opportunities, values creativity and strategic change, and is willing to take calculated risks.
Stability and Consistency: Values predictable routines and works within well-defined boundaries and established procedures.	**Agility and Adaptability:** Navigates in uncertain environments, capable of dealing with changing circumstances, and leverages these changes for strategic advantage.
Internal Networking: Concentrates on strengthening relationships within the organisation and maintaining harmonious relations among staff, musicians, and the artistic team.	**External Networking:** Emphasises robust relationships with donors, sponsors, partners, and the broader community.
Financial Stewardship: Ensures wise if not prudent use of available funds, focusing on budget control, financial responsibility, and reporting.	**Fundraising and Resource Acquisition:** Prioritises fundraising activities and acquiring resources from diverse sources, actively soliciting donations, sponsorships, and partnerships.
Long-term Planning: Engages in long-term strategic planning, benefiting from the stability of their funding.	**Short- to Medium-Term Planning:** Focuses more on medium-term strategic planning, remaining responsive to shifting funding landscapes and seizing emerging opportunities.
Harmony Within Artistic Team: Fosters a collaborative environment, aligning the artistic team, including musicians, with the orchestral vision and enhancing their professional development.	**Leadership in Artistic Direction:** Involves him/herself in the artistic discussions, challenges the artistic team to explore new repertoires, collaborations, or formats to generate audience interest.
Local Community Engagement: Focuses on maintaining good relationships with the local community, primarily through traditional outreach activities such as concerts and educational programmes.	**Broad Community Engagement:** Pursues innovative ways of community engagement, reaching beyond traditional boundaries to tap into new audiences, volunteers, and supporters, potentially leveraging digital platforms and partnerships.
Board Relationship: Aims to maintain a serene relationship with the board, focusing on governance and fulfilling fiduciary duties.	**Board Relationship:** Seeks a more collaborative and productive relationship with the board, leveraging the board's resources and network for strategic initiatives and fundraising.

As we traverse the spectrum of funding models, it becomes clear that each organisation moulds its own management style rooted in its distinct background and context. Government-funded orchestras typically rely on consistent subsidies, which tend to result in an administrative management mindset. The financial safety net often frees managers to concentrate on operational efficiency and artistic programmes, given the lower pressure to secure substantial external funding. Countries such as France and Germany, where the government actively supports the arts, typify this model. Private funding, on the other hand, usually creates a different dynamic. Without guaranteed government subsidies, or limited ones, orchestras turn to private sector agreements, donations, monetisation of content, and patronages to finance their activities. This scenario requires an entrepreneurial management mindset. Such leaders often champion organisational innovation, calculated risk-taking, and robust networking to secure funds, simultaneously leveraging these qualities to advance artistic agendas. Examples of this approach are evident in countries such as the United States, where private funding plays a prominent role in arts and culture.

Some orchestras operate within a hybrid funding model, blending government subsidies with private sector contributions. Here, the management mindset develops from a mix of administrative and entrepreneurial approaches. These leaders juggle the need to ensure efficient operations while also pursuing private funding, essentially functioning in a dual role. Notable instances of this model are observed in Japan and South Korea, but also in the UK or Canada, where both government and private sector funding contribute to the revenue.

Importantly, the prevalent management mindset affects an orchestra's ability to attract certain types of funding. An administrative-focused leadership might lack the agility and proactivity necessary to attract ample private funds, potentially reducing diversification of income sources. Conversely, an entrepreneurial-minded leadership could create robust networks and partnerships, increasing the chances of securing private funding, but might risk overlooking other areas of operations, including the necessary attitude or approach to effectively connect with government funding bodies.

However, no matter the model, each comes with its strengths and challenges. Government funding, while more stable, might be subject to macro-economic downturns and political changes and can foster complacency due to its consistency. Private funding, though potentially empowering, is often unpredictable, requiring constant effort to maintain. Hybrid models offer balance but necessitate managers to shift adeptly between mindsets.

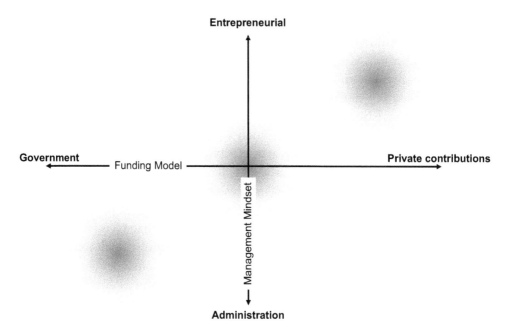

FIGURE 4.4 Funding Model vs Management Mindset

This complexity extends across national borders, each country presenting a unique blend of funding sources and management approaches. A visual representation of these dynamics illuminates the relationships.

To distil the complex interaction between funding models and management mindsets into an accessible, comparative framework, a two-dimensional figure is proposed. One axis shows the dominant funding model, ranging from entirely or mostly government-funded, through a blend of public and private sources, to mostly private sector finance. The orthogonal axis represents the management mindset, which spans from a purely administrative focus, through a balanced mixture, to an entirely entrepreneurial disposition. This graphical representation enables the placement of each country (or region) at a given time on this two-dimensional plane, indicating the prevailing operational model within their orchestras. Countries largely reliant on government funding and an administrative mindset would appear towards one end, such as France, Germany, or Italy. At the opposite extreme, those principally using private funding and adopting an entrepreneurial approach, such as the United States, would occupy a different quadrant. Countries adopting a hybrid funding approach and a mixed managerial mindset, such as the UK and several Asian countries, would naturally gravitate towards the centre of this graph.

Importantly, this visualisation tool recognises the temporal dynamism of the orchestral landscape. As countries experience shifts in political, socioeconomic, and cultural contexts, changes in the dominant funding model occur, necessitating an adjustment in management mindset. Therefore, a country's position within this figure isn't static but moves over time in response to these contextual changes. This acknowledgement of temporal fluidity adds a layer of depth to the model, underscoring the dynamism inherent in the world of orchestras. The case of Middle Eastern countries is highly instructive in this regard when viewed from this two-dimensional perspective: while they were sharply aligned to the German or French model a decade ago, political and funding decisions have been pushing orchestras towards a mixed model, which requires in turn a transformation of the managerial mindset in their senior management teams.

This two-dimensional figure serves multiple purposes. Academically, it offers a concise, comparative (yet still deeply archetypal and vague) snapshot of global operations, facilitating cross-national studies. For practitioners, it provides a crude navigational tool, showing their position relative to international counterparts and offering insights into potential shifts in management mindset in response to evolving funding models. For policy-makers, it offers a simplified overview of the current state and potential future trajectories of orchestral operations, thus informing policy decisions.

***

The complex dynamics between funding sources and management mindsets form the backbone of the operational model within orchestras, shaping the way these cultural institutions navigate their environment and secure their future.

Our examination, although expansive, is not exhaustive – and may very well end up being proven inaccurate if not wrong by additional in-depth research. It, however, paves the way for further studies to delve into the connections of funding sources and management mindsets, extending the inquiry to other cultural institutions, different geographical contexts, and across longer periods of time. As such, it contributes to the burgeoning body of knowledge corpus around the management of arts and culture institutions, serving as a compass for future research and practice.

Box 4.2 Expanding Perspectives: Review Questions

1   Discuss the ongoing evolution in the business models of orchestras, especially in the context of shifting audience preferences, technological disruptions, and the economic landscape. What are some innovative revenue streams that might be considered to expand reach and financial sustainability, and how can these new strategies be balanced with the necessity to uphold artistic excellence?

2   Given the diversification of revenue streams that now include digital platforms, corporate partnerships, and philanthropy, how can orchestras strategically manage their costs to maintain a balance between their financial imperatives and artistic objectives? Discuss the importance of optimised budgeting and resource allocation, particularly with respect to investment in high-quality artists and innovative programming.

3   Considering the challenges of adapting to shifting audience demographics and preferences, what strategies could be employed to engage younger and more diverse listeners? Explore how initiatives such as innovative programming, use of digital technology, and enhanced audience experiences could be utilised.

4   In light of the declining traditional funding sources, explore the implications in terms of seeking alternative funding models and cultivating a culture of philanthropy. In this context, delve into the delicate task of balancing artistic and financial imperatives through strategic planning and resource allocation. Discuss the role of organisational change and resilience in navigating these challenges and capitalising on new opportunities. How can fostering a culture of innovation, strengthening leadership and governance structures, and maintaining alignment with core values and mission contribute to an orchestra's adaptation and success in this evolving landscape?

5   Compare the business models and management mindsets of large international orchestras of your choice, position them in the two-dimensional plan and examine whether and how they have evolved over the last 20 years. This exercise works better when institutions from different parts of the world are selected.

NOTES

1 From mp3.com in 1997, Pandora Radio in 2005, Spotify in 2008 up to the more recent Apple Music Classical in 2023, to name a few.
2 An interesting approach is also provided by Schiuma and Lerro (2017), who use the *Business Model Prism* (BMP) – a multidimensional framework that is utilised to map the structure and logic of the business model of arts and cultural organisations and to drive the design of innovation initiatives – to make a fruitful distinction between business model "as is" and "as should be," and discuss the benefits of introducing the concept of *business model innovation* (BMI) in the art and culture industry.
3 Because of Kickstarter's internal rules on single donations, the Danish National Chamber had to return the donations while requesting the same donors to re-submit their donations in cash.
4 A useful discussion of the concept of programming strategy as methods and approaches used by conductors and programmers to curate a concert programme is given by Gilmore (1993).
5 While focused on the case of Australia, the research conducted by Donelli et al. (2023) provides a valuable overview of philanthropy patterns and culture from a managerial perspective. Its significance extends well beyond the initial geographical scope and is practically useful to the entire industry.
6 The key difference, of course, is the role of public funding, which is not present in the luxury industry.
7 An interesting case study on the London Symphony Orchestra is available from Hackman et al. (2000, 2002).
8 This section should be regarded as an early-stage working hypothesis, based on partial observations and an analysis that drew upon limited data. However, the limited scientific literature available on the subject points to an exciting research gap that is yet to be explored.
9 Some fragmented insights, or perhaps fragments of insights, can be gleaned indirectly from the following research contributions: Zhong (2023), de Wit and Bekkers (2016), Musteen, Barker, and Baeten (2006), McClelland, Liang, and Barker (2010).

BIBLIOGRAPHY

Campbell, R. M. 2006. "Orchestra Deficit Exceeds $3 Million." *Seattle Post-Intelligencer.* www.seattlepi.com/news/article/Orchestra-deficit-exceeds-3-million-1214871.php.

Caves, Richard E. 2002. *Creative Industries: Contracts Between Art and Commerce*, 1st paperback ed. Cambridge, MA and London: Harvard University Press.

Caves, Richard E. 2003. "Contracts Between Art and Commerce." *The Journal of Economic Perspectives: A Journal of the American Economic Association* 17 (2): 73–83. https://doi.org/10.1257/089533003765888430.

Charity Commission for England and Wales. 2023. "Southbank Sinfonia – Charity 1092461." https://register-of-charities.charitycommission.gov.uk/charity-search/-/charity-details/3988191/financial-history.

Cheung Leung, Chi. 2013. "The Development of Cultural Entrepreneurship: Case Studies of Four Community Orchestras in Hong Kong." *Asian Education and Development Studies* 2 (3): 275–294. https://doi.org/10.1108/AEDS-05-2013-0032.

Cicchiello, Antonella Francesca, Serena Gallo, and Stefano Monferrà. 2022. "Mapping Crowdfunding in Cultural and Creative Industries: A Conceptual and Empirical Overview." *European Management Review* 19 (1): 22–37. https://doi.org/10.1111/emre.12510.

Dervan, Michael. 2018. "Why Should the Taxpayer Bail out RTÉ over Orchestra Mess?" *The Irish Times*, May 9. www.irishtimes.com/culture/music/why-should-the-taxpayer-bail-out-rte-over-orchestra-mess-1.3486777.

de Wit, Arjen, and Rene Bekkers. 2016. "Government Support and Charitable Donations: A Meta-Analysis of the Crowding-out Hypothesis." *SocArXiv*. https://doi.org/10.31235/osf.io/9ysjm.

Donelli, Chiara Carolina, Ruth Rentschler, Simone Fanelli, and Boram Lee. 2023. "Philanthropy Patterns in Major Australian Performing Arts Organizations." *Journal of Management and Governance*, January. https://doi.org/10.1007/s10997-022-09657-2.

Downs, James B., and Vivek K. Velamuri. 2018. "Business Model Innovation in a Knowledge Revolution: An Evolutionary Theory Perspective." *Managerial and Decision Economics: MDE* 39 (5): 550–562. https://doi.org/10.1002/mde.2926.

Gałecka, Małgorzata, and Katarzyna Smolny. 2017. "Financing Rules of the Activity of Cultural Institutions in the Context of Economic Efficiency." *Ekonomia I Prawo. Economics and Law* 16 (4): 387–399. https://doi.org/10.12775/EiP.2017.027.

Gilmore, Samuel. 1993. "Tradition and Novelty in Concert Programming: Bringing the Artist Back into Cultural Analysis." *Sociological Forum* 8 (2): 221–242. https://doi.org/10.1007/BF01115491.

Giraud Voss, Zannie. 2020. "Orchestra Facts: 2006–2014." *Americanorchestras.org*. https://americanorchestras.org/orchestra-facts/.

Hackman, J. Richard, et al. 2000. "London Symphony Orchestra (A), Case – Faculty & Research – Harvard Business School." www.hbs.edu/faculty/Pages/item.aspx?num=16468.

Hackman, J. Richard, et al. 2002. "London Symphony Orchestra (B), Case – Faculty & Research – Harvard Business School." www.hbs.edu/faculty/Pages/item.aspx?num=27075.

Kapferer, Jean-Noël, and Vincent Bastien. 2012. *The Luxury Strategy: Break the Rules of Marketing to Build Luxury Brands*, 2nd ed. London and Philadelphia, PA: Kogan Page.

Kennicott, Philip. 2013. "America's Orchestras Are in Crisis." *The New Republic*. https://newrepublic.com/article/114221/orchestras-crisis-outreach-ruining-them.

Lebrecht, Norman. 1997. *Who Killed Classical Music? Maestros, Managers, and Corporate Politics*. Secaucus, NJ: Carol Pub. Group.

Light, Larry. 2022. "Building Luxury Brands with Abundant Rarity." *Branding Strategy Insider*. https://brandingstrategyinsider.com/building-luxury-brands-with-abundant-rarity/.

Loots, Ellen, Diana Betzler, Trine Bille, Karol Jan Borowiecki, and Boram Lee. 2022. "New Forms of Finance and Funding in the Cultural and Creative Industries. Introduction to the Special Issue." *Journal of Cultural Economy* 46 (2): 205–230. https://doi.org/10.1007/s10824-022-09450-x.

McClelland, Patrick L., Xin Liang, and Vincent L. Barker. 2010. "CEO Commitment to the Status Quo: Replication and Extension Using Content Analysis." *Journal of Management* 36 (5): 1251–1277. https://doi.org/10.1177/0149206309345019.

McGreevy, Ronan. 2018. "Cash-Strapped RTÉ Can No Longer Afford Two Orchestras, Says Report." *The Irish Times*, April 23. www.irishtimes.com/culture/music/cash-strapped-rte-can-no-longer-afford-two-orchestras-says-report-1.3471785.

Musteen, Martina, Vincent L. Barker III, and Virginia L. Baeten. 2006. "CEO Attributes Associated with Attitude toward Change: The Direct and Moderating Effects of CEO Tenure." *Journal of Business Research* 59 (5): 604–612. https://doi.org/10.1016/j.jbusres.2005.10.008.

Redmond, Adele. 2021. "Southbank Sinfonia Merges with St John's Smith Square." *ArtsProfessional*. www.artsprofessional.co.uk/news/southbank-sinfonia-merges-st-johns-smith-square.

Rizkallah, Elias G. 2012. "A Non-Classical Marketing Approach for Classical Music Performing Organizations: An Empirical Perspective." *Journal of Business & Economics Research (JBER)* 7 (4). https://doi.org/10.19030/jber.v7i4.6870.

Schiuma, Giovanni, and Antonio Lerro. 2017. "The Business Model Prism: Managing and Innovating Business Models of Arts and Cultural Organisations." *Journal of Open Innovation: Technology, Market, and Complexity* 3 (1): 13. https://doi.org/10.1186/s40852-017-0066-z.

Schweitzer, Vivien. 2006. "Seattle Symphony Posts $3.2 Million Deficit." *Playbill*. www.playbill.com/article/seattle-symphony-posts-32-million-deficit.

Tempo, Il. 2014. "La musica nella Capitale è sempre più a rischio. In crisi un'altra orchestra." *Il Tempo*. LiberoQuotidiano. www.iltempo.it/cultura-spettacoli/2014/05/20/gallery/la-musica-nella-capitale-e-sempre-piu-a-rischio-in-crisi-unaltra-orchestra-939967/.

Van Den Hoogen, Quirijn Lennert. 2020. "Values in Crowdfunding in the Netherlands." *International Journal of Cultural Policy* 26 (1): 109–127. https://doi.org/10.1080/10286632.2018.1433666.

Weber, William. 2008. *The Great Transformation of Musical Taste: Concert Programming from Haydn to Brahms*. New York: Cambridge University Press.

Wikipedia contributors. 2022a. "Nashville Symphony." *Wikipedia, The Free Encyclopedia*. https://en.wikipedia.org/w/index.php?title=Nashville_Symphony&oldid=1111739303.

Wikipedia contributors. 2022b. "National Symphony Orchestra (Ireland)." *Wikipedia, The Free Encyclopedia*. https://en.wikipedia.org/w/index.php?title=National_Symphony_Orchestra_(Ireland)&oldid=1124799605.

Wikipedia contributors. 2023. "Danish Chamber Orchestra." *Wikipedia, The Free Encyclopedia*. https://en.wikipedia.org/w/index.php?title=Danish_Chamber_Orchestra&oldid=1146601358.

Wikipedia contributors. "Orchestra Sinfonica Di Roma." *Wikipedia, The Free Encyclopedia.* https://it.wikipedia.org/w/index.php?title=Orchestra_Sinfonica_di_Roma&oldid= 131962142.

Wise, Brian. 2016. "These Are the 15 Most Popular Orchestras on Spotify." https://brianwise.net/most-popular-orchestras-on-spotify/.

Zhong, Daheng. 2023. "The Government Subsidies Effect on the Company Strategic Change-Theory and Emprical." *BCP Business & Management* 38 (March): 3090–3103. https://doi.org/10.54691/bcpbm.v38i.4240.

Cited content from websites was last accessed on 01 July 2023.

CHAPTER 5

The Fundamentals of Orchestra Management

Managing an orchestra involves a variety of responsibilities, each of which requires specialised knowledge, skills, and expertise. It also requires an unprecedented ability to multitask, for the various responsibilities and areas of activity come in batches rather than one after the other. The following key aspects of management have been widely recognised as best practices. While firmly anchored in the late 1970s and early 1980s American tradition, the *American Symphony Orchestra League* – now known as the *League of American Orchestras* – identified the eight key elements of management, which include governance, financial management, artistic programming, audience engagement, marketing and public relations, fundraising, human resources, and strategic planning (Truskot, Belofsky, and Kittilstad 1983, 1988). The scope of this chapter is to review these eight key responsibility areas, which are grouped slightly differently, as integral components of a larger managerial picture.

WHAT YOU WILL LEARN IN THIS CHAPTER

Section	Key Learning Points
A. Artistic Programming and Strategic Planning	Orchestras shape their growth and audience appeal through a unique artistic vision, which guides their programming. This vision needs to align with strategic, long-term plans to foster artistic innovation and successful collaborations. The leadership, notably the artistic director, plays a pivotal role in enabling these collaborations, enriching the artistic experience, and extending community outreach. Tours and international collaborations offer the opportunity to expand influence and horizons. However, these ventures come with challenges, including logistics, finances, cultural sensitivities, and environmental concerns. Best practices such as strong international partnerships, clear communication, and experience assessment are useful tools to navigate the industry's challenges and ensure long-term success.

DOI: 10.4324/9781032629636-5

Section	Key Learning Points
B. Financial, Fundraising, Legal, and Resource Management	Effective financial management is crucial to success, and managers must excel in strategic budgeting, diversified fundraising, cost management, financial risk assessment, and the unrelenting pursuit of innovative revenue opportunities. Collaborating with other cultural institutions or community groups broadens funding sources and fortifies proposals. Utilising the expertise and passion of board members, staff, and volunteers help identify potential funding opportunities and cultivate relationships with prospective supporters. It is important to recognise that no symphony orchestra earns enough revenue from performances to cover its expenses; therefore, survival is better achieved going beyond traditional commercial practices.
C. The Costs–Revenues Puzzle	Orchestras must conduct a thorough financial analysis to understand their costs and revenue streams, formulate a comprehensive plan to address any gaps, and implement innovative fundraising strategies to diversify their income sources. This involves leveraging a variety of tools such as digital technology, educational partnerships, and merchandise opportunities to mitigate risks associated with over-reliance on any single revenue stream. Artistic innovation and financial sustainability should be balanced through a creative mix of traditional and alternative revenue channels. Examples are given by other performing arts organisations looking to improve their financial sustainability while maintaining artistic integrity and reputation in the community.
D. Operations	A well-managed and efficient operational framework is crucial in supporting artistic programming, financial management, audience development, and overall success of classical music ensembles. Effective planning and execution of concerts require careful consideration of programming, scheduling, managing rehearsals, and coordinating various elements on performance day. Touring and external performances present unique challenges and opportunities that require careful planning, logistics management, and adaptation to diverse venues.
E. Audience Development	Orchestras adapt to changes in demographics and appeal to younger generations with different musical preferences and consumption habits. This requires a re-evaluation of how they interact with new audiences and retain the loyalty of existing aficionados. Classical orchestras must also address the steady decline in overall audiences by understanding the multitude of factors contributing to this phenomenon, including changes in leisure time and the proliferation of musical genres. Finally, innovative programming that combines different art forms or cultural traditions provides opportunities for skill-sharing and professional development among participating artists and organisations.

Section	Key Learning Points
F. Strengthening Governance and Fostering Board Relations	Open communication and collaboration among all stakeholders, as well as the need to understand governance models, ethical considerations, and leadership principles are key to good governance. By aligning strategic goals, legal requirements, and ethical norms, a robust framework can be created that eases stability and growth. Developing a leadership pipeline through mentoring and targeted professional development opportunities helps prepare potential successors for leadership roles and ensure a smooth transition when the time comes for them to step up. Creating a detailed transition plan outlining the steps and timeline for the leadership transition process is essential to ensure that outgoing and incoming leaders understand their roles and responsibilities during the transition period.
G. Human Resources and Conflict Resolution	The success relies not only on artistic vision and execution but also on the people behind the scenes, ensuring that musicians, staff, and volunteers work together harmoniously. The chapter on human resources and conflict resolution delves into the critical aspects of personnel within the management context. It addresses hiring, training, and retaining personnel while promoting professional development and growth to create a positive work culture. The seven components identified for effective human resources management include hiring, training and onboarding, retaining, development and growth, positive culture, conflict resolution, and succession plan. A firm governance structure and positive board relations are also critical aspects that contribute significantly to the organisation's outcome. Ultimately investing in the professional growth and well-being of personnel strengthens not only the ensemble's performance on stage but also its overall impact and resilience.
H. The Role of Unions	The role of unions is a crucial aspect of the global music landscape. Unions provide a collective voice for musicians, safeguarding their welfare by negotiating favourable work conditions, contracts, remuneration, and health and safety. The emergence of unions in the late 19th century was a response to the harsh work conditions and low wages typically endured by workers, including musicians. The relationship between unions and management is complex, requiring careful negotiation and communication. Unions have a critical part to play in challenging traditional norms and biases, an issue often overlooked in the industry, and need to navigate a complex landscape with foresight and adaptability, working collaboratively with management team, funders, and policy-makers to ensure a sustainable future for the classical music industry.

These categories cover the key aspects of orchestra management and provide a comprehensive framework for understanding the roles and responsibilities of a CEO and managers. This structure addresses the main areas of management, including artistic and strategic planning, financial and resource management, audience development, change management, and governance. Let us see them in more detail.

***

Before we explore the fundamental principles of management, we should be aware of a few key cases that have demonstrated excellence in this field. They have achieved success by utilising various levers that we will examine in the following sections of this chapter. Drawing from their experiences, we can better understand the strategies implemented in the 21st century and extract valuable insights that can be applied across the wider landscape.

These exemplary orchestras have not only navigated the cultural and economic environment but also thrived in the face of adversity, pioneering innovative approaches to revenue diversification, cost management, artistic programming, and technological adoption. Their stories serve as a source of inspiration and a testament to the power of effective management in shaping the future of classical music. The twelve cases listed below are not the only successful ones; they are the ones we have selected to develop this chapter. We recognise that any selection is somewhat arbitrary, but we are confident that the selected cases showcase a wide range of measures and actions that contribute to the success of others. As we delve into this chapter, we encourage readers to reflect on the lessons learned from these organisations, drawing parallels to the situations they better know and experiences they may have.

Through the analysis, we aim to identify the key factors that contribute to their achievements and apply them to a broader context, empowering readers to cultivate vigorous organisations. We strongly believe that with the insights and lessons learned from these examples, we attain a deeper understanding of management best practices. This list primarily highlights decisions, actions, and strategies taken or implemented over the last 10 to 20 years, reflecting recent innovations and adaptations only.[1]

Berlin Philharmonic (Germany)	The Berlin Philharmonic has successfully diversified its revenue streams through innovative initiatives, such as the Digital Concert Hall, which allows subscribers to watch live concerts and access an extensive archive of past performances. They have also established fruitful corporate sponsorships with companies such as Deutsche Bank and BMW, as well as implemented successful fundraising campaigns and a strong education programme, which engages young audiences through workshops and outreach events.

London Symphony Orchestra (United Kingdom)	The London Symphony Orchestra (LSO) has effectively explored new revenue sources through initiatives such as LSO Live, their in-house record label that produces and distributes high-quality recordings of their performances. Additionally, the LSO has forged strong corporate partnerships, including collaborations with international financial institutions such as UBS, and they have implemented effective cost management strategies, ensuring the optimal balance between financial stability and artistic excellence.
Royal Concertgebouw Orchestra (Netherlands)	The Royal Concertgebouw has embraced revenue diversification through initiatives such as the RCO House, a facility that serves as their rehearsal space and functions as a revenue-generating event venue. They have also cultivated corporate sponsorships with companies such as ING and KLM, and have executed successful fundraising campaigns, such as the RCO Foundation, which supports long-term financial health and sustainability.
New York Philharmonic (United States)	The New York Philharmonic has effectively diversified its revenue sources by creating a digital streaming platform, NYPhil+, offering subscribers access to a vast library of performances, interviews, and documentaries. It has also successfully partnered with various corporate sponsors, such as Credit Suisse and Breguet, and they have launched successful fundraising campaigns that support their artistic and educational initiatives, ensuring financial stability and artistic excellence.
Los Angeles Philharmonic (United States)	The Los Angeles Philharmonic has successfully explored innovative revenue-generating initiatives, such as their partnership with Deutsche Grammophon to produce and distribute recordings of their performances. They have also established strong corporate sponsorships with companies such as Acura cars and have engaged in effective fundraising campaigns, such as the LA Phil Gala, which supports the artistic and educational programmes.
Oslo Philharmonic (Norway)	The Oslo Philharmonic has effectively diversified its revenue sources by partnering with major Norwegian companies such as Hydro Equinor. They have also launched fundraising campaigns through the Friends of the Oslo Philharmonic program, which invites individuals and organisations to support their artistic and educational initiatives. They have established a strong digital presence, offering streaming and recordings of their performances through their website and other platforms such as their own YouTube channel.
Melbourne Symphony Orchestra (Australia)	The Melbourne Symphony Orchestra (MSO) has diversified its revenue streams by engaging in fruitful corporate partnerships with companies such as Emirates. They have also explored fundraising opportunities through their Support the Future of MSO initiative and the grants received from various trusts and foundations that support important MSO programs and initiatives, both on and off the stage. Additionally, the MSO has embraced digital distribution by offering virtual concerts, special events, and musical experiences from the MSO, other Australian arts companies, and some of the world's great orchestras through its MSO.LIVE platform.

Orchestre Symphonique de Montréal (Canada)	The Montreal Symphony Orchestra has adopted a successful revenue diversification strategy through initiatives such as their OSM Digital programme and Apple Music. They have also cultivated strong corporate alliances with companies such as BMO Financial Group and Hydro-Québec, and they have implemented successful fundraising campaigns.
Seoul Philharmonic Orchestra (South Korea)	The Seoul Philharmonic Orchestra has effectively diversified its revenue sources by engaging in partnerships with major South Korean companies such as Hyundai i40. It has embraced technology through its online presence on YouTube and Apple Music (to name a few), offering audiences greater access to their performances.
Buenos Aires Philharmonic Orchestra (Argentina)	The Buenos Aires Philharmonic Orchestra has adopted technology to engage audiences through streaming concerts and digital archives, which provide access to their performance history, via platforms such as Naxos and Apple Music. In addition, it frequently explores innovative artistic programming, collaborating with renowned guest artists and presenting unique concert experiences that attract diverse audiences.
Vienna Philharmonic Orchestra (Austria)	The Vienna Philharmonic Orchestra has successfully diversified its revenue streams by securing sponsorships (ad hoc or longer-term) from major corporations such as Rolex. They have also formed long-lasting alliances with cultural institutions, such as the Wiener Staatsoper and the Salzburg Festival. It has embraced technology by offering streaming concerts (see the traditional New Year concert) and maintaining a digital archive, which grants audiences access to their historic performances. The Vienna Philharmonic frequently engages in innovative artistic programming, often showcasing a blend of traditional and contemporary music, as well as collaborating with renowned guest artists.
Tonhalle Orchestra Zurich (Switzerland)	The Tonhalle Orchestra Zurich has effectively diversified its revenue sources through corporate partnerships with companies such as Credit Suisse, then LGT Private Banking. It has adopted digital technology, providing streamed concerts and on-demand content for audiences worldwide. The Tonhalle is known for its innovative artistic programming, which includes a mix of classical and contemporary works, as well as unique projects such as the "TonhalleLATE" series, which combines classical music with electronic beats and visual art.

A. ARTISTIC PROGRAMMING AND STRATEGIC PLANNING

Artistic programming and strategic planning[2] form the heart and soul of an ensemble's musical identity. This section describes the process of intertwining a compelling artistic vision with a pragmatic long-term roadmap, ensuring that the orchestra remains relevant and true to its core values.

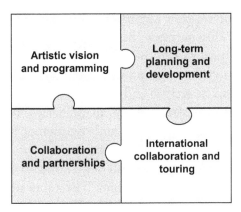

FIGURE 5.1 Key Components of Artistic Programming and Strategic Planning

The following four areas present the various facets of artistic programming and strategic planning, including crafting a unique artistic vision, the importance of long-term planning and development, and the immense potential of collaboration and alliances, as well as touring, as a means of expanding the horizons.

Artistic Vision and Programming

A pivotal aspect of a CEO's role is collaborating with the board, conductor, artistic director, and other stakeholders to elaborate a long-term and comprehensive artistic strategy and roadmap, develop concert seasons, curate repertoire, and organise special events that align with the mission and vision. This responsibility demands a profound understanding of the repertoire, musicians, audience preferences, the community's cultural landscape, and the board's expectations and visions to craft a shared grand design (Rentschler 2014). The process involves balancing artistic excellence with audience appeal and financial viability.

Effective artistic direction and programming go beyond merely selecting pieces and guest artists. Incorporating innovative formats, educational initiatives, and community programs contributes to a more diverse and inclusive offering while increasing the likelihood of attracting a larger audience. As a matter of fact, these efforts help broaden the reach and strengthen connections with new audiences while maintaining commitment to artistic quality. Artistic programming and strategic planning also play a crucial role in creating a narrative about the orchestra and its desired relationship with its surrounding world. The artistic programming becomes a vehicle for storytelling, communicating the orchestra's identity and aspirations to both existing and potential audiences. This narrative-building aspect of artistic programming adds depth and meaning to the overall concert experience, embedding the orchestra within its environment and across time, by infusing purpose, directions, and meaning into its artistic and community offerings.

The unique governance structure of an orchestra, however, sets it apart from other industries. Artistic directors and conductors, though holding senior profiles, do not report to the CEO in the traditional sense. Instead, they operate as quasi-peers of the CEO while still depending on them organisationally and from a financial authority standpoint. The table of delegated authority (ToDA) and the table of financial authority (ToFA) have to introduce mechanisms to deal with this paradoxical situation where senior members of the leadership team both report and do not report to the CEO whilst the musicians are caught in the middle of a double loyalty, to their conductor and artistic department, on the one hand, and their CEO and senior management team, on the other hand.[3] This nuanced relationship creates a dotted reporting line of authority between the CEO, artistic director, and conductor that differs significantly from the more hierarchical structures observed in other sectors (Herman 2021, l. 1344).

BOX 5.1 TABLES OF AUTHORITY

1 **Table of Delegated Authority:** In the domain of management science, a Table of Delegated Authority (ToDA) is a clearly delineated document outlining the decision-making authority vested in different roles within an organisation. The ToDA delineates the boundaries of managerial prerogatives, stipulating who has the capacity to make certain decisions and under what conditions. This encompasses a vast range of organisational functions, from procurement to human resources, strategic direction to operational decisions. The ToDA is instrumental in fostering transparency, mitigating risks associated with unauthorised decisions, and ensuring efficiency by assigning decision-making powers to the most appropriate roles. This mechanism of governance is seen as a tool to uphold accountability, as it provides a clear record of who holds responsibility for various decisions.

2 **Table of Financial Authority:** A Table of Financial Authority (ToFA) is a similar organisational document that specifically pertains to financial

decisions within an organisation. It is a systematic presentation detailing the levels of financial authority entrusted to various roles within the organisation. It provides a clear framework for financial responsibility, specifying who can authorise spending, to what extent, and under which circumstances. This ranges from approval of small expenses to the sanctioning of major capital investments or financial commitments. The ToFA is a key instrument for financial governance, risk management, and control, ensuring that financial decisions are made by appropriately authorised individuals, thereby safeguarding the organisation's financial health and integrity.

In this context, the CEO's authority framework is distinct, requiring exceptional diplomacy, negotiation, and communication skills to navigate these complex relationships. In the cases that we have observed, the CEO ensures successful artistic programming and direction, working closely with the artistic director and conductor, nurturing an environment of collaboration, mutual respect, and shared goals.

Some key considerations for effective artistic planning and programming include:

Audience demographics and preferences	Assessing the preferences, interests, and expectations of the target audience to ensure programming resonates with them.
Financial sustainability	Balancing artistic aspirations with budgetary constraints and revenue-generation goals
Collaborations	Exploring partnerships with guest artists, composers, and other cultural organisations to create unique and captivating experiences.
Innovation	Embracing new technologies, formats, and approaches to raise the performance experience.
Community outreach	Developing programs that educate the local community, take inclusivity into consideration, and boost cultural appreciation.

In summary, artistic vision and programme development require careful collaboration and negotiation among the CEO, artistic director, conductor, board, and a vast array of other stakeholders. The overall success and impact in the cultural sphere are elevated when innovation is accepted, alliances supported, and audience preferences considered, leading to rich, diverse, and sustainable programming that aligns with its mission and vision.

Long-Term Planning and Development

Long-term strategic planning and development demand a comprehensive approach that considers artistic vision and market trends as well as resource constraints and the potential of innovations in every segment of the value chain. Positive outcome and impact are seen where CEOs clearly demonstrate to skilfully manage the resources (people, repertoire, money, time, technology, etc.) and capitalise on emerging opportunities to keep their organisation relevant.

A key aspect of long-term planning is ensuring that operations are carried out within the resource constraints while the expressive potential is maximised. A strategic approach is then preferred to both budgeting, personnel management, and facilities management to optimise the allocation of resources and artistic planning. The scope is to ensure the best possible alignment with potential audiences while taking the required actions to involve the community and educate and attract new listeners. Identifying areas where efficiencies could be seized and potential synergies could be exploited to make the most of the resources appear as a CEO's key abilities. Exploring new revenue sources, such as digital content monetisation or soliciting partnerships with other organisations to share resources and minimise costs, are frequent routes to efficiency gains.

Long-term planning also involves harnessing the power of innovations in every activity, both artistic and operational, to drive artistic growth and overall performance, especially in teams with a clear functional diversification where the leadership's ability to maintain cohesion in transformation is paramount (Hüttermann and Boerner 2011). Another CEO prerequisite that has predominantly emerged in the recent years is the capacity to identify and authorise cutting-edge technologies, such as content digitisation, streaming, augmented and virtual reality, or artificial intelligence which could improve the audience experience, streamline operations, or open up new avenues for artistic expression. At the same time, a culture of creativity, experimentation, and continuous improvement, where new ideas and approaches are encouraged, is essential.

While staying at the forefront of technological advancements is not always required to create an environment that values organisational innovation and adaptability, the orchestra enhances its competitive edge and better positions itself for long-term success when it makes strategic, rather than opportunistic, use of technology. Effective long-term planning and development hinge on a CEO's ability to expertly manage resources, anticipate market trends, and exploit the potential of innovations. As demonstrated by examples of successful management, resource constraints and better usage of emerging technologies enable the charting of a vibrant future in a rapidly changing world. Similarly, innovation in management practices, artistic programming, or community engagement broaden the horizon (while showing that technocentrism is not a panacea to solve all issues).

Collaboration, Partnerships, and the Role of the Artistic Director

In today's ever-evolving and fiercely competitive market, the pursuit of artistic expression and audience retention is a guiding principle for arts and culture institutions seeking to leave a lasting impact on the cultural landscape. Collaborations and partnerships have emerged as crucial components of this quest,[4] providing opportunities to broaden horizons, challenge and enrich identity, and elevate artistic endeavours. This section analyses the significance of alliances and examines the pivotal role of the artistic director in spearheading such initiatives.

The Importance of Collaborations and Partnerships

Over the past few decades, collaborations and partnerships have become integral components in the toolbox of measures aimed at nurturing artistic innovation and creativity. Exploring collaborations with other artists, ensembles, or cultural institutions pushes the boundaries of musical repertoire, exploring diverse genres and creating new experiences for the audiences. Collaborative ventures also facilitate tapping into new demographics, expanding their reach, and establishing a more robust presence in their communities.

These connections manifest in various forms, from co-commissioning new works and cross-disciplinary projects to educational programmes and community outreach initiatives. Not only do they lift artistic credibility, but they also contribute to financial stability through shared resources, joint marketing efforts, and the potential for additional funding opportunities.

The Artistic Director's Role

The artistic director occupies a central position, steering the artistic vision and shaping the overall direction of the ensemble. As the chief creative force, the artistic director plays a crucial role in shaping a collaborative environment, identifying potential partners, and developing joint initiatives that align with the artistic (and financial) goals.

1 **Establishing a Collaborative Environment:** One of the artistic director's primary responsibilities is to create a *culture of collaboration*. This involves forging an atmosphere of trust, openness, collegiality, and mutual respect among musicians, staff, and board members. The artistic director helps cultivate an environment where expressive creativity prospers when everyone champions the merits of collaboration and actively encourages the exchange of ideas.

   It is also essential for the artistic director to maintain strong internal and external communication channels as clear and transparent dialogue with all stakeholders facilitates smoother collaboration and helps manage expectations.

2 **Identifying Potential Partners:** The artistic director plays a vital role in scouting potential partners. This requires a keen understanding of the cultural landscape and a proactive approach to seeking out organisations, ensembles, or artists who share similar values and objectives. They also explore synergies and create opportunities for mutually beneficial partnerships with like-minded entities.

   When evaluating potential collaborators, the artistic director considers factors such as artistic compatibility, shared goals and values, and the capacity to contribute unique resources or expertise to the alliance. A well-chosen partner does not only amplify the artistic output but elevates its reputation and contributes to its long-term sustainability.

3 **Developing Joint Initiatives:** In addition to identifying potential partners, the artistic director is responsible for devising and implementing joint initiatives that resonate with the mission and artistic vision. Careful planning, strategic thinking, and close coordination with various stakeholders, including musicians, staff, partners, and board members, are paramount in this context.

   Joint initiatives may include co-commissioning new works, creating cross-disciplinary performances, or devising educational and community outreach programmes. In developing these initiatives, the artistic director ensures that they align with the strategic objectives, add value to the artistic offering, and contribute to overall growth and development of the organisation.

4 **Involving Diverse Artistic Communities:** In a globalised world, orchestras can collaborate with a wide array of artistic communities, encompassing various cultures, disciplines, and genres (Walker and Scott-Melnyk 2002). The artistic director must possess a broad artistic outlook and a deep appreciation for diversity to identify potential partners and projects that enrich the repertoire and help touch new audiences.

For instance, collaborating with world music ensembles or incorporating elements from non-Western musical traditions offer unique perspectives and constructively challenge conventional musical norms. Similarly, working with artists from other disciplines, such as dance, theatre, or visual arts, results in innovative, multidisciplinary performances that push creative boundaries and captivate audiences.

5 **Balancing Artistic Integrity and Collaboration:** While collaborations and partnerships yield numerous benefits, the artistic director also ensures that the ensemble's artistic integrity remains intact, striking a delicate balance between welcoming new ideas and preserving the core values and identity.

The artistic director must be mindful of the potential risks associated with alliances, such as diluting the brand or compromising the artistic vision. To mitigate these risks, they establish clear goals and guidelines for each collaboration, communicate openly with all stakeholders, and regularly evaluate the partnership's progress and impact.

6 **Nurturing Long-term Relationships:** In addition to initiating collaborations and partnerships, the artistic director plays a vital role in nurturing and maintaining these relationships over the long term. Consistent communication, ongoing support, and a willingness to adapt and grow together are key to this task.

Long-term relationships with partners are the building blocks of a strong network of allies and collaborators that offer sustained artistic, financial, and community benefits. These relationships help establish a reputation for innovation and excellence, bolstering the overall positioning within the cultural sector.

7 **Leveraging Technology and Digital Platforms:** Rapid technological advancements and the widespread diffusion of digital streaming platforms have opened up new possibilities to enrol in collaborations and partnerships, both locally and globally.[5] The 21st-century artistic director is more attuned to the latest technological developments and willing to explore

innovative ways of leveraging these tools to facilitate collaboration and artistic expression.

For instance, digital platforms facilitate collaboration with artists from across the globe, breaking down geographical and cultural barriers. Additionally, through technologies such as streaming, virtual reality experiences, or social media interactions, a dialogue with global audiences is established in new and interactive ways.

8 **Encouraging Innovation and Experimentation:** To stay relevant and competitive in today's soundscape, innovation emerges as a useful lever, even in the time-honoured tradition of classical music. The artistic director, as the creative leader of the ensemble, is the ideal person to champion a spirit of experimentation and risk-taking. An artistic director is also prepared to encourage musicians, staff, and partners to challenge conventional wisdom and explore new ideas that indirectly endorse a culture of innovation.

9 **Measuring the Impact of Collaborations and Partnerships:** Finally, the artistic director is also responsible for measuring and evaluating the impact of alliances – assessing the artistic, financial, and community outcomes of each initiative and using this information to inform future decisions and strategies (Gazley 2010; Weiss, Anderson, and Lasker 2002) and turn past experiences into assets. By adopting a data-driven approach to evaluating collaborations and partnerships, the artistic director verifies that the resources are being invested wisely and that the collaborative efforts are contributing to the overall growth and success.

***

Although not sufficient, collaborations and partnerships drive success and evolution. They provide opportunities for creative growth, audience engagement, artistic innovation, and community impact. As the driving force behind these collaborative endeavours, the artistic director holds significant responsibility for establishing a supportive environment, identifying suitable partners, and developing joint initiatives that align with the mission and artistic vision. Collaboration and strong alliances also fuel relevance by creating transformative experiences for audiences, artists, and the wider community.

International Collaboration and Touring

Today more than ever before, orchestras have the opportunity to expand their horizons beyond their local communities thanks to international collaborations and touring. Embracing these opportunities allows them to widen audience reach, establish a network of cultural exchange, and accelerate artistic development.

This section discusses the numerous benefits, challenges, and best practices associated with international collaboration and touring.

The Benefits

International collaboration and touring yield several benefits that contribute to artistic growth and long-term success:

1 **Expanding Audience Reach and Brand Visibility:** Performing in new countries exposes the ensemble to diverse audiences, potentially garnering new fans and supporters worldwide. Eventually, the increased exposure boosts their international reputation and attracts additional opportunities for collaboration and funding, triggering a virtuous circle of globalisation of the brand.

2 **Enriching Artistic Experiences and Inspiration:** Collaborating with musicians, composers, and other artists from different countries and cultural backgrounds brings fresh perspectives and ideas to the repertoire. These interactions usually inspire new works, unique interpretations, and innovative programming.

3 **Fostering Cultural Exchange and Diplomacy:** Music has the power to transcend cultural and political boundaries. Participation in international tours and collaborations contributes to cultural diplomacy, building bridges between communities (Panasiuk et al. 2022; Statler 2012; Ahrendt, Ferraguto, and Mahiet 2014).

4 **Enriching the Reputation and Credibility:** Successful international tours and collaborations elevate the orchestra's standing in the eyes of critics, peers, and potential funders. A strong international reputation attracts more top talent, additional resources, and increased support from the local community.

BOX 5.2 MUSIC DIPLOMACY

One notable example of music diplomacy is the New York Philharmonic's visit to North Korea in February 2008 (Associated Press 2008; PBS 2008). The orchestra was invited by the North Korean government to perform in Pyongyang, the nation's capital, in a rare cultural exchange between the United States and the isolated country. Under the baton of then-Music Director Lorin Maazel, the New York Philharmonic performed works by American composers such as George Gershwin and Leonard Bernstein, as well as the national anthems of both the United States and North Korea. The concert was broadcast on North Korean state television and radio, allowing millions of citizens to experience the performance.

Other notable examples of "political touring" are the Trieste Philharmonic's tour in Serbia in the spring of 1946 (Sukljan 2018) and the foreign tours of the Moscow State Symphony Orchestra headed by Veronika B. Dudarova in the 1970s (Andreev 2021).

The Challenges

While international collaborations and touring offer significant benefits, they also come with a broad spectrum of challenges that require careful consideration for both operational and branding reasons:

1 **Logistics and Planning:** Coordinating an international tour is a complex undertaking that involves travel arrangements, visa applications, shipping of instruments and equipment, and adapting to different venues and performance conditions. Thorough planning and attention to detail are essential to a smooth and successful experience.

2 **Financial Implications:** International touring is often costly, particularly for large ensembles with numerous musicians, staff, and equipment. Even if the absolute cost for smaller ensembles is contained, the impact on their sometimes meagre finances might be much higher. Orchestras must carefully weigh the potential benefits against the financial risks and work to secure funding from multiple sources, including grants, sponsorships, and ticket sales, to cover expenses.

3 **Balancing Local and International Commitments:** Even when the financial implications of touring are not an issue, participating in international activities always takes away a considerable share of time from daily

operations. It is therefore crucial that orchestras strike a balance between maintaining their presence and commitments in their local community and pursuing international opportunities.

4 **Navigating Cultural Sensitivities and Differences:** Collaboration with external artists and performances for audiences from different cultural backgrounds should reflect a genuine appreciation and respect for diverse cultural norms, traditions, and sensitivities. This involves adjusting programming, presentation, or communication styles to ensure a positive and inclusive experience for all involved.

5 **Environmental Impact and Audience Perception:** In an age of growing environmental awareness, the carbon footprint associated with international touring has become a concern. Younger audience members, particularly active on social media, may express disapproval of the environmental impact caused by a large group of musicians and staff travelling around the world on planes to deliver a performance that lasts no more than a few hours. These concerns are increasingly being addressed by considering and implementing simple measures to mitigate the environmental impact.

Best Practices for International Collaboration

Several quite well-established levers are increasingly available to maximise the benefits of international collaboration and limit potential challenges:

1 **Building Partnerships With International Organisations and Venues:** Establishing strong relationships with cultural institutions, venues, and festivals in other countries facilitates collaboration and touring opportunities. These alliances provide valuable support, resources, and local knowledge to help navigate the complexities of international activities.

2 **Leveraging Existing Networks and Relationships:** Generally, the international connections of individual musicians, staff, board members, and supporters abound with unforeseen possibilities to identify potential collaborations. Personal connections are an invaluable asset in initiating and sustaining international initiatives.

3 **Showcasing Diverse and Innovative Programming:** To stand out on the international stage, orchestras have a strong interest to present programming that showcases their unique strengths and artistic identity. Premiering new works, exploring diverse genres and styles, or collaborating with artists from different disciplines all contribute to create innovative performances.

4 **Investing in Marketing:** To attract audiences and create a buzz around their international activities, targeted marketing and visibility efforts are a must. Leveraging social media, partnering with local media outlets, and working with relevant cultural influencers in the host country play a vital role in maximising the reach and impact of international engagements.

5 **Ensuring Clear and Open Communication:** Successful international collaborations rely on effective communication among all parties. Establishing clear lines of communication with international partners ensures that expectations are understood and any challenges or concerns are addressed promptly.

6 **Evaluating and Learning From the Experience:** After completing an international tour or collaboration, conducting a thorough evaluation of the outcomes and extracting insights from the experience is essential. This exercise comprises a couple steps: (i) gathering feedback from musicians, staff, partners, and audiences and (ii) using this information to inform future international activities.

International collaboration and touring greatly enrich artistic development and contribute to long-term success. Careful consideration of the challenges associated with these activities, coupled with the identification of best practices, enables orchestras to maximise the potential of their international activities, expanding their horizons of cultural exchange on a global scale.

CASE STUDY 5.1

The Integration of Artistic Programming and Strategic Planning

The integration of artistic programming and strategic planning is essential to ensure long-term success and audience engagement. This case study examines how a regional orchestra navigated the process of aligning its artistic vision with its long-term strategic objectives.

ESTABLISHING THE ARTISTIC VISION AND LONG-TERM OBJECTIVES
- Defining the artistic identity and values
- Identifying target audiences and community needs

- Setting measurable goals for artistic growth, audience development, and financial sustainability

COLLABORATING WITH KEY STAKEHOLDERS

- Involving the artistic director, music director, and other artistic staff in the planning process
- Involving the board, musicians, and administrative staff in discussions and brainstorming sessions
- Soliciting input from audience members, donors, and community partners

DEVELOPING THE ARTISTIC PROGRAMMING STRATEGY

- Balancing innovative and traditional repertoire
- Showcasing diverse composers, genres, and musical styles
- Incorporating collaborative projects with local artists and cultural organisations
- Integrating educational and outreach initiatives to attract new audiences

ALIGNING ARTISTIC PROGRAMMING WITH STRATEGIC OBJECTIVES

- Ensuring programming supports audience development goals
- Evaluating the financial feasibility of proposed projects and initiatives
- Assessing the potential for grant funding and sponsorship opportunities
- Identifying ways to leverage digital platforms for increased audience satisfaction

BUILDING A FLEXIBLE AND ADAPTABLE PROGRAMMING SCHEDULE

- Creating multi-year programming plans with room for adjustments based on audience feedback, financial considerations, and external factors
- Establishing a contingency plan for unexpected changes or challenges, such as pandemics or economic downturns

IMPLEMENTING AND COMMUNICATING THE INTEGRATED PLAN

- Developing a marketing and communication strategy to promote the artistic vision and programming
- Ensuring consistent messaging across all channels, including print materials, website, social media, and public relations efforts

- Creating excitement and anticipation among stakeholders and the community

MONITORING PROGRESS AND ADAPTING THE PLAN

- Collecting data on audience attendance, activities, and demographics
- Regularly reviewing financial performance and fundraising results
- Soliciting feedback from stakeholders to inform future planning efforts
- Adjusting the artistic programming and strategic plan as needed to address changing circumstances and opportunities

The integration of artistic programming and strategic planning resulted in a more cohesive artistic vision, increased audience engagement, and a stronger financial foundation. Key lessons learned from this case study include the importance of collaboration among stakeholders, balancing innovation with tradition, adapting to changing circumstances, and effectively communicating the vision to the community.

QUESTIONS:

1 Discuss how the integration of artistic programming and strategic planning could be accomplished in a way that balances the creative vision, financial sustainability, and changing needs of audiences and the community. How might the orchestra navigate potential conflicts between these areas?

2 In the process of involving key stakeholders (the artistic director, artistic staff, board members, musicians, administrative staff, audience members, donors, and community partners), what techniques could be employed to ensure all voices are heard and considered? How might this broad input strengthen the integration of artistic programming and strategic planning?

3 The case study highlights the necessity of balancing innovative and traditional repertoire and showcasing diverse composers, genres, and musical styles. How can these elements be woven into a cohesive and engaging programming strategy that resonates with existing audiences and attracts new ones?

4 With the need for flexibility and adaptability, especially in light of potential unexpected changes such as pandemics or economic downturns, how should the orchestra approach the definition of its programming

schedule? What factors are to be considered when establishing a contingency plan?

5   Assess the implementation process of the integrated plan from a communications and marketing perspective. What methods can be employed to ensure consistent messaging across all channels and to create excitement and anticipation among stakeholders and the community?

B. FINANCIAL, FUNDRAISING, LEGAL, AND RESOURCE MANAGEMENT

Financial Management

Managing the finances is a challenging and intricate task: while essential for long-term sustainability, it also commands the application of an analytical approach to an artistic and emotional activity, which is fundamentally and historically alien to quantification. The financial stability implies an approach that goes beyond traditional corporate financial management best practices. As Flanagan (2012, l. 158) sharply put it, "no symphony orchestra earns enough from performances to cover its performance expenses. Second, that fact is not likely to change in the foreseeable future. Third, the survival of orchestras depends on the resources provided by guarantors."

As with all arts and culture institutions, orchestras operate in a unique ecosystem that presents both opportunities and challenges, although they often

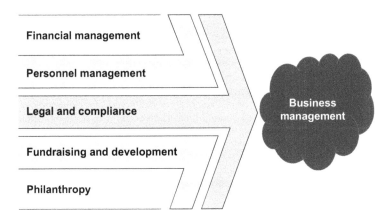

FIGURE 5.2 Key Aspects of Business Management

go beyond those specific to the world of arts and culture.[6] This requires managers not only to master the standard principles of financial management but also to develop a deeper understanding of the particularities of the cultural sector.

Managers must be proficient in strategic budgeting, comprehensive fundraising, cost management, financial risk assessment, and pursuing innovative revenue streams, all while maintaining a strong focus on the organisation's artistic vision and values. This delicate balancing act necessitates a keen awareness of the mission, the cultural landscape, and the diverse needs of its stakeholders, including musicians, staff, board members, and audiences. It is within this context that the following ten points have been developed to provide a framework for effective financial management, stability, and resilience of an organisation.

Function	Description
Strategic Budgeting and Financial Planning	The manager formulates detailed financial plans that align with the organisation's strategic goals and artistic vision – key components of the plan are setting financial objectives, forecasting revenues and expenses, and creating contingency plans for unexpected situations. Regular monitoring and adjustments are required to ensure the orchestra remains on track to meet its financial goals.
Diversified Fundraising and Development	A fundraising strategy involves pursuing diverse funding sources. Managers identify and approach potential donors, sponsors, and grant-makers while maintaining existing relationships. This requires understanding the unique value proposition and tailoring communication to resonate with different target groups, leveraging digital channels and social media platforms to their expand reach towards a broader audience.
Cost Management and Operational Efficiency	Effective cost management involves identifying areas where resources could be optimised and expenses reduced without compromising the artistic mission. Managers scrutinise all aspects of their organisation, from staffing and marketing to venue management and production costs, to uncover opportunities for improved efficiency and cost savings.
Financial Risk Assessment and Mitigation	Managers evaluate potential financial risks, such as fluctuations in ticket sales, changes in funding sources, or economic downturns, that impact their organisation's stability. Managers develop strategies to mitigate risks and safeguard the financial health by assessing these risks regularly and understanding their potential consequences.

Function	Description
Financial Opportunities from Innovation	To diversify income and reduce dependency on traditional funding sources, exploring innovative revenue streams is essential. Managers consider opportunities that generate additional income, such as digital content creation, streaming, merchandising, collaborations with film or other media, and licensing arrangements. Pursuing these ventures requires a willingness to embrace new risks and innovate within the organisation while keeping a focus on financial returns.
Financial Reporting and Transparency	Accurate financial records, regulatory compliance, and transparent communication of financial information to the board, staff, and other stakeholders are critical components of effective financial management. This helps build trust, enables informed decision-making, and ensures accountability.
Cash Flow Management	Managers closely monitor cash inflows and outflows to ensure short-term financial stability and long-term business sustainability. This includes ensuring the timely collection of receivables, managing payables, and optimising the use of available cash. Effective cash flow management helps avoid liquidity crises and supports the organisation's ongoing operations.
Long-term Financial Sustainability	Beyond day-to-day financial management, managers also consider the long-term financial sustainability of their organisation. This requires identifying and addressing structural financial challenges, investing in the future, and building financial reserves to withstand economic fluctuations and uncertainties.
Financial Analysis and Decision-making	Managers are proficient in analysing financial data to inform strategic decision-making. This includes evaluating the financial implications of various programming choices, assessing the cost-effectiveness of marketing efforts, and determining the return on investment for fundraising initiatives.
Adaptability and Resilience in Revenue Generation	Managers demonstrate adaptability and resilience in the face of unexpected situations or crises, such as the Covid-19 pandemic,[7] which disrupted live concerts for extended periods. Managers who are proactive and responsive to challenges can identify and seize opportunities to transform adversity into new revenue streams. Adaptability and resilience are sine qua non conditions to navigate unforeseen circumstances and ensure the financial stability and continued success of their organisation.[8]

In conclusion, effective financial management is crucial to sustainability. Due to the financial peculiarities of orchestras, managers must excel in strategic budgeting, diversified fundraising, cost management, financial risk assessment, and the unrelenting pursuit of innovative revenue opportunities.

The seamless integration of financial analysis into artistic decision-making and vice versa, a commitment to transparency, and a steadfast focus on long-term financial sustainability in alignment with artistic objectives all serve to fortify an orchestra's financial position and safeguard the ongoing realisation of its artistic vision.

Personnel Management

In the field of management, one of the vital components is personnel, which is centred on drawing in the best possible talents and maintaining their commitment, excitement, and well-being over time, including the smooth treatment of all related bureaucratic procedures. Given the globalised nature of today's classical music industry, orchestras are vying not only for the attention of audiences but also for the most accomplished musicians, conductors, managers, and supporting staff. As a result, personnel management demands a strategic and empathetic approach to secure the finest talents in the industry and keep their satisfaction at the highest level.

Personnel management encompasses several key elements, including hiring, contracting, and the ongoing development of musicians and staff. The process of hiring musicians and conductors significantly influences the artistic orientation, quality, and overall success. To excel in this aspect, managers must possess a comprehensive understanding of the classical music landscape (as both an industry and a form of art) and demonstrate an aptitude for identifying and recruiting remarkable talents.

Contracting is another crucial aspect of personnel management. Managers should have a solid grasp of the market trends, employment law, and contract negotiations to ensure fair compensation and career opportunities for musicians and staff. To draw and retain outstanding talents is better achieved by implementing transparent compensation structures, career paths, and development frameworks. Moreover, a positive work environment, which supports creativity, collaboration, and teamwork, is an indispensable asset for musical success.

Effective personnel management also encompasses the non-artistic staff, which includes marketers, accountants, finance, legal professionals, etc., all of whom play pivotal roles in the organisation's business life. In the competitive global market, securing top management talent requires a strategic approach to recruitment, compensation, and retention. To ensure long-term sustainability, managers usually pay attention to employee development, offering opportunities for growth and, above all, for training while addressing any concerns that arise. Creating a sense of belonging is vital. To accomplish this, managers prioritise open communication, encourage collaboration, and value feedback from musicians and staff. Constructively and fairly addressing performance issues allows managers to create an environment of trust and respect, contributing to a healthy corporate culture. Another essential factor is work-life balance. Recognising the importance of balancing professional and personal lives, effective managers favour flexible working arrangements, address scheduling conflicts, and are understanding of the unique demands placed on musicians and staff that are, more than others, often requested to work on weekends, late evenings, or special celebration days.

It is important to recognise and celebrate the achievements of musicians and staff, both individually and collectively. In successful orchestras, the senior management tends to often cultivate ownership and pride in the organisation's accomplishments when they acknowledge and reward hard work and dedication.

Ultimately, effective personnel management relies on a deep understanding of the classical music industry and the capability to identify, attract, and retain the best musicians, conductors, and staff. Long-term success in a highly competitive global market is usually easier in the presence of a positive work environment, fair compensation, and ongoing development of the artistic and admin staff.

Compliance and Legal Matters

Compliance and legal matters should not be underestimated. They require a deep understanding of legal frameworks, contracts, and intellectual property. Adhering to relevant laws and regulations, including labour laws, tax laws, and performance rights, maintains the operations within legal boundaries while protecting assets.

BOX 5.3 ORCHESTRAS AS CHARITIES

An interesting trend at the crossroad between tax, fundraising, and legal is the growing number of orchestras registering as charities in the US (Cooper 2016). As government funding for the arts declines, registering as a charity enables US arts and culture institutions to receive tax-deductible donations from individuals, corporations, and foundations, providing an alternative source of revenue.

In today's digital age, the ease of content circulation – and the difficulty of controlling it – has made legal rights more complex to manage. Orchestras now have no other choice than dealing with intricate international copyright laws and licensing agreements to protect their intellectual property while being compelled by the market to expose their content to a wider audience. Managing compliance and legal matters requires a CEO capable of identifying the right professionals with the skills and expertise necessary to navigate legal complexities while also protecting the assets. Orchestras cannot ringfence their long-term options in a rapidly changing industry without effectively mastering legal frameworks and protecting intellectual property.

Artist Agencies

In the classical music industry, soloists, conductors, and choirs are often contracted by artist managers and agencies that serve as intermediaries[9] while taking care of their career, marketing, and image (O'Reilly 2014). Managers and CEOs must be well-versed in the financial implications of recruiting these agencies and the legal and compliance requirements involved in hiring their services. These requirements extend to regulations surrounding tenders and the procurement process, particularly when working with public funding or collaborating with other institutions.

It is recommended that managers develop a strong understanding of the contractual agreements and negotiation processes associated with commissioning artists through artist managers and agencies that sometimes appear or behave like oligopolistic intermediary bodies. This involves profiting from the competition between artist managers or agencies, carefully reviewing and negotiating contract terms (such as fees, scheduling, cancellation policies, and performance rights) to preserve the orchestra's interests and proceed smoothly with the collaborations. Additionally, they must be aware of any specific legal requirements or regulations that govern the hiring of artists, especially when working across international borders or within certain jurisdictions.

When navigating the legal complexities of dealing with artist agencies, it is vital for managers and CEOs to collaborate with legal professionals who possess the necessary expertise in this area. This objective is achieved by either retaining in-house counsel or working closely with external legal advisors who specialise in entertainment law and the intricacies of the classical music industry – this usually depends on the size and importance of the organisation as smaller ensembles usually do not have internal legal expertise. Managers usually see an interest in maintaining open lines of communication with artist managers and agencies to foster strong professional relationships, facilitate smoother negotiations, and help address any potential issues or misunderstandings before they escalate. Managers who understand the roles and responsibilities of both the orchestra and the agency better anticipate the needs and expectations of the artists they hire, leading to trouble-free collaborations for all parties involved.

In conclusion, managers and CEOs must be adept at handling the legal and compliance requirements associated with artist agencies in the classical music industry. A solid grasp of the financial and legal implications of working with agencies, as well as the relevant regulations surrounding tenders and procurement processes, eases successful collaborations with soloists, conductors, and choirs while operating within the boundaries of the law. This requires a combination of market awareness, strong negotiation skills, a thorough understanding of contracts and legal frameworks, and the ability to work effectively with legal professionals and artist agencies alike.

Fundraising and Development

Although funding models substantially vary across geographies, fundraising is a critical aspect of the cultural industry overall.[10] It involves soliciting financial support from individuals, corporations, foundations, and government institutions to sustain the organisation's operations, artistic programmes, and community initiatives. As public funding for the arts dwindles, and competition for resources intensifies, fundraising has become fundamental to long-term viability. This section delves into the importance of fundraising, discusses various fundraising methods, and shares best practices for relationship building, donor stewardship, and addressing the challenges and opportunities that arise when securing funding for initiatives and endowment campaigns.

The Importance of Fundraising

Although fundraising is far from being a new practice in Western societies (Hufton 2008), in the last 50 years only it came to play a vital role in the financial health of arts and culture institutions, helping to bridge the gap between earned revenue (such as ticket sales) and the actual costs of running the organisation. Philanthropic support, licensing, sales of content and merchandising, to name a few, generated the much-needed income to maintain high artistic standards, develop innovative programming, expand their reach to diverse audiences, and invest in education and outreach activities. Additionally, a robust fundraising programme serves as a buffer during economic downturns, providing a degree of financial stability and resilience.

Fundraising, whilst undeniably a critical activity, must be approached with a holistic understanding of the overall funding model. A myopic focus on fundraising alone potentially leads to the cannibalisation of other revenue streams. This was sharply highlighted by Flanagan (2012, l. 2837):

> The full effect of government support for symphony orchestras depends on how that support influences private contributions. If government support for orchestras discourages private support from individuals, businesses, and foundations, nonperformance income will increase by less than the amount of government subsidies. If potential supporters of orchestras believe that their inclination to contribute has been fulfilled by tax-financed government subsidies, government expenditures on orchestras would displace or crowd out private donations.

Real-life examples show that to avoid the cannibalisation of revenue streams, managers recognise the delicate balance among various sources of income, such as ticket sales, merchandising, corporate sponsorships, government grants, and individual donations. Therefore, a well-conceived funding strategy is paramount to giving long-term financial sustainability and artistic success.

A common pitfall for smaller or less wealthy ensembles lies in concentrating fundraising efforts at the expense of other revenue-generating initiatives. For instance, overly aggressive fundraising campaigns may alienate potential guarantors (ticket buyers or corporate sponsors), who may in turn perceive an orchestra as too reliant on philanthropy, thereby diminishing their willingness to invest in the organisation. A single-minded focus on fundraising could inadvertently result in the neglect of audience development activities, which are equally important for sustaining financial health and artistic vitality.

A comprehensive approach to revenue generation, striking an equilibrium among the various income sources in order to avoid (or control) the cannibalisation of revenue streams, seems to be the winning managerial attitude. This entails rearing philanthropic alongside nurturing and diversifying ticket sales, exploring new partnership opportunities, and lobbying for increased public funding. Additionally, embracing innovative strategies, such as digital content monetisation or developing unique experiences for audiences, further bolsters the financial resilience.

In essence, real-life examples show that although fundraising remains an indispensable component of a funding model, it should not overshadow other equally crucial revenue streams. Only through a balanced and strategic approach to income generation can orchestras safeguard their financial stability and artistic ambitions while avoiding cannibalising revenue streams. As the old adage goes, one should not put all their eggs in one basket; instead, managers must skilfully juggle various revenue sources, aiming at a harmonious and sustainable funding symphony.

Fundraising Methods

Various fundraising methods are usually employed to diversify revenue streams and maximise support from different sources.

- **Individual Giving**
  Soliciting donations from passionate individuals. Donor categories may include annual fund contributors, major gift donors, and planned giving participants. Effective strategies for individual giving include targeted appeals, special events, and personalised stewardship.
- **Corporate Sponsorship**
  Private companies – usually larger, but not always – may be eager to align themselves with reputable cultural institutions to obtain more brand visibility and networking opportunities. There are numerous examples of orchestras that developed mutually beneficial alliances with businesses offering tailored sponsorship packages that include logo placements, exclusive event access, and customised employee programmes. A special form of corporate sponsorship that does not affect the sponsor's balance sheet is investing in reputable musical instruments. These are then borrowed by the musicians against visibility to the sponsor while their value still appears in the sponsor's books. Given the market expansion for (and constant value increase of) reputable music instruments, corporate sponsors like to consider this investment option more and more often.
- **Government Support**
  Orchestras (more so in Europe, the Middle East, Asia, and Oceania than the US) receive considerable subsidies from local, regional, and national government agencies that support the arts and culture. However, a capacity to demonstrate a clear contribution to the community's cultural vibrancy, economic growth, and social cohesion is sometimes a prerequisite to subsidy renewal. Even though the legal framework strictly regulates public subsidies, the ability of managers to maintain good relationships with funding bodies nevertheless facilitates the process, highlighting the importance of a fundraising attitude to government financial support that should not be underestimated.
- **Grant Writing**
  Foundations, trusts, and sometimes even government-affiliated authorities provide financial support through competitive grant programmes to implement new initiatives. A well-crafted grant proposal clearly articulates the

project's objectives, expected outcomes, and impact, budget, and degree of alignment with the funder's priorities.

Best Practices for Relationship Building and Donor Stewardship

A successful fundraising programme hinges on strong relationships with donors and stakeholders. Here are some best practices for lasting connections and ensuring continued support:

1 **Communicate the Impact**: Regularly share the impact of donors' contributions on the artistic work, highlighting how their support has facilitated transformative experiences for audiences, musicians, and the broader community.

2 **Personalise Stewardship**: Tailor the stewardship efforts to each donor's interests and preferences. This includes, amongst others, personalised updates, invitations to exclusive events, or opportunities to interact with musicians and artistic staff.

3 **Express Gratitude**: Ensure that donors feel valued and appreciated by sending timely thank-you letters, acknowledging their contributions in printed materials and online platforms, and recognising their support at events.

4 **Invest in Donor Relationships**: Develop a comprehensive donor relations strategy that covers regular touchpoints, increased involvement, and plans for long-term relationships.

Challenges and Opportunities in Securing Funding for Initiatives and Endowment Campaigns

Searching for funding for new initiatives or endowment campaigns does not come without many obstacles, some of which include competition for resources, changing donor priorities over time, and broader economic uncertainties. However, the same challenges also show ways for strategic growth, intense collaboration, and artistic innovation:

1 **Craft a Compelling Narrative**: Clearly communicate the value and impact of orchestral work by weaving a compelling story that resonates with potential supporters, illustrating the significance of their investment.

2 **Favour Innovative Collaboration**: Explore fresh programming concepts, partnerships, and delivery models that attract funding from diverse sources or more funding from existing sources (or both). Collaborating with

other cultural institutions, educational organisations, or community groups usually fortifies a proposal and broadens its funding base.

3 **Activate Your Network**: Utilise the expertise, connections, and passion of board members, staff, and volunteers to identify potential funding opportunities and cultivate relationships with prospective supporters.

4 **Diversify Funding Sources**: Develop a comprehensive fundraising strategy that targets multiple revenue streams, including individual giving, corporate sponsorships, foundation grants, and government support. This approach helps mitigate the risks associated with relying on a single funding source.

5 **Invest in Fundraising Capacity and Expertise**: Ensure that an organisation possesses the necessary skills, resources, and infrastructure to successfully execute its fundraising strategy. This involves hiring dedicated development staff (or volunteers), providing training and professional development opportunities, and implementing effective systems for donor management and stewardship.

Fundraising and (business) development are essential components of overall sustainability. Long-term viability and continuous enrichment of the cultural landscape often have a profoundly erosive impact on the budget; implementing a variety of fundraising methods, consolidating relationships with donors and stakeholders, and addressing the challenges and opportunities inherent in securing funding for initiatives and endowment campaigns are costly actions that cannot be skipped.

Philanthropy

Especially in contexts with limited public or government support, philanthropy is instrumental to the financial sustainability of cultural institutions, as it provides a vital source of funding that complements other revenue streams. This section reviews the importance of philanthropy in financial management, focusing on the motivations behind philanthropic giving, strategies to attract donors, and the potential impact of this form of financial support on long-term stability.

The Importance of Philanthropy in Financial Management

In the face of increasing economic difficulties and the decline of public funding for the arts, philanthropic support has become an indispensable component of financial management. Although this might be more relevant to the US than, for example, Germany, France, or South Korea, philanthropy nonetheless helps to:

Bridge the funding gap

As earned revenues never cover the entire costs of operations, philanthropic contributions help bridge the gap between income and expenses, ensuring financial stability and resilience.

Maintain artistic excellence

Generous donations allow managers to invest in the highest-quality musicians, conductors, and guest artists, as well as commission new works and produce innovative programming.

Boost community relationships

Philanthropic support could cover a new class of costs related to the production of more and better content for social media, as well as the implementation of educational initiatives and outreach programmes that broaden access to classical music and nurture the next generation of musicians and audiences.

Improve long-term viability

A strong base of philanthropic support provides a foundation for future growth and development, offering a financial cushion that orchestras rely upon to adapt to changing circumstances and maintain their cultural relevance.

Understanding Philanthropic Motivations

At any moment in time, managers need to have a clear understanding of the underlying (and evolving) motivations behind philanthropic giving to effectively leverage potential donors. Motivations may be more personal or more collective; however, they may also be rooted in a positive attitude or a selfish sentiment, and, above all, they emerge from a mix that is specific to each donor. Some common reasons for providing support include:

1 **Passion for Music and the Arts**: Many donors are driven by a deep love for classical music and a desire to preserve and advance this art form for future generations.

2 **Personal Connection**: Some donors have a personal connection to an orchestra, such as being a former musician, staff member, or having a family member involved in the organisation.

3 **Social Responsibility**: Philanthropic individuals may view their contributions as an expression of their civic duty, supporting cultural institutions that enrich the community and bolster social cohesion.

4 **Prestige and Recognition**: Donors may appreciate the social and reputational benefits of being associated with a prestigious cultural institution and may be motivated by opportunities for public acknowledgement of their support.

Attracting Donors

Effectively securing philanthropic support requires a strategic approach to donors rather than relying solely on sporadic or *ad hoc* initiatives. Some key strategies are better deployed following a staged approach:

Identifying potential donors	Conduct thorough research to identify individuals, foundations, and trusts with a demonstrated interest in supporting the arts and a potential alignment with the mission and vision.
Building relationships	Invest time and effort in getting to know potential donors, understanding their interests and motivations, and developing a genuine rapport.
Communicating impact	Share compelling stories and evidence of the positive impact that donors' contributions have on the orchestra's work, both artistically and within the community.
Personalising engagement	Tailor your approach to each donor, offering unique experiences, opportunities for involvement, and recognition that align with their interests and preferences.
Stewarding relationships	Maintain strong connections with donors through regular communication, updates on the activities, and expressions of gratitude for their support.

The Impact of Philanthropy on Long-Term Success

Philanthropy has the potential to transform financial outlook, providing the resources for artistic innovation, organisational growth, and community impact. Orchestras, therefore, have a strong interest in cultivating a committed base of philanthropic supporters to improve their long-term financial resilience and continue to contribute to the cultural enrichment of society.

In a nutshell, where government financial support is limited, philanthropy is a crucial aspect of financial sustainability, helping to secure the resources needed for artistic excellence, operations, and community outreach. Understanding the motivations behind philanthropic giving, attracting and retaining donors effectively, and demonstrating the impact of their support are rewarding strategies for securing this vital source of funding. Philanthropy is a cornerstone of financial management to build a strong foundation for long-term success and to continue enriching the cultural landscape with transformative artistic contributions.

CASE STUDY 5.2

Navigating Financial Challenges and Implementing Effective Fundraising Strategies

This case study presents a quantitative analysis of an ensemble with an annual budget of $8.3 million, which faced financial difficulties due to declining ticket sales, reduced government support, and stagnation in donations.

A. ASSESSING THE FINANCIAL SITUATION AND IDENTIFYING KEY CHALLENGES

The recently appointed management team conducted a thorough financial analysis that revealed the following.
  Over the last two years:

- 12% decline in ticket sales, from $2.5 million to $2.2 million
- 16.7% reduction in government support, from $3 million to $2.5 million
- stagnant donors' contribution at $2 million and corporate contribution at $500,000
- $4.8 million in staff costs, up $100,000
- $2.5 million in production and marketing costs, up $100,000
- $1 million in other expenses, up $100,000

Overall, the costs had increased by $300,000 while the revenue lost $800,000.

	Two Years Ago	Current Situation
Costs		
– Staff Costs	4,700,000	4,800,000
– Production & Marketing Costs	2,400,000	2,500,000
– All Other Expenses	900,000	1,000,000
Revenue		
– Ticket Sales	2,500,000	2,200,000
– Government Support	3,000,000	2,500,000
– Donor Contributions	2,000,000	2,000,000
– Corporate Sponsorships & Partnerships	500,000	500,000
Balance		–1,100,000

B. FORMULATING A STRATEGIC FINANCIAL PLAN

- The leadership team worked closely with the board to develop a comprehensive financial plan aiming to increase revenue by $750,000 and reduce costs by $350,000 over the next two years.
- The plan included clear and quantifiable objectives and milestones, such as securing new corporate sponsorships worth $200,000 and increasing annual donations by $200,000.
- Alternative funding opportunities were explored too, targeting an increase in corporate sponsorships, partnerships, and venue rentals.
- A robust membership and loyalty programme was planned to encourage recurring donations, with a goal of boosting contributions by 10%.
- The plan also looked at grant opportunities (aiming to secure an additional $100,000) and fundraising campaigns, such as crowdfunding (with an objective of $50,000 revenue increment).

- The management team agreed to be fully transparent on the financial challenges and strategic plan with its stakeholders, including musicians, staff, volunteers, and the wider community.
- The management committed to cut non-staff costs only and made it a bold element in its internal and external communication.

The orchestra regularly reviewed its financial performance, assessing progress towards strategic objectives and adjusting the plan as needed.

	Current Situation	Planned Changes	Expected Final Situation
Annual Budget Breakdown			
– Staff Costs	4,800,000		4,800,000
– Production and Marketing Costs	2,500,000	-250,000	2,250,000
– All Other Expenses	1,000,000	-100,000	900,000
Revenue			
– Ticket Sales	2,200,000	+200,000	2,400,000
– Government Support	2,500,000		2,500,000
– Donor Contributions	2,000,000	+200,000	2,200,000
– Corporate Sponsorships and Partnerships	500,000	+200,000	700,000
– Crowdfunding and Planned Giving		+50,000	50,000
– Grants		+100,000	100,000
Total Revenue Increase		+750,000	
Total Cost Reduction		-350,000	

QUESTIONS:

1   With a significant drop in ticket sales and government support, as well as stagnation in donations, how could the leadership team have possibly foreseen these financial difficulties? What warning signs or market trends might they have overlooked?

2   The financial plan aimed to increase revenue by $750,000 and reduce costs by $350,000 over two years. What factors would you consider in order to determine the feasibility of these goals? Are there potential risks or obstacles that might impede their achievement?

3   The diversification of revenue streams and innovative fundraising strategies played a crucial role in the financial turnaround. What considerations should orchestras review when seeking alternative funding opportunities? How can they ensure these strategies align with their brand and mission?
4   Stakeholder communication was a key part of the strategy. Discuss the role of transparency in building trust and securing support during financial hardships. What strategies could be employed to maintain open lines of communication and foster strong relationships with stakeholders?
5   In the context of deciding the allocation of the budget to marketing and audience development efforts, discuss how a significant investment in marketing and audience development could lead to increased revenue. What challenges might be faced in implementing these efforts, and how might they overcome them?

C. THE COSTS–REVENUES PUZZLE

By this point, it should be clear that managing an orchestra is complex and requires a delicate balance between a variety of factors: artistic vision, audience mobilisation, financial stability, and many more components of operations and aesthetics. One of the most pressing issues faced by managers is the persistent disparity between costs and revenues, a puzzle that has troubled the classical music industry for decades.

At its core, the costs–revenues puzzle stems from the fact that orchestras, by nature, are all at once labour-intensive, high-skilled, experience-oriented, and expensive to maintain (Flanagan 2012).

BOX 5.4 HR PECULIARITIES OF ORCHESTRAS

Professional full-size orchestras typically employ around 100–120 musicians, a significant number of whom hold at least a master's degree (sometimes two or more, or a PhD). As a result, the salaries and benefits required to attract and retain these highly qualified staff members represent a higher cost to the organisation overall. Additionally, it's worth noting that older, more experienced musicians are generally not replaced by younger, less expensive counterparts purely for cost-saving reasons.

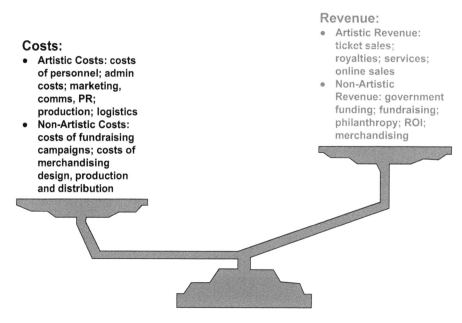

Costs:
- Artistic Costs: costs of personnel; admin costs; marketing, comms, PR; production; logistics
- Non-Artistic Costs: costs of fundraising campaigns; costs of merchandising design, production and distribution

Revenue:
- Artistic Revenue: ticket sales; royalties; services; online sales
- Non-Artistic Revenue: government funding; fundraising; philanthropy; ROI; merchandising

FIGURE 5.3 The Costs–Revenues Puzzle

The fixed costs associated with artistic activities, such as musician salaries, rehearsal spaces, concert venues, and production, often far exceed the income generated through ticket sales, royalties, and other streams related to performance activities. This has led to a financial tension that has persisted throughout history.

Several factors contribute to this disparity. Firstly, the sheer number of musicians required to perform the symphonic repertoire is substantial (approximately 100–120), and each musician must be highly trained and skilled, resulting in significant salary and benefits expenses. The cost of maintaining, renting, or owning a suitable venue for performances is considerable too, as are production costs, such as technicians, sound engineers, stage design, lighting, and sound equipment.

Meanwhile, the revenue generated by ticket sales is insufficient to cover these expenses, and the gap between ticket price and real costs has been widening for the last five decades (Bertolini 2018). Factors such as audience demographics, regional economic disparities, and competition from other entertainment options contribute to this challenge. In recent years, the growth of digital media and online platforms has also impacted traditional revenue sources (Reesman 2019), such as royalties, as consumer preferences shifted towards digital content consumption or digital content from unauthorised and illegal reproduction or distribution (Arditi 2014; Lee 2018; Cronin 2014; Perry and Sinnreich 2022).

Faced with this financial impasse, orchestras have had to become increasingly creative in identifying alternative revenue streams to supplement their primary yet meagre income sources. Some of the approaches adopted to address this challenge include, as seen previously: fundraising and donor development, government and public funding, educational and outreach programs, ancillary services, digital media and streaming, merchandising and licensing, partnerships, etc.

While these alternative revenue streams have helped alleviate the financial pressure, the costs–revenues puzzle remains a persistent challenge for the industry. It is essential for managers to repeatedly evaluate and adapt their business models, seeking innovative ways to generate income while maintaining the artistic integrity and cultural value of their organisations. As a result, we strongly advocate for orchestras of the future to be agile, adaptive, and creative in their approach to financial sustainability, prepared to change and seize any relevant opportunity in a competitive cultural and economic landscape.

The costs–revenues puzzle is an ongoing problem that demands innovative solutions and a strategic approach to financial sustainability. The costs associated with running a professional ensemble recurrently exceed the revenue generated from traditional sources. Therefore, management teams devote significant energy and brain bandwidth to explore alternative revenue streams and adapt their business models to remain financially viable in an ever-evolving cultural and economic environment.

BOX 5.5 A NEW COLLEAGUE IN TOWN: AI

Interestingly, as we conclude the writing of this book (June 2023), we are receiving the first testimonies from working groups that are beginning to utilise the power of generative models such as chatGPT to fuel brainstorming sessions on potential new sources of revenue and artistic initiatives.

The evolution of LLMs heralds transformative opportunities for the management of classical orchestras. In this era of rapid technological development, there's a compelling case for leveraging this innovative tool to foster dynamic brainstorming sessions aimed at identifying potential new revenue streams. As semantic models, LLMs' prowess lies in their ability to generate human-like text based on specific inputs. The models thus can act as a virtual colleague, offering an alternative lens through which to view traditional revenue streams and strategise novel financial avenues. To tap into these benefits, some management teams have input a broad array of data – historical ticket sales, demographic information, social media engagement metrics, donor contributions, and even qualitative data on audience perceptions of various performances. In response, the LLM (mainly chatGPT) delivered possible scenarios and insights that were collectively discussed by the group. For instance, it suggested altering performance times to suit different demographic groups and creating new digital offerings to target a younger, tech-savvy audience. It also suggested experimenting with the duration of the concerts and proposed compact performances that last 45 minutes only to attract busy people and people who are not yet fully used to classical music. Through AI-enhanced brainstorming sessions, the management fosters an environment of "ideational equity" where no notion is too outrageous, and every potential income source is exhaustively analysed. It is too early to say if this open-minded, iterative process will lead to innovative breakthroughs, but it is interesting to notice how new technological tools are used with an unexpected scope to help orchestras.

In this example, the application of an LLM in management is a remarkable illustration of how AI pushes the boundaries of conventional thinking and stimulates the development of ingenious business models. In a landscape where the survival of arts and culture institutions depends on their ability to adapt and innovate, the embrace of AI becomes not only strategic but pivotal.

Some of the key strategies that have been employed to bridge the gap between costs and revenues include fundraising and donor development, government and public funding, educational and outreach programs, ancillary services, digital media and streaming, and merchandising and licensing. Each of these strategies not only contributes to the financial health of the organisation but also helps strengthen the connection with the community and expand its reach to new audiences.

However, there is no one-size-fits-all solution to the costs–revenues puzzle. Each orchestra is unique in its artistic vision, organisational structure, institutional ecosystem, and community context. For example, the Philadelphia Orchestra found a legal solution with strong financial implications to solve the decrease in US federal subsidies over time. After emerging from bankruptcy protection in 2012, it turned to charitable status to support its financial recovery. While the move is not without challenges (due to the need to balance a search for donations with artistic integrity and independence within the framework of mandatory strict rules or regulations on increased transparency in financial reporting and governance), it facilitated tax-deductible donations from individuals, corporations, and foundations (Cooper 2016).

Therefore, flexible and adaptive managers are more likely to survive the pressure to adapt their approach to the specific needs and circumstances of their organisation while maintaining a commitment to artistic excellence and cultural value.

The future of the industry will undoubtedly continue to be shaped by the interplay between artistic innovation and financial sustainability. Pursuing creative solutions and staying focused on delivering exceptional musical experiences fertilises the development of the cultural landscape for future generations.

***

The overarching financial structure, as shown in the following table, is far from a black-and-white scenario, as numerous factors influence the equilibrium between expenses and income. Local and specific factors such as regional audience preferences, government policies, philanthropic tendencies, and cultural values all contribute to the distinctiveness of each orchestra's financial background. However, the most critical aspect in shaping the financial and funding model is the underlying funding framework within which it operates, which varies significantly from one country to another (Herman 2021).

Artistic Revenues	Artistic Costs
• Ticket sales • Royalties • Services and private concerts • Online sales	• Costs of personnel • Admin costs • Marketing, comms, PR • Production • Logistics
Income Gap	
Non-Artistic Revenues	Non-Artistic Costs
• Government and public funding • Fundraising • Philanthropy • Return on investments • Merchandising	• Costs of fundraising campaigns • Costs of merchandising design, production, and distribution
Annual Balance	

Note: This table is indicative and not exhaustive; it does not list all possible costs and revenue streams and provides the main ones only.

Arts and culture institutions worldwide are embedded in diverse economic and funding systems, each with its own unique set of socioeconomic features. In some nations, public funding plays a significant role, helping to keep the focus on artistic excellence without the permanent pressure of generating more income from ticket sales or private donations. This approach, however, may expose orchestras not only to innovation laziness but also to fluctuations in political priorities and economic cycles.

In contrast, other countries rely heavily on private funding and philanthropy to support their cultural institutions, emphasising the need for strong relationships with individual donors, corporations, and foundations. While this model encourages innovation, adaptability, and resilience in response to audience preferences and market forces, it also creates financial uncertainty due to the potential volatility of these funding sources.

Additionally, orchestras operating in diverse economic and funding environments always navigate an intricate web of legal, regulatory, and tax implications. These factors profoundly impact their revenue streams and cost structure, from labour regulations affecting musicians' remuneration to tax policies influencing donors' willingness to contribute. Consequently, managers have no other choice than to be well-versed in the nuances of their local funding landscape to develop a sustainable financial model tailored to their specific circumstances.

Regardless of the prevalent economic and funding system, agility and creativity in looking for alternative revenue streams give a clear advantage in supporting artistic endeavours. This involves the capacity to quickly leverage a variety of tools, such as consenting to new digital technology to reach broader audiences, partnering with educational institutions to deliver outreach programmes, or developing innovative merchandise and licensing opportunities. Such strategies lead to the diversification of income sources and mitigate the risks associated with over-reliance on any single revenue stream.

The financial and funding model is an intricate puzzle shaped by a complex interplay of local, specific factors and the broader economic and funding environment. Managers who have demonstrated their capacity to recognise and understand these dynamics are instrumental in crafting a sustainable financial framework for their organisation to flourish artistically and significantly impact their community. To achieve this, they usually opt for an agile, inventive, and forward-looking attitude, adapting to a perpetually changing landscape that persistently tests the delicate equilibrium between expenses and revenues.

Funding Models

A large variety of funding models have emerged worldwide, each shaped by their respective country's unique historical, cultural, political, and economic contexts. They have also evolved over time in accordance with specific priorities and concerns. Pinpointing a singular model for each nation proves elusive, as these models cover a wide spectrum, ranging from those predominantly reliant on government subsidies to those heavily dependent on private funding sources.

In some countries, orchestras receive significant government support, reflecting the belief in the importance of culture and the arts as a public good. This funding comes in a variety of forms: direct subsidies or grants, tax incentives and tax shelters, or other support mechanisms. Government support is nevertheless not always guaranteed, and changes in political priorities or economic conditions may lead to fluctuations in funding levels. As a result, even orchestras that primarily rely on public subsidies still need additional private funding for their financial stability.

At the opposite end of the spectrum, some orchestras find their lifelines primarily in private sources: fundraising, sponsorships, donations, patrons, etc. This model often prevails in countries with a strong culture of philanthropy or limited public funding for the arts. A mixed funding model, fusing government support with private sector contributions, is also frequent, reflecting a blended approach that harnesses both public and private resources to sustain ongoing operations and artistic aspirations.

Regardless of the specific funding model, arts and culture institutions continually adapt to changes in their financial landscape and develop diverse, sustainable revenue streams. The examples provided in the following tables[11] illustrate different ways in which orchestras across the globe navigate these varying financial models, offering insights into the challenges and opportunities they face.

Country	Funding Model	Main source of funding	Examples of Funding Institutions/Entities
Belgium	Mix of government subsidies (national, regional, and local levels), private funding, corporate sponsorships, ticket sales, and individual donations	• Government subsidies	Belgian Federal Government, Flanders Ministry of Culture, Wallonia-Brussels Federation, Wallonia Government

Country	Funding Model	Main source of funding	Examples of Funding Institutions/Entities
Netherlands	Mix of government subsidies (national and local levels), private funding, corporate sponsorships, ticket sales, and individual donations	• Government subsidies	Dutch Ministry of Education, Culture, and Science, Municipality of Amsterdam
UK	Mix of government subsidies (through organisations such as Arts Council England, Creative Scotland, and Arts Council of Wales), private funding, corporate sponsorships, ticket sales, and individual donations	• Government subsidies • Private funding	Arts Council England, Creative Scotland, Arts Council of Wales
Germany	Mix of government subsidies (national, regional, and local levels), private funding, corporate sponsorships, ticket sales, and individual donations	• Government subsidies	German Federal Government, state governments, municipalities
US	Mix of private funding, corporate sponsorships, ticket sales, individual donations, and limited government support (national, state, and local levels)	• Private funding • Individual donations	National Endowment for the Arts, state arts agencies, local arts agencies
Australia	Mix of government support, private funding, corporate partnerships, ticket sales, donations, endowments	• Government subsidies	Australia Council, Creative Victoria, APRA AMCOS
Austria	Mix of government support, private funding, corporate partnerships, ticket sales, donations, endowments	• Government subsidies	Bund, Länder, Municipalities
Japan	Mix of government support, private funding, corporate sponsorships, ticket sales, and individual donations	• Government subsidies • Private funding and corporate sponsorships	Government agencies, mmunicipalities
France	Mix of government subsidies (national, regional, and local levels), private funding, corporate sponsorships, ticket sales, and individual donations	• Government subsidies	French Ministry of Culture, regional governments, municipalities

Country	Funding Model
Belgium	In Flanders, a region in Belgium, the management model is characterised by a mix of government support, private sponsorship, and ticket sales. The Flemish government plays a significant role in providing the lion's share of financial assistance, with funds primarily distributed through the Flemish Ministry of Culture. This funding ensures long-term stability and helps artistic excellence. Besides government subsidies, orchestras in Flanders also rely on private sponsorships and individual donations. These sources of funding are essential to expand outreach and diversify programming. Ticket sales contribute to the financial stability of orchestras in Flanders. In Wallonia, the French-speaking region of Belgium, the funding model follows a similar scheme, with the government's financial support provided by the relevant agencies and ministries of the Walloon governments.
Netherlands	The music organisation landscape in the Netherlands features a unique model that includes a mix of government support, private funding, and ticket sales. The Dutch government, both at the national and local levels, provides significant financial assistance to orchestras in the Netherlands, helping to maintain high artistic standards and ensuring accessibility for audiences. However, private funding plays an essential role in the Dutch music scene, including corporate sponsorships and individual donations. This additional financial support allows for embarking on ambitious projects and reaching a broader audience.
UK	The Anglo-Saxon model, particularly prevalent in the United Kingdom, is characterised by a combination of government funding, private support, and ticket sales. Government support is mainly provided by institutions such as Arts Council England, which distributes funds to cultural institutions across the country. Despite government funding, private support plays a more significant role in the Anglo-Saxon model compared to the models in Belgium and The Netherlands. Orchestras in the UK rely heavily on private donations, corporate sponsorships, and foundations to maintain their financial stability and artistic endeavours. This model demands effective management to balance the various funding sources and ensure the continued success and relevance of orchestras. Overall, the management models in Belgium, The Netherlands, and the UK highlight the unique features and challenges of each model.
Germany	In Germany, the funding model is characterised by a strong emphasis on government support at various levels, alongside ticket sales and (more limited) private funding. German orchestras benefit from significant financial assistance provided by the federal and state governments, and municipalities. This comprehensive support framework ensures stability and promotes artistic excellence within the country. However, government subsidies, although massive, are not the sole source of funding. They also rely on private sponsorships, corporate partnerships, and individual donations to supplement their income. This additional financial flow eases the undertaking of ambitious projects and the reach of a wider audience. Ticket sales play an important role in sustaining financial stability too.

Country	Funding Model
	The German funding model requires effective management to balance the various funding sources. Management navigates the funding landscape, builds relationships with funding institutions, and explores new opportunities for financial support. Overall, the German funding model is unique in its strong emphasis on government support while incorporating elements of private funding and ticket sales, requiring strategic and agile management to ensure long-term success and sustainability.
US	The funding model in the United States is distinct from its European counterparts, with a greater emphasis on private funding, corporate sponsorships, individual donations, and ticket sales. While government support is available at the national, state, and local levels, it is generally much more limited than in European models, making private funding the main source of income for many American orchestras.
	This reliance on private support leads to a more diverse funding landscape, with management teams working diligently to secure funding from various sources, such as foundations, corporate partners, and individual donors. This approach demands a proactive and entrepreneurial spirit from the management as they seek to maintain financial stability and promote artistic excellence in the face of a competitive and fluctuating funding environment.
	Ticket sales also play a crucial role in sustaining American orchestras, as they often account for a significant portion of their annual revenue. Consequently, management focuses on audience development, marketing, and community collaboration to ensure a consistent and growing audience base.
	In summary, the US funding model is characterised by its emphasis on private funding and entrepreneurial management while also incorporating limited government support and ticket sales. This model requires a strategic and adaptive approach to leadership to navigate the complex and competitive funding landscape and ensure long-term relevance within the cultural sphere.
Australia	Australian orchestras operate within a mixed funding model, which includes government support, private funding, and ticket sales. The Australia Council for the Arts, a government agency, plays a significant role in providing financial support, ensuring their sustainability and artistic excellence.
	Private funding, including corporate sponsorships and individual donations, is also vital in Australia, as it allows organisations to pursue ambitious projects and expand the audience base. Ticket sales also contribute to the financial stability of these organisations. Effective management is essential to balance their diverse funding sources and maintain their artistic integrity and financial stability in a competitive cultural landscape.
Austria	Austrian orchestras predominantly receive financial support from the government, with funds distributed at the federal, regional, and local levels. This substantial backing from the government ensures the sustainability and artistic quality, enabling them to maintain high standards and offer accessible performances for audiences.

Country	Funding Model
	Aside from government support, Austrian orchestras also rely on private funding, including sponsorships and individual donations, as well as revenue from ticket sales. Skilled management is vital to balance these funding sources and continue thriving in the competitive musical landscape.
Japan	In Japan, the management model is characterised by a combination of government support, private funding, and ticket sales. Japanese orchestras receive financial assistance from various levels of government. Japanese orchestras also benefit from corporate sponsorships, individual donations, and ticket sales, which contribute to their financial stability and help diversify their artistic offerings.
France	In France, the management model is heavily reliant on government support, which provides financial stability and promotes artistic excellence. The French Ministry of Culture allocates funds to cultural institutions, ensuring the longevity and accessibility of these organisations. Regional and local governments also contribute to their financial backing. In addition to government funding, French orchestras benefit from private sponsorships, individual donations, and ticket sales. These additional sources of income help diversify programming and extend outreach initiatives.

These examples undeniably highlight the paramount significance of proficient management in securing the long-term viability and realising artistic ambitions, all while navigating the complexity of national and local funding landscapes.

Within the classical music industry, these examples portray how each country has crafted its own distinctive funding model, shaped by its unique historic, cultural, economic, and political contexts. Yet, upon closer examination, a comprehensive analysis unveils three overarching frameworks that broadly encapsulate the funding approaches prevalent across different nations. Understanding these distinctions holds immense value for scholars and practitioners in the fields of management, music, and arts and culture. It equips them with the ability to discern the unique challenges and opportunities encountered by operating within each paradigm, empowering them to forge strategies that optimise financial sustainability within the respective contexts.

1   The first framework is characterised by countries where arts and culture institutions receive substantial financial support from the government and

local authorities. This public funding model ensures stability and promotes artistic excellence. It helps to maintain high standards and offer accessible performances for audiences. In these countries, government subsidies are typically the primary source of income, and they often cover a significant portion of the organisations' costs. Examples of countries that predominantly follow this model include Germany, Austria, Belgium, and France.

2   The second framework is exemplified by countries where public subsidies are more limited, and cultural institutions develop entrepreneurial activities to generate additional revenue. These activities include business partnerships, fundraising initiatives, sponsoring agreements with the private sector, and the development of patronage support. In this model, orchestras rely heavily on private funding, corporate sponsorships, individual donations, and ticket sales to maintain their financial stability and promote artistic excellence. The United States is a prime example of a country that adheres to this funding model, with orchestras often operating in a more competitive and fluctuating funding environment.

3   The third framework is a combination of government and private funding. When examining the funding models adopted by Asian countries, a striking pattern emerges – a blend, striking a balance between the European and American approaches. In nations like Japan and South Korea, orchestras benefit from the support of public finances, yet they also actively pursue revenue generation through various entrepreneurial activities. This hybrid model allows them to capitalise on the stability offered by government subsidies while also leveraging the flexibility and innovation inherent in private sector partnerships. Consequently, orchestras operating within this mixed framework navigate the intricate terrain of both public and private funding sources, necessitating a mastery of entrepreneurial skills and a profound comprehension of the cultural and economic contexts in which they operate.

The funding landscape is diverse and complex, shaped by the unique cultural, economic, and political contexts of each country. While some countries predominantly rely on government support, others emphasise entrepreneurial activities and private funding. Additionally, Asian countries tend to adopt a mixed model, blending aspects of both the European and American frameworks. As the classical music industry continues to evolve, it is essential for researchers, practitioners, and stakeholders to understand these funding models, their challenges and their impact, and the array of possible strategies required to prosper within their respective contexts.

BOX 5.6 FUNDING MODELS AND INDIVIDUALS

Although beyond the scope of this book, the impact of the funding model should be considered not only from the perspective of the organisation but also from the individual standpoint of the musicians who comprise it. While the focus of Park and Kim's (2020) quantitative study is on the Korean case, the findings suggest that the type of funding received by performing artists has a noticeable impact on their overall satisfaction. By investigating how grant characteristics influence performing artists' satisfaction levels, this study sheds light on potential policy implications for sustainable management of performing arts in Korea. This research highlights the importance of considering not only the amount but also the type of government support provided in order to better promote creative activities and well-being of the artists.

The following concise and overarching comparative table presents a high-level summary of costs and revenues models across geographies. It is, however, essential to emphasise that the figures presented in this table serve merely as indicative average approximations, constructed upon fragmented and incomplete information.[12]

in %	Europe	Hybrid	USA
Revenue			
Public Subsidies (government, municipality, etc.)	65	45	5
Performance (tickets sales, subscription, etc.)	25	30	35
Private Donations, Grants, and Business Activities	5	20	45
Investment Income	–	2	10
Other Income[13]	5	3	5
Costs			
Artistic (incl. salaries)	60	65	50
Admin (incl. salaries)	15	10	10
Marketing	7	10	10
Production	10	10	15
Fundraising	–	2	5
Other costs	8	3	10

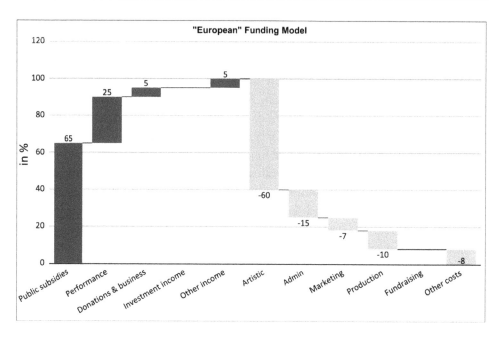

FIGURE 5.4 The "European" Model (Public Funding)

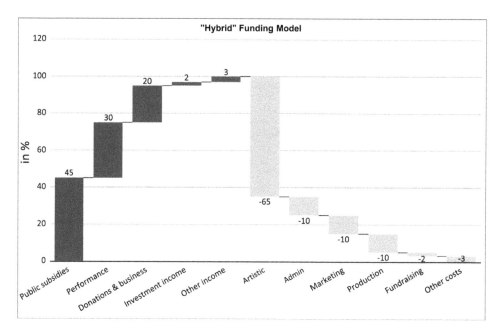

FIGURE 5.5 The "Hybrid" Model

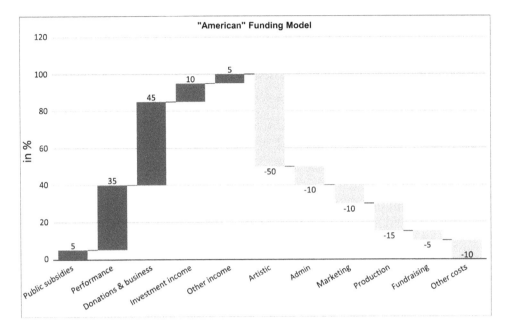

FIGURE 5.6 The "American" Model (Private Funding)

CASE STUDY 5.3

Ticket Pricing for Financial Sustainability[14]

ABSTRACT

This case study examines the challenge faced by a symphony orchestra management team in determining the optimal ticket pricing strategy for the season to achieve financial sustainability. The study utilises quantitative data related to ticket sales, costs, funding, and additional revenue, and employs a systematic approach to derive the ideal average ticket price to reach a lossless Profit and Loss (P&L) position.

After the management team has calculated the ticket pricing, they also explore a different avenue where the ticket price is set to half the calculated point.

INTRODUCTION

In the field of arts and culture management, financial sustainability remains a critical concern for organisations such as symphony orchestras.

These institutions typically rely on a combination of ticket sales, public funding, and other revenue sources to cover their operational and artistic costs. This case study presents a fictitious scenario where a management team establishes a ticket pricing strategy for the season to ensure financial stability.

DATA

Based on previous years, the financial data are as follows:

- The symphony season consists of 48 concerts, with an average of 720 tickets sold and 50 complimentary tickets issued per concert (maximum capacity of concert hall: 900 seats).
- The annual total cost, including fixed and variable costs, amounts to $22 million.
- The total annual funding from government, municipality, and other public authorities is $16.5 million.
- Additional annual revenue of $1.6 million, excluding ticket sales.

RESULTS

To determine the average ticket price needed to achieve a lossless P&L, we first calculate the total revenue required to cover the annual total costs. We subtract the annual funding and additional revenue from the total costs:

$22 million (Total Costs) – $16.5 million (Annual Funding) – $1.6 million (Additional Revenue) = $3.9 million (Revenue Required from Ticket Sales, if no additional income sources)

Next, we calculate the total number of tickets sold during the season:

48 concerts × 720 tickets = 34,560 tickets

Finally, we divide the revenue required from ticket sales by the total number of tickets to be sold:

$3.9 million (Revenue Required from Ticket Sales) / 34,560 (Total Tickets) = $113

CONCLUSION

In order to achieve a lossless P&L, the management team sets an *average* ticket price of $113 per unit. This pricing strategy would ensure that the annual costs are covered by overall revenue.

However, if the orchestra wishes to decrease the average ticket price by 50% to $57, it must explore alternative strategies to offset the reduction in ticket revenue. To calculate the required additional revenue or the increased number of concerts, we first determine the revenue generated with the new ticket price:

57 (New Ticket Price) × 34,560 (Total Tickets) = $1,969,920 (New Ticket Revenue)

We then calculate the shortfall in revenue, given the reduced ticket price:

$3,900,000 (Revenue Required from Ticket Sales) – $1,969,920 (New Ticket Revenue) = $1,930,080 (Revenue Shortfall)

Option 1: Generate Additional Revenue

The orchestra could generate an additional $1,930,080 in revenue through alternative means, such as sponsorships, donations, or other entrepreneurial activities.

Option 2: Increase the Number of Concerts

To calculate the required increase in concerts, we first determine the average revenue per concert with the $57 ticket price:

720 (Tickets Sold per Concert) × 57 (New Ticket Price) = $41,040 (Revenue per Concert)

Next, we divide the revenue shortfall by the revenue per concert:

$1,930,080 (Revenue Shortfall) / $41,040 (Revenue per Concert) ≈ 47 additional concerts

Assuming a similar proportion of fixed to variable costs and concert hall occupancy rate, the orchestra would need to increase the total number

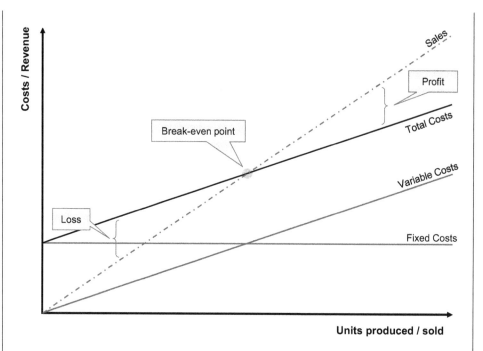

FIGURE 5.7 Managing Fixed and Variable Costs in Price Definition

of concerts to 95 (48 original + 47 additional) to maintain a lossless P&L with the reduced average ticket price of $57.

To accommodate a lower average ticket price of $57, the orchestra must either generate an additional $1,930,080 in revenue or increase the total number of concerts to 95, or maximise the concert hall occupancy, or a combination of all the above.

QUESTIONS:

1   Given the calculations presented in the case study, how might the pricing strategy influence its perceived value among its audience and wider community? What potential advantages or disadvantages might be associated with a higher ticket price of $113, compared to a lower price of $57?

2   In the context of reducing the average ticket price by half to $57, what are the possible implications of this strategy on audience accessibility and diversity? How might such a decision influence the demographic profile of the attendees?

3   If $1,930,080 in additional revenue is generated through alternative means, such as sponsorships, donations, or other entrepreneurial

activities, what kind of strategies could be implemented? What challenges might be faced in these attempts?

4   With an increased number of concerts to maintain a lossless P&L, what might be the potential impacts on the musicians, administrative staff, and overall quality of performances? How could these effects influence the reputation and long-term financial sustainability?

5   Given the current financial situation and potential strategies for achieving a lossless P&L, what additional strategies might be considered to ensure financial sustainability? Could there be a middle ground between raising additional revenue, increasing the number of concerts, and adjusting ticket prices?

D. OPERATIONS

Over the past 50 years, arts and culture institutions have had to adapt to broader industrial practices in the world of consumer industries (O'Regan 2002). Although – as highlighted by Peter Drucker (1990) in the late 1980s – the distinctive and truistic characteristic of not-for-profit organisations is precisely the lack of profit generation in their scope statement, it is undeniable that expectations towards these entities have progressively yet plainly shifted towards commercial concerns. This paradox has resulted in operations playing a pivotal role in the overall success of classical music ensembles, serving as the organisational backbone that both supports and sustains their artistic endeavours, and is responsible for maximising the value extracted from all the available resources. In a society that increasingly views the arts and culture as a mere subset of the business world, while still expecting them to provide beauty and inspiration detached from material reality, this has created a complex incongruity that sees orchestras compelled to balance competing demands and irreconcilable objectives. A well-managed and efficient operational framework, therefore, ensures that rehearsals and concerts proceed seamlessly, musicians receive the necessary resources and support, the orchestra is well-equipped to navigate and, hopefully, flourish in an evolving industry, and all the assets (human, material, and intangible) are used at their optimum. In this section, we delve into the effective operations and show how they intersect with other key aspects of management, including artistic programming, financial management, and audience development.

To lay the groundwork for this exploration, we will first examine the operational structure, delineating the key roles and their associated responsibilities. This foundational understanding will enable us to appreciate the complex interaction between various operational functions and underscore the importance of clear communication and collaboration in fostering an efficient and harmonious environment. Following this, we will turn our attention to the planning and execution of concerts, exploring the logistical difficulties involved in organising and delivering world-class performances. We will also consider the unique challenges associated with touring and external performances, offering insights into how orchestras effectively manage these aspects of their operations.

Our investigation will include a brief digression on the management of equipment and instruments, delving into the strategies and best practices for maintaining, transporting, and safeguarding these valuable assets. Lastly, we will touch on the critical issue of health and safety, discussing the measures to ensure the well-being of musicians, staff, and audiences.

Looking ahead, we will contemplate the future of operations and assess the potential impact of technological advancements on this essential facet of management. We will emphasise the need for innovation and adaptability as orchestras confront a rapidly changing landscape marked by new technologies, shifting audience expectations, and evolving industry standards.

In conclusion, we will distil the core facets of operations, reaffirming their vital significance in the overall sustainability paradigm. By casting a spotlight on the fundamental role operations play within the broader context of management, this section underlines the need for ongoing development, adaptation, and refinement, ensuring that orchestras continue to thrive and excel in an ever-changing world.

The following table offers a concise compendium of this section that encapsulates the vital elements of operations. By reviewing these key aspects, one gains a comprehensive understanding of the interconnected components that contribute to successful management, emphasising the need for effective communication, strategic planning, and adaptability.

The Operational Structure	Discusses the key roles and responsibilities, including administrative, artistic, and logistical aspects. Emphasises the need for clear communication and cooperation among various operational functions to ensure a harmonious environment.
Planning and Executing Concerts	Explores the process of organising and delivering concerts, from programming and scheduling to managing rehearsals and coordinating the various elements on performance day. Examines the complexities and interdependencies of the concert planning process.

Touring and External Performances	Examines the unique challenges and opportunities associated with touring and external performances, including planning, logistics, and adapting to diverse venues. Explores the financial, cultural, and artistic implications of performing away from the home base.
Equipment and Instrument Management	Addresses the strategies and best practices for maintaining, transporting, and safeguarding valuable assets such as instruments and equipment. Discusses the importance of inventory management and the role of instrument specialists in ensuring optimal performance conditions.
Health, Safety, and Risk Management	Highlights the measures that are taken to ensure the well-being of their musicians, staff, and audiences. Discusses the identification and mitigation of potential risks and the importance of creating a safe and secure environment for everyone involved.
Sustainability, Environmental, and Diversity, Equity, and Inclusion Considerations	Introduces the importance of sustainable practices, environmental awareness, and diversity, equity, and inclusion in operations. Emphasises the need to align operations with broader societal values and to look forward to more detailed analysis later in the book.
The Future of Operations	Contemplates the impact of technological advancements on operations, such as the use of digital tools for planning and communication. Underscores the importance of innovation and adaptability in navigating a rapidly changing landscape and staying relevant in the classical music industry.

The Operational Structure

With its unbalanced costs and revenue structure, and its ambivalent positioning in both business and the arts, the management of a cultural institution is a complex system (Kostylev 2015) that is constantly required to achieve the impossible reconciliation between contradictory objectives and competing expectations. In order to ensure the effective functioning of an orchestra, it is essential to establish a robust and efficient operational structure. The operational structure covers a range of roles, each with specific responsibilities and areas of expertise, working in unison with the aim of creating a cohesive and harmonious environment for musicians and staff alike.

The core operational roles can be divided into several categories, including artistic, administrative, technical, and production – and each category comprising several functional layers.

- The **artistic** roles are typically fulfilled by the artistic director, conductor, concertmaster, section leaders, and musicians, who work together to interpret the music and provide artistic guidance to the ensemble.

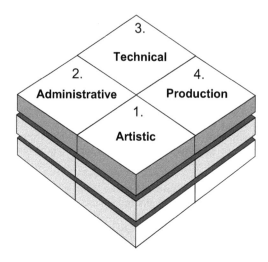

FIGURE 5.8 Operations Structure

- The **administrative** roles, such as operations manager and education and outreach coordinator, focus on the strategic planning and execution of activities and projects, as well as ensuring the smooth running of the organisation.
- The **technical** roles encompass the stage manager, audio engineers, and lighting technicians, who ensure that the performance environment is properly set up and maintained.
- Finally, the **production** roles involve the librarian, who is responsible for organising and distributing the musical scores, and the personnel manager, who oversees the hiring and management of musicians and other staff members.

The operational structure is marked by a complex interaction between various roles and functions, calling for unambiguous communication and dynamic teamwork amongst all involved. For instance, the concertmaster and conductor's artistic choices need to be properly relayed to the administrative team, who then plans and executes the necessary activities to bring the artistic vision to life. This might involve coordinating with the education and outreach coordinator to craft educational materials for audience members or liaising with the stage manager and technical crew to ensure that the performance environment aligns with the performance requirements. In a similar vein, the librarian needs to maintain close ties with the conductor and musicians, ensuring that the right scores are ready for rehearsals and performances. Meanwhile the personnel manager attentively alternates between the artistic and administrative teams to oversee the musicians and auxiliary staff members.

Transparent communication and teamwork stand as a cornerstone in maintaining an effective operational structure.[15] This is achieved through routine meetings, both internally and across departments, as well as defining distinct lines of communication and reporting structures. Leveraging digital resources, such as project management applications and online communication platforms, further boosts collaboration and streamlines the sharing of information amongst various operational roles. In addition, cultivating a culture of open dialogue, mutual respect, and shared goals aids in constructing a supportive and cohesive environment. This ensures that all team members are pulling in the same direction – the collective aim being to deliver compelling performances and forge meaningful connections with audiences.

By unravelling the complex operational structure and the interactions among various functions and roles, those engaged in management can work together to craft a seamless and productive environment for both musicians and staff. This way, they underpin the continued success and resilience of the organisation, whilst simultaneously nurturing artistic brilliance and stimulating audience involvement.

Planning and Executing Concerts

To capture audiences and ensure they are offered a gratifying experience, the planning and executing of concerts are critical aspects of operations (Marín and University of La Rioja 2018), necessitating robust coordination, communication, and meticulous attention to details amongst all team members. The process begins with the artistic director and conductor selecting the repertoire for the concert season, taking into account considerations such as audience preferences, artistic balance, and programming requirements. The selection and engagement of guest artists, be they soloists, choirs, or conductors, also forms an intrinsic part of this process.[16]

Once the artistic programme has been determined, the administrative crew, steered by the CEO and operations manager, collaborates with the artistic team to define a comprehensive timetable for rehearsals and performances. This involves liaising with musicians and guest artists to confirm availability, along with securing suitable venues and, when needed, procuring permits or licences. Additionally, artistic and administrative teams also cooperate to develop a marketing strategy to promote the concerts, which includes advertising, public relations, and social media campaigns, alongside targeted outreach efforts to engage diverse audiences and community groups.

Simultaneously, the technical and production crews collaborate to ensure that the performance environment is configured and equipped to satisfy the artistic requirements of the programme. This includes coordination with the stage manager, audio engineers, and lighting technicians to optimise stage setup and acoustics, as well as procuring and prepping any necessary equipment or instruments. The librarian plays a crucial role in this process, working closely with the conductor and musicians to procure and distribute the (right editions of the) scores, while the personnel manager supervises the recruitment and management of additional musicians, as needed.

As the concert date approaches, rehearsals kick off, providing the conductor and musicians with an opportunity to refine their interpretation and rendition of the music and address any technical issues. During this period, communication among the artistic, administrative, and technical teams is vital, with any changes or problems requiring prompt resolution to ensure a successful performance. It is also essential to maintain regular contact with guest artists, to verify that they are well-prepared and supported throughout the rehearsal process.

On the day of the concert, the stage manager and technical team take on the responsibility for the smooth execution of the event, coordinating with front-of-house staff, musicians, and guest artists to deliver a flawless experience for both performers and audience members. This includes managing the logistics of the stage and overseeing the technical aspects of the performance, such as lighting and sound.

After the concert, the administrative team undertakes a thorough evaluation of the event, analysing audience feedback, ticket sales, and any issues that arose during the planning and execution process. This intelligence is instrumental in guiding future programming decisions and operational improvements.

The planning and execution of concerts is a complex enterprise that demands the joint efforts of the artistic, administrative, technical, and production teams. By collaborating in a spirit of mutual support, they can stage outstanding performances that captivate audiences and reinforce the reputation for artistic excellence.

Touring and External Performances

Touring and external performances offer a unique opportunity to broaden reach and showcase artistic prowess on a larger scale, be it nationally or globally. This is likely the best way to foster connections with diverse audiences and cultural institutions. However, these occasions also present a vast array of logistical and operational problems that require meticulous planning and coordination amongst the various departments.

Whether they plan a large tour or a single external performance, the artistic team, led by the artistic director and conductor, first identify the scope of the event (artistic, branding and image, diplomatic, etc.) and determine accordingly the repertoire that resonates with the target audience, then define the programme that best showcases the orchestra's strengths. This decision-making process involves consultations with local promoters, venue managers, and cultural organisations to optimise alignment with specific expectations, regional preferences, and cultural sensitivities.

Once the programme has been established, the administrative crew sorts out the logistical aspects of the tour. This includes negotiating contracts with agents, promoters, and venues, securing visas and work permits for musicians and staff, and arranging travel and accommodation. They also develop a comprehensive budget and financial plan that take into account not only the direct costs of transportation, lodging, and venue hire, but also indirect expenses such as marketing, insurance, and per diem allowances for personnel, amongst others.

The technical and production teams play a vital role in ensuring the delivery of performances in unfamiliar environments, often with limited time and resources. They coordinate with local venue staff to address any technical requirements, such as stage dimensions, acoustics, lighting, and sound equipment. In addition, they are responsible for the transportation and handling of instruments and equipment, taking care to safeguard these valuable assets from damage or loss during transit.

Touring also places additional pressure on the musicians and guest artists, who must adapt to the travel, changing time zones, and varying performance conditions. It is essential to provide adequate support for their well-being and performance readiness, including ensuring sufficient rest and practice time, as well as access to healthcare and other essential services as needed. Keeping musical instruments at a relatively stable temperature during longer trips may also be a tough challenge under exceptional circumstances. A key aspect of successful touring and external performances is the cultivation of partnerships with local arts organisations, educational institutions, and community groups. Common examples of possible initiatives are educational workshops, masterclasses, and outreach programmes, aimed at fostering cultural exchange, nurturing local talent, and deepening the connection with the host community.

Touring and external performances present significant opportunities for artistic growth, audience development, and cultural diplomacy. By approaching these ventures with careful planning, clear communication, and a spirit of collaboration, orchestras surmount the associated challenges and deliver memorable performances that resonate with audiences worldwide, thereby enhancing their global reputation and enriching the cultural fabric of the communities they visit.

Equipment and Instrument Management

Although this is often seen as a practical issue of minor importance that does not demand leadership's attention, effective management of equipment and music instruments is crucial to maintaining high-quality performance standards. This encompasses the procurement, maintenance, transportation, and storage of a variety of music instruments and related equipment to ensure that they remain in optimal condition and readily available for use by the musicians. As if this wasn't complicated enough, a piano, a double bass, a harp, a marimba, or a tuba should not be stored in the same way and require quite different conditions to be ready to use at any time.

Acquisition and Service

One of the primary responsibilities of management is the acquisition and service of instruments. This involves selecting suitable instruments in consultation with relevant musicians and conductors, ensuring their quality and compatibility with the ensemble's existing inventory. The acquisition process involves purchasing or leasing instruments, as well as seeking donations or sponsorships from patrons and benefactors. Once procured, the instruments are insured and regularly maintained by skilled technicians, who perform tasks such as tuning, cleaning, and repairs to prevent deterioration and secure longevity.

Transportation and Handling

The transportation and handling of instruments present logistical challenges, particularly when the performance is carried out at external venues or on tour. Careful planning and coordination are essential for the safe and timely arrival of these valuable assets. To this end, frequent practical measures are engaging specialised transport services, adhering to strict handling protocols to minimise the risk of damage or loss, or even partnering with carriers.

Storage

Storage of instruments and equipment is another critical aspect. The orchestra allocates sufficient space, both at their primary venue and any external locations, to store instruments securely and in a controlled environment. Climate control is particularly important, as fluctuations in temperature and humidity or prolonged direct sunlight exposure adversely affect the instruments' materials and performance characteristics. Additionally, the storage area should be organised to allow for easy retrieval and return of instruments, minimising disruption and delays during rehearsals and performances while preserving the economic value of the assets.

Inventory

Finally, inventory management systems play a key role in maintaining an accurate record of the instruments and equipment portfolio. This may involve the use of digital databases, barcoding, radio-frequency identification (RFID), or other tracking technologies to monitor the location, condition, and maintenance history of each item. Such systems help identify and address potential issues proactively, streamlining operations and reducing the risk of unexpected disruptions.

Diligent management of equipment and instruments is essential to the smooth functioning of an orchestra and the delivery of performances. By adopting a proactive and systematic approach to instrument management, the single musicians are provided with the tools necessary to realise the collective artistic vision while the organisation protects its assets.

Health, Safety, and Risk Management

The operations department prioritises health, safety, and risk management to safeguard the well-being of musicians,[17] staff, and audience members, and to protect the organisation's reputation and financial sustainability. A thorough assessment of potential hazards is the first step to define and implement preventive measures, and to respond effectively to any incidents that may arise.

A crucial component of health and safety is the evaluation of potential hazards within the operations. This includes physical risks, such as those associated with equipment, instruments, and performance spaces, as well as occupational risks, such as repetitive strain injuries, hearing loss, and mental health concerns. Regular risk assessments are conducted to identify areas of concern, with input from musicians, staff, and external experts, as appropriate.

Once potential hazards are identified, the operations team recommends policies and procedures to mitigate these risks. This involves, amongst other tasks, circulating health and safety guidelines, providing training for musicians and staff, and securing compliance with relevant regulations and standards. Measures include the provision of personal protective equipment, the adjustment of performance schedules to prevent fatigue, the adoption of ergonomic practices to minimise the risk of injury, and partnerships with physiotherapy clinics and wellness centres.

In addition to preventive measures, orchestras must be prepared to respond effectively to incidents that do arise, whether they involve injuries, equipment damage, or other emergencies. This necessitates the development of contingency plans, the designation of responsible personnel, and the regular review and rehearsal of emergency procedures. Effective communication and coordination among all stakeholders are vital in these situations to ensure swift, appropriate action.

A crucial aspect of health and safety lies in the mental well-being of its members. While the operations crew might not be directly involved in addressing these issues, they play a significant role in monitoring the conditions that either enhance or undermine staff well-being. Through regular investigation of factors such as job satisfaction, professional autonomy, and the impact of organisational hierarchies, the operations team observes the evolution of the equilibrium between artistic expression and the demands inherent to the workload. One particularly fascinating area of this investigation is the study of musicians' adaptation to the stringent discipline and hierarchical structure of orchestras, which frequently conflict with their creative inclinations. The operations team has a distinct vantage point in observing the tensions between individual artistry and collective harmony, unravelling the intricate network of relationships that ultimately shape the public performance (Allmendinger, Hackman, and Lehman 1996).

Lastly, ongoing monitoring and evaluation of health, safety, and risk management practices are essential to spot areas for improvement and maintain a culture of vigilance. This includes soliciting feedback from musicians, staff, and external experts, as well as staying informed about emerging risks and best practices in the field.

In summary, a proactive approach to health, safety, and risk management is vital for the well-being of all involved in operations and for the organisation's long-term success. A safer and more supportive environment for all is usually created by identifying and addressing potential hazards, implementing preventive measures, and maintaining a culture of vigilance.

Sustainability, Environmental, and Diversity, Equity, and Inclusion Considerations

Nowadays, cultural institutions not only focus on artistic excellence and effective management but also consider the broader social, environmental, and cultural contexts in which they operate. This section highlights the importance of sustainability, environmental stewardship, and diversity, equity, and inclusion as essential considerations overall,[18] with each aspect playing a crucial role in the long-term success and relevance of these organisations. It is worth mentioning that these topics will be examined in greater depth later in the book.

Following a general social trend, sustainability has become an increasingly important topic in the arts and cultural industry too, that seeks optimal ways to reduce its carbon footprint and minimise waste. Environmental considerations extend to energy consumption, the use of eco-friendly materials (for example, for stage design), and the promotion of green initiatives.

Diversity, equity, and inclusion are equally vital, with organisations striving to create a more respectful and representative environment for musicians, staff, and audiences. This entails recognising and addressing historical biases and barriers to entry, as well as actively promoting diversity and equity across various dimensions, including ethnicity, gender, socioeconomic background, and disability.

In addition to addressing these issues within the organisation, collaborating with external parties and stakeholders to promote a shared vision of sustainability, stewardship, and diversity, equity, and inclusion is essential. This may entail partnerships with schools and community groups to provide educational programmes and outreach initiatives, as well as participating in cross-sector collaborations to drive systemic change.

The incorporation of environmental sustainability, as well as diversity, equity, and inclusion considerations, into operations is quite recent but vital for long-term relevance in today's world. All-round responsible practices, along with an inclusive mindset, facilitate the alignment of the orchestra with the values of audiences who are increasingly sensitive to arguments of equity, fairness, diversity, and environmental protection.

The Future of Operations

As we consider the future of operations, we must recognise the ongoing evolution of the classical music industry and the need to adapt practices to protect success and relevance. This section explores several key trends that are shaping the future of operations and the innovative approaches being employed to address these issues.

One significant and potentially destabilising trend is the increasing integration of technology into every step of operations. This already includes the use of digital tools and platforms for scheduling, communication, marketing, ticket sales, inventory, archiving, and data analysis; it may also soon encompass the burgeoning applications of artificial intelligence tools and services. As orchestras continue to embrace the digital age, they invest in the appropriate infrastructure, software, and staff training to maximise the benefits of these technologies. In particular, the use of data analytics helps organisations better understand audiences, improve marketing strategies, and tailor artistic offerings to meet the needs and preferences of diverse listeners. Similarly, Large Language Models are being used already to test the automation of some managerial workflows in the arts and culture industry or to feed brainstorming sessions devoted to tackling an array of issues specific to arts and culture institutions.

As already highlighted, the growing importance of sustainability and environmental concerns is another factor shaping the future of operations. It is increasingly common to observe orchestras taking steps to reduce their environmental footprint and promote sustainable practices, both in their own operations and in the broader classical music industry. Indeed, there has been a recent increase in demand for the installation of energy-efficient lighting and low-carbon climate control systems in performance venues, as well as a search for partnerships with environmentally conscious suppliers and sponsors. Demonstrating a sincere commitment to sustainability helps to enhance public image and appeals to the values of increasingly eco-conscious audiences.

Given the rapid change in mentality over the last decade, we strongly believe that the need for greater diversity, equity, and inclusion within the industry is a key challenge that may shape the future of operations. Orchestras make concerted efforts to attract, support, and retain musicians, staff, and board members from diverse backgrounds. Similarly, they engage with diverse communities through innovative and courageous programming and outreach initiatives. This requires a genuine commitment to an inclusive organisational culture, addressing systemic barriers to entry and advancement, and cultivating a more representative and diverse repertoire.

The ongoing challenges presented by the global Covid-19 pandemic have underscored the importance of adaptability and resilience in the face of unforeseen circumstances. As for any other professional organisation, the capacity to respond quickly and effectively to emerging risks and opportunities now enters the DNA of not-for-profit institutions as well. Indeed, it appears that the development of broader contingency plans and the cultivation of a flexible organisational culture that can accommodate change and innovation have increased significantly since the outbreak of the pandemic. Financial sustainability and artistic vitality in an uncertain landscape also depend upon the capacity to anticipate and explore alternative performance formats and revenue sources.

Last but not least, the future of operations will be shaped by the evolving expectations and tastes of audiences, musicians, and stakeholders. As the classical music industry continues to change, responsiveness to the needs and preferences of increasingly fragmented audiences becomes also paramount.

The importance of a clear mission-driven management (Drucker 1990) in guiding an organisation's operations is particularly relevant to management, as it helps them focus on their artistic vision and purpose while making strategic decisions. This may involve embracing new forms of artistic expression, such as multimedia and interdisciplinary collaborations, or adopting innovative approaches to audience engagement, such as interactive concert formats and immersive experiences.

The future of operations is marked by a variety of trends and challenges, ranging from technological advancements and sustainability concerns to the need for greater diversity, inclusion, equity, and adaptability. By proactively addressing these issues and embracing innovative approaches, the uncertainties of the future are approached in a structured manner as they arise, if at all.

***

Operations cover a myriad of interconnected activities and responsibilities that collectively contribute to the functioning of a professional organisation. By examining the different aspects of operations, we gain a holistic understanding of the complexities and challenges faced by those tasked with managing these systems, who navigate an ever-evolving landscape, marked by technological advancements, shifting audience preferences, an increased emphasis on diversity, equity, and inclusion, and the need for sustainable and environmentally conscious practices.

The future of operations calls for adaptability, ongoing training, and strategic planning to nurture the relevance of these esteemed institutions. As we have explored in this section, embracing technology streamlines processes, enhances communication, and enables data-driven decision-making, all of which contribute to a more efficient and effective operational framework. Prioritising sustainability and environmental stewardship not only addresses pressing global concerns but also aligns with the values of eco-conscious audiences, thereby strengthening the public image and appeal.

Diversity, equity, and inclusion, while often discussed in relation to musicians and artistic programming, must also be addressed in the realm of operations to create an inclusive organisational culture at every level of the organisation, fostering diverse representation among staff and ensuring equitable opportunities for individuals from all backgrounds.

Adaptability and resilience are vital qualities for operations as they navigate an uncertain future marked by global challenges such as the pandemic. The ability to respond quickly and effectively to emerging risks and opportunities, develop contingency plans, and cultivate a flexible organisational culture is essential to thrive in this dynamic landscape. Furthermore, exploring alternative performance formats and revenue streams bolsters financial sustainability and artistic vitality.

Ultimately, the management of operations demands a delicate balance between preserving time-honoured traditions and embracing innovation. As orchestras continue to evolve and adapt to the changing landscape of the classical music industry, they stay true to their artistic mission and vision while remaining responsive to the needs and preferences of their constituents. By approaching operations with a forward-looking, strategic mindset, managers ensure the longevity, success, and impact of their organisations in a rapidly transforming world.

E. AUDIENCE DEVELOPMENT

A pressing issue in the 21st century is the progressive decline in the audience, a phenomenon that derives from a multitude of factors (Bouder-Pailler 2008; Onditi 2020), including changes in demographics, a long-term reduction in music education among the general population, the transformation of leisure time, a significant increase in time spent on electronic (mobile) devices for both professional activities and entertainment, and the tremendous proliferation of musical genres over the last half-century. The latter has led to the emergence of a plethora of niche music markets, thereby intensifying competition and posing a considerable threat to classical music's appeal.

1   The **shift in demographics** poses a substantial challenge, as the ageing population that has traditionally constituted the core audience for classical music is gradually being replaced by a younger generation with different musical preferences and consumption habits (Montoro-Pons, Caballer-Tarazona, and Cuadrado-García 2021). This generational shift imposes a re-evaluation of the ways in which orchestras appeal to and interact with new audiences, as well as how they retain the loyalty of their existing aficionados.

2   The overall **decline in music education** (Lowe 2012; Whittaker 2021; Freer and Evans 2018; Ng and Hartwig 2011) is a long-standing issue that has far-reaching implications for the future of classical music. As schools and educational institutions continue to de-prioritise music in favour of more practical or quantitative subjects, the general population's exposure to and appreciation of classical music is dwindling. This, in turn, translates into a shrinking reservoir of potential audience and a potentially contracting pool of aspiring musicians who might be interested in pursuing a career in classical music.

FIGURE 5.9 Key Components of Audience Development

3   The **transformation of leisure time** (Rooksby et al. 2015; Foley, Holzman, and Wearing 2007) is yet another factor that has contributed to the diminishing appeal of classical music. As our society has evolved, so too have the ways in which we spend our free time. The myriad options now available for leisure activities, coupled with the ever-increasing pace of life and the pervasive availability of mobile devices, have resulted in a reduction in the time and attention that people devote to classical music concerts.

4   The substantial **increase in the use of electronic devices** for both work and entertainment has profoundly impacted how people consume music. Streaming platforms, social media, and other digital technologies have revolutionised the way we discover, consume, and share music (Datta, Knox, and Bronnenberg 2018; Aguiar and Waldfogel 2018). While this has opened

up new opportunities for classical music to reach a wider audience, it has also led to a substantial drop in the industry's revenues (Reesman 2019) and an increasingly fragmented and competitive market, as the sheer volume of content available vies for the attention of potential listeners.[19] The increase in the use of electronic devices has also had a knock-on effect on the overall time people have available for other activities, such as the enjoyment of classical music.

5   The exponential **growth in musical genres** over the last 70 years has further compounded the challenges facing classical music.[20] As the market becomes saturated with an ever-expanding array of musical styles, the competition for listeners' attention and loyalty has intensified, leading to a more challenging environment for classical music institutions.

In light of these challenges, classical orchestras that are worried about their audience vanishing have developed and implemented robust community-oriented strategies[21] that not only sustain their revenue streams but also contribute to the long-term survival of classical music as an art form. Active orchestras bind with their communities, deploy educational initiatives, and experiment with new technologies to reach a wider audience, revitalise the classical music scene, and secure their place in the cultural fabric of the 21st century.

As highlighted by Borwick (2012), a key issue in arts management and audience development is caused by an increasing disconnection between arts and the wider society over the last century, with a growing focus on attracting and retaining audiences rather than forming authentic connections with local communities. This disconnection threatens the long-term sustainability and relevance of arts organisations, as it fails to address the evolving needs and expectations of the public. To tackle this issue, a possible solution is a fundamental shift in how arts organisations operate, transitioning from an audience-centric model to one that actively seeks to bridge and serve the needs of diverse communities. This approach does not only fortify the arts sector but also contributes to the social structure and well-being of society as a whole.

In the historical and cultural context in which American arts organisations have developed, there has been a considerable emphasis on the factors that have contributed to the widening disconnect between the arts and the public. The traditional role of arts organisations as cultural gatekeepers, that presented high-quality art to audiences who were expected to adapt their tastes and preferences accordingly, has led to the perception that the arts are elitist and inaccessible, alienating numerous potential participants. To construct a more inclusive and sustainable future for the arts, a model of arts management that prioritises community engagement and social impact has been more and more recommended in the last two decades, demonstrating the advantages of forming deep and meaningful connections with local communities. One of the key components of this community-focused model is the importance of working with community organisations, local businesses, and other partners to identify shared goals and co-create arts experiences that resonate with the needs and interests of the community.

Marketing, Communications, and PR

In the world of arts and culture institutions, marketing, communications, and public relations have always played a pivotal role in building their reputation and fuelling public's interest. Since the 19th century, long before the concepts of marketing, communication, and public relations took shape, reputation and image were heavily influenced by the ways artistic vision was conveyed. Even in those early days, deft communication strategies played an integral role in shaping an orchestra's standing, paving the way for future recognition. However, with the dawn of the digital age, the complexity of these tasks has multiplied, demanding cultural institutions to venture into unfamiliar territories, such as digital channels and a plethora of social media platforms. Nowadays, mastering platforms such as Spotify, YouTube, Instagram, and TikTok to diffuse music, captivate new audiences, and secure loyalty is viewed as a common practice and no longer an exception. Navigating the ever-evolving digital marketing and social media landscape may be daunting, particularly for those unacquainted with the latest trends, influencers, and best practices.

It has been observed that managers are becoming increasingly proactive in building an online presence, seeking innovative ways to connect with their fickle audiences, such as streamed performances, educational content, and interactive experiences. Attaining success in this domain necessitates personnel with a profound understanding of the digital landscape, including the digital generation that will constitute tomorrow's audiences. Additionally, creativity, a willingness to take risks, and relevant new technologies are all essential elements for thriving in the digital arena.

To create an effective marketing and PR strategy (Janičić 2021), a clear understanding of their unique selling points (USPs) helps the organisation to tailor the messaging to highlight their strengths. Identifying the target audience and their preferences is crucial in crafting a bespoke marketing strategy, which involves segmenting the audience based on demographics, interests, and behaviours. This approach allows an organisation to deliver highly personalised and relevant content, increasing the likelihood of building meaningful connections with potential and existing patrons.

Collaborating with key stakeholders, such as artists, sponsors, and partner organisations, is another important aspect of marketing and PR strategy.

Through the pooling of resources and the utilisation of shared networks, arts and culture institutions progressively expand their reach and establish mutually beneficial partnerships that enhance their reputation and result in increased visibility.

The power of structured storytelling cannot be understated either as it harnesses the capacity to craft compelling narratives that showcase artistic vision, share stories of musicians and staff, and provide consistent insights into the creative process behind performances. This approach not only stimulates audiences emotionally but also generates connection and loyalty.

Effective marketing strategies also prioritise audience development, aiming to expand and diversify their fan base. Therefore, several orchestras have already found it useful to experiment with new formats, venues, and collaborations that appeal to different audience segments. Educational outreach initiatives, workshops, and community programmes play a significant role in attracting new audiences and encouraging a lifelong appreciation for classical music.

Examples of musical and performance experiments cover:

Aurora Orchestra (United Kingdom)	Known for their trailblazing approach to performance, the Aurora often plays entire symphonies by heart, leaving sheet music behind. They captivate new audiences by venturing into unconventional venues such as gardens and parks. Their collaborations with artists across diverse genres, including jazz and electronic music, further broaden their appeal.
Los Angeles Philharmonic (United States)	Embracing genre-blending and innovative collaborations, the LA Phil has garnered attention with their popular "Americas and Americans" festival, which features cross-genre and cross-cultural performances. Their annual "Sound/Stage" series showcases multimedia performances, fusing live music with visual arts and immersive experiences.
Philharmonie de Paris (France)	The Philharmonie de Paris has delved into experimental projects such as "Démos," a programme designed to introduce classical music to underprivileged children from various cultural backgrounds. By performing in alternative venues such as schools and community centres, they can connect with a wider audience.
Sydney Symphony Orchestra (Australia)	Venturing into unique formats, the SSO has presented events such as "Symphony in the Domain," an outdoor concert series set in the Royal Botanic Gardens.
Tokyo Metropolitan Symphony Orchestra (Japan)	By collaborating with other art forms, such as dance and visual arts, the Tokyo Metropolitan creates innovative performances that captivate diverse audiences. They have also partnered with local businesses and organisations to host more intimate concerts, reaching out to new audience segments.

Measuring the impact of marketing, communications, and PR efforts is key to refining these strategies. Managers tend to adopt measurable key performance indicators (KPIs) to gauge the effectiveness of their campaigns and utilise data-driven insights to make informed decisions on future initiatives.

Success in the digital age also hinges upon the ability to navigate the complexities of the digital landscape and deploy innovative marketing, communications, and PR strategies. Understanding USPs, targeting the right audience, collaborating with stakeholders, utilising storytelling, and focusing on audience development allow orchestras to forge meaningful connections with existing and potential patrons. Ultimately, a willingness to take risks, onboard new technologies, and continually optimise their strategies based on data-driven insights contributes to long-term success in an increasingly competitive global market.

Branding and Positioning

A strong brand identity is a decisive prerequisite of marketing and public relations efforts (Baumgarth and O'Reilly 2014; Jyrämä et al. 2015), as it encapsulates the essence of the organisation and distinguishes it from competitors. To define a unique brand identity, four elements must be considered:

1 **Vision and Mission:** The vision and mission statements reflect its core values and artistic aspirations, conveying its purpose and desired impact on audiences and the broader community. Managers are free to involve key stakeholders, including musicians, staff, board members, and patrons, in the development of these statements to ensure that they are truly representative of the ethos.

2 **Artistic Direction:** The artistic direction, including repertoire, collaborations, and commissioning of new works, should be aligned with its brand identity, emphasising unique strengths and areas of specialisation. The appointment of a charismatic and visionary artistic director or conductor can significantly enhance the brand by providing a distinct and recognisable artistic voice.

3 **Visual Identity:** A consistent visual identity, including its logo, colour palette, typography, and overall design language, across all marketing materials, reflects the organisation's personality and values.

4 **Brand Storytelling:** Crafting a compelling brand narrative that captures the history, values, and artistic vision is an essential aspect of building a strong brand identity. This narrative is woven throughout the marketing and communication efforts, helping to create an emotional connection with audiences and fostering a sense of loyalty and affinity.

Positioning in the Competitive Landscape

In the increasingly competitive world of classical music, orchestras have an interest to effectively position themselves to stand out amongst their peers (Campelo and Pasquinelli 2017). Managers use several tools and methods to achieve this goal:

1 **Market Research:** Conduct thorough market research to identify the main competitors and their respective strengths and weaknesses. This analysis provides valuable insights into potential opportunities and niches in which the orchestra can excel. Surveying audience members and analysing audience data also helps managers understand their target market's preferences, motivations, and unmet needs, enabling them to tailor their marketing and programming strategies accordingly.

2 **Unique Selling Proposition (USP):** Develop a clear and compelling USP that highlights the unique features, differentiating it from other ensembles. This USP should resonate with the target audience and be consistently communicated across all marketing channels. Examples of USPs might include a focus on contemporary music, an emphasis on community outreach and engagement, or a commitment to nurturing emerging talent.

3 **Competitive Advantages:** Identify and leverage the competitive advantages, whether they are rooted in its artistic excellence, innovative programming, community engagement, or other factors. By emphasising these strengths, the orchestra further distinguishes itself in the competitive landscape. For instance, a musical group that excels in its educational programme may position itself as a leader in community development, while an ensemble with a rich and diverse repertoire could emphasise its versatility and breadth of offerings. And should the same educational programme be available online as a Massive Open Online Course (MOOC), the marketing narrative to promote it would be of a different nature.

Consistency and Coherence in Branding and Messaging

Maintaining consistency and coherence in branding and messaging is essential for building a strong and recognisable brand. A variety of routes are possible to this aim:

1 **Develop Brand Guidelines:** Create comprehensive brand guidelines that outline the organisation's visual identity, tone of voice, and key messaging. These guidelines should be shared with all staff, ensuring that everyone

involved in the marketing and communication efforts adheres to a unified approach. They should also be shared with staff not directly involved in marketing, such as musicians, who can therefore adhere to the same set of rules when publishing about life behind the scenes or activities and performances on their personal social media. Regular training and updates on the guidelines help keep the team aligned and reinforce the importance of brand consistency.

2 **Align Internal and External Communications:** Ensure that internal communications, such as newsletters and intranet content, align with the brand identity and external messaging. This consistency fosters a cohesive organisational culture that reinforces the brand.

3 **Monitor and Evaluate Brand Consistency:** Regularly review marketing materials, public relations efforts, and audience feedback to ensure that the brand identity remains consistent and coherent. This ongoing evaluation enables managers to identify and address any discrepancies or areas for improvement. Monitoring key performance indicators (KPIs) related to brand awareness, perception, and loyalty give managers the right input to modify or fine-tune their branding efforts and make data-driven decisions to enhance the brand equity.

Brand Management and Reputation

In addition to developing a strong brand identity, it is crucial to proactively manage reputation, addressing any potential risks or crises that could damage the brand. This may involve closely monitoring social media and traditional media coverage, developing a crisis communication plan, and engaging in proactive public relations efforts to maintain positive relationships with the press and key influencers. Carefully managing the reputation also means that managers take the needed actions to shield the organisation's brand and guarantee that it remains strong and resilient in the face of adversity.

In conclusion, by defining a unique brand identity, effectively positioning the orchestra within the competitive landscape, maintaining consistency and coherence in branding and messaging, exploring partnerships and cross-promotional opportunities, and proactively managing the reputation, managers build a strong and recognisable brand that resonates with audiences, enhances the organisation's reputation, and supports long-term success. Embracing these strategies does not only contribute to the continued vitality and evolution of classical music but also helps the art form remain a cherished and integral part of our global culture.

Traditional Marketing Channels

In today's rapidly evolving digital landscape, it may be tempting to focus solely on online marketing strategies; however, traditional marketing channels continue to hold significant value. Despite the phenomenal expansion of digital media and online marketing formats, traditional channels such as print, outdoor, radio, and television presence remain important to reach diverse audiences, improve brand visibility, and reinforce the unique selling proposition. Time, energy, and budget allocated to traditional marketing efforts are not a waste of resources as they complement digital strategies, especially in light of generational preferences in content consumption. A balanced and integrated approach to marketing is a paying method to optimise the reach and impact of every campaign.

Print Advertising

Despite the growing importance of digital marketing and the increased attention to sustainable and green measures, print advertising remains a valuable channel for promoting concerts and other activities:

1 **Targeted Publications:** Identify publications that cater to the target audience, such as local newspapers, magazines, and specialised music publications. This targeted approach aims at reaching the most relevant readers that better align with the classical music experience and values.

2 **Ad Design and Copywriting:** Develop eye-catching, well-designed print commercials that reflect the brand identity and convey key messages. Engaging copywriting that speaks directly to the target audience helps elicit an emotional response and encourage ticket sales.

3 **Advertising Schedule and Frequency:** Develop a strategic advertising schedule that follows the concert calendar and seasonal patterns. Accurately timed print ads usually maximise their impact (without harming the sustainability efforts).

4 **Measuring Effectiveness:** Track the success of print advertising campaigns by using unique promo codes, URLs, or phone numbers that can be attributed to specific ads. This data enables managers to evaluate the effectiveness of their print advertising efforts and make informed decisions about future campaigns.

Outdoor Advertising

Outdoor advertising (billboards, posters, and transit commercials) also provides high-impact visibility and helps build brand awareness:

1 **Strategic Placement:** Select high-traffic locations for outdoor ads to maximise visibility and reach. Consider the target audience's habits and preferences when choosing locations, aiming to reach potential concertgoers where
   they live, work, and socialise. In addition to traditional outdoor advertising
   spaces, managers should explore unconventional locations and formats, such
   as large-scale building projections or interactive installations, which can generate buzz and create memorable impressions.

2 **Design and Messaging:** Develop visually striking outdoor commercials
   that convey the unique selling proposition and showcase upcoming concerts
   or events. A concise and compelling design, if consistent with the brand identity, increases the effectiveness of outdoor advertising.

3 **Monitoring and Maintenance:** Again, managers should track the performance of outdoor advertising campaigns, including metrics such as impressions, reach, and conversions, to inform future decisions and optimise their
   marketing efforts.

Radio and Television Presence

Radio and television advertising and presence in high audience shows offers a
powerful platform for reaching a broad audience, particularly when targeting
specific demographics or geographic areas, or when happening in thematic
shows.

1 **Demographic and Geographic Targeting:** Identify radio and television stations that cater to the target audience and geographic market. By
   being visible on stations that align with the demographics and geographies,
   managers maximise the impact of their ad spend. Additionally, managers can
   explore opportunities for partnerships with local broadcasters, which provide
   easier access to discounted ad rates, sponsored content, or in-kind media
   support.

2 **Advertising/Presence Schedule and Frequency:** Develop a strategic schedule that takes into account the concert calendar, target audience's
   media consumption habits, and seasonal patterns. This may involve airing
   ads or shows during specific times of day or programming that aligns with
   the target demographic, as well as adjusting the frequency to optimise reach
   and maintain cost efficiency.

3 **Cross-Promotion and Synergy:** Explore opportunities for cross-promotion with other arts and cultural organisations, broadcasters, or advertisers, which amplify the reach and impact of radio and television advertising
   campaigns.

4 **Measuring Success:** Use unique call-to-action elements, such as promo codes or contests, to track the success of radio and television campaigns. This data is a good indicator to assess the return on investment and make informed decisions about future advertising efforts. In addition to quantitative metrics, managers should gather qualitative feedback from audience members, broadcasters, and other stakeholders to gain a comprehensive understanding of the effectiveness of their radio and television initiatives.

Managers should always consider strategically utilising traditional marketing channels, including print, outdoor, radio, and television advertising, to effectively promote their organisations and cultivate brand recognition among their intended audiences. These efforts, combined with digital marketing initiatives, help achieve a comprehensive marketing strategy that maximises their reach and impact.

Community and Audience Engagement

Establishing robust relationships with the local community, educational institutions, and organisations elevates the orchestra's profile and opens valuable opportunities overall. As mentioned by Emily Dollman at the very beginning of her recent book *Opening Doors: Orchestras, Opera Companies and Community Engagement*, as if to immediately underscore the inescapable centrality of the argument, "education and community engagement programming has evolved to be a crucial counterpoint to main stage performance programming for orchestras and operas companies" (Dollman 2023). This entails partnering with local businesses, schools, not-for-profit organisations, activist groups, or charities to devise mutually beneficial programmes and events that bring the orchestra closer to its audience. Although this may seem easy on paper, it has to happen at a time of profound changes in the sociodemographics of the audience, the transformation in leisure patterns and the increased competition for attention. As noted by Flanagan (2012, 1. 1009),

> the decline in attendance at classical music concerts (and other arts performances) may reflect broad social shifts in the use of leisure time that have little to do with orchestra policies (or policies of the performing arts industry in general). These patterns are all the more puzzling because they are occurring during a period in which leisure time has increased.

In light of these changes, it becomes even more imperative to adapt and innovate in community and audience strategies.

Grasping the diverse needs and interests of their communities is crucial for managers, and translating them into outreach programmes that captivate a broad spectrum of audiences holds even greater significance. For example, offering educational programmes for young people, collaborating with local musicians or artists from other disciplines, or performing in non-traditional venues to reach new audiences are examples of artistic innovations that are leveraged to compete for interest and attention, proposing novel experiments. Hence, the need for a quasi-sociological understanding of the local community – as this varies from one urban or rural area to another, and one country to another – to allow the service offerings to closely align with the expectations of the target audiences.

Effective community and audience engagement requires creativity, empathy, and a deep understanding of the local culture and socioeconomic fabric. It is essential to devise innovative strategies to involve various community segments, including youth and underserved populations. Educational initiatives and outreach programmes help instil a love for music among young people and prepare future generations of music enthusiasts. This involves offering workshops, masterclasses, or open rehearsals, allowing the community to witness the creative process. Moreover, collaborative approaches lead to the creation of richer and more original artistic experiences. Collaborations with local artists, theatre groups, and dance companies result in multidisciplinary performances that appeal to a broader audience. Additionally, immersive experiences that blend classical music, visual arts, technology, and storytelling into a single performance present an inventive and compelling approach to refresh the artistic palette of the offering. This method not only renders the music more accessible but also captivates audiences, creating an opportunity to inspire curiosity (if not excitement) and facilitate a broader comprehension of the vast cultural and historical contexts within which the music exists. Also, increasingly tailored programming that better reflects a community's cultural diversity (for example, incorporating a variety of musical genres and cultural backgrounds) helps draw new audiences while laying the ground for community belonging. Similarly, reaching out to community groups and organising performances in unconventional venues, such as parks, community centres, industrial brownfields, railways stations, and public spaces, make classical music more accessible to people who might not typically attend concerts.

In the last two to three decades, maintaining an ongoing dialogue with the audience and requesting their feedback and input on programming and outreach initiatives has emerged as a common practice for many arts and culture institutions. This is achievable through traditional tools such as surveys and focus groups or more recently by smart usage of social media platforms, providing granular quantitative insights for a better alignment of the service offerings with the community's needs and desires.

In summary, successful community and audience-oriented initiatives necessitate creativity, empathy, and a deep understanding of the local culture and community. Strong relationships, impactful outreach programmes, and attentiveness to community needs broaden the reach, enhance the audience, and secure long-term success.

Content Production

Content production constitutes a crucial aspect of management, spanning concert production and developing compelling visual and audio material for a range of channels, including social media. The mastery of content production lies in a profound comprehension of music production, technical requirements, and the capacity to identify – if not "sense" – first-rate content that captivates audiences. Organising the production of a concert involves meticulous attention to logistics, technical requirements, and stage management, culminating in a seamless and immersive concert experience. This entails addressing the various technical elements for each performance, such as sound systems, lighting arrangements, and stage setups. Beyond the realm of concert production, content creation also encompasses the generation of visually striking and sonically impactful material that resonates with diverse audiences across multiple channels.

Aiming at excellence in content production demands creativity, proficiency, and a discerning eye for detail. It also calls for the adept coordination of musicians, technicians, and resources, which may involve integrating shooting sessions amidst rehearsals or other activities linked to the seasonal programme. Staying attuned to evolving audience preferences and emerging trends in content consumption help adapt content strategies to better connect with the target audience.

Observation shows that investing in innovative approaches to content production, such as immersive concert experiences or interactive digital content, further raises audience interest and elevates the overall impact. This may happen through harnessing cutting-edge technology, exploring interdisciplinary collaborations, or venturing into unconventional performance formats. In today's booming digital landscape, a vast portfolio of technologies and platforms contribute to reaching a broader audience. For instance, streaming, virtual reality, or social media storytelling help expand reach, connect with younger demographics, and cultivate a more diverse and global fanbase. Ultimately, effective content production is pivotal to success. Meticulous coordination of content production, from live concerts to digital materials, provides the needed material to craft memorable experiences that resonate with in-person and online audiences.

Education and Outreach Programmes

Education and outreach programmes not only may inspire a love for music from a young age but also may deepen the impact within the community. Effective education programmes necessitate a profound understanding of pedagogy and curriculum design to ensure that the material presented is suitable and effective for learners of all ages. Additionally, active community participation is vital to forge partnerships and support while ensuring alignment with the needs and interests of the community. Successful education and outreach programmes strengthen the connections and inspire future music enthusiasts. We have seen that successful ensembles prioritise the diverse learning needs and preferences of their target audience rather than their own preferences. This might include developing age-appropriate content for children, teenagers, and adults or tailoring programmes to suit the interests and skill levels of participants. In the quest for an inclusive and accessible learning environment, various teaching methods, approaches, and channels can be further explored. This encompasses a blend of hands-on activities, group discussions, and multimedia presentations, augmenting the traditional sphere of lectures and demonstrations.

One effective approach to educational programming is to provide learners with opportunities to actively participate in the music-making process. Organising youth ensembles, workshops, or masterclasses led by professional musicians increases participants' confidence as they gain first-hand experience and develop their musical skills. In a similar vein, creating collaborative projects with local schools also offer students opportunities to attend rehearsals, meet musicians, or even perform alongside the ensemble in special concerts.

There is a growing trend in the classical music ecosystem to develop programmes that connect music with other subjects or disciplines, such as history, literature, or science. This interdisciplinary approach allows learners to appreciate the broader context of classical music and its relevance to other aspects of their lives. Programmes that explore the relationship between music and mathematics or highlight the cultural and historical significance of a specific composer or musical period are now quite common. Outreach programmes are also designed to reach a broad audience and extend beyond traditional concert venues. Performances in public spaces, such as parks, community centres, or hospitals, make classical music more accessible to people who might not typically attend concerts. These unconventional performances break down barriers and preconceived notions about classical music, promoting a more inclusive and diverse musical landscape.

Another essential aspect of education and outreach programmes is the possibility they offer to establish a network of alliances with community organisations, businesses, and educational institutions. Collaboration with various entities may pave the way to additional resources, to an extended reach, and to more impactful programmes. Partnerships with local businesses may aim to sponsor educational events or work with community organisations to provide music lessons for underprivileged youth.

Evaluation and assessment of any education and outreach programme ensure that the initiatives remain relevant, effective, and aligned with the community's needs. Measurable goals and objectives and regular collection of feedback from participants, educators, and community partners are used to fine-tune and improve the programme for a better impact.

Education and outreach programmes are integral to the success of management, inspiring a passion for music and extending the influence within the community. Creating exciting, inclusive educational content, forging community partnerships, and consistently evaluating and refining initiatives solidify connections with the community, attract new audiences, and inspire future music aficionados.

The Social Impact of Community Engagement

Orchestras hold a unique position within their local communities: not only do they serve as a source of cultural dynamism, but they may also become a potent catalyst for social change. As institutions rooted in tradition, they have the potential to connect with diverse audiences and contribute positively to society. This section will examine their role in the larger community to which they belong, exploring the importance of connecting with various groups and the significance of measuring and communicating any social impact.

The Role in Local Communities

Orchestras have long been considered cornerstones of cultural expression, contributing to the vibrancy and artistic identity of the communities they serve. Onboarding local audiences forges a sense of belonging and shared heritage, trying to unite people from diverse backgrounds through music. In that sense, they back cultural cohesion and address social challenges, as they often collaborate with community organisations, educational institutions, and other stakeholders to create inclusive and diverse programming.

Strategies for Connecting With Diverse Community Groups

To maximise their social impact, orchestras define strategies to connect with a wide range of community groups. This includes forging alliances with local organisations, hosting public performances in accessible venues, and undertaking collaborative projects that draw upon the strengths of each partner. Some of these strategies are outlined as follows:

Approach	Description
Partnerships With Local Organisations	Collaborations with community-based groups open new horizons as orchestras tap into networks and additional resources, increasing their reach and impact. These partnerships involve working with schools, social service agencies, or cultural institutions to develop and deliver programs that cater to the needs of specific communities.
Public Performances	Hosting free or low-cost concerts in public spaces such as parks, community centres, and libraries makes orchestral music more accessible to a wider audience. These performances also serve as a platform for showcasing local talents and encouraging audience participation.
Collaborative Projects	Joint initiatives with other arts organisations or community groups lead to innovative programming that combines different art forms or cultural traditions. These projects also provide opportunities for skill-sharing and professional development among participating artists and organisations.

Defining Social Impact

Social impact refers to the positive effects that an organisation's activities have on society. It covers various aspects such as educational outreach, cultural enrichment, and economic contributions, and manifests in several ways:

1 **Educational Outreach:** Orchestras often embark on educational initiatives that aim to inspire the next generation of musicians, as well as incentivise an appreciation for music among young people. These programs include workshops, masterclasses, and school visits (Mall 2020), providing valuable learning opportunities for students and teachers alike.

2 **Cultural Enrichment:** Diverse and innovative programming contributes to the cultural landscape of communities, exposing audiences to new perspectives and artistic expressions. This, in turn, leads to increased cultural understanding and tolerance and inspires creative thinking and dialogue.

3 **Economic Contributions:** A vibrant cultural scene generally also plays a part in the economic vitality of the community, as musical activities often generate both direct and indirect revenue. Moreover, a local rootedness contributes to the attractiveness of a city as a cultural destination, drawing tourists and stimulating local businesses.

BOX 5.7 ABOUT TOURISM

It is difficult to determine the exact amount of tourism a large orchestra generates for its city, as there is no specific data publicly available on this subject. However, the large and well-known orchestras are undeniably significant cultural institutions and prominent attractions for tourists interested in classical music. An ensemble that has a world-class reputation attracts numerous concertgoers, both locally and internationally. For example, visitors to Berlin who are interested in classical music may plan their trips around the Berliner Philharmoniker's concert schedule or include a performance at the Philharmonie in their itineraries. It is worth noting that the impact of the Berliner Philharmoniker on tourism should be considered within the broader context of Berlin's overall cultural scene, which includes various other attractions such as museums, galleries, historical sights, and other performing arts venues.

Glückler and Panitz (2023) managed to collect original data and employed a regional economic impact analysis to determine both the financial resilience of the Mannheim Philharmonic Orchestra and its impact on the urban economy.

Measuring and Communicating Social Impact

To demonstrate their value and relevance to the communities, orchestras increasingly adopt a more structured approach, measuring and communicating regularly their social impact. In the last couple of decades, collecting and analysing data on programs and initiatives and gathering feedback from stakeholders have become routine activities to identify areas of success and improvement, as well as inform future strategies and decision-making processes. Communicating their social impact effectively helps build trust and credibility within their communities, potential funders, and supporters. Various channels, such as annual reports, social media, and public events, contribute to this goal, allowing to showcase accomplishments and the positive outcomes of their work.

Some methods for measuring and communicating social impact include:

1 **Surveys and Feedback Forms:** Collecting feedback from participants and audience members to gauge the success of programs and events, and identify areas for improvement. Surveys are conducted online, in person, or through mail and email, depending on the target audience and available resources.

2 **Data Analysis:** Tracking data on programme attendance, ticket sales, and other performance indicators provide insights into the reach and impact. Analysing this data over time reveals trends and patterns, informing future decision-making and strategy development. Data analysis is also taken to a much higher level when it leverages the data produced by digital media, as this leads to a more granular understanding of the actual and potential audience in quantitative terms and the possibility of carrying out sentiment analysis or similar statistical methods that extract value from language (for example, comments to social media posts).

3 **Case Studies and Stories:** Sharing personal stories and anecdotes from participants and community members is a powerful way to illustrate the social impact. These stories are showcased on the website, social media channels, or printed materials to humanise the data and statistics.

4 **Public Events and Presentations:** Hosting public events (open rehearsals, community forums, or panel discussions) provide opportunities to connect directly with audiences and stakeholders, as well as share updates on progress and impact. It may also give a general feeling of proximity to the local community of journalists who see the life of their city ensemble from behind the scenes.

The social impact of community engagement is a crucial aspect of the orchestra's role in a given society,[22] for they create meaningful connections and contribute to the well-being of their communities when they actively involve diverse community groups and employ strategies such as partnerships, public performances, and collaborative projects. Additionally, measuring and communicating their social impact effectively is vital for maintaining credibility and ensuring continued support from stakeholders and contributors. Ultimately, prioritising social impact leads to remaining relevant and vibrant cultural institutions, enriching the lives of their audiences, and stimulating change within their communities.

Audience Segmentation and Personalisation

In modern management, audience segmentation and personalisation are indispensable tools (Raitaluoto 2023), and management of arts and culture institutions is no exception. In today's fast-paced world, where consumers are constantly bombarded with numerous choices, understanding the audiences' diverse needs, preferences, and behaviours paves the way to targeted marketing campaigns, customised experiences, and more pertinent content.

Understanding Audience Segmentation and Personalisation

The process of audience segmentation involves analysing and categorising audience members into distinct groups based on shared characteristics.[23] These characteristics include sociodemographic factors such as age, education, gender, and income level; geographic factors such as location and distance to the venue; and psychographic factors, which encompass interests, values, and lifestyles. Accurate segmentation provides the analytical insights to develop a deeper understanding of their audience and create marketing messages, as well as programmes that resonate with each specific segment, increasing the likelihood of long-term relationships. In addition to improving marketing efficiency, audience segmentation also informs artistic programming. Data-driven decisions regarding repertoire,[24] guest artists, and programming elements are better made when the preferences of diverse audience segments are well understood. This strategic approach to programming aims to diversify the audience, attract new patrons, retain existing ones, and ensure the long-term financial viability of the organisation.

Personalisation takes audience segmentation one step further by tailoring experiences and content to individual audience members. With the help of granular data collection and data analysis, it is possible to dissect the audience's preferences and deliver personalised experiences that deepen connections and build loyalty. A simplistic example is when personalised emails are sent to patrons, suggesting upcoming performances based on their past attendance history or favourite composers. More sophisticated examples are inspired by the airline industry, where loyalty programs are designed to align with the tastes and preferences of small groups of users, if not single users. It is also possible to implement a high level of personalisation in the concert experience, such as offering pre-concert talks, post-concert receptions, or special family-friendly events designed to target micro-segments of the audience or patrons and sponsors of all ages, or offer diversified and tailored online content.

Collecting and analysing data is a crucial aspect of implementing audience segmentation and personalisation strategies. Various data sources, including ticketing information, website analytics, social media utilisation, and mobile device background info, are used nowadays to build comprehensive audience profiles. Data analysis tools and customer relationship management (CRM) systems help organise and interpret this data to make informed decisions about marketing, programming, and audience. As a more extreme example, we also cite new AI tools coupled with CCTV in the venues that allow to refine the segmentation of the audience (as long as it is carried out in complete adherence to privacy rules and regulations).

The following are some potential applications of audience segmentation and personalisation within the context of orchestra management:

Applications of segmentation	Description
Targeted Marketing Campaigns	Tailored marketing messages and materials for each audience segment increase the effectiveness of the communication campaigns, driving ticket sales and boosting revenue.
Customised Concert Experiences	Offering unique experiences for different audience segments, such as pre-concert talks, post-concert receptions, or special family-friendly events, retain patrons of all ages and encourage repeat attendance.
Personalised Content and Communications	Data insights are used to send personalised emails, social media content, and other communications that align with individual audience members' interests and preferences, aiming at stronger connections and loyalty.
Data-informed Artistic Programming	Audience insights improve strategic decisions about programming, ensuring that the repertoire, guest artists, and other elements resonate with the diverse audience and contribute to long-term financial stability.
Tailored Education and Outreach Programmes	A detailed understanding of the needs and interests of various audience segments optimises targeted community outreach and education initiatives that support connections with new audiences and the value of classical music within their communities.
Elevating the Digital Experience	Audience data is utilised to create personalised digital experiences, such as customised website content, interactive mobile apps, and social media campaigns that resonate with patrons and promote bi-directional participation.
Improved Audience Retention and Loyalty	The delivery of tailored experiences and content that align with audience preferences and needs is a key element to a long-lasting relationship with patrons, sponsors, and even public funders, ensuring ongoing support and loyalty.

Implementing audience segmentation and personalisation strategies requires a commitment to data collection, analysis, and ongoing refinement. A prerequisite step to consider involves the articulation of clear objectives and measurable goals, as these are instrumental in evaluating the effectiveness of segmentation and personalisation initiatives. Subsequently, a way to increase the yield of segmentation and personalisation is to adapt and evolve strategies based on the insights from the data collected. To maintain a data-driven approach to audiences, investments in staff training and professional development, as well as collaborations with local research institutes and data scientists, are no longer exceptions. Ensuring that team members directly or indirectly access the necessary skills and expertise to collect, analyse, and interpret data leads to more informed decision-making and more effective audience strategies.

Orchestras also explore opportunities to work with external partners, such as arts organisations, educational institutions, and technology providers, to expand their data collection capabilities and learn from best practices in audience segmentation and personalisation. These partnerships provide valuable insights and resources that develop innovative audience strategies and stay ahead of industry trends.

Methodologies for Audience Segmentation and Personalisation

- **Demographic Segmentation**: This approach divides the audience based on demographic factors such as age, gender, income, or education level. These factors often influence musical tastes and preferences, making demographic segmentation a useful starting point for targeting communications and offers.
- **Behavioural Segmentation**: This method focuses on audience behaviours, such as attendance patterns, ticket purchasing habits, or consumption of digital content. Making the internal logic of the audience's behaviours evident is the first step to pinpoint trends and opportunities for targeted marketing campaigns or bespoke offers.
- **Psychographic Segmentation**: This approach considers the attitudes, interests, and lifestyles of audience members, revealing the motivations and values that drive their connection to classical music.
- **Geographical Segmentation**: A properly executed location-based segmentation of the audience provides the necessary insights to adequately tailor communications and offers aligned with tastes, preferences, and cultural context.

These four forms of segmentation – demographic, behavioural, psychographic, and geographical – should not be seen as mutually exclusive. In fact, the most

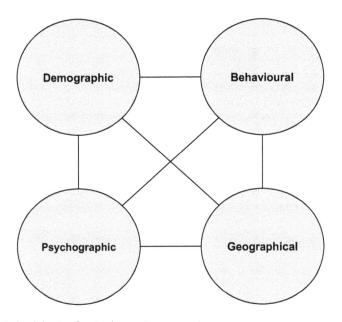

FIGURE 5.10 Methodologies for Audience Segmentation

comprehensive and effective results can be achieved when these segmentation methodologies are blended. By combining demographic factors, audience behaviours, psychographic insights, and geographical context, orchestras can gain a better and more granular understanding of their audience and create more targeted and impactful marketing strategies. A blended holistic approach enables orchestras to connect with their audience on multiple levels and deliver experiences that resonate with their unique preferences and values.

Practical Applications of Audience Segmentation and Personalisation

Targeted Marketing and Communications

Use audience segmentation to create targeted marketing campaigns and communications that resonate with specific audience groups, customising advertising materials, tailoring email campaigns, or creating segment-specific social media content.

Personalised Content and Offers

Leverage personalisation techniques to create tailored content and offers for individual audience members. This may include personalised concert recommendations, targeted special offers, or customised digital experiences.

Data-Driven Artistic Programming

The analysis of audience segmentation data provides a strong quantitative backbone to more informed decisions about repertoire selection, concert formats, and collaborative projects that cater to the preferences and interests of different audience segments. Although concert programming is usually driven by qualitative heuristics and common musical wisdom, the introduction of a complementary quantitative approach is now eased by the amount and variety of data collected (and archived) on a variety of variables related to audiences (Yanchenko 2020).

Community Outreach and Education

Use audience segmentation to identify opportunities for community outreach and educational initiatives, targeting programmes and resources to the needs of specific demographic groups or communities.

Audience segmentation and personalisation are valuable tools to better understand and cater to the diverse needs of audiences. The implementation of these measures provides a competitive advantage to those who employ them in the arts and culture ecosystem, boosting marketing efficiency, and perhaps increasing revenue growth. There is little doubt that the insights gleaned from audience segmentation and personalisation play a key role in shaping artistic programming decisions, while concurrently broadening the reach through focused community outreach and educational initiatives.

CASE STUDY 5.4

Boost Audience Development and Engagement

One of the primary paradoxes is the need to deal with fragmented audiences and forge a (somehow) united community. This case study examines an innovative outreach programme aimed at expanding the reach towards diverse audiences. The programme's success demonstrates the power of creativity, adaptability, and strategic thinking.

IDENTIFYING THE TARGET AUDIENCE AND PROGRAMME GOALS

* A thorough research identified underrepresented and underserved communities.

- Clear objectives were established to increase audience diversity, community connections, and social impact.

PARTNERING WITH LOCAL ORGANISATIONS

- The orchestra forged alliances with local schools, community centres, and non-profit organisations to deliver various outreach activities.
- These partnerships helped to establish trust within the community and facilitated access to the target audience.

DESIGNING TAILORED EDUCATIONAL AND PERFORMANCE INITIATIVES

- A range of activities was developed to cater to different age groups and interests, including workshops, masterclasses, and open rehearsals.
- Special performances were organised at non-traditional venues, such as community centres, public parks, and local festivals, making them more accessible to the target audience.

INTEGRATING TECHNOLOGY AND DIGITAL MEDIA

- Digital platforms were used to promote its outreach activities, share multimedia content, and dialogue with the community.
- Streaming technology enabled remote participation in workshops and concerts, increasing accessibility for those unable to attend in person.

MONITORING AND EVALUATING THE PROGRAMME'S IMPACT

- Data and feedback collected from participants, partners, and the broader community served as a foundational layer to assess the programme's effectiveness.
- The results were used to refine and expand the outreach initiatives, ensuring their continued success and alignment with the overall objectives.

LEVERAGING THE PROGRAMME'S SUCCESS FOR FUNDRAISING AND PUBLICITY

- The achievements were communicated to existing supporters and potential donors, demonstrating commitment to community and social impact.
- The programme garnered positive media attention, boosting reputation and attracting new audiences.

This case study showcases an innovative outreach programme in developing the audience. Through targeted audience identification, strategic partnership development, custom initiative design, and technology integration, the orchestra made a significant community impact and broadened its reach. The lessons in this case study can be applied to other arts and culture institutions that are keen to develop similar outreach initiatives, highlighting the importance of creativity, adaptability, and strategic thinking in audience management.

QUESTIONS:

1   Reflecting on the approach to identify and reach underrepresented and underserved communities, what considerations should be taken into account when identifying and defining a target audience for such outreach programmes?

2   Evaluating the partnerships with local entities such as schools, community centres, and not-for-profit organisations, what strategies can be employed to ensure these partnerships are mutually beneficial and sustainable in the long term?

3   Given the range of activities developed for different age groups and interests, what considerations should managers bear in mind when designing educational and performance initiatives tailored for diverse audiences? How might cultural, socioeconomic, and educational factors come into play?

4   How might the integration of digital platforms and streaming technology evolve in the future, and what implications could these developments have on the outreach activities?

5   Considering the process of monitoring and evaluating the programme's impact, what methods or approaches could be used to ensure that evaluation is robust, fair, and meaningful? Additionally, how might this evaluation feed into broader organisational strategies, including fundraising and publicity?

F. GOVERNANCE AND BOARD RELATIONS

In orchestra management, a strong partnership with the board is paramount, as it encompasses strategic planning, artistic programming, and high-level business objectives. Building on Chapter 3's discussion on organisation, this brief section explores the intricacies of managing relationships with the board, facilitating mutual understanding, and working cohesively towards the collective objectives.

To establish fruitful board relations, it is essential to understand governance models, ethical considerations, and leadership principles thoroughly. This knowledge enables the alignment of the organisation's strategic goals with ethical norms and legal requirements, creating a robust framework that eases stability and growth. A crucial component of nurturing positive board relations is for the CEO to actively listen to the opinions and concerns of board members, musicians, and staff. Through this attentive approach, the needs and interests of all stakeholders are considered to create a collaborative environment where all parties contribute to the initiatives.

The role of the CEO in managing board relations cannot be overstated, as their leadership skills and ability to collaborate with diverse stakeholders play a vital role in guiding the organisation.[25] Observation has highlighted that only the executive team's strong connections with the board lead to good governance, transparent communication, and the adept handling of the challenges inherent in the industry.

In addition to these skills, the following concrete measures are employed to enhance board relations and improve governance:

Regular Communication	Keep board members informed about the activities, successes, and challenges. This encourages their active involvement and helps them make well-informed decisions.
Board Development	Invest in ongoing board education and development programs, which enable members to stay updated on governance best practices, industry trends, and fiduciary responsibilities.
Board Evaluation	Conduct periodic board evaluations to review performance, identify areas of improvement, and ensure that the board's composition aligns with the strategic goals.
Celebrate Achievements	Acknowledge and celebrate the accomplishments of the board, staff, and musicians, honouring pride and ownership in the organisation's success.

A firm governance structure and positive board relations are critical aspects of management that contribute significantly to the organisation's outcome. Orchestras create a solid foundation for their growth and ongoing success in understanding governance models whenever they can prioritise open communication and collaboration among board members, musicians, and staff. In turn, these efforts lead to a thriving organisation that enriches the cultural landscape and serves its community with excellence.

G. HUMAN RESOURCES AND CONFLICT RESOLUTION

Success relies not only on artistic vision but also on the people behind the scenes who facilitate harmonious work among musicians, technical crews, admin staff, and volunteers. This chapter delves into the critical aspects of human resources and conflict resolution within the management context, addressing hiring, training, and retaining personnel, promoting professional development and growth, aiming at a positive work culture, and resolving conflicts that may arise within the organisation.

We have identified seven components that require particular attention for effective management of human resources:

Hiring Musicians, Staff, and Volunteers

The process of hiring musicians, staff, and volunteers is delicate, requiring a keen understanding of the unique skills and attributes needed for each role. When recruiting musicians, a rigorous audition process should be in place to evaluate the candidates' technical proficiency, musicianship, and ability to blend with the existing ensemble. For non-musical and non-artistic staff positions, as in any organisation a well-defined job description and a thorough

FIGURE 5.11 Main Aspects of HR Management

interview process helps in identifying candidates with the right experience, expertise, and cultural fit. In the case of volunteers, a clear outline of their responsibilities and expectations is essential, along with a genuine passion for the mission and values.

Training and Onboarding

Once new members are recruited, it is vital to provide a comprehensive onboarding process that introduces them to their specific responsibilities and the organisation's culture and values. For musicians, this involves orientation sessions, mentoring programmes with experienced players, or workshops to help them adapt to the ensemble's unique dynamics. To build unity and collaboration, staff members may benefit from cross-departmental training sessions and team-building activities. Volunteers should receive training on their specific tasks and the organisation's policies and procedures to ensure they are equipped to fulfil their roles effectively.

Retaining Personnel

Retaining talented musicians, staff, and volunteers is crucial to maintaining stability and reducing recruitment budgets over time. Competitive remuneration packages, opportunities for professional growth, and a supportive work environment are essential for employee retention. Additionally, it is vital to acknowledge and reward outstanding performance, offering incentives and regular feedback to encourage continuous improvement. For volunteers, acknowledging their contributions, providing meaningful tasks, offering specific training, and creating a cohesive atmosphere within the organisation keep them committed.

Professional Development and Growth

Investing in the professional development of musicians, staff, and volunteers is vital for cultivating artistic excellence, ensuring operational efficiency, and nurturing a vibrant and cohesive organisational culture. This entails offering workshops, masterclasses, or mentoring programmes to help musicians refine their skills, explore new repertoire, or develop leadership qualities. Staff members benefit from training in specific areas relevant to their roles, such as project management, marketing, or fundraising. Volunteers can also be encouraged to develop their skills through targeted training sessions or by taking on more significant responsibilities within the organisation.

Creating a Positive Work Culture

A positive work culture is key to ensuring everyone feels valued, respected, and motivated to contribute their best efforts. This is achieved through communicating, facilitating collaboration, and creating opportunities for social interaction among musicians, staff, and volunteers. Emphasising the importance of diversity and inclusion creates a welcoming environment where everyone feels comfortable sharing their perspectives and suggestions.

Resolving Conflicts

Conflicts are unavoidable in any organisation, and art and culture institutions may even prove to be a more fertile ground for tensions to arise. The unique blend of creative personalities, sparkling minds, high-pressure situations, and varying opinions sometimes leads to disagreements and misunderstandings. Dissatisfaction with contracts or complaints about venues, programs, selection of guest conductors, soloists, and musicians are not uncommon (Sigurjónsson 2022). When conflicts arise, it is imperative to address them promptly and constructively, by facilitating open dialogues between the parties involved, offering mediation or conflict resolution training, and implementing clear policies to guide behaviour and expectations. Management's fair and transparent handling of conflicts helps restore harmony and maintain a positive working environment. Managing human resources and conflict resolution in the framework of an industry primarily based on the open expression of emotions requires a delicate balance of skill, empathy, and foresight. By focusing on hiring the right people, providing comprehensive training and onboarding, building a positive work culture, and addressing conflicts promptly and constructively, orchestras ensure that their musicians, staff, and volunteers are well-equipped to work together seamlessly and contribute to the organisation's artistic and operational success. Ultimately, professional growth opportunities and the well-being of personnel strengthen not only the ensemble's performance on stage but also its overall impact and resilience.

Succession Planning: Continuity and Stability

Special consideration must be given to the need for careful succession planning, both for the CEO and the artistic leadership, as well as the section principals, to avoid harming the continuity and stability of a musical organisation. This section covers the extreme importance of succession planning, outlining the steps involved in creating a comprehensive plan and offering practical guidance on how to navigate the challenges associated with leadership transitions.

Succession planning involves the strategic identification of individuals with the potential to take on critical leadership roles within an organisation, to preserve continuity, agility and resilience, and a culture of growth and innovation. This includes the roles of the executive director and artistic director but also other critical positions such as principal conductor, concertmaster, and department heads. Typically, a robust succession plan serves as a strong assurance to minimise disruption during transition periods, preserving both the artistic vision and operational efficiency. A well-thought-out succession plan begins with a clear understanding of the organisation's needs, values, and strategic objectives. It is essential to consider the unique characteristics, including size, resources, and artistic direction, when identifying potential successors and assessing their suitability for leadership roles. The main scope of this approach is to choose candidates who possess the necessary skills, experience, and qualities to lead the organisation effectively, but also to mitigate the uncertainties that may arise from an extended period of interregnum.

Developing a succession plan involves several key steps:

1 **Assessing Current Leadership:** Identify the strengths and weaknesses of the existing leadership team and highlight any gaps or areas for improvement. This assessment provides insights into the skills and competencies required for future leaders.

2 **Identifying Potential Successors:** Create a list of internal and external candidates who possess the desired skills, experience, and qualities for leadership roles. This list should be regularly updated to account for changes in personnel and organisational needs or objectives.

3 **Developing a Leadership Pipeline:** Implement strategies to develop the talents of potential successors (mentoring, job rotation, and targeted professional development opportunities). This approach prepares candidates for leadership roles and facilitates a smooth transition when the time comes for them to step up.

4 **Creating a Transition Plan:** Develop a detailed plan outlining the steps and timeline for the leadership transition process. This plan includes information on the roles and responsibilities of the outgoing and incoming leaders, as well as any necessary resources required during the transition period.

5 **Communicating the Plan:** Keep stakeholders informed about the succession plan, including the board, staff, musicians, and patrons. Transparent communication helps to manage expectations and maintain trust during times of change.

6 **Evaluating and Refining the Plan:** Regularly review the succession plan and adjust it to ensure its effectiveness and relevance. This ongoing process enables the organisation to stay ahead of changes in the industry and adapt to new situations.

One of the challenges associated with succession planning is managing the emotional aspects of leadership transitions. It is crucial to approach these transitions with sensitivity and empathy, acknowledging the contributions of outgoing leaders while also considering the fresh perspectives and ideas of incoming leaders. A culture of openness and support allows for the successful navigation of the complexities of leadership transitions.

H. THE ROLE OF UNIONS

Introduction and Overview of Unions

Unions, an integral yet frequently overlooked part of the global music landscape,[26] provide a pivotal role in safeguarding the welfare of staff and musicians (work conditions, contracts, remuneration, health and safety, etc.). Originating in the late 19th century, unions emerged as a response to the harsh working conditions and low wages typically endured by workers, including musicians. They were conceived to serve as a collective voice for the often disparate and potentially disenfranchised individual musicians, providing them with the power to negotiate more favourable working conditions and salaries.

In the orchestral sphere, the inception of unions was a transformative development, reshaping the relationship between musicians and management. Prior to their existence, musicians, despite their high skill level and significant contribution to the arts, were often left vulnerable to financial instability and precarious employment conditions. Unions offered an avenue for musicians to seek redress and advocate for their rights collectively. The role of unions is varied and extends far beyond mere financial negotiations. They represent the interests of musicians, negotiate contractual agreements on their behalf, and seek to ensure fair treatment from management. The introduction of collective bargaining, a direct result of union influence, significantly altered the power dynamics between management and musicians. Collective bargaining is a process where the union and management negotiate terms of employment, including wages, working hours, working conditions and any other relevant terms and conditions. This has brought about considerable improvements in musicians' lives, including better pay, more reasonable working hours, and enhanced job security.[27]

Unions have been instrumental in advocating for better health and safety standards for musicians. They have made strides in campaigning for appropriate noise levels in rehearsals and performances, sufficient rest periods, and ensuring the provision of adequate physical conditions for musicians, such as chair ergonomics and room temperatures.

In essence, unions have served as a pivotal bridge between management and musicians, mitigating potential conflicts and fostering a cooperative atmosphere. They have been instrumental in initiating dialogue, facilitating negotiations, and resolving disagreements, leading to a more harmonious and productive working environment. As such, understanding the role and function of unions is fundamental to comprehending the broader orchestral ecosystem, particularly given the complexities and potential tensions inherent in the management-musician relationship. This interaction and negotiation of power, represented through the existence and activities of unions, offer a fascinating lens through which to view the operational intricacies inherent within such ensembles, inextricably linking labour relations to the art of music-making.

Unions and Management: A Complex Relationship

The relationship between unions and the management team is complex, characterised by a delicate equilibrium of cooperation and conflict, negotiation and tensions, disagreements and mutual understanding. While the union represents the collective interests of musicians and functions as their advocate, the management is charged with the responsibility of ensuring the overall operational efficiency and financial viability. This dichotomy creates a unique interplay of power and negotiation, with both entities needing to balance their respective interests and objectives against the broader goal of a common success. One of the most prominent facets of this relationship is the process of collective bargaining. This is a negotiation process where unions and management arrive at agreements concerning terms of employment, including wages, working conditions, working hours, etc. Collective bargaining is central to the relationship between unions and management, as it provides a structured and formalised forum for both parties to articulate their concerns and find an acceptable middle ground. However, these negotiations are often challenging and fraught with tension, as unions strive to secure the best possible conditions for musicians, while management balances these demands with financial sustainability.

Another critical aspect of the relationship between unions and management is the negotiation of contracts. Contracts typically detail the terms of employment, including remuneration, bonuses if any, performance assessment process, working hours, health and safety provisions, and other employment benefits and duties. These contracts, often renegotiated every few years, are a significant focus of union and management interaction. The negotiation process can be intense, with unions pushing for improvements and better terms for musicians.

The relationship between unions and management is further complicated by the precarious nature of employment in the music industry. Many musicians work on a freelance basis, leading to a lack of job security and unpredictable income in a highly competitive market that requires an ever-expanding host of skills beyond their creative specialisations (Walzer 2020). Unions play a vital role in advocating for these musicians, ensuring that they receive fair treatment and are protected from exploitation.[28] However, this creates tension with management, particularly in situations where financial resources are limited and, perhaps, decreasing.

The role of unions extends beyond negotiation and advocacy. They also play a crucial role in dispute resolution. In instances of conflict or disagreement between musicians and management, the union often steps in to mediate and resolve the issue. This function is critical in maintaining a harmonious working environment, as unresolved conflicts negatively impact the performances and reputation.

Yet, it's not always a tale of contention. There are moments of synergy, where unions and management collaboratively work towards shared objectives, such as promoting the brand, advocating for music education, and fundraising. These collaborative efforts underscore the mutual interdependence of unions and management and highlight the necessity for a functional, cooperative relationship between the two. Unions also play a significant role in educating musicians about their rights and responsibilities. This educational role is especially important in helping young and emerging musicians navigate the complexities of the music industry. Management, on the other hand, also benefits from a knowledgeable and informed workforce, as this facilitates more effective communication and negotiation processes.

The relationship between unions and the management team is complex and not always an easy one. It is characterised by an intricate dance of power and negotiation, conflict, and cooperation. Understanding this relationship is crucial, as it illuminates the challenges inherent in the management of orchestras, offering a lens into the complexity of labour relations within the music industry. It underscores the balance that must be struck between advocating for the rights and welfare of musicians and ensuring the financial and operational viability. It is a balance that requires skill, understanding, and a mutual commitment to the shared goal of producing and promoting exceptional music.

Union–Orchestra Relationship Frameworks Around the World

The relationship frameworks of unions and orchestras vary greatly around the world, reflecting the diversity in social, economic, and political contexts, cultural norms, regulatory frameworks and, above all, historical backgrounds. In this section, we explore the distinct nature of these relationships in six regions: the United States, Europe, the Gulf countries, South Korea, Japan, and Australia.

1 In the **United States**, a more corporatist model is generally observed. American orchestras, like other sectors of the American economy, operate within a robust unionised environment (by professional activities or categories of activities – hence the corporatist model) characterised by collective bargaining. The American Federation of Musicians (AFM), originally established in 1896, represents professional orchestra musicians, and contracts are negotiated and disputes resolved through this body. These contracts encompass a wide range of conditions, from salaries and benefits to working conditions and job security. The rigidity of these contracts sometimes leads to high-profile disputes, as seen in various strikes over the years. However, the strength of the unions also provides significant protection for musicians, offering a higher degree of stability and security within a volatile industry.

2 In contrast, **European** orchestras generally operate within a different model. While situations vary across countries, unions are typically present and actively engaged, their role is less centralised and more diversified than in the US (i.e., more generalist, less focused on professions or categories), reflecting both the heterogeneity of Europe's sociopolitical landscape and its pluralistic unions model. In some countries, such as Germany and Austria, arts and culture institutions often benefit from substantial public funding, resulting in greater job security for musicians and less contentious union–management relationships – with musicians representing the unions that sit in the board or the management committee. In others, such as the UK, orchestras commonly follow a mixed funding model, leading to a different dynamic between unions and management. Here, the Musicians' Union (MU) advocates for musicians, but the relationships are less formalised than in the US, with a greater emphasis on individual orchestras and their specific contexts.

3   In the **Gulf countries**, along with several other regions, the presence of unions is not as pronounced or sometimes entirely absent. Here, orchestras usually function within a unique "sort of" patronage system. Contrary to common misconceptions, it is not royal families or affluent individuals acting as benefactors. Instead, the orchestras are initiated, owned, and financially supported, directly or indirectly, predominantly by institutional patrons such as governments and government-funded organisations. These institutions foster a cultural environment that encourages the growth and flourishing of arts and culture. Consequently, the concept of unionisation is less applicable within this context. Musicians' working conditions and remunerations are not subject to individual whims but follow structured, institutional policies. While the absence of unions might suggest potential vulnerability in terms of employment security and bargaining power for musicians (especially if looked at from a Western point of view that is used to 130 years of unionised background), the government patronage model in these countries often offers substantial opportunities ruled by clear policies and procedures. The generous funding from governments and/or governmental organisations leads to a supportive environment that encourages artistic development. However, the dynamics of such a system vastly differ from the union–orchestra relationship frameworks common in the West, highlighting the diversity and complexity of management models worldwide.

4   In East Asia, and specifically **South Korea**, the union–orchestra relationship framework again presents a distinct model. South Korea has a vibrant classical music scene, with numerous orchestras and a highly appreciative audience. Yet, the presence and influence of musician's unions are notably different from their Western counterparts. The unionisation of musicians is relatively recent, with the Korean Symphony Orchestra's musicians forming the country's first orchestra union in 2007. The orchestra unions often function within a complex sociocultural environment that intertwines Confucian work ethics with a modern emphasis on workers' rights. As such, the unions frequently encounter the challenge of striking a delicate balance between advocating for their members and maintaining harmonious relationships with management, a dynamic that is quite distinctive from the more confrontational stance often observed in the West. The unions do negotiate contracts and working conditions, but these negotiations are often nuanced by cultural values and norms that prioritise cooperation and consensus-building. South Korean orchestras, much like their counterparts in Japan, operate within a mixed funding model. They receive substantial public support while also seeking private funding and revenue from ticket sales and other entrepreneurial activities. This funding model impacts the union–orchestra relationship, as

both sides need to navigate the pressures of financial sustainability while ensuring fair remuneration and working conditions for musicians. In contrast to the corporatist model of the US, the diversified model in Europe, and the institutional patronage model in the Gulf countries, the South Korean case illustrates another variant of the union–orchestra relationship. The cultural context, historical development, and funding structure all influence how unions operate and interact with orchestras.

5   In **Japan**, the relationship between orchestras and unions is an intriguing reflection of the country's unique sociocultural landscape, characterised by a blend of time-honoured traditions and modern sensibilities. Unions do exist within the orchestral sphere, but they are not as prevalent or influential as their Western counterparts. The Japanese orchestras operate within an ethos heavily influenced by the *Nemawashi* approach, a deeply ingrained aspect of Japanese culture. This approach is based on informal, behind-the-scenes consensus-building, which often precedes formal negotiations and decision-making. In practice, this results in a collaborative environment that respects the rights and roles of musicians but also places significant emphasis on harmony, mutual understanding, and maintaining group cohesion. Conflicts and disputes are seen as disruptions to this harmony and are therefore avoided where possible. Consequently, high-profile disputes and strikes, as seen in other parts of the world, are relatively rare within orchestras. The nuanced and complex union–orchestra dynamics, therefore, offer valuable insights into how cultural norms and values shape industrial relations within the orchestral sector.

BOX 5.8 *NEMAWASHI*: A JAPANESE WORK ETHOS

Nemawashi (根回し or ねまわし) is a traditional Japanese approach to decision-making and consensus-building. The term literally translates to "preparing the roots" and originates from the practice of gardening, where it refers to the process of preparing the roots of a plant or tree before transplanting it. In a business context, *Nemawashi* involves gathering the support of key stakeholders prior to a decision being formally proposed. It is a process of informal, behind-the-scenes discussions and negotiations, allowing for concerns to be addressed and consensus to be built before a formal meeting takes place. This helps the smooth implementation of decisions and reduces the likelihood of opposition. *Nemawashi* is reflective of the emphasis on harmony and consensus in Japanese society. See Machizawa (2013).

6   In contrast, the musical landscape in **Australia** presents yet another distinct model shaped by the country's sociopolitical history and geographical context. Orchestras operate within a broader national framework characterised by robust union representation and a strong culture of collective bargaining. The Media, Entertainment and Arts Alliance (MEAA),[29] the principal body representing musicians, plays a central role in this landscape. The relationship between unions and orchestras is formalised, with contracts typically negotiated collectively. However, Australia's geographical position and unique cultural context also shape these relationships. This necessitates a balance between adhering to global industry standards and addressing national considerations, which include everything from the country's geographic dispersion to its cultural diversity. For instance, the negotiation of contracts might need to account for the logistical challenges of touring within a geographically vast country, or the promotion of local, native cultural forms within the broader repertoire. The Australian case, therefore, underscores the importance of context in shaping union–orchestra relationships, and the ways in which these relationships need to adapt to specific local realities.

These variances in union–orchestra relationships across the globe highlight both the complexity of the orchestral landscape and the importance of context in understanding these dynamics. Each model presents its unique features and background, and navigating them requires a deep understanding of the sociopolitical, historical, economic, and cultural contexts.

A comparison table summarising these different frameworks is provided as follows:

Region	Union-Orchestra Relationship	Key Characteristics
United States	Corporatist Model	• Robust union representation through AFM • Centralised collective bargaining with clearly defined contracts • Better degree of job security, balanced by possibility of high-profile disputes • Union protection offering some stability in a volatile industry

Region	Union-Orchestra Relationship	Key Characteristics
Europe	Generalist Models	• Varied union roles reflecting the heterogeneity of Europe's sociopolitical landscape, and unions are more generalist (not focused on professions) • In countries with significant public funding such as Germany and Austria, union–management relationships tend to be less contentious • In countries such as the UK with mixed funding models, relationships are less formalised, with an emphasis on individual organisations and their specific contexts
Gulf Countries	Government Patronage Model	• Absence or minimal presence of union representation • Orchestras funded directly or indirectly by institutional patrons (governments, government-funded organisations) • Working conditions and remuneration follow structured, institutional policies • Generous funding from institutional patrons encourages artistic development
South Korea	Confucian Modern Hybrid Model	• Unionisation of musicians is relatively recent; first orchestra union formed in 2007 • Unions function within a complex sociocultural environment, balancing worker rights with Confucian work ethics • Cooperative and consensus-building approach to negotiations • Orchestras operate within a mixed funding model, combining public support and private funding
Japan	Nemawashi Model	• Nemawashi approach to consensus-building guides negotiation and decision-making • Emphasis on harmony and mutual understanding, with disputes and strikes being relatively rare
Australia	Balanced Model	• Strong union representation through MEAA and its musicians' sections (SOMA, TOMA, MA) • Formalised contracts negotiated collectively • Contextual balance between global industry standards and national considerations

In conclusion, the relationship frameworks of unions and orchestras around the world exhibit great diversity, reflecting the unique conditions and contexts in each region. Understanding these frameworks is essential for effectively managing and advocating for musicians' rights and welfare.

Unions in the Future of Orchestras

As the classical music industry keeps evolving, the role of unions in the future of orchestras has become a subject of debates. The dynamism of the sector, coupled with the impact of macro factors such as economic flux and technological innovations (if not disruptions), suggests a future that will require adaptability, resilience, and forward thinking from all stakeholders, unions included.

Within the United States, the future may see a shift towards more flexible union arrangements. The existing model that provides protection and stability for musicians may need to pivot to more fluid structures that accommodate the changing nature of work, the increasing prevalence of gig economy practices, and the new forms of performing arts allowed by the digital transformation of the industry. This may entail a rethinking of the collective bargaining process, with a shift of focus on achieving a balance between security and flexibility, to better prepare orchestras to adapt to changing economic circumstances, audiences' tastes, and technological background.

In Europe, the diversity of union models across countries presents a unique set of challenges. However, pan-European policies and initiatives may lead to greater harmonisation of practices across the region. The European group of the International Federation of Musicians, for example, might play a more prominent role in advocating for common standards and practices across the continent. This could enhance the mobility of musicians within Europe, while developing a consistent approach to union representation and musicians' rights.

In the Gulf countries, where unions are currently absent or have a minimal role, there could be an emergence of new forms of musician representation and advocacy: this might take the form of professional associations or guilds that cater to the specific needs and contexts of the region. Such intermediary bodies could promote fair working conditions and adequate compensation for musicians, while also liaising with patrons and government bodies to fertilise the growth and sustainability of the musical scene overall.

Technological advancements will undoubtedly have a significant impact on the future role of unions. The digital transformation has already begun to reshape the classical music industry, from the proliferation of audio streaming services to the advent of video platforms that offer recorded or real-time virtual performances. And not least, the digital transformation of the industry clearly disregards borders and therefore blurs the distinction between national regulations, making it even more complex to protect the rights of musicians. Unions will need to adapt their practices and policies to account for these changes, advocating for fair compensation for digital performances and ensuring that musicians' rights are protected nationally and globally.[30]

The growing awareness of social issues, such as diversity, equity, and inclusion, will likely influence the role of unions in the future. Unions will have a critical part to play in this respect, challenging traditional norms and biases.

The future of orchestras will invariably be shaped by the interactions between various stakeholders, with unions playing a role in this ecosystem. As catalysts for change and advocates for musicians, unions will need to navigate this complex landscape with foresight and adaptability, working collaboratively with managers, funders, and policy-makers to ensure a vibrant and sustainable future for the classical music industry.

Conclusion

As this exploration of the role of unions concludes, it becomes evident that the relationship with unions is layered with complexities deeply embedded in the sociocultural and economic fabrics of their operating contexts. Unions play a pivotal role in advocating for musicians' rights, negotiating fair wages and working conditions, and providing a collective voice to the artists. However, their influence extends far beyond these core functions, impacting the strategic management and operations.

The intricacies of this relationship are further magnified when examined from a global perspective. The comparative analysis of the relationship frameworks of unions and orchestras revealed a rich tapestry of practices and norms, shaped by the unique cultural, economic, and legislative landscapes of different regions. The corporatist model prevalent in the United States, the diverse European models, the absence of unions in regions such as the Gulf countries, and the connections with specific features of the local culture in South Korea and Japan, or the local geography in Australia, all paint a picture of an industry grappling with the complexities of balancing artistic integrity, economic viability, and the welfare of musicians.

Looking towards the future, the role of unions will continue to evolve in response to macro-level changes. Technological developments, sociocultural shifts, and economic fluctuations will all influence the dynamics of this relationship. Unions will need to navigate these complexities with adaptability, innovativeness, and a commitment to safeguarding the interests of musicians.

The role of unions is a topic of profound importance and complexity. It is a field ripe for further research, dialogue, and action, necessitating a deeper understanding and appreciation of its nuances by researchers, practitioners, and stakeholders alike. The classical music world is at a crossroads between several influences – tradition and ultra-modernity, ageing audiences and digital transformation, to name a few – all contributing to the harmony and dissonance that define the orchestra's collective voice. The future of this relationship, much like the future of the industry, will undoubtedly be a fascinating interplay of challenge and opportunity, discord and harmony.

CASE STUDY 5.5

Wage Negotiations and Financial Sustainability

To illustrate the complexities of the union–orchestra relationship and its impact on financial and operational viability, let's consider a hypothetical case study involving the fictitious *Metropolis Symphony Ensemble* (MSE) in the United States.

MSE is a well-established large chamber ensemble with an annual operating budget of $20 million, approximately 40% of which is derived from ticket sales, 30% from private donations, 20% from government, state, and county subsidies, and the remaining 10% from other sources such as recording royalties and educational programmes. Musicians' salaries, which are negotiated through collective bargaining with the local chapter of the American Federation of Musicians (AFM), constitute approximately 40% of the annual operating budget.

In the recent contract negotiation, the musicians' union has proposed a 10% wage increase over the next three years, citing the rising cost of living in Metropolis. If approved, this would increase the ensemble's annual operating expenses by approximately $800,000 by the end of the three-year period. Given the tight budget, the management is concerned about the financial viability of this proposal, although being aware of the rising costs of living in the Metropolis area.

To assess the financial implications, the management conducts a detailed analysis. First, they project future revenues, assuming a modest

2% annual growth in ticket sales and flat private donations and government funding. Under this scenario, the total revenue increases by about $400,000 over the next three years, falling short of the $800,000 additional cost incurred by the proposed wage increase.

The management then considers potential cost-saving measures. Cutting back on performance schedules or educational programmes could adversely impact ticket sales and community support. Reducing administrative or marketing costs could limit the operational efficiency and visibility. Reducing musicians' salaries is not an option given the current union negotiations.

In the face of the impending impasse, one might ask, what solutions could be proposed to resolve the situation. Given the constraints of the existing financial structure and the legitimate concerns of the musicians, the management team needs to devise a strategy that respects both the sustainability of the ensemble and the financial welfare of the musicians. The management, thus, proposes a compromise that seeks a balance between the union's demands and the ensemble's financial viability: a 7% wage increase over three years. This figure is less than the 10% initially proposed by the union, but it is arrived at after careful consideration of various factors:

1   A 7% increase would cost the ensemble approximately $560,000 over three years, which is closer to the projected revenue increase of $400,000. This makes the wage proposal more sustainable, yet still responsive to the cost-of-living increase raised by the musicians.
2   To further offset this wage increase and bolster the organisation's financial health, the management proposes an intensified fundraising campaign. This campaign would target not just larger donations from affluent patrons, but also smaller, recurring donations from a broader base of supporters, thereby increasing the financial resilience. Similarly, musicians will be requested to actively promote the ensemble via their personal social media accounts to increase overall visibility.
3   The management team suggests implementing cost-saving measures in non-core areas, which could include streamlining administrative processes or reducing non-essential expenses. These savings, although small individually, could collectively create a buffer for the additional wage costs.
4   Slightly increasing the number of concerts per year is a measure that the management team is prepared to propose to bring more ticket sales.

5 Recognising the inherent uncertainties in revenue and cost projections, the management introduces a contingency clause in the contract. This clause would allow for a wage adjustment based on the actual financial performance over the three years, ensuring that both the management and the musicians share the financial risks and rewards.

With this compromise, the management not only addresses the immediate wage negotiation issue but also initiates longer-term measures to improve financial sustainability. This careful and holistic approach is accepted by the union, who appreciates the management's transparency and willingness to share the financial risk. This case exemplifies the importance of a nuanced, strategic approach in managing union–orchestra relationships, highlighting the balance between financial sustainability and fair remuneration in this unique industry.

QUESTIONS:

1 When evaluating the MSE's proposed compromise, what factors should be considered in understanding the implications of a 7% wage increase over three years versus the initial 10% proposed by the union? How might this affect the ensemble's relationships with its musicians and its public image?

2 Reflecting on the strategy of intensified fundraising, what are the potential benefits and risks associated with targeting smaller, recurring donations from a broader base of supporters? What tactics can be employed to ensure the success of such a campaign, considering the diverse interests of potential donors?

3 In contemplating the cost-saving measures proposed by the management, what criteria should be used to identify 'non-core' areas that can be streamlined or reduced? How can the potential impact of these cuts on the operations and reputation be mitigated?

4 Analyse the effectiveness of introducing a contingency clause in the wage contract. How could such a clause influence the dynamic of the relationship between the management and the musicians' union? What are the potential long-term implications of this clause for the financial sustainability and the musicians' job satisfaction?

5 In a broader context, how might the strategies employed in this case study be adapted to other cultural organisations facing similar financial pressures and union negotiations? How might different socioeconomic and cultural contexts influence the applicability of these strategies?

Box 5.9 Expanding Perspectives: Review Questions

1 Discuss how the artistic vision and strategic planning are linked and contribute to its growth, audience appeal, and overall success. In this context, evaluate the potential benefits, challenges, and impacts of international collaborations and touring.

2 Explore the vital role of effective financial management in the survival and resilience of orchestras. How do strategic budgeting, diversified fundraising, and the pursuit of innovative revenue opportunities work together to strengthen the financial position? Reflect on the role of collaborations with cultural institutions and community engagement in fortifying proposals and broadening funding sources.

3 With the backdrop of an orchestra's unique cost-revenue structure, analyse how financial risk management strategies and innovative revenue-generation methods can help maintain a balance between artistic ambition and financial sustainability.

4 How does a well-managed operational framework influence the ability to successfully execute artistic programming and audience development initiatives? Discuss the challenges and opportunities presented by touring and external performances, with a particular focus on logistics management and venue adaptation.

5 Shifting demographic and evolving consumption habits are a typical condition of the contemporary music industry. How can ensembles adapt to these changes to develop their audiences? Discuss the role of innovative programming in this context. Finally, explore the critical role of human resources management, board relations, and the involvement of unions in fostering a healthy, resilient organisation.

NOTES

1 Some of the actions presented in this list, particularly those related to sponsorship or partnerships with private companies, may have been modified or terminated by the time this book is published. The information and details in this list come from public sources, mainly news websites, magazines, and press releases.

2 An indispensable resource to gain deeper insights into strategic planning in not-for-profit organisations is Allison and Kaye (2015).

3 During a lecture on aircraft system engineering at MIT in the Fall 2005 semester, Professor Cones highlighted a common frustration and confusion experienced by

engineers when they have to report to two different managers and demonstrate loyalty to multiple individuals (OpenCourseWare 2008). While this situation is exceptional in most industries and often occurs during special projects under matrix management framework, it is, conversely, a standard practice within orchestras.

4 The key idea developed by Walmsley (2019) is that audience engagement is part of a process where the performing artists (or institutions) and the audience exchange value.

5 We refer here to the legal streaming platforms, for the actual impact of illegal streaming platforms is harder to assess as they harmed intellectual property rights while stimulating the audience to pivot to new forms of cultural content consumption.

6 Remarkable overviews and analysis of cultural organisations management are provided by DeVereaux (2019, 2023) and Saintilan and Schreiber (2018).

7 There is a wealth of literature on how the Covid-19 pandemic has transformed orchestra management. Beyond the exceptional nature of the events and the transformations introduced as a result of an unprecedented increase in the usage of technological means, this theme is more suited for specific study than for a practical management handbook.

8 For example, during the pandemic, production of high-quality digital content for online media, subscriptions or pay-per-view access to online performances allowed organisations to maintain a connection with audiences and yield much-needed revenue in challenging times.

9 Although the publication is related to the cultural industries overall, Morrow (2018) provides an excellent comprehensive *summa* of the artist management's role in the industry, from both standpoints of artist and artist manager relationship, and artist manager to industry connection and implications.

10 For a thorough study of fundraising in the cultural industry, including its practical aspects, see Wright, Walmsley, and Simmons (2022).

11 Details for Belgium, The Netherlands, and UK cases are based upon Herman (2021).

12 Nonetheless, data reported here are quite aligned with (and not far from) Flanagan (2012), Giraud Voss (2020), and Herman (2021) – at least as "orders of magnitude." We are well aware that financials of single organisations may substantially diverge from the models shown in the table depending on a variety of factors (size, type – fully professional or semi-professional or amateur – local vs national, etc.)

13 From both or either private sector and/or public authorities.

14 A broad framework for pricing in art is available in Rhine and Pension (2022).

15 Although centred on a very different industry, Gluyas's paper (2015) boldly underlines the crucial role played by communication in operations management, as it enables effective teamwork, cooperation, and coordination in teams.

16 In addition, the selection of a guest conductor should consider the potential reactions of the orchestral body to the imposition of an external authority figure (Khodyakov 2014).

17 There is an extensive literature on musicians' specific health issues, but it falls outside the scope of this book. Interested readers will refer to the following publications: Gembris, Heye, and Seifert (2018), O'Brien, Driscoll, and Ackermann (2012), Raymond,

Romeo, and Kumke (2012), Sousa et al. (2017), and Laitinen (2005), among many others.

18 The importance of diversity for sustaining transformational leadership is highlighted by Boerner and Gebert (2012).

19 The fragmentation of the market should not be considered outside of the concentration effect that the major streaming platforms impose on the music industry overall (Im, Song, and Jung 2019).

20 Glenn McDonald's findings reveal a staggering growth in the number of music genres on Spotify. In 2018, he identified 1,742 genres (Johnston 2018), but by June 2023, that figure more than tripled to 6,234 (McDonald 2023).

21 For a detailed analysis of the difference between audience and community, see Borwick (2012). The author challenges traditional notions of arts management and audience development, advocating for a more community-centred approach that prioritises social impact.

22 A notable demonstration of community engagement is observed through the efforts of Conductor Ms. Speranza Scappucci, who not only captivates audiences through her uncommon, if not unique, Italian television show on classical music but also envisions demystifying opera for British audiences in her upcoming position (June 2023) as the first principal guest conductor of the Royal Opera House in London (Bryant 2023).

23 For data-driven segmentation and personalisation, see the remarkable contribution of Jansen and Salminen (2022).

24 Despite the potential offered by a data-driven approach, limited attention has been paid thus far to the study of repertoire. Notable exceptions are Zabanal (2021) and Pope (2019).

25 The concept of "ecology of participation" developed by Sutherland and Cartwright (2022) following a data-driven analysis is a useful tool to deepen this section of the analysis.

26 Literature on this subject is quite limited, and mostly, but not exclusively, focused on history. See Miller (2021), Spitzer (2012), Lizé, Greer, and Umney (2022), Moon (2012), Mazzola (1984), and Kraft (1995).

27 This latter point applies mainly to staff musicians (as opposed to freelancers).

28 As demonstrated by the French case of freelance artists (known as *intermittents du spectacle*), union involvement can be pivotal in shaping cultural landscapes. This unique system provides unemployment insurance for artists and technicians between projects, recognising the intermittent nature of performing arts work. Unions and stakeholders fiercely defended the system during recent scrutiny, staging demonstrations and strikes that underscored their influence. This example highlights how creative solutions address challenges in the arts sector. See Issehnane and Merchaoui (2020), Sigalo Santos (2014), and Grégoire (2013).

29 The MEAA has a musicians section that comprises the Symphony Orchestra Musician Association (SOMA), the Theatre Orchestra Musicians Association (TOMA), and, since December 2018, a trade union specifically for musicians, Musicians Australia (MA).

30 It is interesting to observe how unions are already grappling with a new type of demand from their members. In the United States, actors in the film industry, another pivotal component of the performing arts, have requested their union SAG-AFTRA, among other things, to safeguard them against the non-remunerated utilisation of their own past work to train Artificial Intelligence models (Pulliam-Moore 2023; Yandoli 2023).

BIBLIOGRAPHY

Aguiar, Luis, and Joel Waldfogel. 2018. "As Streaming Reaches Flood Stage, Does It Stimulate or Depress Music Sales?" *International Journal of Industrial Organization* 57 (March): 278–307. https://doi.org/10.1016/j.ijindorg.2017.06.004.

Ahrendt, Rebekah, Mark Ferraguto, and Damien Mahiet. 2014. *Music and Diplomacy from the Early Modern Era to the Present*. New York: Springer.

Allison, Michael, and Jude Kaye. 2015. *Strategic Planning for Nonprofit Organizations: A Practical Guide for Dynamic Times*. NJ: John Wiley & Sons.

Allmendinger, Jutta, J. Richard Hackman, and Erin V. Lehman. 1996. "Life and Work in Symphony Orchestras." *The Musical Quarterly* 80 (2): 194–219. https://doi.org/10.1093/mq/80.2.194.

Andreev, Mikhail A. 2021. "Organization and Conduct of Foreign Tours of the Moscow State Symphony Orchestra Headed by V. B. Dudarova in the 1970s." *History and Archives* 3: 65–75. https://doi.org/10.28995/2658-6541-2021-3-65-75.

Arditi, David. 2014. "Downloading Is Killing Music: The Recording Industry's Piracy Panic Narrative." edited by Victor Sarafian and Rosemary Findley. *Civilisations, The State of the Music Industry* 63: 13–32. https://publications.ut-capitole.fr/id/eprint/21698/1/Sarafian_21698.pdf#page=13.

Associated Press. 2008. "N.Y. Philharmonic Plays Concert in North Korea." *NBC News*. www.nbcnews.com/id/wbna23347082.

Baumgarth, Carsten, and Daragh O'Reilly. 2014. "Brands in the Arts and Culture Sector." edited by Carsten Baumgarth and Daragh O'Reilly. *Arts Marketing: An International Journal* 4 (1/2): 2–9. https://doi.org/10.1108/AM-08-2014-0028.

Bertolini, Daniel. 2018. "Management and Structure of the Symphony Orchestra: A Professional Orchestra Case-Study into the Techniques and Philosophy Applied Within the Industry." https://doi.org/10.13140/RG.2.2.30708.19846.

Boerner, Sabine, and Diether Gebert. 2012. "Fostering Artistic Ensemble Performance: Exploring the Role of Transformational Leadership: Fostering Artistic Ensemble Performance." *Nonprofit Management & Leadership* 22 (3): 347–365. https://doi.org/10.1002/nml.20058.

Borwick, Doug. 2012. *Building Communities, Not Audiences: The Future of the Arts in the United States*. Winston-Salem, NC: ArtsEngaged.

Bouder-Pailler, Danielle. 2008. "Personal Time and Social Time: Their Role in Live Performance Attendance." *International Journal of Arts Management* 10 (3): 38–48.

Bryant, Miranda. 2023. "'We Can't Just Be in Our Ivory Tower': The Italian Conductor Aiming to Open Up the Royal Opera House to Everyone." *The Guardian*, June 3. www.theguardian.com/music/2023/jun/03/we-cant-just-be-in-our-ivory-tower-the-italian-conductor-aiming-to-open-up-the-royal-opera-house-to-everyone.

Campelo, Adriana, and Cecilia Pasquinelli. 2017. "The Cultural Branding Matrix: Framing the Relation Between Cultural Institutions and City Branding." In *Handbook on Place Branding and Marketing*, 41–55. Edward Elgar Publishing. https://doi.org/10.4337/9781784718602.00012.

Cooper, Michael. 2016. "It's Official: Many Orchestras Are Now Charities." *The New York Times*, November 15. www.nytimes.com/2016/11/16/arts/music/its-official-many-orchestras-are-now-charities.html.

Cronin, Charles. 2014. "I Hear America Suing: Music Copyright Infringement in the Era of Electronic Sound." https://doi.org/10.2139/ssrn.2394339.

Datta, Hannes, George Knox, and Bart J. Bronnenberg. 2018. "Changing Their Tune: How Consumers' Adoption of Online Streaming Affects Music Consumption and Discovery." *Marketing Science* 37 (1): 5–21. https://doi.org/10.1287/mksc.2017.1051.

DeVereaux, Constance, ed. 2019. *Arts and Cultural Management: Sense and Sensibilities in the State of the Field*. New York: Routledge.

DeVereaux, Constance, ed. 2023. *Managing the Arts and Culture: Cultivating a Practice*. Abingdon, Oxon: Routledge.

Dollman, Emily. 2023. "Introduction." In *Opening Doors: Orchestras, Opera Companies and Community Engagement*, 1–17. London: Routledge. https://doi.org/10.4324/9781003198512-1.

Drucker, Peter Ferdinand. 1990. *Managing the Non-Profit Organization: Practices and Principles*. New York: HarperCollins.

Flanagan, Robert J. 2012. *The Perilous Life of Symphony Orchestras: Artistic Triumphs and Economic Challenges*. New Haven: Yale University Press.

Foley, Carmel, Caryn Holzman, and Stephen Wearing. 2007. "Moving Beyond Conspicuous Leisure Consumption: Adolescent Women, Mobile Phones and Public Space." *Leisure Studies* 26 (2): 179–192. https://doi.org/10.1080/02614360500418555.

Freer, Elisabeth, and Paul Evans. 2018. "Psychological Needs Satisfaction and Value in Students' Intentions to Study Music in High School." *Psychology of Music* 46 (6): 881–895. https://doi.org/10.1177/0305735617731613.

Gazley, Beth. 2010. "Linking Collaborative Capacity to Performance Measurement in Government – Nonprofit Partnerships." *Nonprofit and Voluntary Sector Quarterly* 39 (4): 653–673. https://doi.org/10.1177/0899764009360823.

Gembris, Heiner, Andreas Heye, and Andreas Seifert. 2018. "Health Problems of Orchestral Musicians from a Life-Span Perspective: Results of a Large-Scale Study." *Music & Science* 1 (January): 1–20. https://doi.org/10.1177/2059204317739801.

Giraud Voss, Z. 2020. "Orchestra Facts: 2006–2014." *Americanorchestras.org*. https://americanorchestras.org/orchestra-facts/.

Glückler, Johannes, and Robert Panitz. 2023. "Live Music in the Time of Corona: On the Resilience and Impact of a Philharmonic Orchestra on the Urban Economy." *Sustainability: Science Practice and Policy* 15 (4): 3611. https://doi.org/10.3390/su15043611.

Gluyas, Heather. 2015. "Effective Communication and Teamwork Promotes Patient Safety." *Nursing Standard: Official Newspaper of the Royal College of Nursing* 29 (49): 50–57. https://doi.org/10.7748/ns.29.49.50.e10042.

Grégoire, Mathieu. 2013. "Les intermittents du spectacle." *Mouvements* 73 (1). La Découverte: 97–104. https://doi.org/10.3917/mouv.073.0097.

Herman, Arne. 2021. *Orchestra Management: Models and Repertoires for the Symphony Orchestra*, 1st ed. Abingdon, Oxon and New York: Routledge.

Hufton, Dame Olwen. 2008. "Faith, Hope and Money: The Jesuits and the Genesis of Fundraising for Education, 1550–1650." *Historical Research: The Bulletin of the Institute of Historical Research* 81 (214): 585–609. https://doi.org/10.1111/j.1468-2281.2008.00456.x.

Hüttermann, Hendrik, and Sabine Boerner. 2011. "Fostering Innovation in Functionally Diverse Teams: The Two Faces of Transformational Leadership." *European Journal of Work and Organizational Psychology* 20 (6): 833–854. https://doi.org/10.1080/1359432X.2010.524412.

Im, Hyunsuk, Haeyeop Song, and Jaemin Jung. 2019. "The Effect of Streaming Services on the Concentration of Digital Music Consumption." *Information Technology & People* 33 (1): 160–179. https://doi.org/10.1108/ITP-12-2017-0420.

Issehnane, Sabina, and Wided Merchaoui. 2020. "Trajectoires des intermittents du spectacle indemnisés." *Culture Chiffres* 4 (4): 1–36. https://doi.org/10.3917/culc.204.0001.

Janičić, Radmila. 2021. "Strategic Marketing Planning in Development of Arts and Cultural Institutions." In *40th International Conference on Organizational Science Development Values Competencies and Changes in Organizations*, 351–363. University of Maribor Press. https://doi.org/10.18690/978-961-286-442-2.25.

Jansen, Bernard J., and Joni Salminen. 2022. *Data-Driven Personas*. New York: Springer.

Johnston, Maura. 2018. "How Spotify Discovers the Genres of Tomorrow." *Spotify for Artists*. https://artists.spotify.com/blog/how-spotify-discovers-the-genres-of-tomorrow.

Jyrämä, Annukka, Sami Kajalo, Tanja Johansson, and Anni Sirèn. 2015. "Arts Organizations and Branding: Creating a New Joint Brand for Three Arts Organizations." *The Journal of Arts Management, Law, and Society* 45 (3): 193–206. https://doi.org/10.1080/10632921.2015.1062444.

Khodyakov, Dmitry. 2014. "Getting in Tune: A Qualitative Analysis of Guest Conductor – Musicians Relationships in Symphony Orchestras." *Poetics* 44 (June): 64–83. https://doi.org/10.1016/j.poetic.2014.04.004.

Kostylev, Sergey V. 2015. "Art Management as a Complex System of Managerial Activity in the Field of Culture, Art and Education." *Journal of Siberian Federal University. Humanities & Social Sciences* 8 (8): 1611–1624. https://doi.org/10.17516/1997-1370-2015-8-8-1611-1624.

Kraft, James P. 1995. "Artists as Workers: Musicians and Trade Unionism in America, 1880–1917." *The Musical Quarterly* 79 (3): 512–543.

Laitinen, Heikki. 2005. "Factors Affecting the Use of Hearing Protectors Among Classical Music Players." *Noise & Health* 7 (26): 21. https://doi.org/10.4103/1463-1741.31643.

Lee, Jonathan F. 2018. "Purchase, Pirate, Publicize: Private-Network Music Sharing and Market Album Sales." *Information Economics and Policy* 42 (March): 35–55. https://doi.org/10.1016/j.infoecopol.2018.01.001.

Lizé, Wenceslas, Ian Greer, and Charles Umney. 2022. "Artistic Work Intermediaries as Industrial Relations Institutions: The Case of Musicians." *Economic and Industrial Democracy* 43 (2): 793–809. https://doi.org/10.1177/0143831X20945789.

Lowe, Geoffrey. 2012. "Lessons for Teachers: What Lower Secondary School Students Tell Us About Learning a Musical Instrument." *International Journal of Music Education* 30 (3): 227–243. https://doi.org/10.1177/0255761411433717.

Machizawa, Sayaka. 2013. "Nemawashi (根回し)." In *The Encyclopedia of Cross-Cultural Psychology*. Wiley. https://doi.org/10.1002/9781118339893.wbeccp380.

Mall, Peter. 2020. "Reaching Out to the Orchestra – Concert Visits as a Curricular Link to Extracurricular Musical Activities?" *Hungarian Educational Research Journal* 10 (2): 123–130. https://doi.org/10.1556/063.2020.00013.

Marín, Miguel Ángel, and University of La Rioja. 2018. "Challenging the Listener: How to Change Trends in Classical Music Programming." *Resonancias: Revista de Investigación Musical* 42 (June): 115–130. https://doi.org/10.7764/res.2018.42.6.

Mazzola, Sandy Raymond. 1984. "When Music Is Labor. Chicago Bands and Orchestras and the Origins of the Chicago Federation of Musicians, 1880–1902." Ann Arbor: Northern Illinois University.

McDonald, Glenn. 2023. "Every Noise at Once." https://everynoise.com/.

Miller, Rachel. 2021. "Talent on Strike: The Musicians' Union and the Early Agonies of the Creative Class." *Labor Studies in Working-Class History of the Americas* 18 (3): 8–36. https://doi.org/10.1215/15476715-9061395.

Montoro-Pons, Juan D., María Caballer-Tarazona, and Manuel Cuadrado-García. 2021. "From Pirates to Subscribers: 20 Years of Music Consumption Research." *International Journal of Consumer Studies* 45 (4): 690–718. https://doi.org/10.1111/ijcs.12660.

Moon, Krystyn R. 2012. "On a Temporary Basis: Immigration, Labor Unions, and the American Entertainment Industry, 1880s–1930s." *Journal of American History* 99 (3): 771–792. https://doi.org/10.1093/jahist/jas413.

Morrow, Guy. 2018. *Artist Management: Agility in the Creative and Cultural Industries.* London and New York: Routledge.

Ng, Chi-Hung Clarence, and Kay Hartwig. 2011. "Teachers' Perceptions of Declining Participation in School Music." *Research Studies in Music Education* 33 (2): 123–142. https://doi.org/10.1177/1321103X11423598.

O'Brien, Ian, Tim Driscoll, and Bronwen Ackermann. 2012. "Hearing Conservation and Noise Management Practices in Professional Orchestras." *Journal of Occupational and Environmental Hygiene* 9 (10): 602–608. https://doi.org/10.1080/15459624.2012.715519.

Onditi, David. 2020. *Symphony Orchestra Challenge.* 1. Auflage, digitale Originalausgabe. München: GRIN Verlag.

OpenCourseWare, M. I. T. 2008. "Lec 19 | MIT 16.885J Aircraft Systems Engineering, Fall 2005." *Youtube.* www.youtube.com/watch?v=IHVf3ukiIiA.

O'Regan, Tom. 2002. "Too Much Culture, Too Little Culture: Trends and Issues for Cultural Policy-Making." *Media International Australia* 102 (1): 9–24. https://doi.org/10.1177/1329878X0210200104.

O'Reilly, Daragh, ed. 2014. *The Routledge Companion to Arts Marketing.* London and New York: Routledge.

Panasiuk, Valerii, Ihor Borko, Taisiia Khvostova, Andrii Maslov-Lysychkin, and Anastasiia Yermukanova. 2022. "Music as a Communication Factor in Foreign Policy." *Studies in Media and Communication* 10 (3): 160–167. https://doi.org/10.11114/smc. v10i3.5847.

Park, Hyun-Seung, and Hyeon-Cheol Kim. 2020. "Impact of Government Support on Performing Artists' Job and Life Satisfaction: Findings from The National Survey in Korea." *International Journal of Environmental Research and Public Health* 17 (20). https://doi.org/10.3390/ijerph17207545.

PBS. 2008. "The New York Philharmonic Live from North Korea." *Great Performances.* www.pbs.org/wnet/gperf/the-new-york-philharmonic-live-from-north-korea-introduction/157/.

Perry, Neil W., and Aram Sinnreich. 2022. "Global Music Piracy." In *Oxford Research Encyclopedia of Communication.* Oxford: Oxford University Press. https://doi.org/10.1093/acrefore/9780190228613.013.1038.

Pope, David A. 2019. "An Analysis of the Repertoire Performed by Youth Orchestras in the United States." *String Research Journal* 9 (1): 35–49. https://doi.org/10.1177/1948499219851378.

Pulliam-Moore, Charles. 2023. "Hundreds of Actors Are Ready to Strike If SAG-AFTRA Doesn't Secure a Truly 'Transformative Deal'." *The Verge.* www.theverge.com/2023/6/28/23776829/sag-aftra-strike-letter?ref=futuretools.io.

Raitaluoto, Teemu. 2023. "The Importance of Customer Segmentation in Growth Marketing." www.markettailor.io/blog/importance-of-customer-segmentation-in-growth-marketing.

Raymond, Delbert M., June Hart Romeo, and Karoline V. Kumke. 2012. "A Pilot Study of Occupational Injury and Illness Experienced by Classical Musicians." *Workplace Health & Safety* 60 (1): 19–24. https://doi.org/10.1177/216507991206000104.

Reesman, Ward M. 2019. "Music in the Digital Age: An Analysis of Declining Revenue in the U.S. Recorded Music Industry." University of South Dakota.

Rentschler, Ruth. 2014. *Arts Governance: People, Passion, Performance.* London: Routledge.

Rhine, Anthony, and Jay Pension. 2022. "Price and the Arts." In *How to Market the Arts: A Practical Approach for the 21st Century.* Oxford: Oxford University Press. https://doi.org/10.1093/oso/9780197556078.003.0014.

Rooksby, John, Timothy E. Smith, Alistair Morrison, Mattias Rost, and Matthew Chalmers. 2015. "Configuring Attention in the Multiscreen Living Room." In *ECSCW 2015: Proceedings of the 14th European Conference on Computer Supported Cooperative Work, 19–23 September 2015, Oslo, Norway,* 243–261. https://doi.org/10.1007/978-3-319-20499-4_13.

Saintilan, Paul, and David Schreiber. 2018. *Managing Organizations in the Creative Economy: Organizational Behaviour for the Cultural Sector.* Abingdon, Oxon and New York: Routledge.

Sigalo Santos, Luc. 2014. "Intermittence de L'emploi, Permanence Des Luttes: Le Cas Des Salariés Du Spectacle." *Revue Française de Socio-économie* 14 (2): 249. https://doi.org/10.3917/rfse.014.0249.

Sigurjónsson, Njörður. 2022. "Orchestra Leadership." In *Managing the Arts and Culture,* edited by Constance DeVereaux, 1st ed., 240–262. London: Routledge.

Sousa, Cláudia Maria, Jorge Pereira Machado, Henry Johannes Greten, and Daniela Coimbra. 2017. "Playing-Related Musculoskeletal Disorders of Professional Orchestra Musicians from the North of Portugal: Comparing String and Wind Musicians." *Acta Médica Portuguesa* 30 (4): 302–306. https://doi.org/10.20344/amp.7568.

Spitzer, John. 2012. "American Orchestras and Their Unions in the Nineteenth Century." Oxford University Press. https://doi.org/10.7208/chicago/9780226769776.003.0004.

Statler, Kathryn C. 2012. "The Sound of Musical Diplomacy." *Diplomatic History* 36 (1). Oxford Academic: 71–75. https://doi.org/10.1111/j.1467-7709.2011.01010.x.

Sukljan, Nejc. 2018. "The Trieste Philharmonic in Serbia." *Muzikologija* 25: 135–158. https://doi.org/10.2298/MUZ1825135S.

Sutherland, Andrew, and Phillip A. Cartwright. 2022. "Working Together: Implications of Leadership Style for the Music Ensemble." *International Journal of Music Education* 40 (4): 613–627. https://doi.org/10.1177/02557614221084310.

Truskot, Joseph, Anita Belofsky, and Kittilstad Kittilstad. 1983. *Principles of Orchestra Management: 1984–1985 Orchestra Management Seminars*. New York: American Symphony Orchestra League.

Truskot, Joseph, Anita Belofsky, and Kittilstad Kittilstad. 1988. *Principles of Orchestra Management*. New York: American Symphony Orchestra League.

Walker, Chris, and Stephanie Scott-Melnyk. 2002. "Reggae to Rachmaninoff: How and Why People Participate in Arts and Culture." *PsycEXTRA Dataset*. American Psychological Association (APA). https://doi.org/10.1037/e717882011-001.

Walmsley, Ben. 2019. *Audience Engagement in the Performing Arts: A Critical Analysis*. New Directions in Cultural Policy Research. Cham: Palgrave Macmillan.

Walzer, Daniel. 2020. "Leadership in the Creative Industries: Addressing an Uncertain Future." *Journal of the Music and Entertainment Industry Educators Association* 20 (1): 147–172. https://doi.org/10.25101/20.5.

Weiss, Elisa S., Rebecca Miller Anderson, and Roz D. Lasker. 2002. "Making the Most of Collaboration: Exploring the Relationship Between Partnership Synergy and Partnership Functioning." *Health Education & Behavior: The Official Publication of the Society for Public Health Education* 29 (6): 683–698. https://doi.org/10.1177/109019802237938.

Whittaker, Adam. 2021. "Teacher Perceptions of A-Level Music: Tension, Dilemmas and Decline." *British Journal of Music Education* 38 (2): 145–159. https://doi.org/10.1017/s0265051720000352.

Wright, Michelle, Ben Walmsley, and Emilee Simmons. 2022. *Fundraising in the Creative and Cultural Industries: Leading Effective Fundraising Strategies*. Abingdon, Oxon: Routledge.

Yanchenko, Anna K. 2020. "Network Analysis of Orchestral Concert Programming." *arXiv [stat.AP]*. arXiv. https://doi.org/10.48550/ARXIV.2009.07887.

Yandoli, Krystie Lee. 2023. "Jennifer Lawrence, A-List Actors Threaten to Strike in Letter to SAG." *Rolling Stones*. www.rollingstone.com/tv-movies/tv-movie-news/jennifer-lawrence-meryl-streep-actors-threaten-strike-sag-aftra-letter-exclusive-1234779586/.

Zabanal, John Rine A. 2021. "An Examination of Orchestras and Repertoire Performed at the Midwest Clinic From 1990 Through 2019." *Update: Applications of Research in Music Education* 39 (3): 29–38. https://doi.org/10.1177/8755123320978776.

Cited content from websites was last accessed on 01 July 2023.

CHAPTER 6

Contemporary Issues in Orchestra Management

In addition to the historical elements of orchestra management examined in Chapter 2 and the fundamentals reviewed in Chapter 5, over the past three decades, the demands for revenue diversification, enhanced resilience and adaptability, streamlined and agile operations, increased diversity, equity, and inclusion, and the ability to address the disruptive influence of technology have contributed to the piling up of additional layers of concerns that the management team must now take into careful consideration, increasing the overall complexity of the task and workload.

WHAT YOU WILL LEARN IN THIS CHAPTER

Section	Key Learning Points
A. Innovative Revenue Streams	Alternative funding channels are key to diversify income sources for long-term sustainability. Traditionally, a mix of earned income, contributed income, and endowment income have supported operations. However, in recent years, these funding sources have become increasingly volatile, prompting orchestras to explore new ways of generating more resilient forms of revenue. This section provides a practical overview of options that are readily accessible, regardless of their funding model or background.
B. Resilience, Adaptability, and Change Management	Strategic planning and adaptability ensure long-term financial sustainability of arts and culture institutions without compromising artistic excellence. The optimisation of the financial position and adaptation to a challenging landscape also involves the careful evaluation of different cost-saving scenarios and the pursuit of innovative revenue-generation strategies, alongside the renegotiation of public funding and amplification of fundraising efforts.

DOI: 10.4324/9781032629636-6

Section	Key Learning Points
C. Diversity, Equity, and Inclusion	Diversity, equity, and inclusion contribute to creating a vibrant community that reflects the diverse audiences served. By embracing diversity in all its forms, orchestras foster a culture of inclusivity that promotes creativity, innovation, and excellence. The search for equity ensures more cohesion amongst the staff and demonstrates the manager's commitment to respect and honesty.
D. Crisis Management and Contingency Planning	This section provides practical guidance on how to prepare for unexpected crises by developing robust contingency plans that prioritise the safety of musicians, staff, and audiences while maintaining artistic integrity. Anticipating potential risks and developing clear communication protocols with stakeholders at all levels of the organisation is the ideal way to respond effectively to crises while minimising disruption to operations.
E. Embracing Sustainability	Embracing sustainability by adopting environmentally responsible practices reduces the footprint while promoting social responsibility. Sustainable practices such as reducing energy consumption, promoting waste reduction and recycling, and supporting local communities demonstrate commitment while enhancing their reputation as responsible cultural institutions.
F. Digital and Physical Accessibility	Digital and physical accessibility ensure that musical performances are equally enjoyable by all audiences, regardless of their location or ability status. Digital technologies such as (live) streaming, social media, and online ticketing reach new audiences and enhance engagement with existing ones. At the same time, physical accessibility measures such as wheelchair access, audio description, and sign language interpretation lower the barriers and make performances open to a variety of audiences that had been excluded for decades.

A. INNOVATIVE REVENUE STREAMS: EXPLORING ALTERNATIVE FUNDING OPPORTUNITIES

As financial pressure increases, developing innovative revenue streams has become essential. This section explores various alternative funding channels, examining their potential benefits and drawbacks and providing a practical overview of diversified income sources for long-term sustainability.

Traditionally, a mix of earned income (such as ticket sales, merchandising, and performance fees), contributed income (including donations, sponsorships, and government subsidies and grants), and endowment income have supported operations. However, in recent years, these funding sources have become increasingly volatile and unpredictable (or, more precisely, predictably downwards), prompting orchestras to explore new ways of generating forms of revenue that are more resilient and adaptable.

While we recognise that there are numerous new revenue avenues, we have narrowed our focus to ten common options amongst orchestras, regardless of the funding model or background.

a. Collaborations and Partnerships

Forming strategic alliances with other arts organisations (and across arts disciplines), businesses, and community groups opens new revenue-generating opportunities. These partnerships commonly involve co-productions, shared resources, or cross-promotional activities that broaden the audience base and increase ticket sales. Additionally, partnering with not-for-profit organisations or educational institutions leads to grants and funding opportunities that might not be available otherwise.

b. Educational and Outreach Programs

Expanding the educational and outreach initiatives could generate additional income by attracting new audiences, increasing ticket sales, and securing funding from government agencies, foundations, and corporate sponsors. These programs conventionally include school concerts, workshops, masterclasses, and civic empowerment events that connect the orchestra with a diverse range of audience members and stakeholders.

c. Merchandising and Licensing

Additional revenue streams can be generated from the sales of branded merchandise, such as digital downloads, apparel, and souvenirs. Although they may be a bit outdated for the large public, vinyl discs, CDs, and DVDs still have aficionados ready to pay the price for a limited series or rare edition (perhaps with great visual art from a renowned artist). Licensing music, image, and brand for use in ads, films, television shows, and other media also generate income.

d. Digital Media and Streaming

The rapid growth of digital media and streaming technology offers new avenues to monetise content and reach a global audience. High-quality video and audio recordings of concert performances already serve as a complementary source of revenue generation for many, as they harness the potential of subscription-based streaming platforms (Negus 2019), pay-per-view events, and digital downloads for dissemination and monetisation. Additionally, existing digital content can be released to attract sponsors and advertisers interested in reaching a broad online audience. Sharing fragments of digital content on social media platforms such as Instagram, TikTok, and others serves as trailers to pique interest in both live performances and complete online content.

e. Venue Rentals and Ancillary Services

Additional income can come from renting out performance spaces, rehearsal facilities, and other venues for events, meetings, and conferences. Offering ancillary services, such as event planning, catering, and technical support, further enhances the return on real estate investment.

f. Corporate Sponsorships and Partnerships

Developing relationships with corporate sponsors and partners provide a valuable source of revenue. In addition to direct financial support, these partnerships offer in-kind contributions, such as products, services, or marketing support, that help reduce operating costs. For example, a partnership with an advertising agency can lead to the remunerated creation of soundtracks for commercials.

g. Membership and Loyalty Programs

Establishing membership and loyalty programs not only generates recurring revenue by incentivising patrons to make ongoing financial commitments but also provides a variety of benefits (such as priority seating, exclusive access to special events, and discounts on tickets and merchandise), which foster long-term relationships with audience members and supporters.

h. Crowdfunding and Online Fundraising

Online crowdfunding platforms and social media campaigns offer an opportunity to raise funds for specific projects (Gamble, Brennan, and McAdam 2017), such as commissioning new works, supporting community outreach initiatives, or financing the production of a recording. A direct connection with audience and supporters definitely fosters a stronger sense of ownership and investment in their artistic endeavours, potentially leading to increased support.

i. Planned Giving and Endowment Campaigns

Encouraging planned giving and launching endowment campaigns helps with long-term financial stability. Robust relationships with donors interested in leaving a legacy through bequests, trusts, or other planned giving vehicles also establish a reliable source of future income. Similarly, endowment campaigns provide a financial cushion to alleviate economic downturns and maintain artistic programming and operations.

j. Grant Writing and Funding Research

Applying for grants regularly offered by government agencies, foundations, and other funding organisations can prove to be a lucrative activity. Staying current on funding opportunities coupled with a strong grant-writing capacity can lead to additional financial support with limited upfront investment.

In conclusion, the key to successfully diversifying revenue sources lies in championing a proactive, innovative, and entrepreneurial mindset. Exploring new funding routes and alternative income-generating strategies fortifies the financial resilience and maintains artistic vitality and sustainability.

CASE STUDY 6.1

Optimisation Strategies for a Large Symphonic Under Financial Pressure

This case study explores the financial challenges faced by a symphonic ensemble comprising 92 musicians and 34 other staff members based in its own venue holding a 1,300-seat concert hall. The orchestra contends with a government subsidy reduced by half and a stipulation that the average ticket price must not exceed $150. Consequently, the management explores a variety of cost-saving measures and innovative revenue-generation strategies while maintaining its artistic integrity and reputation.

DATA:

- Musicians' average annual package: $95,000[1]
- Staff average annual package: $65,000
- All other expenses (annual): $8.75 million
- Government (and other agencies) funding: $6 million
- Number of concerts per year: 45
- Average number of tickets sold per concert: 1,150
- Average price per seat: $150

COSTS		$
Musicians	92	90,000
Other Staff	34	65,000
Other Expenses		8,750,000
TOTAL		**19,240,000**
INCOME		
Government Funding		6,000,000
Additional Income		5,500,000
Ticket Sales		7,762,500
NBRE Concerts per Year[2]	45	
Max Seats	1150	

COSTS	$
Max Average Price $	150
TOTAL	**19,262,500**
BALANCE	**22,500**

Following the cut of government funding by $3 million, the orchestra explores two scenarios of staff reduction and a series of opportunities for new income.

TWO COST-SAVING SCENARIOS:

A   Limited staff reduction. A reduction by five musicians and three non-musicians, resulting in savings of $735,000.
B   Larger staff reduction. A reduction by twelve musicians and nine non-musicians, resulting in savings of $1,665,000.

REVENUE-GENERATION STRATEGIES:

1   Sales of online concerts: Assuming the orchestra has 150,000 followers on social media, and 5% of them purchase a mix of single tickets at $2 per online concert or subscriptions at $29 per year, this could generate $75,000.
2   Collaboration with advertising agencies: Producing music for commercials for large luxury brands could yield additional income. Assuming five contracts per year with an average revenue of $50,000 per contract, this would generate $250,000.
3   Creation of small chamber ensembles: The orchestra could form chamber ensembles comprising three to six musicians to give private concerts. Assuming 75 chamber concerts per year, with each concert generating an average of $2,000, this would result in $150,000 in additional revenue.
4   Merchandising and licensing: Selling branded merchandise and licensing the music for commercial use could potentially generate an additional $100,000 annually.
5   Venue rentals and ancillary services: Renting out the concert hall and offering ancillary services such as catering and event planning during non-performance days could generate an estimated $75,000 annually.

6 Crowdfunding and online fundraising: Engaging supporters through crowdfunding and online fundraising campaigns could yield approximately $50,000 annually.
7 Grant writing and funding research: Actively pursuing grants and funding opportunities from both public and private sources could result in an additional $50,000 in annual funding.

FINANCIAL ANALYSIS:

Given the savings from the staff reduction, the additional income from the revenue-generation strategies ($750,000), and a $3 million decrease in government subsidy, the ticket sales should generate at least:

A Scenario with limited staff reduction: $9,255,000
B Scenario with larger staff reduction: $8,325,000

If the orchestra manages to increase the average number of tickets sold per concert from 1,150 to 1,200, the total number of concerts needed per year will be:

A 9,255,000 / 150 / 1200 = 52
B 8,325,000 / 150 / 1200 = 47

STRATEGIC CONSIDERATIONS:

Explore a combination of cost-saving measures and revenue-generation strategies to maintain financial sustainability while preserving the artistic mission. Given the various scenarios, the management considers adopting the following strategies:

1 Pursue a limited staff reduction to strike a balance between cost savings and maintaining a high-quality ensemble. This would result in an estimated annual saving of $735,000 in staff costs.
2 Increase the number of tickets sold per concert to no less than 1,200.
3 Increase the number of concerts to 52 per year.
4 Invest more time and energy in fundraising, sponsorship, and patronage activities to further increase the flow of money from these sources. If this measure proves successful, the increase in the number of annual concerts could be limited or perhaps could even be avoided.

Through careful evaluation of different cost-saving scenarios and the implementation of innovative revenue-generation strategies, as well as increasing fundraising efforts, the philharmonic can optimise its financial position and adapt to a challenging landscape. This case study highlights the importance of strategic planning and adaptability for arts and cultural institutions, ensuring long-term financial sustainability without compromising artistic excellence.

B. RESILIENCE, ADAPTABILITY, AND CHANGE MANAGEMENT

Resilience

Resilience prepares organisations to withstand challenges and recover from setbacks. The classical music industry, like any other field, faces its share of uncertainties, such as economic fluctuations, changes in audience preferences, and unforeseen disruptions like the Covid-19 pandemic (Yu, Chiu, and Chan 2023). Developing resilience requires creating a robust organisational culture, establishing financial stability, and a mindset of adaptability and innovation among its members. As a result, the capacity to leverage new solutions to respond to unexpected harmful situations (Szedmák 2021) becomes the central tenet of resilience, acting as the linchpin in navigating the orchestra through the tumultuous seas of uncertainty towards the safest shores of

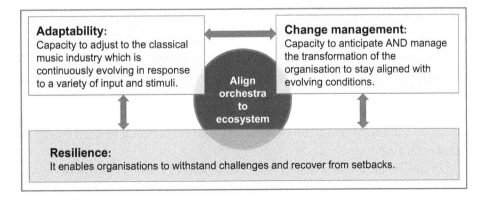

FIGURE 6.1 Resilience, Adaptability, and Change Management

stability and growth. A resilient management team prioritises a culture of mutual support and constructive collaboration, an atmosphere of optimism, and a faith in the future. As Deborah Borda, executive director of the New York Philharmonic, simply put it during the Covid crisis, "try to believe there will be a future because there is going to be a future" (Tan 2020). Managers foster trust and unity within an organisation when they encourage an environment of free idea exchange and open discussion of concerns without fear of reprisal. This, in turn, helps facing challenges collegially and finding creative solutions to problems.

Financial stability is another essential component of resilience. Maintaining diverse income streams, including ticket sales, grants, sponsorships, and individual donations, contributes to insulate an orchestra from economic downturns or unexpected funding cuts. Developing a prudent financial strategy, with contingency plans and emergency funds, also provides a safety net when faced with unforeseen expenses or revenue shortfalls.

Finally, a mindset of adaptability and innovation among staff empowers them to evolve with the changing landscape of the classical music industry. Encouraging continuous learning, experimentation, and risk-taking helps the organisation stay relevant and thrive in an increasingly competitive environment.

Adaptability

Adaptability is here seen as the capacity to adjust to the classical music industry, which is continuously evolving in response to shifting demographics, changing audience preferences, and technology disruptions. Adaptability is a prerequisite to seize new opportunities, remain relevant, and ultimately facilitate long-term action. An adaptable management team is open to change and willing to reassess and revise strategies and practices as needed. This flexibility is crucial when faced with unexpected challenges, such as pivoting to digital performances during the Covid-19 pandemic or adjusting programming to accommodate diverse audiences. Being adaptable also involves staying informed about industry trends and new relevant technologies and incorporating innovative approaches to artistic programming, audience management, and revenue generation. One aspect of adaptability is establishing a constructive dialogue with the community and responding to their needs and preferences.

Adaptability among musicians and staff is also crucial. A culture of ongoing learning and professional development allows for providing all staff with the necessary skills and knowledge to succeed in a fast-paced industry. Offering training in new technologies, cross-disciplinary collaborations, or non-traditional performance formats are real-life examples of actions taken to adjust to 21st-century society.

Change Management

Effective change management lets organisations smoothly navigate transitions and concurrently mitigate the associated risks. This process is all but simple or easy as it encompasses three demanding actions:

- Understanding the diverse perspectives and concerns of all stakeholders.
- Shaping a culture of teamwork and collaboration.
- Employing a balanced approach that combines structured processes with creative problem-solving.

By honing their change management capabilities, managers empower their organisations to tackle new challenges while upholding the highest standards of artistic and operational excellence.

One critical aspect of change management involves **understanding the potential impact** of proposed changes on various stakeholders, including musicians, staff, board members, donors, and audiences. Managers empathetically consider each group's concerns and needs, actively soliciting suggestions and feedback to ensure that decisions are well-informed and considerate of all perspectives.

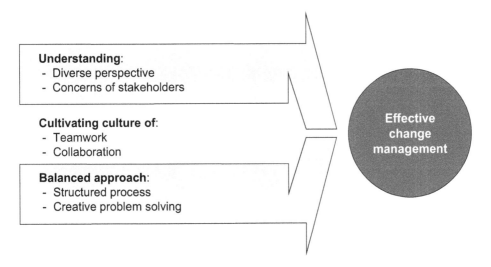

FIGURE 6.2 Change Management

A **culture of teamwork** and collaboration is essential for effective change management (Hoegl and Gemuenden 2001). Managers therefore pay attention to shared ownership and responsibility for the success of the organisation, encouraging open communication, trust, and mutual support among all members. This collective approach empowers the staff and artistic personnel to work together to overcome challenges and implement changes more seamlessly.

Additionally, change management requires a **balanced approach** that blends structured processes with creative problem-solving. On the one hand, implementing systematic processes, such as project management methodologies and risk assessment frameworks, helps manage change in an organised and efficient manner. On the other hand, creativity and flexibility are crucial for addressing unforeseen challenges and finding innovative solutions to complex problems. Managers effectively and holistically navigate change when they adopt a combination of process-driven and creative strategies.

Training and support create a founding layer to change management. Managers provide staff and musicians with the necessary resources, guidance, and encouragement to adapt to new situations and practices. Common examples of resources are offering workshops, mentoring, or other professional development opportunities to equip all members with the skills and knowledge needed to succeed in a changing environment.

Effective change management is a critical skill that enables organisations to navigate transitions smoothly, mitigate risks, and seize new opportunities. Comprehending stakeholders' concerns, pursuing collaboration, and using balanced problem-solving techniques enable managers to lead organisations through change without sacrificing artistic and operational excellence.

C. DIVERSITY, EQUITY, AND INCLUSION

Given the nature and the extent of inequalities in the classical music industry (Bull, Scharff, and Nooshin 2023), the significance of diversity, equity, and inclusion cannot be overstated (League of American Orchestras 2023). Welcoming a wide range of backgrounds, perspectives, profiles, and experiences enriches the creative process and feeds a sentiment of belonging among musicians, staff, and audiences while ensuring an equitable treatment to all staff shows the management's commitment to respect and honesty. As orchestras strive to remain relevant in the arts, culture, and entertainment industries and work with their communities, they prioritise a culture that values diversity and inclusivity in all aspects of their operations to expand their horizons as well as the boundaries of the potential audience.

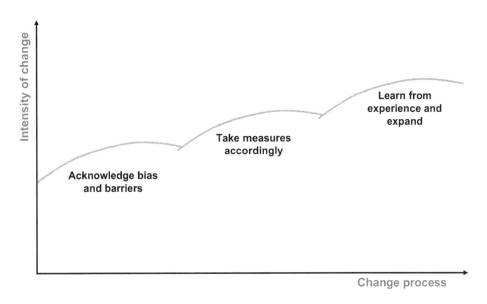

FIGURE 6.3 Phases of a Change Process

One of the initial steps towards diversity, equity, and inclusion involves acknowledging and addressing any existing biases or barriers that might hinder equal opportunities. This process requires a genuine commitment from the leadership, staff, and musicians to inspect and evaluate their current practices, policies, and beliefs. Identifying areas for improvement is the first step to define action plans that address these issues, resulting in a more inclusive environment for everyone.

Recruitment and audition processes offer a critical starting point for diversity, equity, and inclusion (Goldin and Rouse 1997). Traditionally, blind auditions have been employed to reduce unconscious bias and create a level playing field for all applicants. As reported by Heymann, Sprague, and Raub (2023), "after orchestras began holding auditions in which prospective members played behind a curtain, the share of women rose to 40 percent." However, this approach alone does not suffice. Orchestras also expand their talent pool by actively reaching out to underrepresented groups, providing mentorship opportunities, and establishing alliances with institutions that nurture diverse talent. Offering workshops, masterclasses, and internships to musicians from diverse backgrounds breaks down barriers and builds a more inclusive culture. Partnering with music academies and conservatories also contributes to breaking inequality barriers from a younger age.

Additionally, programming is a fair reflection of the rich tapestry of human experience. This means presenting works by composers and artists from diverse backgrounds, exploring different musical traditions, and collaborating with a variety of art forms (Biernoff and Blom 2002). When presenting various creative voices, orchestras defy preconceived ideas, encourage dialogue, and deliver a more inclusive and captivating experience for their audiences. Incorporating local communities' cultural heritage into performances also contributes to creating shared ownership.

Education and outreach initiatives are vital platforms to share diversity, equity, and inclusion initiatives. Through the creation of programmes tailored to diverse audiences, orchestras connect with underrepresented communities, motivate aspiring musicians, and establish enduring relationships. It is essential to design educational content that is both accessible and culturally sensitive, taking into account the unique needs and interests of various groups. Collaborating with schools, community organisations, and cultural institutions helps nail down this goal and develop a love for music across diverse audiences (Kimpton and Lestz 1985). Productive communication is essential to diversity, equity, and inclusion. It is essential that messaging and marketing materials reflect the commitment to these values, highlighting the diverse range of artists, repertoire, and programmes offered. Utilising inclusive language, imagery, and narratives conveys a message of belonging and encourages a broader audience to bind with the message.

Accessibility is another crucial aspect of diversity, equity, and inclusion. This includes ensuring that concerts, education programmes, and outreach initiatives are tailored to the needs and preferences of a wide range of community members. Accessible programming involves offering performances in non-traditional venues, collaborating with artists from various cultural backgrounds, or using technology to reach broader audiences. In addition, accessibility encompasses the financial aspect, exploring different pricing structures or offering discounted (or free) events to lower financial barriers to participation. Finally, measures are taken to accommodate individuals with physical or cognitive impairments (such as by providing ramps, visual or auditory aids, sign language interpretation, and sensory-friendly performances), thereby creating an inclusive and welcoming environment for all.

It is crucial to establish systems for continuous improvement and accountability too. Establishing a routine of assessing progress in diversity, equity, and inclusion, as well as gathering data and feedback from musicians, staff, and audiences, presents a straightforward yet highly impactful management practice whose value should never be underestimated. This information is useful in identifying areas for further growth, refining existing strategies, and developing new initiatives. A culture of continuous learning and improvement is a minimal condition to ensure an ongoing commitment to diversity and inclusion.

Embracing diversity, equity, and inclusion is an essential aspect of any workplace (Patrick and Kumar 2012; Triguero-Sánchez, Peña-Vinces, and Guillen 2018), in particular in orchestra management that not only enriches the artistic process but also generates belonging and connection within the organisation and its audiences. Addressing biases and barriers, promoting inclusive recruitment and programming practices, implementing education and outreach initiatives, and communicating effectively enables an orchestra to cultivate an inclusive environment that benefits all involved.

Diversity in Music: Expanding the Artistic Palette

The concept of diversity and inclusion extends beyond human resources and touches the core of artistic programming. A broader understanding of diversity in music programming encompasses both the inclusion of non-classical music genres and the integration of various cultural and anthropological backgrounds. As orchestras strive to remain relevant and appealing to a wide range of audiences, it is vital to challenge traditional programming norms and explore new artistic avenues. This approach involves incorporating pieces by composers from diverse backgrounds, collaborating with artists representing different cultures, and experimenting with varied musical forms and traditions.

One way to introduce diversity in music programming is by welcoming contemporary and non-classical genres, such as jazz, world music, and popular music. Not only does this broaden the appeal to new audiences, but it also allows musicians to explore fresh creative challenges in a more vibrant and dynamic artistic environment.

Another key aspect of diverse programming is the inclusion of compositions by underrepresented composers. Concerts shed light on lesser-known musical treasures and provide a platform for a wider range of creative voices when they champion works from historically marginalised communities. This strategy both enriches the repertoire and challenges conventional notions of what constitutes classical music and encourages audiences to welcome new and exciting musical narratives.

A third option is to include in the artistic programming compositions belonging to the classical repertoire of non-Western cultural backgrounds. Classical compositions from Asia or the Arabic-Muslim tradition are often, at best, underrepresented in classical performances or, most of the time, absent from the programming or special events.

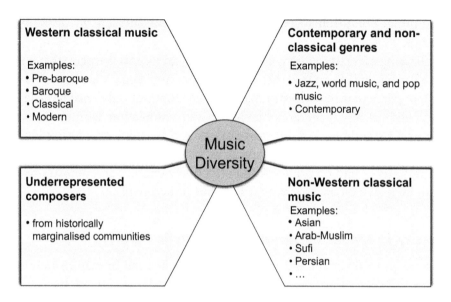

FIGURE 6.4 Diversity in Music

Collaborations with artists from different cultural and artistic backgrounds are instrumental in introducing diversity in music programming. Innovative and culturally rich performances that resonate with a diverse audience are created when orchestras work with musicians, composers, and performers who bring unique perspectives, skills, and traditions. This approach entails fusing different musical styles, incorporating traditional instruments, or even exploring new performance formats, such as multimedia installations and interdisciplinary collaborations.

Integrating local communities' cultural heritage into performances is another vital aspect of diverse programming. An example is commissioning new works inspired by regional folklore, traditions, or stories or collaborating with local ensembles and artists to create unique and culturally relevant performances. The cultural wealth of the communities they serve allows orchestras to forge a sense of belonging and shared ownership, ultimately making classical music more accessible and relevant to a broader audience.

Diverse programming offers an opportunity to challenge traditional concert formats and settings. Presenting performances in unconventional venues or adopting new presentation styles helps make music more approachable and appealing to a wider range of spectators. Site-specific performances, immersive experiences, or even participatory events encourage audience interaction.

Education and outreach initiatives are also crucial in music diversity. Incorporating diverse repertoire and artistic perspectives into educational content allows orchestras to inspire the next generation of musicians, composers, and music enthusiasts. Collaborations with schools and community organisations that serve diverse populations ensure that the educational offerings resonate with and reflect the cultural richness of the audiences.

In conclusion, diversity in music is a vital aspect of management that enriches the artistic experience and the sense of inclusivity and belonging among musicians, staff, and audiences. A vibrant and dynamic creative environment that is accessible and exciting for all is instilled by a stance of openness to non-classical genres, underrepresented composers, collaboration with artists from diverse backgrounds, and challenge to conventional performance formats.

Equity

The pursuit of equity is increasingly seen as integral to all aspects of management, influencing decisions and processes from the stage to the office (Byrnes 2022; Worth 2021; Garrett 2018; McClelland 2021). The concept of equity, that includes fairness and justice, transcends the theoretical and permeates the organisation's practical operations, establishing a benchmark for the treatment of all individuals – musicians, conductors, administrative personnel, and audience members alike. At its core, equity relies on an unbiased distribution of opportunities and treatment. This implies not merely adhering to a policy of non-discrimination but actively fostering an environment that is positively receptive to differences and nurtures the personal and professional potential of all individuals. Such an environment treats all individuals with the highest respect and consideration, offers fair remuneration and working conditions, and provides equal opportunities for professional growth and personal development. A simple yet tangible example would be to guarantee fair audition, impartial recruitment, and promotion processes, pay equity (Goldin and Rouse 1997), and the provision of necessary accommodations for staff with disabilities, thereby demonstrating the manager's commitment to respect and honesty.

In seeking equity, arts and culture institutions also strive to afford access to opportunities for those groups that have historically been marginalised or underrepresented. This might entail forming partnerships with music education programmes in less advantaged communities, establishing scholarships for aspiring musicians, or initiating efforts to ensure greater representation within the organisation. However, the quest for equity is not limited to the provision of opportunities. It extends to the provision of the resources that each individual needs to succeed. This includes tangible resources such as instruments or rehearsal space, but most importantly, also intangible resources such as mentorship, professional development opportunities, and psychological support. Such an environment, one that values and supports everyone, cultivates a sense of belonging and empowers all staff to reach their full potential.

Equity insists on diversifying voices in artistic leadership roles, programming decisions, and the board of directors. This inclusive approach ensures that decision-making processes draw from the richness of diverse perspectives. It contributes to a more vibrant, resonant artistic output that appeals to a broader audience base. A crucial outcome of this pursuit of equity is an enhanced sense of cohesion among the staff. When fairness and justice underpin all aspects of an organisation's operation, it fosters a shared sense of commitment and unity amongst staff members. They perceive that their contributions are valued, leading to increased job satisfaction, engagement, and commitment.

The notion of equity is expansive. The integration of equitable practices requires a consistent commitment from all artistic and non-artistic staff, necessitating regular monitoring and adaptation to ensure progress. The resulting organisation, underpinned by a culture of inclusivity, respect, and honesty, not only enjoys a richer, more varied artistic output but also benefits from enhanced staff cohesion and commitment.

D. CRISIS MANAGEMENT AND CONTINGENCY PLANNING

Crisis management and contingency planning might not – fortunately – be part of the day-to-day toolbox of a senior manager, but they are functional and helpful – although demanding to design and test – instruments to run any organisation (McConnell and Drennan 2006; Eriksson and McConnell 2011). In an increasingly uncertain society, orchestras face a myriad of challenges and emergencies (such as financial difficulties, natural disasters, pandemics, or the sudden loss of key personnel) that range at any level of the predictability scale from the most anticipated to the most unlikely. Being prepared to navigate these unforeseen situations is vital for the long-term stability and for the well-being of musicians, staff, and stakeholders.

In this section, we explore how orchestras prepare for and manage crises effectively, covering topics such as creating a crisis management plan, maintaining transparent communication, and adapting to new circumstances. As orchestras understand and implement these best practices, they emerge

FIGURE 6.5 Crisis and Contingency

from challenging situations more resilient and better equipped to face future uncertainties.

Crisis management covers three essential steps in a circular approach: (i) getting prepared for a hypothetical crisis, (ii) implementing the plan to manage the crisis if it occurs, and (iii) debriefing after the crisis to consolidate the lesson learned and amend the plan accordingly.

Preparing for Crises: The Importance of Contingency Planning

One of the most important aspects of crisis management is being prepared for potential emergencies before they occur (Beehive 2020). This involves developing a comprehensive contingency plan that outlines the procedures and protocols to be followed in the event of a crisis.

BOX 6.1 CONTINGENCY PLANNING

Contingency planning is a method of risk management that promotes effective crisis management. It involves anticipating potential crises and allocating resources, personnel, equipment, crisis control rooms, tasks, responsibilities, and decision guidance/rules to maximise the chances of a successful response in the event of a crisis. The relationship between crisis planning and crisis management outcomes is complex and nuanced. The concept of contingency planning comes from the field of crisis management and is widely considered to be an essential role of public authorities. See Eriksson and McConnell (2011).

A contingency plan is not just a formality. It's an essential blueprint for navigating the unexpected:

1 **Risk Assessment:** Identify the most likely risks and threats that could jeopardise the organisation, such as financial instability, natural disasters, or personnel issues. Assess the potential impact of each class of risk and prioritise them accordingly (by likelihood, or magnitude of impact, or any other criteria more relevant to the organisation).

2 **Defining Roles and Responsibilities:** Assign roles and responsibilities for crisis management to specific individuals or teams within the organisation, including a designated crisis management team responsible for coordinating the response and making key decisions.

3 **Communication Plan:** Develop a communication plan that outlines how the information will be disseminated during a crisis, both internally and externally, including the prioritisation of communication channels, such as email, phone, and social media, as well as key messages and talking points to be conveyed.

4 **Decision-making Processes:** Establish clear decision-making processes and protocols to be followed during a crisis, ensuring that decisions are made quickly and effectively, even under pressure.

5 **Resource Allocation:** Identify the resources that are required during a crisis, such as financial reserves, personnel, or equipment, and plan how these resources will be allocated and deployed as needed.

6 **Training and Simulation:** Conduct regular training sessions and simulations to ensure that all personnel are familiar with the contingency plan and their roles and responsibilities during a crisis.

Managing Crises Effectively: Best Practices and Key Principles

When a crisis does occur, the way it is managed impacts significantly the outcome and the orchestra's ability to recover. Some best practices and key principles for managing crises effectively include:

1 **Transparent Communication:** Maintain open and transparent communication with all stakeholders, including musicians, staff, board members, and the public. This builds trust, reduces uncertainty, and ensures that everyone is kept informed of the situation and any actions being taken.

2 **Prioritising Well-Being:** In times of crisis, the well-being of musicians, staff, and other stakeholders is a top priority. And providing support, such as counselling services, financial assistance, or flexible working arrangements, helps individuals cope with the challenges they may be facing.

3 **Adapting to New Circumstances:** Crises often require organisations to adapt quickly to new circumstances and find innovative solutions to the challenges they are facing. Be prepared to reassess and modify existing plans and strategies and explore new opportunities for growth and development.

4 **Collaborative Decision-making:** Encourage a collaborative approach to decision-making during a crisis, involving relevant stakeholders and drawing on the diverse expertise and perspectives within the organisation. This ensures that decisions are well-informed and the needs and priorities of all those affected are considered.

Post-Crisis Debrief and Continuous Improvement

After a crisis has been resolved or managed, it is essential to conduct a thorough evaluation of the response, identifying what worked well and any areas for improvement to facilitate the recovery. This provides valuable learning opportunities and insights to refine the contingency plan and better prepare the organisation for future crises (Ndlela 2019). Key components of the post-crisis debrief include:

1 **Review and Analysis:** Conduct a thorough review of the crisis management process, analysing the decisions and actions taken, and outcomes, gathering feedback from all relevant stakeholders to gain a comprehensive understanding of the effectiveness of the response.

2 **Identification of Lessons Learned:** Identify the key lessons learned from the crisis management process, focusing on both the successes and areas that require improvement. Examining the effectiveness of communication, decision-making, resource allocation, and other aspects of the response is key to bring out the pros and cons of the measures previously adopted.

3 **Amendments to Contingency Plan:** Based on the lessons learned, amend the contingency plan to better address potential future crises, and update risk assessments, revise roles and responsibilities, improve communication plans, or refine decision-making processes.

4 **Ongoing Training and Development:** Provide ongoing training and development opportunities for personnel involved in crisis management, ensuring they are well-equipped to respond effectively to future crises. This includes regular refresher training, participation in simulations, or access to relevant resources and support.

Systematic post-crisis debriefs and continuous refinements of the contingency plan improve the ability to navigate future crises more effectively and efficiently while mitigating the potential impact on the organisation and stakeholders.

To better illustrate the principles and practices of crisis management and contingency planning, let's explore some case studies.

CASE STUDY 6.2

Responding to a Pandemic: The Covid-19 Crisis

The Covid-19 pandemic had a significant impact on the performing arts industry worldwide. This case study examines how a symphony orchestra managed to adapt its operations and performances during the pandemic, showcasing resilience, adaptability, and innovative thinking. The orchestra faced the challenge of maintaining audience involvement, generating revenue, preserving its artistic integrity, and fighting the prevailing demoralisation and pessimism during a period of lockdowns and social distancing measures.

RAPID TRANSITION TO DIGITAL PERFORMANCES

- Rapid transition to online performances was made, leveraging tools such as Acapella (Mixcord) to register, edit, and share original music, and video streaming platforms to broadcast it.
- Professional recording and editing equipment were utilised to ensure high-quality audio and video for the online audience.
- As soon as the lockdown was partially lifted and small groups of musicians could meet in person again, a mix of livestreamed and recorded performances was offered, catering to different preferences.

CREATIVE PROGRAMMING AND COLLABORATIONS

- Innovative programming ideas were explored, including themed concerts, chamber music ensembles, and performances featuring guest artists.
- Collaborations with other local and international ensembles, dance companies, and visual artists were initiated to create unique experiences for the audience.
- These initiatives not only expanded the repertoire but also attracted new audiences.

AUDIENCE ENGAGEMENT AND COMMUNICATION

- A dedicated team was responsible for maintaining communication with the audience through social media, newsletters, and online events.
- Online Q&A sessions, behind-the-scenes content, and interviews with musicians and guest artists were regularly released on social media.
- The scope of all the initiatives was to maintain the connection with the audiences and the community at large despite the lack of physical proximity.

REVENUE GENERATION AND FUNDRAISING

- "Pay-what-you-can" model for online concerts was inaugurated, making performances accessible to a broader audience.
- Online fundraising campaigns and gala events were organised to generate revenue and maintain donor interest.
- Special grants and government relief packages were sought to partially offset the lack of revenue during the challenging period.

SUPPORTING MUSICIANS AND STAFF

- Well-being of musicians and staff was prioritised, offering mental health resources and professional development opportunities.
- Flexible working arrangements were implemented, allowing musicians and staff to balance work and personal responsibilities.
- Open lines of communication were maintained between the management and employees, ensuring transparency and a supportive work environment.

This case study illustrates adaptability and resilience during the Covid-19 pandemic. Using digital platforms, innovative programming, audience engagement, and effective revenue-generation strategies contributed to the survival. The lessons learned from this experience could be applied to a broad range of performing arts organisations facing similar challenges, emphasising the importance of adaptability, creativity, and strong leadership.

QUESTIONS:

1   Reflecting on the swift transition to digital performances, what challenges might they have encountered during this process, and how could they have overcome them? How did this shift impact the artistic vision, and how might they have mitigated any adverse effects?

2   The case study mentions innovative programming and collaborations as a strategy to attract new audiences. How might the choice of thematic concerts, chamber music ensembles, and collaborations with other artistic groups have influenced the audience reach? Given different audience demographics and interests, what factors should be considered when planning collaborations?

3   Considering the economic impact of the Covid-19 pandemic, how effective do you think the "pay-what-you-can" model for online concerts was in both maintaining accessibility and generating revenue? Are there other creative revenue-generation strategies the orchestra could have employed during this period, while still ensuring accessibility and inclusivity?

CASE STUDY 6.3

The Fire at a Historic Theatre

When a massive fire destroys a historic performance venue, significant challenges emerge for both the users of the facility and the surrounding community. Drawing some inspiration from the experience of Teatro La Fenice in Venice, Italy, which was devastated by a fire in 1996, the following are some strategies to maintain cohesion and ongoing work during such a challenging period:

1 **Temporary Performance Venues:** Identify and secure alternative performance spaces, such as local theatres, churches, and public spaces, to continue presenting concerts and maintaining visibility within the community.
2 **Fundraising Efforts:** Launch significant fundraising campaigns to support both the rebuilding of the venue and the ongoing operations during the reconstruction period. This effort helps maintain the financial stability of the organisation.
3 **Community Engagement:** Continue to bind with the community through various initiatives, such as educational programs, workshops, and collaborations with local organisations. This approach maintains a strong connection with the audience and reinforces the orchestra's role as a cultural ambassador.
4 **Internal Communication and Support:** Maintain strong internal communication among musicians, staff, and management to keep the team cohesive during challenging times. The organisation also provides support and resources to help members adapt to the changing circumstances.

The resilience and adaptability during a rebuilding process after a disaster demonstrate the importance of strong leadership, innovative thinking, and collaborative problem-solving in crisis management.

QUESTIONS:
1 In the face of such an overwhelming disaster as the fire that destroyed the historic venue, what strategies could be employed to ensure that the reputation, standing, and sense of identity are not similarly devastated?
2 Given the critical role that location and physical space can play, how can the organisation work to maintain its unique brand and connection with its historical roots while operating from temporary venues during a reconstruction period?
3 In response to the inevitable financial strain incurred by the disaster, how could they effectively engage patrons and the broader community in fundraising efforts without creating donor fatigue or over-reliance on a narrow group of major donors?

Crisis management and contingency planning are essential aspects of management, enabling organisations to prepare for and navigate unforeseen challenges and emergencies, and facilitate recovery. Organisations that understand and implement best practices, such as providing transparent communication, prioritising well-being, and adapting to new circumstances, emerge from crises more resilient and better equipped to face future uncertainties. The example of the Berliner Philharmoniker is emblematic, as they used the Covid lockdown time to strengthen their digital reach, expanding their audience to new profiles and demographics that they now leverage to increase visibility and revenue.

E. EMBRACING SUSTAINABILITY

Sustainability has become an increasingly significant concern in various industries, and the world of performing arts is no exception to this underlying trend. As orchestras aim to create a lasting impact on their audiences, they also consider their environmental footprint and sustainable practices. This section explores the levers of environmental impact and offers high-level guidance on how to implement sustainable practices in various aspects of management, from operations to touring and beyond.

The Environmental Impact

Orchestras contribute to environmental concerns through various aspects of their operations, such as energy consumption, waste generation, and carbon emissions resulting from a variety of activities (Prado-Guerra et al. 2020). It is essential to start the sustainability journey by gaining a clear understanding of environmental impact and determining areas where improvements can be made accordingly.

1   **Energy Consumption:** Concert halls, offices, and rehearsal spaces have a substantial energy consumption. The non-publicly visible area is often just as large, if not larger, than the hall and stage, which makes the energy demand much more significant than it may initially appear. This includes lighting, heating or cooling, and powering all kinds of equipment. It also includes indirect energy use, such as fuel used by musicians when many of them take their car to go to rehearsals, performances, and other activities.

2   **Waste Generation:** Organisations produce waste through various means such as paper usage, disposable items related to food and beverages, and

other materials utilised during events or performances, as well as during routine work. Marketing collateral, and at times merchandise, also significantly add to the overall waste accumulation throughout a given operational season.

3 **Carbon Emissions:** Travel for performances, tours, and transporting equipment contributes to the carbon footprint, as it often involves air and road transportation, which are significant sources of greenhouse gas emissions. The daily trips to and from the home of the musicians and other staff should also be included in the carbon footprint.

BOX 6.2 CLIMATE CHANGE AND THE PERFORMING ARTS: NEW YORK UNDER SIEGE IN JUNE 2023

While the environmental impact of the performing arts has been a topic of increasing concern, it is equally crucial to consider the reverse – how rapidly deteriorating environmental conditions, exacerbated by climate change, have profound and far-reaching effects on orchestras, operas, and the performing arts sector at large.

As we write these lines in June 2023, unprecedented wildfires have been ravaging Canada for several weeks, casting a pall of toxic smoke that has drifted southwards to infiltrate the United States, resulting in the worst air pollution in the nation's recent recorded history (Gabbatt 2023). This calamitous event, seemingly distant from the typical concerns of the cultural sector, has nonetheless revealed a pressing and underacknowledged challenge for the performing arts: information filtering through from those working on the ground in New York over the past few days reveals that the deteriorated air quality is already having a detrimental impact on operatic and orchestral performances.

The severity of the current climate crisis is highlighted by both a recent alarming update published in the *Earth System Science Data* (Smith et al. 2023) and the research from Stanford University Echo Lab, which reveals that on 7 June 2023 the average American was exposed to 27.5 micrograms per cubic metre of small particulate matter carried within the plumes of smoke (Milman 2023), the highest level ever recorded. These microscopic particles, known as PM2.5, penetrate deep into the lungs when inhaled and are linked to a variety of health conditions, even causing premature deaths. This level of pollution is notably higher than previous records, painting a worrying picture of the potential health implications for all citizens, including artists and performers. As the climate crisis escalates, and these occurrences become more frequent, it is imperative to consider how this reality can disrupt the world of performing arts. As currently observed in New York, some opera and orchestral performances are being perturbed by the execrable air quality resulting from these wildfires. The breath control required for operatic singing and the playing of wind instruments is a delicate art, balanced on the knife-edge of physical capability. Awful air quality tips this balance, making performances challenging and potentially hazardous to the health of performers. This issue is particularly novel for regions such as the US East Coast, which is unaccustomed to such disasters and the associated risks. The eastern seaboard has been largely spared from the direct impact of wildfires, with most large-scale fires occurring in the western regions of North America. However, the current situation has brought an unthinkable and distant problem uncomfortably close to home, affecting areas that are unfamiliar with such a crisis (Anguiano 2023).

As we will likely face this new reality more and more frequently, it necessitates a change in the way we approach the management of cultural events. Common advice for dealing with poor air quality, such as staying indoors, using air purifiers, and wearing masks, while essential for maintaining health, brings with it a host of implications for the performing arts. Rehearsals, performances, and even the simple act of practising one's craft are hampered significantly by these precautions. The invisible nature of the threat is particularly insidious. Wildfire smoke at the level seen on the East Coast permeates everything, and the risk from air pollution remains even when one cannot see or smell it. The potential implications of this for performing arts spaces are substantial. Even after the visible signs of smoke have subsided, particulate matter remains in the air and on surfaces, necessitating rigorous cleaning protocols and ongoing air filtration measures in venues.

In the face of these challenges, the call for adaptive strategies within the performing arts community becomes louder. For some, this may involve investing in air filtration systems for their venues, a solution that may be beyond the reach of smaller and amateur orchestras or opera houses. Others may seek alternative venues, potentially even exploring outdoor performances where air quality permits. Such solutions, while not without their challenges, reflect the creativity and resilience intrinsic to the arts community. However, it is essential to recognise that these are merely reactive measures, serving to mitigate rather than solve the underlying problem. The increasing frequency and intensity of wildfires, fuelled by climate change, pose a severe threat to the performing arts.

Consider the lyric soprano, the choir, or the brass players, all of whom depend on good respiratory health to carry out their duties. The complex physiological processes that these artists engage in to produce and modulate sound are exquisitely sensitive to air quality. The inhalation of polluted air irritates the respiratory tract, reduces lung capacity, and triggers allergic reactions, all of which impair a performer's ability to control their breath – a vital factor in the delivery of a powerful musical performance. Also, the audience, the lifeblood of any performance, is not immune to these effects. Awful air quality discourages attendance at live performances, leading to a decrease in ticket sales and revenues, and ultimately threatening the financial viability of these cultural institutions. The recent reports of disturbances at performances due to the smoke from the Canadian wildfires are not isolated events but symptoms of an escalating crisis in the domain of arts and culture.

Looking ahead, it is clear that the intersections between climate change, air quality, and the performing arts are far from straightforward. The challenges are significant, but they also offer opportunities for innovation, resilience, and leadership. The current predicament underscores the need for a paradigm shift in the management of arts and culture – one that acknowledges and addresses the interconnectedness of the environment, human health, and the arts. The effects of climate change on music performance, particularly in relation to air quality, are far-reaching and require urgent attention.

Implementing Sustainable Practices

Sustainable practices involve a comprehensive and in-depth approach to reducing the environmental impact. The following are key areas where facility managers focus their efforts already:

1 **Reducing Energy Consumption:** Concert halls invest in energy-efficient technologies, such as LED lighting, and implement energy-saving practices, such as turning off equipment when not in use. Sometimes, adapting office hours to align activities with daylight also contributes to reducing energy consumption and, most importantly, to increasing awareness of the significant impact caused by small actions.

2 **Minimising Waste:** Reduce the quantity of material used overall, encourage utilisation of repairable equipment, offer recycling and composting at events and performances, use digital materials whenever possible, and provide reusable or compostable food and beverage items.

3 **Sustainable Touring:** Plan tours with environmental considerations in mind, such as optimising travel routes to reduce emissions, selecting eco-friendly accommodations and venues, considering carbon emissions as criteria to select an airline, and partnering with local organisations to offset the environmental impact.

4 **Green Procurement:** Choose suppliers and partners who prioritise sustainability and implement environmentally friendly practices in their operations.

Onboarding Stakeholders in Sustainable Initiatives

To enhance the chances of achieving a more comprehensive environmental impact and bringing sustainable initiatives to fruition, it is crucial for any organisation to educate its entire ecosystem of stakeholders. This includes its personnel, volunteers, contractors, and the audiences they serve. Such an educative effort ensures that everyone involved understands and aligns with the mission of sustainability, thereby potentially fostering a more profound and widespread effect.

1 **Internal Education and Training:** Provide training and resources to all staff on sustainable practices, and encourage them to onboard these practices in their daily work routines.

2 **Audience Engagement:** Communicate the sustainability efforts to audiences and encourage them to participate in sustainable practices during events and performances.

3 **Collaborating with Local Organisations:** Partner with local environmental organisations to support sustainable initiatives, such as tree planting or clean-up campaigns, and give the community a key, if not leading, role in these efforts.

Measuring and Communicating Success

To demonstrate their dedication to sustainability, organisations quantify their advancements, establish tangible targets for enhancement, and maintain open lines of communication with their stakeholders. This process not only makes progress measurable but also keeps all parties invested and informed about the strides being made towards a more sustainable future.

1 **Establishing Sustainability Metrics:** Define measurable success indicators of sustainability efforts, such as energy savings, waste reduction, and carbon emission reductions.

2 **Setting Goals and Monitoring Progress:** Set ambitious but realistic goals for improving sustainability and regularly monitor progress towards these goals.

3 **Transparent Communication:** Share the sustainability efforts with stakeholders, such as through annual reports, social media, and press releases, to demonstrate their commitment to environmental stewardship and inspire others to take action.

Sustainability goes beyond being a moral imperative; it also offers a potent avenue to deepen bonds with patrons and the wider community. Entities that embrace shared sustainable practices exhibit not only their allegiance to environmental values but also their ability to heed the civil appeals of their stakeholders. This dual commitment resonates with today's conscious audiences, positioning these arts and culture institutions as both cultural and environmental leaders.

***

Each of these sectors demand an in-depth understanding and specific skill sets. The unique facets of each are not only critical, but provide an integral understanding of the whole. Managers, in the face of constant change, often witness the necessity to adapt, aligning themselves with the progression of technology, shifting audience, and community demands.

CASE STUDY 6.4

A Journey to Sustainability and Environmental Protection

Sustainability and environmental protection are becoming increasingly important to navigate the complex landscape of audience expectations and environmental concerns. This case study explores how a specialised consulting firm was called to conduct a sustainability and environmental protection audit and make recommendations on the path to becoming a more responsible and environmentally conscious organisation.

IDENTIFYING THE NEED FOR A SUSTAINABILITY AUDIT

- Recognising the growing importance of sustainability and environmental responsibility in the cultural sector
- Evaluating the current environmental impact and identifying areas for improvement
- Gaining board and staff support for the audit process and subsequent initiatives

TENDER PROCESS FOR SELECTING THE CONSULTING FIRM

- Developing a request for proposals (RFP) outlining the objectives, scope of work, and desired outcomes
- Advertising the RFP to potential consulting firms specialising in sustainability and environmental protection
- Assessing proposals based on experience, methodology, and alignment with the values and goals
- Selecting the most suitable consulting firm and negotiating the contract terms

CONDUCTING THE SUSTAINABILITY AND ENVIRONMENTAL PROTECTION AUDIT

- Assessing the environmental impact, including energy consumption, waste generation, and carbon footprint
- Evaluating the existing sustainability policies and practices
- Identifying areas for improvement and potential environmental risks
- Benchmarking the performance against industry standards and best practices

DEVELOPING A COMPREHENSIVE SUSTAINABILITY STRATEGY

- Collaborating with the consulting firm to create a tailored sustainability strategy
- Setting specific goals and targets for reducing environmental impact
- Identifying potential partnerships and collaborations with other organisations and stakeholders to support sustainability initiatives

- Incorporating sustainability considerations into the artistic programming, operations, and communications

IMPLEMENTING THE SUSTAINABILITY STRATEGY

- Communicating the strategy to staff, musicians, board members, and stakeholders
- Providing training and resources to support the implementation of new policies and practices
- Establishing monitoring and reporting mechanisms to track progress toward sustainability goals
- Continuously evaluating and refining the strategy as needed

COMMUNICATING THE COMMITMENT TO SUSTAINABILITY

- Developing a marketing and public relations campaign to promote the sustainability efforts
- Sharing success stories and progress updates through various communication channels, such as the website, social media, newsletters, and other channels
- Cooperating with audiences, donors, and community partners to raise awareness and support for the sustainability initiatives

The collaboration with a specialised consulting firm led to a comprehensive sustainability and environmental protection audit, resulting in the development and implementation of a tailored strategy to reduce its environmental impact. This case study highlights the importance of relying on expert guidance, setting clear goals, seeking internal support, and effectively communicating the commitment to sustainability and environmental protection.

QUESTIONS:

1 How might the initial identification and assessment of the environmental impact challenge traditional operational processes and attitudes within the organisation, and how can these challenges be effectively managed?

2 In what ways could the selection process of the consulting firm potentially reflect or affect the organisation's commitment to sustainability, and what factors should be given priority in the evaluation of proposals? How can the orchestra ensure that the developed sustainability strategy

aligns with its core values and mission, while also achieving tangible environmental improvements?

3 Given the potential resistance to change and the additional workload that may accompany the implementation of a sustainability strategy, what strategies can be employed to foster widespread support and active participation among staff, musicians, and board members?

4 How can the orchestra effectively leverage its commitment to sustainability as a marketing tool, and what considerations should be made to ensure authenticity and transparency in communicating its efforts to audiences, donors, and community partners?

F. DIGITAL AND PHYSICAL ACCESSIBILITY

Ensuring that performances are accessible to all audiences, regardless of physical or sensory limitations, is a crucial aspect of modern management.[3] The pursuit of accessibility not only aligns with principles of inclusivity and social corporate responsibility but also broadens the potential reach and impact, attracting diverse audiences and forging a feeling of belonging within the classical music community. Several complementary strategies could be implemented to improve physical accessibility in venues and incorporate technologies that enable greater access for individuals with disabilities. Five

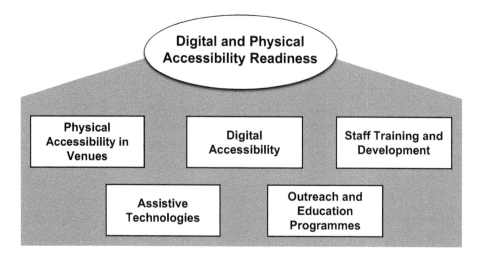

FIGURE 6.6 Digital and Physical Accessibility Readiness

key components are involved in aligning a performing organisation with the common practices of a digital business ecosystem:

a **Physical Accessibility in Venues:** Indeed, the consideration given to the design and layout of performance spaces to accommodate mobility impairments, including the provision for wheelchair users and those who struggle with stairs, as well as the incorporation of aids for the visually and hearing impaired, is often an integral aspect of good practice and a demonstration of comprehensive accessibility. This involves the provision of accessible seating areas, ramps, lifts, and appropriate signage to facilitate movement and ensure a positive experience for all patrons. In response to the growing awareness of inclusivity, management increasingly collaborates with venue staff to develop policies and procedures catering to the needs of individuals with disabilities. This practice often involves reserving specific seating areas and offering early entrance to the venue. Along with this, augmenting the physical infrastructure of performance spaces, there is a burgeoning attention towards the accessibility of ancillary services such as refreshments and merchandise stands. The idea is to ensure these facilities are conveniently reachable and navigable for all.

b **Assistive Technologies:** Incorporating assistive technologies into performances significantly enhances the experience for individuals with sensory impairments, such as hearing or visual disabilities. For example, audio description services provide real-time narration of visual elements, such as the conductor's movements or stage design, through individual headsets or a smartphone app. Alternatively, some captioning systems already display the spoken or sung text of a performance, allowing spectators with hearing impairments to follow the narrative or lyrics. In some cases, providing sign language interpreters for performances or pre-concert talks helps people with hearing conditions to fully follow the content.

c **Digital Accessibility:** Although more recent, digital accessibility has also become vital for managers: websites, advertising materials, and digital content are now designed following standards or best practices to make them accessible to individuals with disabilities, using features such as screen readers, alternative text for images, and adjustable font sizes. Additionally, digital accessibility extends to the provision of online performances and streams, which offer a more comfortable and accessible experience to all those who find it challenging to attend a physical event. An investment in digital accessibility helps create a more inclusive online presence and demonstrates their commitment to reaching the widest possible audience.

d   **Outreach and Education Programs:** Outreach and education programs are instrumental in raising awareness about accessibility issues and a culture of inclusivity within the classical music community. Engaging in collaborations with disability organisations, schools, and community groups paves the way for offering workshops, performances, and other events designed to introduce individuals with disabilities to the world of classical music, providing them an avenue for cultural enrichment and enjoyment.

e   **Staff Training and Development:** An effective implementation of accessibility initiatives also requires investment in staff training and development, ensuring that all team members possess the necessary knowledge and skills to support patrons with disabilities. This may include training in the use of assistive technologies, understanding accessibility requirements and best practices, and developing effective communication skills. A corporate culture of empathy and understanding better serve the diverse needs of audiences and create a more welcoming environment for all.

Incorporating digital and physical accessibility into the fundamentals of management is essential for creating a more inclusive experience, regardless of physical or sensory limitations. When orchestras invest in physical accessibility in venues, incorporate assistive technologies, ensure digital accessibility, and deploy outreach and education programmes, they demonstrate their commitment to social responsibility and broaden their reach and impact within the classical music community. Staff training and development in accessibility best practices cultivate empathy that permeates all aspects of the organisation.

As digital and physical accessibility concerns are addressed, orchestras create opportunities for individuals with disabilities to enjoy the transformative power of classical music as a form of enrichment of the cultural landscape overall.

***

In essence, the world of orchestra management can be distilled into five key driving forces, which encapsulate the essential aspects required for success in today's competitive environment. These forces ensure the long-term sustainability and prosperity of an orchestra, enabling it to continue inspiring and enriching the lives of countless individuals through the power of music.

This five-forces framework provides a comprehensive yet succinct representation of the fundamental pillars of management. A proactive approach towards resilience, diversity, equity, inclusion, sound governance, and environmental sustainability keeps orchestras in tune with the evolving world,

FIGURE 6.7 Five Forces: Fundamentals of Orchestra Management

subsequently enabling them to make a substantial positive contribution to the wider society.

The five forces that stand out as particularly significant in determining the ability to thrive in today's competitive market are:

1 **Financial Equilibrium:** Ensuring financial health is crucial for long-term survival, for example, maintaining a diverse mix of revenue streams, including ticket sales, corporate sponsorships, philanthropy, and government funding.

2 **Appealing Artistic Programming:** Attracting and retaining audiences is essential for success. A well-curated artistic programme that balances innovative and traditional works and promotes diversity and inclusion draws in diverse audiences and generates excitement around the performances.

3 **Visionary or Charismatic Senior Management Team, Talent Acquisition, and Diversity, Equity, and Inclusion:** Effective leadership is a key factor in success. A visionary and charismatic senior management team inspires confidence in the organisation, provides strategic direction, and fosters a collaborative environment that promotes artistic excellence. Embracing diversity, equity, and inclusion across all levels of the organisation, both

on stage and behind the scenes, is vital for fostering a rich and dynamic artistic community. Additionally, attracting and retaining top talent, both musicians and administrative staff, is crucial for maintaining the high standards and reputation.

4   **Adaptability and Innovation:** The ability to adapt to changes in the cultural and technological landscape is vital for long-term success. Embracing new technologies, forging strategic partnerships, and staying abreast of trends in the industry helps organisations remain relevant in an ever-evolving and highly competitive market.

5   **Good Governance, Resilience, and Sustainability:** The deployment of robust governance protocols, the endorsement of diversity and inclusion, and the integration of resilience and sustainability measures throughout operational procedures are fundamental tactics for securing enduring viability. This includes fostering environmental sustainability through responsible resource management and considering the ecological impact of all activities. It also entails resilience of the institution as a good governance practice to face acute crises, if any occur.[4]

Box 6.3 Expanding Perspectives: Review Questions

1   Given the trend towards more innovative revenue streams due to volatility in traditional funding, what potential opportunities and challenges does this shift present? How can orchestras navigate these challenges, striking a balance between ensuring their long-term sustainability and maintaining their artistic integrity?

2   In the current volatile economic landscape, reflect on the pivotal role of strategic planning, adaptability, and change management in ensuring long-term financial sustainability. How do these elements contribute to various facets of management, including budgeting, and programming decisions?

3   What benefits and challenges come from fostering a culture of diversity, equity, and inclusion? How might an active commitment to these principles impact the creative, innovative, and excellence quotient of renowned musical institutions? How can an equitable work environment contribute to staff cohesion and management transparency? How can it facilitate engagement with the community at large?

4 Discuss the significance of having a robust contingency plan to mitigate the impact of potential crises. How does having such a plan in place safeguard the interests of musicians, staff, and audiences, while also preserving artistic integrity? What role do clear communication protocols play in ensuring effective crisis response?

5 What are the implications of embracing sustainability in the broader sense, beyond financial longevity, to include environmentally responsible practices? How might adopting sustainable practices enhance the public image and demonstrate the commitment to social responsibility?

6 Discuss the role of physical and digital accessibility in expanding the reach to a more diverse audience. What impact might this increased accessibility have on audience engagement, and potentially, on reputation and influence?

NOTES

1 Based on US high-end values from Salary.com (2023).
2 This number includes all concerts (season concert, pops concerts, family concerts, special events concerts, etc.).
3 For a case study of the physical accessibility of Cracow's cultural institutions, see Bac et al. (2020). Physical accessibility as a prerequisite to cultural appropriation is discussed by Benente and Minucciani (2020). While there is a massive volume of scientific literature produced over the last two decades on digital accessibility of cultural institutions, an interesting case is given by Latvia (Krūmiņa 2014).
4 A captivating data-driven case of cultural institutions resilience is provided by Marian-Potra et al. (2022).

BIBLIOGRAPHY

Anguiano, Dani. 2023. "Surviving the Smoke-Pocalypse 101: Californians Offer Advice to New Yorkers." *The Guardian*, June 8. www.theguardian.com/environment/2023/jun/08/wildfire-smoke-survival-guide-california-new-york.

Bac, Aneta, Karolina Kowal, Paulina Aleksander-Szymanowicz, Katarzyna Filar-Mierzwa, and Edyta Janus. 2020. "An Assessment of Adaptation of Cracow's Cultural Institutions to the Needs of Wheelchair Users." *Advances in Rehabilitation* 34 (1): 13–18. https://doi.org/10.5114/areh.2020.93094.

Beehive. 2020. "Crisis Management: Using the Power of Communication to Maintain Business Continuity." *Beehive*. https://beehivepr.biz/crisis-management-communication/.

Benente, Michela, and Valeria Minucciani. 2020. "Inclusive Museums: From Physical Accessibility to Cultural Appropriation." In *Advances in Industrial Design*, 189–195. Advances in Intelligent Systems and Computing. https://doi.org/10.1007/978-3-030-51194-4_25.

Biernoff, Lara, and Diana Blom. 2002. "Non-Western Ensembles: Crossing Boundaries and Creating Interstices in Cross-Cultural Educational Contexts." *Research Studies in Music Education* 19 (1): 22–31. https://doi.org/10.1177/1321103X020190010401.

Bull, Anna, Christina Scharff, and Laudan Nooshin. 2023. *Voices for Change in the Classical Music Profession: New Ideas for Tackling Inequalities and Exclusions*. Oxford: Oxford University Press.

Byrnes, William J. 2022. *Management and the Arts*, 6th ed. New York: Routledge.

Eriksson, Kerstin, and Allan McConnell. 2011. "Contingency Planning for Crisis Management: Recipe for Success or Political Fantasy?" *Policy and Society* 30 (2): 89–99. https://doi.org/10.1016/j.polsoc.2011.03.004.

Gabbatt, Adam. 2023. "Canada Wildfires Smoke Could Linger Over Parts of US for Days, Officials Warn." *The Guardian*, June 8. www.theguardian.com/world/2023/jun/08/canada-wildfires-smoke-linger-us-days-officals-warn.

Gamble, Jordan Robert, Michael Brennan, and Rodney McAdam. 2017. "A Rewarding Experience? Exploring How Crowdfunding Is Affecting Music Industry Business Models." *Journal of Business Research* 70 (January): 25–36. https://doi.org/10.1016/j.jbusres.2016.07.009.

Garrett, Karen. 2018. "Inextricably Connected: Recognizing the Power of Equity and Inclusion in Arts and Culture Philanthropy." My University. https://doi.org/10.13016/M22B8VG0C.

Goldin, Claudia, and Cecilia Rouse. 1997. *Orchestrating Impartiality: The Impact of "Blind" Auditions on Female Musicians*. w5903. Cambridge, MA: National Bureau of Economic Research. https://doi.org/10.1257/aer.90.4.715.

Heymann, Jody, Aleta Sprague, and Amy Raub. 2023. "Gender Discrimination at Work." In *Equality Within Our Lifetimes: How Laws and Policies Can Close – or Widen – Gender Gaps in Economies Worldwide*, 21–53. University of California Press. https://doi.org/10.1525/luminos.147.c.

Hoegl, Martin, and Hans Georg Gemuenden. 2001. "Teamwork Quality and the Success of Innovative Projects: A Theoretical Concept and Empirical Evidence." *Organization Science* 12 (4): 435–449. https://doi.org/10.1287/orsc.12.4.435.10635.

Kimpton, Jeffrey, and Glenn M. Lestz. 1985. "Selling Young People on the Symphony." *Music Educators Journal* 72 (1): 44–45. https://doi.org/10.2307/3396576.

Krūmiņa, Līga. 2014. "Accessibility of Cultural Heritage in the Virtual Environment of Latvia Memory Institutions." *Bibliotheca Lituana* 3 (December): 196–208. https://doi.org/10.15388/bibllita.2014.3.15572.

League of American Orchestras. 2023. "Racial/Ethnic and Gender Diversity in the Orchestra Field in 2023." *League of American Orchestras*. https://americanorchestras.org/racial-ethnic-and-gender-diversity-in-the-orchestra-field-in-2023/.

Marian-Potra, Alexandra-Camelia, Ana-Maria Pop, Gheorghe-Gavrilă Hognogi, and Júlia A. Nagy. 2022. "Resilience of the Romanian Independent Cultural Sector under COVID-19 Pandemic Using the Grounded Theory." *Sustainability: Science Practice and Policy* 14 (8): 4564. https://doi.org/10.3390/su14084564.

McClelland, Christina. 2021. "Exploring Needs for Diversity, Equity, and Inclusion Practices in Arts and Culture Nonprofits in Denver, Colorado." *The Foundation Review* 13 (1): 5. https://doi.org/10.9707/1944-5660.1550.

McConnell, Allan, and Lynn Drennan. 2006. "Mission Impossible? Planning and Preparing for Crisis." *Journal of Contingencies and Crisis Management* 14 (2): 59–70. https://doi.org/10.1111/j.1468-5973.2006.00482.x.

Milman, Oliver. 2023. "Air Pollution in US from Wildfire Smoke Is Worst in Recent Recorded History." *The Guardian*, June 8. www.theguardian.com/environment/2023/jun/08/air-quality-record-smoke-hazard-wildfire-worst-day-ever-canada-new-york.

Ndlela, Martin N. 2019. "A Stakeholder Approach to Crisis Evaluation." In *Crisis Communication: A Stakeholder Approach*, edited by Martin N. Ndlela, 151–156. https://doi.org/10.1007/978-3-319-97256-5_8.

Negus, Keith. 2019. "From Creator to Data: The Post-Record Music Industry and the Digital Conglomerates." *Media Culture & Society* 41 (3): 367–384. https://doi.org/10.1177/0163443718799395.

Patrick, Harold Andrew, and Vincent Raj Kumar. 2012. "Managing Workplace Diversity: Issues and Challenges." *SAGE Open* 2 (2): 1–15. https://doi.org/10.1177/2158244012444615.

Prado-Guerra, Alba, Sergio Paniagua Bermejo, Luis Fernando Calvo Prieto, and Monica Santamarta Llorente. 2020. "Environmental Impact Study of Symphony Orchestras and Preparation of a Classification Guide." *The International Journal of Environmental Studies* 77 (6): 1044–1059. https://doi.org/10.1080/00207233.2020.1746546.

Salary.com. 2023. "Orchestra Musician Salary in the United State." www.salary.com/research/salary/hiring/orchestra-musician-salary.

Smith, Chris, Tristram Walsh, Alex Borger, Piers Forster, Nathan Gillett, Mathias Hauser, Willam Lamb, et al. 2023. "Indicators of Global Climate Change 2022." https://doi.org/10.5281/zenodo.8000192.

Szedmák, Borbála. 2021. "Business Model Innovation and the First Steps of Digitalization in the Case of Symphony Orchestras." In *New Horizons in Business and Management Studies*. Corvinus University of Budapest. https://doi.org/10.14267/978-963-503-867-1_15.

Tan, Cheryl Lu-Lien. 2020. "Music, and Work, Never Stop for New York Philharmonic's Borda." *Reuters*, October 23. www.reuters.com/article/us-world-work-borda-idUSKBN2781DP.

Triguero-Sánchez, Rafael, Jesus Peña-Vinces, and Jorge Guillen. 2018. "How to Improve Firm Performance Through Employee Diversity and Organisational Culture." *Review of Business Management* 20 (3): 378–400. https://doi.org/10.7819/rbgn.v20i3.3303.

Worth, Michael J. 2021. *Nonprofit Management: Principles and Practice*, 5th ed. Thousand Oaks, CA: SAGE Publications.

Yu, Hilson Hiu Kai, Dickson K. W. Chiu, and Cheuk Ting Chan. 2023. "Resilience of Symphony Orchestras to Challenges in the COVID-19 Era: Analyzing the Hong Kong Philharmonic Orchestra with Porter's Five Force Model." In *Handbook of Research on Entrepreneurship and Organizational Resilience During Unprecedented Times*, 586–601. IGI Global. https://doi.org/10.4018/978-1-6684-4605-8.ch026.

Cited content from websites was last accessed on 01 July 2023.

CHAPTER 7

Tech Innovation in Modern Orchestra Management

In the last two decades, the landscape of the classical music industry has undergone a rapid transformation, propelled by a variety of factors: the ever-evolving role of technology and digital content, the changing demography of audiences, the fast obsolescence of trends and tastes amongst the younger generations, the emergence of new leisure habits, and the very recent improvement and diversification of AI applications, to name a few. As we venture further and deeper into the digital age, orchestras face unprecedented disruptions, challenges, and opportunities of a magnitude and a nature never seen before. Navigating this shifting terrain requires a forward-thinking approach, a good knowledge of emerging trends, and harnessing the potential of cutting-edge technologies to revolutionise the way performing institutions operate and onboard their audiences (Bibu, Brancu, and Teohari 2018; Poulios and Kamperou 2022).

One of the key trends shaping the future of orchestras is the integration of advanced technologies in music performance, operations, and consumption. The increasing prevalence of digital tools, such as virtual reality (VR), augmented reality (AR), and artificial intelligence (AI), has opened up new possibilities for both the audience experience and management.[1] For instance, VR and AR technologies could be used to create immersive concert experiences, transporting audiences to visually and sonically stunning virtual environments. Additionally, AI-driven platforms have the potential to revolutionise operations (and the way they are managed), from automating administrative tasks to curating personalised marketing campaigns and implementing predictive assets and equipment maintenance or replacement.

The pandemic has further accelerated the growing trend of community-building through the use of digital platforms and social media. When attention becomes an increasingly scarce commodity and all the more valuable, the search for ways to connect with existing and potential patrons and audiences assumes a central role. Leveraging the power of social media and digital

DOI: 10.4324/9781032629636-7

content broadens the reach and forges a shared identity among classical music enthusiasts worldwide. As seen in a previous chapter, data-driven marketing strategies also improve the understanding of audiences and allow granular tailored programming that suits a variety of better-known preferences.

The market for IT solutions catering to various aspects of management has grown significantly in recent years, reflecting the industry's increasing reliance on technology. These solutions encompass a wide range of new functionalities beyond the traditional finance or HR features, from ticketing and scheduling to performance analytics and donor management. The availability of such comprehensive and specialised tools has fundamentally transformed operations and execution, enabling them to streamline processes, improve decision-making, and monitor business and artistic performance against key indicators. This shift towards technology-driven management has made today's administration vastly different from that of just three decades ago.

In light of the recent global pandemic, the importance of resilience and adaptability in the face of adversity has been underscored. The readiness to pivot quickly and adjust becomes a significant determinant in ensuring success within a fiercely competitive industry. This might involve exploring opportunities such as online concerts and digital content subscriptions, or cultivating creative collaborations with other artistic organisations. The rapidity of these adaptive responses becomes paramount to stay abreast of digital shifts but also to grasp the more profound, overall metamorphosis reshaping the industry itself.

The future of the industry, and the way it is managed, lies therefore at the intersection of technology, audience development, demographics, adaptability, and resilience. The assessment and adoption of emerging trends enable both the navigation of the digital wave and a prospective confluence with the expectations of classical music enthusiasts around the globe.

WHAT YOU WILL LEARN IN THIS CHAPTER

Section	Key Learning Points
A. The 1990s Legacy of IT Pervasiveness	In the 1990s and early 2000s, the integration of information technology into the classical music industry has created a paradigm shift in the way major ensembles operate and interact with their audiences. Management software, ERPs, and CRMs have been a game-changer for the industry, providing automation of numerous administrative tasks such as budgeting, scheduling, human resources, and audience management. These tools allow for streamlined operations, improved planning, and mitigated risks.

Section	Key Learning Points
B. The Importance of Social Media	Since the mid-2010s, social media platforms have become an essential channel to engage with audiences and promote performances. A strategic usage of social media expands the reach to a wider audience, builds brand awareness, and creates a sense of community among followers. Social media also provides an opportunity to showcase behind-the-scenes content and connect with fans on a more personal level.
C. Digital Transformation	Digital transformation extends far beyond the mere introduction of new technologies into the operations, communications, and music performances. It involves a multi-branch concept that explores its understanding, implications, opportunities, and challenges. The complex process of digital transformation plays a significant role in maintaining competitiveness within the music industry in the digital age. This often involves the integration of new business models, leveraging technology to bolster audience engagement and streamline execution efficiency.
D. The Potential Impact of Artificial Intelligence on the Classical Music Industry	Artificial intelligence (AI) has an enormous potential to revolutionise the classical music industry by enhancing creativity, improving performance quality, and increasing accessibility for audiences worldwide. AI-powered tools can help musicians compose music more efficiently by generating melodies or harmonies based on specific parameters or styles. AI can also be used to analyse performance data to identify areas for improvement or provide real-time feedback during rehearsals.
E. The Role of Immersive Technologies in the Future of Performances	Immersive technologies such as virtual reality (VR) and augmented reality (AR) have an enormous potential to transform orchestral performances by creating immersive experiences that engage audiences in new ways. VR can transport audiences to different locations or time periods, while AR can enhance live performances by overlaying digital content onto the physical world. These technologies provide an opportunity to create unique and memorable experiences that appeal to a wider audience.
F. Examples of Leveraging Technology and Digital Media	Several renowned large ensembles have successfully leveraged technology and digital media to enhance their operations and engage with audiences. The London Symphony Orchestra has implemented a digital platform that allows musicians to access sheet music, rehearsal schedules, and other resources from their mobile devices. The New York Philharmonic has launched a mobile app that provides information about upcoming performances, behind-the-scenes content, and interactive features such as live polls and quizzes. The Berlin Philharmonic has created a digital concert hall that allows audiences to access streamed live performances and an archive of past concerts. These examples demonstrate the potential of technology and digital media to enhance the classical music industry by improving operational efficiency, increasing audience engagement, and expanding access to performances.

A. THE 1990S LEGACY OF IT PERVASIVENESS

In the 1990s and early 2000s, the rapid integration of information technologies into the classical music industry has created a paradigm shift in the way orchestras operate and interact with their audiences. As technology continues to advance and permeate various aspects of our lives, managers have to face a tide of IT solutions that all claim to upgrade the efficiency and effectiveness of their organisations. The implementation of management software in the 1990s, primarily ERPs and CRMs, has been a game-changer for the industry, providing automation of numerous administrative tasks such as budgeting, scheduling, human resources, and audience management. These tools allow for streamlining operations, improving planning, and mitigating the risk of human error.

Staying informed about relevant technological innovations and selecting the most suitable solutions has become an additional aspect of management. Identifying the right app or service requires a thorough understanding of the organisation's specific needs and objectives. This, in turn, ensures that investments in technology yield the desired results, contributing to the organisation's overall success.

Implementing IT solutions has also opened new avenues for audience engagement and revenue generation. The use of digital platforms and streaming services since the 2000s and 2010s facilitates the reach of wider audiences thanks to the disconnection from time and space constraints (Bergman 2021). Moreover, the integration of IT has spurred the development of innovative marketing strategies, leveraging data analytics and social media platforms to better understand and cater to audience preferences. The data-driven approach supports targeted marketing campaigns and helps a more accurate definition of artistic programming that appeals to a broader demographic by soliciting a variety of previously ignored niches. In the field of artistic collaboration, IT has facilitated seamless communication and coordination among musicians, conductors, and composers. Cloud-based platforms and file-sharing services also support the instantaneous exchange of ideas, annotated music sheets, and recordings, facilitating a collaborative environment that transcends geographical boundaries.

The pervasiveness of IT in the classical music industry has irrevocably changed the landscape of management in a process that started decades ago and is now well established. Embracing technology and adapting to the ever-evolving digital landscape help stay relevant, sharpen operations, and ultimately ensure long-term success in the competitive world of classical music.

B. THE IMPORTANCE OF SOCIAL MEDIA

From the early to mid-2010s until now, social media platforms such as You-Tube, Instagram, Facebook, Twitter, WhatsApp, TikTok, Twitch, Discord, LinkedIn, and many more have emerged as vital instruments to cooperate with audiences or facilitate and stimulate revenue generation.[2] These digital channels also enabled orchestras to capitalise on multiple benefits, transforming the way they function, communicate, and excel in the competitive realm of classical music. We have identified five key advantages of social media.

1 **Attracting New Audiences:** Social media grants orchestras the opportunity to create captivating content, showcasing their unique qualities and artistic offerings. Collaboration with influencers and content diffusion over diverse platforms broaden the demographic reach and draw in new audiences who may have had limited exposure to classical music. For instance, the Berliner Philharmoniker's YouTube channel, featuring performances, interviews, and behind-the-scenes content, now counts half a million subscribers and more than 185 million views.

2 **Fostering Loyalty Among Existing Patrons:** Social media platforms ease and strengthen connections with current and prospective audiences.

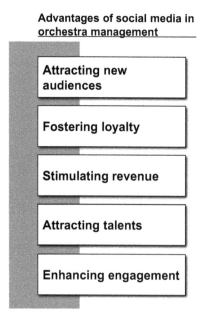

Advantages of social media in orchestra management

- Attracting new audiences
- Fostering loyalty
- Stimulating revenue
- Attracting talents
- Enhancing engagement

Digital channels enable orchestra management to capitalise on multiple benefits, transforming the way they function, communicate, and excel in the competitive realm of classical music.

FIGURE 7.1 Role of Social Media

Orchestras use them to cultivate community and loyalty among their patrons in different ways; sharing behind-the-scenes content, involving followers, and offering exclusive access to events and experiences are one of them. For example, the New York Philharmonic utilises Instagram to share photos and videos of rehearsals, backstage moments, and interviews with musicians, giving followers an insider's perspective not only on the artistic activities but also into the social life of musicians.

3 **Stimulating Revenue Generation:** Social media creates monetisation opportunities. Through sponsored content, online concerts, and streamed events, new avenues for revenue are put in place. This has proven particularly valuable in the wake of the Covid-19 pandemic, which led to the cancellation of numerous live performances. The London Symphony, for instance, has a YouTube channel where they stream concerts, allowing audiences to experience the concerts from the comfort of their own homes but also allowing aficionados who couldn't find tickets not to miss their favourite performers.

4 **Attracting Talented Musicians and Staff:** Apart from drawing new audiences, social media aids in constructing the narrative of an appealing destination for skilled musicians and staff. To tempt potential employees in the search for a vibrant and collaborative work environment, orchestras offer an image that differentiates them from the competition – that is why showcasing their artistic excellence, distinctive programming, and behind-the-scenes culture is not a benign action but a strong means to go beyond the professional image and ignite positive sentiments. The National Symphony Orchestra (Washington, D.C.), for example, has used social media to promote its fellowship programmes and showcase the experiences of its musicians, attracting a diverse pool of talented applicants worldwide.

5 **Enriching Audience Experience:** Key ideas from Travis Newton's handbook (Newton 2022) indicate that audience engagement in the digital age is crucial to success. Digital platforms allow reaching new audiences, establishing a dialogue with existing patrons, and creating communities around their work. Interactive live chats during streaming events facilitate real-time communication between musicians and viewers. Additionally, social media platforms are also used to conduct polls, quizzes, and surveys, encouraging audience interaction and providing valuable insights into audience preferences.

Social media supplies enough data and functionalities to monitor audience preferences, customise marketing efforts, and assess the success of digital strategies. Granular data collection and metrics analysis, such as likes, shares, comments, time of connection, location, hashtags, and more, provide valuable insights into audience-resonating content, enabling for fine-tuning of marketing strategies accordingly.

Incorporating technology for immersive experiences, such as virtual reality and augmented reality, also creates unique ways to connect with audiences. Although still new and largely untapped in the performing arts industry, these data-driven technologies allow virtual tours, interactive educational content, and immersive concert experiences, further shaping audience and stakeholder mobilisation.

Beyond conventional social media platforms, a new generation of innovative applications, such as the well-known Acapella (Mixcord Inc), is pushing the boundaries of how musicians interact, collaborate, and create music. Acapella offers musicians an easy way to connect, share ideas, and, most importantly, seamlessly record joint pieces remotely, without the need to be all present in a studio. This technology transcends geographical limitations, enabling musicians to forge global artistic partnerships and productions that might have been impossible otherwise. During the Covid-19 lockdown, a few orchestras have capitalised on such ground-breaking tools to broaden their creative horizons, explore diverse musical influences, and propose to their audiences collective pieces that could not have been recorded otherwise. Developing innovative projects that blend various cultural and musical traditions becomes possible when the barriers to collaboration with musicians otherwise inaccessible due to physical constraints or logistical challenges are lifted. This approach backs a multicultural soundscape, captivates new audiences, and lifts the global reputation. Collaborative-work applications strongly contribute to audience widening by offering exclusive glimpses into the creative process.[3] Orchestras share their collaborative journey on social media, providing fans with an intimate, behind-the-scenes perspective of the music-making experience. This transparency demystifies the world of classical music and brings audiences to develop a deeper appreciation for the art form. Online masterclasses, workshops, and mentoring programs are good ways to spot new talents and create a strong link to the musicians. The Covid-19 pandemic has made the migration of content and learning opportunities on online platforms more acceptable, although this is not always ideal in the field of music. The pandemic has also made these online platforms more important tools to support distant learning as well as a resource for information and a tool for sharing and keeping the relationship with audiences alive (Serdaroglu 2020). Yet, this remains an excellent solution when the physical distance between the musician and their potential audience is an obstacle. More importantly, this gives aspiring musicians a chance to gain access to valuable learning opportunities that may have been geographically restricted in the past. This inclusive approach expands the boundaries of a global community of classical music enthusiasts, encouraging the growth and development of future generations of musicians.

A whole new generation of applications (for computers and, even more, mobile devices and tablets) is actually revolutionising the classical music landscape, offering the whole industry unprecedented occasions for collaboration, creativity, and global participation. The incorporation of these tools into their repertoire breaks down barriers, unites musicians in a shared creative endeavour, and creates unique, collaborative projects that resonate with audiences worldwide.[4]

Despite inevitable excesses or mishaps, social media has become an indispensable tool, offering numerous opportunities for audience development, revenue generation, and talent attraction. Expressing the potential of social media and other digital technologies is critical to growth in an ever-competing landscape.

As we move forward, flexibility and openness to innovation prove crucial to explore novel ways of integrating social media and a plethora of new technologies into new formats of performance. This does not only help orchestras remain competitive but also enhances their ability to share the beauty and power of classical music with audiences worldwide. While creative use of social media is commendable, utilising it from a strategic perspective yields even greater benefits to overcome challenges, seize new opportunities, and secure a bright future for the art form they passionately represent.

C. DIGITAL TRANSFORMATION

The rapid advancements in technology have brought forth a digital revolution that has permeated nearly every aspect of modern life, including the classical music industry. This section explores the multi-branch concept of digital transformation in orchestra management, delving into its understanding, implications, opportunities, and challenges. Digital transformation extends far beyond the mere introduction of new, cutting-edge (and often fancy and overrated) technologies into the operations, communications, and concerts. Rather than simply adding a layer of innovation to existing processes, digital transformation allows orchestras to deeply examine and address underlying fierce issues, enabling them to realign their goals and adapt to the ever-evolving landscape of the classical music industry (Parviainen et al. 2022; Ng Kea Chye 2021). Through this profound change, orchestras reassess their artistic direction, forge stronger connections with their audiences, and identify opportunities for improvement in areas such as operational efficiency, revenue generation, and community outreach. As rightfully highlighted by Ian Jefferson, expert of the culture sector, in a 2021 interview, "the cultural sector is at an existential moment. When organisations have an acute, important problem, there can also be an amazing opportunity to change their trajectory" (McKinsey & Co. 2021). The significance of digital transformation within the management shell is further underscored by the strategic focus of prominent industry organisations. For instance, in its 2023–2026 Strategic Framework, the League of American Orchestras has identified digital transformation as a key priority (League of American Orchestras 2023). The organisation is committed to transitioning into a digital-first entity, recognising the transformative power of digital technologies to revolutionise its operations and engagement with its constituents.

BOX 7.1 DIGITAL TRANSFORMATION STRATEGY 2023–2026

As part of its digital transformation strategy 2023–2026, the League of American Orchestras is planning to invest in innovative digital learning modalities, enhancing its League360 platform, refining its email marketing and survey reporting processes, and improving its internal IT infrastructure. The objective is to leverage digital technologies to streamline processes, bolster communication channels, and enhance the overall efficiency of operations. Additionally, the League is also directing efforts towards expanding and improving the Resource Centers on its website. The League recognises the importance of adequately resourcing and supporting its remote staff team in the current era of hybrid and remote work arrangements.

Digital transformation in the context of management can be categorised into four primary dimensions: artistic innovation, audience engagement, organisational and operational efficiency, and financial sustainability. Each of these dimensions plays a crucial role in shaping the trajectory of a digital transformation journey.

a   **Artistic Innovation:** Digital transformation offers a wealth of opportunities to push the boundaries of artistic expression, incorporating cutting-edge technologies to create unique and immersive experiences for their audiences. From integrating multimedia elements into live performances to experimenting with virtual reality and augmented reality technologies, the possibilities for artistic innovation are vast. Furthermore, the adoption of digital tools and platforms enables composers, conductors, and musicians to collaborate more effectively, fostering creativity and enhancing the quality of their artistic output.

b **Audience Engagement:** In the digital age, audiences expect more personalised, interactive, and accessible experiences. The digital transformation toolbox is packed with options to connect with audiences in new and innovative ways, utilising data analytics to gain insights into audience preferences and behaviours, and tailoring the offerings accordingly. In addition to facilitating it, digital platforms also extend the reach, making musical performances accessible to a global audience, transcending geographical and socioeconomic barriers. Digital transformation is a guarantee of both deeper and improved connections with audiences, enhancing their levels of loyalty and satisfaction.

c **Organisational/Operational Efficiency:** The integration of digital technologies significantly improves the efficiency of operations happening behind the scenes across arts and culture institutions (Wong and Chiu 2023), streamlining processes, simplifying procedures, and reducing costs. For example, the implementation of project management tools, resource management software, and data analytics platforms facilitate more informed decision-making and enhance the overall effectiveness of operations. Moreover, digital transformation helps create more flexible and agile organisational structures, fostering a culture of innovation and collaboration.

d **Financial Sustainability:** Digital transformation offers the potential to develop new revenue streams, diversify their income sources, and build financial resilience. Online performances, workshops, and digital merchandise are all opportunities for monetisation created by the new digital platforms and services. Moreover, the incorporation of data-driven marketing strategies has the potential to enhance the efficacy of promotional campaigns, likely resulting in increased ticket sales and overall revenue growth.

The journey towards digital transformation is not without its challenges and drawbacks. Striking a delicate balance between fostering innovation and upholding cherished artistic heritage and values is crucial. Digital transformation holds profound implications that considerably alter the very fabric of these organisations, affecting not only their ecosystems but also the platforms they employ and the data-driven processes they rely upon (Cennamo et al. 2020). To successfully embark on this transformative journey, performing arts institutions engage in thorough consideration and strategic

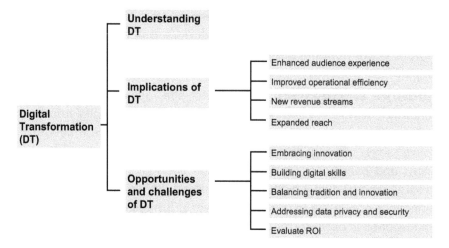

FIGURE 7.2 Diagram of Digital Transformation

planning, identifying areas where digitalisation can enhance their operations and artistic offerings without compromising their core principles. As part of this process, orchestras recognise the importance of cultivating digital skills and competencies within their organisations, providing staff, musicians, and board members with the necessary resources and training for professional development. The increasing reliance on digital platforms (both internal, such as ERPs, CRMs, inventory . . . and external such as social media) for storing and processing personal information necessitates first and foremost to address concerns surrounding data privacy and security, ensuring that appropriate measures are in place to safeguard sensitive information, maintaining the trust of audiences, stakeholders, and employees. The opportunity for organisations to address these challenges and redefine their artistic offerings and operations to flourish in an ever-evolving digital landscape precisely lies in the power of a strategic (rather than opportunistic) use of digitalisation.

Understanding Digital Transformation

Digital transformation refers to the integration of digital technology into various aspects of an organisation, resulting in fundamental changes to its operations, culture, and value delivery. In the context of our discussion, this encompasses technological innovations in areas such as artistic programming and execution, audience engagement, marketing, operations, and even governance.

Drawing upon the digital transformation framework developed by Jefferson et al. (2020) for public sector organisations and tailoring it to the orchestra industry offers an in-depth comprehension of the overarching landscape and the obstacles encountered. This approach, once contextualised for the world of classical music, brings a clearer perspective on how to navigate the process of digital transformation to ultimately achieve more sustainable and impactful outcomes. Also, a "purpose-driven anchor" allows for ambitious objectives that encourage solidarity among members while simultaneously recognising the feasible accomplishments demonstrated by other entities in the arts and cultural sectors.

In the modern era, the challenge lies in selecting and implementing the few right solutions out of countless proposed by the digital age, where technology has drastically changed the way music is consumed and created. As for any not-for-profit organisation (private or public sector), digital transformation strengthens their capacity to remain relevant and ensure sustainability (Ng Kea Chye 2021). Drawing from Ng Kea Chye's key ideas on transformation in public sector organisations, this section will discuss the application of these principles to orchestra management, focusing on setting a high aspiration, driving a rapid and inclusive planning process, and relentlessly focusing on execution, accountability, and sustainability.

Setting a High Aspiration: A clear vision of the objectives and expected outcomes of digital transformation, considering aspects such as audience engagement, operational efficiency, and financial sustainability, is a prerequisite. Ambitious yet achievable aspirations are key, with measurable outcomes to track progress. An orchestra may aim to increase ticket sales by 20% and double its online streaming audience within three years through the adoption of digital technologies and marketing strategies – this is precisely the type of clarity expected in defining trackable objectives.

Driving a Rapid and Inclusive Planning Process: To achieve their digital transformation goals, the involvement of staff members from all levels of the organisation, including musicians, administrative staff, and the board, in the planning process plays a crucial role. This approach will ensure diverse perspectives are considered and foster a sense of ownership in the transformation. The planning process is divided into four key stages:

a **Develop a Shared Understanding:** Engage all stakeholders in a dialogue to create a shared understanding of the need for digital transformation and the expected benefits. Identify the digital skills gap, review existing technological infrastructure, and assess potential opportunities for digital innovation in performance, audience engagement, and revenue generation.

b **Establish a Transformation Team:** Appoint a dedicated team of individuals with relevant expertise in music, management, and technology to drive the transformation effort. This team should be empowered with decision-making authority, a clear mandate, and adequate resources.

c **Evaluate Ideas Rigorously:** Solicit bottom-up ideas from the organisation and develop business cases for each initiative, with clear value propositions, trackable metrics, and dependencies, including initiatives such as adopting a fully integrated ticketing system to collect individual data, implementing data-driven marketing strategies, or investing in virtual reality concert experiences.

d **Lock the Plan:** Once the planning process is complete, lock the plan and commit to it. Stakeholders should remain flexible and adaptable to changes but strive to maintain the overall direction and timeline.

Focusing on Execution, Accountability, and Sustainability: The execution of the digital transformation plan also serves to emphasise rigorous tracking, accountability, and a focus on sustainability. Known success factors are:

a **Courageous Leadership:** Leaders are expected to communicate effectively, prioritise initiatives, and empower the organisation to embrace change. They celebrate successes, acknowledge setbacks, and are transparent about progress.

b **Radical Transparency:** Establish mechanisms to track progress toward milestones and the impact of change. Track outcomes, such as increased ticket sales, improved audience engagement, and enhanced operational efficiency.

c **Relentless Cadence:** Monitor progress at least every week to maintain momentum, focus, and identify and remove roadblocks quickly. Establish a transformation office to lead the cadence and maintain accountability for outcomes.

d **Painstaking Prioritisation:** Make difficult choices about which initiatives to scale back or abandon to focus energy and resources on the most promising ones.

Digital transformation requires a strategic approach, underpinned by a high aspiration, inclusive planning, and a relentless focus on implementation, execution, and smooth operations.

The Implications of Digital Transformation

As organisations embark on their digital transformation journey, the potential implications of this process must be thoroughly understood. The following four points provide an overview of the key areas in which digital transformation impacts the most.

1 **Enhanced Audience Experiences:** In the digital age, audiences (especially the younger generations) increasingly seek engaging experiences that resonate with their individual preferences and tastes. Digital technologies have the intrinsic capacity to deliver such experiences, both online and offline, by tailoring the offerings to meet the evolving needs of audiences. This may include incorporating multimedia elements, such as visuals and animations, into live performances, offering virtual reality experiences that transport audiences to virtual concert halls, or utilising interactive digital platforms that enable audiences to participate in the creative process. Through the adoption of these technologies, unforgettable and impactful experiences that forge stronger connections with audiences, nurturing a sense of community and belonging are crafted. The recent development of music-to-image AI tools opens even more doors, although it is too early to understand the quality of the rendering and the overall appeal.

2 **Improved Operational Efficiency:** The adoption of digital technologies and practices significantly enhances the operational efficiency of both business and artistic execution, streamlining processes and reducing costs. This is achieved through the accurate planning and well-executed automation of manual tasks, as well as the implementation of data-driven decision-making processes. Adopting project management tools facilitates effective communication and collaboration among team members, while resource management software optimises the allocation of assets, such as rehearsal spaces and equipment. Additionally, utilising data analytics to inform decision-making helps identify areas for improvement and optimises operations, ultimately resulting in cost savings and increased productivity.

3 **New Revenue Streams:** Digital transformation provides the opportunity to explore and develop new revenue streams, not only diversifying the income sources and building financial resilience but also offering a chance to shift towards a different business model overall (Shevchenko and Mihaylov 2021). Online performances and workshops can be monetised through pay-per-view models, subscription services, or digital memberships, while digital and physical merchandise, such as downloadable music sheets or

branded merchandise, can be sold through e-commerce platforms. Digital marketing and advertising strategies are proven tools to promote artistic offerings and attract new audiences, increasing the overall revenue potential. The more monetisation opportunities are seized, the greater ability to secure financial sustainability and invest in the continued development of artistic endeavours. All of this, however, does not mean an immediate or easy translation of the opportunities into an actual monetisation. On the contrary, the increased number and variety of digital content available on the market implies a fiercer competition to catch the audience's attention and money.

4 **Expanded Reach and Accessibility:** Digital platforms offer the unique advantage of reaching wider audiences, transcending geographical and socioeconomic barriers that may have previously limited their reach. Through livestreaming, on-demand services, and digital archives, performances – even the most niche ones – are made accessible to audiences around the world, regardless of their location or financial circumstances. This not only promotes cultural and generational inclusivity but also makes classical music more accessible to diverse groups, fostering a more inclusive and vibrant classical music ecosystem.

Examples of generic digital streaming platforms include:

PeopleSound	PeopleSound, established in 1999, was the first European music streaming platform, attracting millions of registered users at its peak. The platform offered a new approach to music distribution, particularly benefiting unsigned artists. Artists were incentivised with £100 per song submitted and earned 50% royalties on physical copies sold. This ground-breaking model had a profound impact on classical music orchestras by creating a platform for them to distribute their music independently from traditional record labels. This allowed for a wider exposure without the need for a record deal, transforming the way music was distributed and consumed.
Pandora Radio	Pandora Radio, launched in 2005, initially did not include classical music in its offerings. However, observing a growth in the classical listenership and a decline in classical programming on traditional radio stations, Pandora expanded its classical catalogue in 2008. The addition of classical music stations provided displaced listeners a new platform to consume their preferred music. This move offered orchestras a new platform for their music to be streamed and appreciated. It also gave them an opportunity to reach a broader audience beyond traditional radio listeners. This expansion into classical music by Pandora showcased the potential for classical music, encouraging other online platforms to follow suit.

YouTube	YouTube has revolutionised the accessibility and reach of classical music, breaking barriers that once confined performances to live concerts, radio, and commercial recordings. Capitalising on YouTube's ubiquity and ease of access, orchestras and labels have been able to disseminate performances globally at no cost to the listener. This platform, used by over 2.68 billion monthly active users as of mid-2023 (Ruby 2023a), has undoubtedly broadened exposure and potentially increased interest in live performances. Notably, the Berlin Philharmonic's Digital Concert Hall channel on YouTube has reached millions of viewers while Warner Classics has totalled almost 410 million views thus far (June 2023). The platform has also opened avenues for creative experimentation, such as virtual concerts and behind-the-scenes content, deepening audience engagement. Despite these strides, monetising YouTube content remains challenging due to low payments (about $0.00074 per view in 2020), necessitating additional revenue sources.
Spotify	Spotify has democratised the listening experience with its algorithmic music recommendation, exposing a variety of music to listeners through features such as "Discover Weekly." By 2023, this platform hosted over 100 million tracks and catered to over 515 million active users (Ruby 2023b), dramatically increasing the accessibility of classical music. This translates into broader awareness and the potential development of new fanbases. However, debates about equitable compensation persist within the classical music community, with arguments that Spotify's per-stream rates (between $0.003 and $0.005 as of 2021) are disproportionately low, particularly considering the length and complexity of many classical compositions.
Apple Music	Apple Music, with its 108 million users as of 2023 (Turner 2023), mirrors Spotify in its substantial role in democratising access to classical music. By providing a vast library of orchestral music to a global audience, Apple Music aids in promoting lesser-known executions and compositions, thus possibly sparking a surge in their popularity. This platform distinguishes itself through exclusive content and high-quality audio offerings, which cater to the discerning audiophile market often found within classical music listeners.

Examples of specific classical music digital streaming platforms include:

Platform	Impact
Apple Music Classical	The introduction of Apple Music Classical in late March 2023 represents a seminal moment in the sector, with the potential to significantly disrupt how classical music is consumed and distributed. Building on Apple's legacy of innovation that began with iTunes and continued with Apple Music, iPod, and the iPhone, Apple Music Classical aims to provide a dedicated platform with an extensive selection of classical music, cutting-edge search and browse features, Spatial Audio for superior sound, and exclusive recordings. The service can notably boost the visibility and

Platform	Impact
	accessibility of orchestral music in a landscape where digital platforms have become the primary medium for music consumption. It can help ensembles to reach a wider audience and potentially increase their revenue from streaming. However, the full impact of this service depends on its evolution, particularly given the initial lack of dedicated applications for Mac, iPad, and CarPlay. While Apple Music Classical holds substantial potential to shape the industry, further research is necessary to understand its longer-term effects and compare it with the impact of Apple's previous initiatives. This involves exploring how orchestras can leverage the platform for audience development and income generation and identifying effective strategies for navigating this new digital terrain.
Idagio	Launched in 2015, Idagio has positioned itself as a specialist platform dedicated exclusively to classical music. This focus enables it to offer features tailored to the unique nature of classical music, such as search by composer, work, or artist, solving a common categorisation problem in other music streaming platforms. Idagio's Lossless Audio offers high-quality sound to appeal to classical music audiophiles. By facilitating ease of discovery and enhancing listening quality, Idagio provides a robust platform to reach global audiences that appreciate the nuances of classical music.
Qobuz	Founded in 2007, Qobuz has distinguished itself as a high-resolution music streaming and downloading platform. Catering to an audience that values audio quality, Qobuz's unique selling proposition lies in its superior sound experience, which can significantly enhance the listening experience for classical music lovers. This emphasis on audio fidelity provides an engaging platform for orchestras to share their performances with discerning listeners who value the nuances of high-quality sound.
Primephonic	Primephonic, another streaming platform dedicated to classical music, has become known for its extensive catalogue and innovative search engine, which allows users to search by composer, work, artist, or period. Primephonic's in-depth liner notes and artist interviews offer listeners rich information about the music they are listening to, facilitating deeper engagement. Primephonic provides a platform that not only showcases performances but also contextualises the works within the broader classical tradition.
medici.tv	Since its inception in 2008, medici.tv has emerged as a leading platform for classical music videos, offering a unique proposition within the digital classical music space. With an extensive library of live concerts, ballets, operas, documentaries, master classes, and artist portraits, medici.tv offers a comprehensive visual and auditory experience for classical music enthusiasts. This presents orchestras with a unique opportunity to visually showcase their performances, providing a richer, more immersive experience for viewers. However, monetisation strategies and audience reach compared to audio-only platforms are aspects to be carefully considered.

Opportunities and Challenges of Digital Transformation

The digital transformation journey presents a unique set of opportunities to keep the offer relevant in the market; it strongly contributes to the re-design and re-structuring of organisational processes and practices where all members of the staff, artistic and non-artistic, play an important role (Edelmann, Steiner, and Misuraca 2023). These opportunities and challenges arise from the need to assess and adopt innovation, build digital skills within the organisation, balance tradition and innovation, address data privacy and security concerns, and evaluate the return on investment. Orchestras unlock the full potential of their digital transformation journey by understanding and addressing these factors:

1 **Assessing and Onboarding Innovation:** The openness to experiment with new technologies and explore inventive approaches in creating and delivering artistic content is essential. This requires a proactive and agile approach to innovation, involving collaborations with high-tech companies, testing new devices, equipment, and platforms, and staying up to date with the latest digital trends. In doing so, orchestras have the opportunity to discover and embrace cutting-edge technologies that amplify their creative and operational capabilities, resulting in the delivery of more immersive and captivating experiences for their audiences. However, it is essential to critically assess each innovation, considering its potential impact on the artistic quality and audience experience, as well as its compatibility with the existing infrastructure and resources.

2 **Building Digital Skills:** The successful navigation of the digital landscape necessitates investment in building the digital skills and competencies of the staff, musicians, and board members (Kokolek, Jakovic, and Curlin 2019). This may include offering training, mentorship, and professional development opportunities to develop digital literacy and expertise. These efforts cultivate a skilled workforce, enabling them to fully leverage the potential of digital technologies and seamlessly integrate them into both operational processes and concert performances. Moreover, building digital competencies within the organisation fosters a culture of innovation, encouraging staff and musicians to continually explore and experiment with new digital tools and practices.

3 **Balancing Tradition and Innovation:** One of the key challenges in the digital age is striking a balance between honouring artistic heritage and embedding new technologies. This requires careful consideration of how digital transformation aligns with the mission, values, and artistic vision.

Orchestras navigate this delicate balance by ensuring that the adoption of digital technologies serves to enhance, rather than detract from, their artistic integrity and identity. This entails employing digital tools and practices that complement the traditional repertoire, as well as exploring new, innovative ways of interpreting and presenting classical music that resonate with contemporary audiences. The adoption of a deliberate and reflective approach to digital transformation maintains the essence of the artistic heritage as a central aspect of the (brand) identity, while simultaneously embracing the opportunities that arise in the digital age.

4 **Addressing Data Privacy and Security Concerns:** An increased reliance on digital platforms for storing and processing various forms of data, including personal information, requires appropriate measures to ensure the protection of data privacy and security. The implementation of robust data protection policies and practices, as well as regular monitoring and assessment of the digital infrastructure to identify and address potential vulnerabilities, are no longer considered as a nice-to-have approach, but it often is a regulatory obligation. In addition, it is imperative that organisations stay informed about evolving data protection regulations and adhere to all relevant legislation. With a strong emphasis on data privacy and security, arts and culture organisations as well can nurture trust among their audiences and stakeholders, showcasing their steadfast dedication to safeguarding the personal information entrusted to their care.

5 **Evaluating the Return on Investment:** Given the significant resources required to implement digital initiatives, a careful assessment of the potential return on investment and weighing the benefits against the costs is a necessary condition. The development of clear, measurable objectives and key performance indicators (KPIs) to evaluate the success of digital initiatives, as well as the implementation of rigorous monitoring and evaluation processes to track progress and assess impact exemplify this trend to the quantification of impact and outcome. The final scope is therefore to always ensure that investments in digital transformation yield tangible benefits, such as confident audience engagement, improved operational efficiency, and enhanced artistic quality.

Digital transformation presents a wealth of opportunities to deepen artistic offerings, streamline operations, and reach out to diverse audiences. A clear picture of the implications, opportunities, and challenges associated with digital transformation make decisions on how to harness technology to drive success in an increasingly digital world more and better informed.

CASE STUDY 7.1

Digital Transformation to Enhance Audience Engagement and Revenue Generation

The rapid advancement of digital technology has significantly impacted the classical music industry, presenting both challenges and opportunities. This case study explores how digital transformation is used to uplift the audience, develop new revenue streams, and secure its future in an increasingly competitive landscape. The lessons learned from this case study underscore the importance of adaptability, forward-thinking, and collaboration in the digital age.

ASSESSING THE DIGITAL LANDSCAPE AND IDENTIFYING OPPORTUNITIES FOR GROWTH

- The management team conducted a comprehensive analysis of its current digital presence, audience behaviour, and industry trends.
- Key opportunities included expanding the online presence, leveraging digital platforms, and exploring new revenue streams.

FORMULATING A DIGITAL TRANSFORMATION STRATEGY

- The leadership team, in collaboration with the board and external experts, developed a strategic digital transformation plan with clear objectives, milestones, and performance indicators.
- The plan encompassed artistic programming, marketing, audience engagement, and revenue-generation initiatives.

ENHANCING THE ONLINE PRESENCE AND DIGITAL INFRASTRUCTURE

- Investment was made in a modernised website, mobile app, and customer relationship management system with data analysis capabilities to streamline its online presence and improve audience experience.
- Priority was given to the development of high-quality digital content, including video recordings, podcasts, and interactive materials.

LEVERAGING DIGITAL PLATFORMS FOR AUDIENCE DEVELOPMENT

- Social media, email marketing, and digital advertising were utilised to reach new audiences, publicise events, and create a sense of community among supporters.

- Educational and outreach initiatives were extended to digital platforms, broadening access and participation.

EXPANDING INTO STREAMING AND ONLINE PERFORMANCES

- New streaming technology was used to broadcast concerts and events, reaching global audiences and generating additional ticket revenue.
- Online (live or recorded) performances and digital archives offered subscribers exclusive access to an extensive catalogue of performances and events, further diversifying revenue streams.

ESTABLISHING PARTNERSHIPS AND COLLABORATIONS FOR DIGITAL GROWTH

- Strategic partnerships were formed with digital platforms, technology providers, and other industry stakeholders to optimise its digital capabilities and expand its reach.
- Collaborations with artists and ensembles from diverse genres and cultural backgrounds stimulated innovation and cross-promotion opportunities.

MONITORING PROGRESS AND ADAPTING THE DIGITAL TRANSFORMATION STRATEGY

- The performance of digital initiatives were regularly assessed, utilising data analytics to make informed decisions and refine strategy.
- This data-driven approach allowed the organisation to remain agile and responsive to emerging trends and opportunities.

This case study demonstrates the potential of digital transformation to revolutionise audience engagement, revenue generation, and overall sustainability. The orchestra expanded its reach, diversified its revenue streams, and secured its future in a rapidly evolving industry by assessing the digital landscape, formulating a strategic plan, and turning to innovative technologies and platforms. The lessons learned from this case study could be applied to other organisations seeking to navigate the digital age, emphasising the importance of adaptability, forward-thinking, and collaboration in ensuring long-term success.

QUESTIONS:

1 How can we identify specific digital opportunities that are congruent with its core values, mission, and unique offerings, while ensuring relevance in the rapidly changing digital landscape?

2   In the development of a digital transformation strategy, what balance should be struck between embracing innovative practices and preserving the inherent traditional aspects of the orchestral experience?

3   What considerations should be borne in mind when modernising their digital infrastructure, particularly regarding the accessibility and user experience for diverse audience segments?

4   What are the potential opportunities and risks associated with livestreaming and online performances, and how can usage of these platforms be optimised for audience engagement and revenue generation?

5   How can data analytics and continuous performance monitoring support adaptability and responsiveness, and what potential challenges may arise in interpreting and acting upon these data?

D. THE POTENTIAL IMPACT OF ARTIFICIAL INTELLIGENCE ON THE CLASSICAL MUSIC INDUSTRY

Although artificial intelligence (AI) applications such as ChatGPT have taken the world by storm in recent months, the impact of AI on many industries, including classical music, has been slowly but steadily felt for the past few years. AI is already quietly present in a variety of aspects of our lives, from X-ray readings to consumers' recommendations, from credit card fraud detection to the prediction of electricity production. In music, it offers exciting possibilities, such as innovative compositions (MusicAlly 2022), but it also brings certain risks. One major concern is that the growing presence of AI in music may result in a loss of human touch and authenticity, which are crucial to artistic expression.

Nevertheless, AI could provide numerous benefits to the classical music industry. For example, it leads to cost savings by partially automating traditionally human-driven tasks such as copywriting, marketing, accounting, and legal work. These cost savings free financial resources to be allocated more efficiently in new artistic projects or community outreach programs.

On the other hand, concerns about AI's impact on employment in the classical music industry persist. As more tasks become automated, human professionals' roles are under threat of termination, leading to job displacement

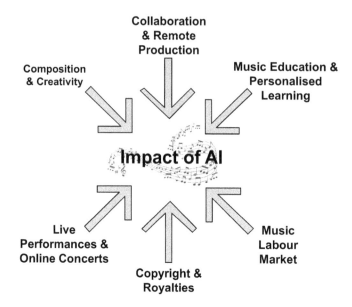

FIGURE 7.3 Impact of AI

and potential ethical concerns regarding technology's role in human-centric industries.

In the end, it will be up to each single orchestra – and to the industry as a whole – to find the right balance between embracing the opportunities presented by AI and addressing the potential risks and challenges associated with this rapidly evolving technology.

A more granular approach shows that the impact of AI on the classical music industry spans the following six areas:

1 **Composition and Creativity:** Imagine a world where AI tools become the Bach, Beethoven, Springsteen, Kraftwerk, or BB King of our time, providing musicians with inspiration from a vast reservoir of musical patterns. Classical musicians could push boundaries by exploring new forms of harmonies, while pop artists might find themselves crafting the catchiest tunes, all with the help of our AI toolbox.

   - Risk: AI-generated content may blur the lines of originality and authenticity, leading to over-reliance on AI-generated patterns and stifling human creativity. It may degrade creativity and originality and push towards more standardisation.

BOX 7.2 COMPOSED BY TECHNOLOGY

The way novel technologies impact music composition falls outside of the scope of this book. Although the significance of technology in shaping the modern music industry cannot be underestimated, this particular work does not explore the subject in detail. However, this experimental trend paves the road for an unpredictable future of music, and a few examples would not be superfluous to provide an idea. The Laptop Orchestra of Louisiana (LOL!) exemplifies music composition driven by IT (Albert 2012). Another relevant example happened in 2020, when the Shanghai Symphony Orchestra Concert Hall hosted a special concert of Mozart's imaginary works . . . as if he had lived to be 80 years old. The last three symphonic pieces were generated by an AI, based on learning a large amount of Mozart's past music (Shaw 2020).

2 **Collaboration and Remote Production:** Cloud-based platforms could take centre stage in connecting musicians across the globe, making possible virtual ensembles, jam sessions, or choirs that know no boundaries (Parr 2020). With AI-driven communication platforms, artists have at their disposal one more tool to compose, arrange, and produce together, paving the way for truly unique and innovative harmonies.

- Risk: The nuances of face-to-face interactions might be lost in unreal environments, impacting the dynamics of in-person collaboration.

3 **Music Education and Personalised Learning:** A new development in music education might be on the horizon, as AI-powered tools offer tailored lessons and feedback for students already. This applies to subjects such as music theory or history but not to instrumental learning that requires manual training. A personalised AI approach to music theory and history education adds an option to learning experiences, making them more accessible.

- Risk: Over-reliance on AI-generated content for learning might hinder the development of creativity and critical thinking in students.

4 **Live Performances and Online Concerts:** The grand entrance of generative AI into live performances could be the encore we never knew we needed. Musicians can leverage AI for real-time visualisations or immersive soundscapes,

taking the concert experience to new heights. Plus, online concerts could bring live music to fans worldwide, making the arts more inclusive. Generative AI may not replace an orchestra any time soon, but it may add to performances.

- Risk: Online concerts would miss the excitement and energy of in-person performances, potentially diminishing the live event atmosphere.

5 **Copyright and Royalties:** After the streamed music revolution, the music industry once again needs to confront the complex issue of copyright and royalties, this time in both the new age of AI-generated compositions or interpretations and the remuneration shift from contract to new forms including resale of royalties and equity (Van Haaften-Schick and Whitaker 2022; Whitaker and Kräussl 2020). Striking the right balance between human composers, interpreters, technicians, and AI-generated works will require innovative policies and legal frameworks to ensure fair play for all.

- Risk: Complex disputes over ownership arise as the line between human creativity and AI contributions becomes blurred, leading to unfair compensation practices.

6 **Music Labour Market:** There is little doubt that a variety of professions in the music industry will soon benefit from generative AI, increasing efficiency and productivity through automation and leaving more time for creative tasks.

- Risk: While increased efficiency is a positive outcome, generative AI might lead to job displacement in certain professions, such as technicians, software engineers, and PR people, due to a reduced need for their services, while composers and interpreters are less exposed to the competition introduced by AI tools (at least in the very near future).

In summary:

Area of Impact	Pros	Cons
Composition and Creativity	Generative AI offers a wealth of new musical patterns, inspiring musicians to explore novel harmonies, rhythms, and melodic lines.	Originality suffers as AI-generated content becomes prevalent, potentially leading to increased standardisation and stifled human creativity.

Area of Impact	Pros	Cons
Collaboration and Remote Production	AI-based platforms to bridge distances, enabling virtual jam sessions and collaborative composition, arrangement, and production across the globe.	The subtleties of face-to-face interactions are lost in online settings, affecting the dynamics of in-person collaboration.
Music Education and Personalised Learning	AI-powered platforms to revolutionise music theory and history education by providing tailored lessons and feedback, increasing accessibility.	Excessive reliance on AI-generated content hinders students' creativity and critical thinking, particularly in music theory and history.
Live Performances and Online Concerts	AI to enhance live performances with real-time visualisations and immersive soundscapes, while online concerts bring the arts to a global audience.	The energy and excitement of in-person concerts is diluted in virtual settings, potentially undermining the live event experience.
Copyright and Royalties	The rise of AI-generated compositions and interpretations necessitates new legal frameworks and policies, innovation in copyright and royalties.	Blurred lines between human and AI contributions lead to complex ownership disputes and potentially unfair compensation practices.
Music Labor Market	Greater adoption of generative AI could boost efficiency and productivity across various music industry professions, allowing more time for creative tasks.	While composers and interpreters are less exposed to AI competition for the time being, job displacement may occur in professions like technicians, software engineers, and PR people due to reduced service needs.

In today's context (May 2023), the risk table for AI "taking over" the music industry is as shown in Figure 7.4.

The reverberations of generative AI's influence on the music industry are both intriguing and diverse, offering a medley of opportunities and challenges, new horizons, and scary risks for musicians and the industry at large. As we march to the beat of this new technological drum, it is essential to thoughtfully navigate the implications for musicians, the industry, and society overall. Striking the balance enables a more harmonious future for the world of music.

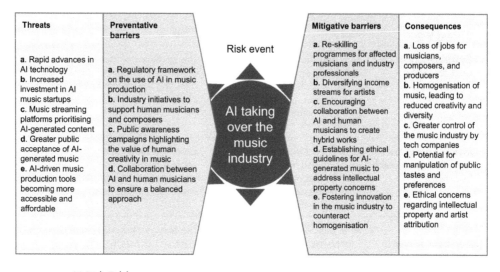

FIGURE 7.4 AI Risk Table

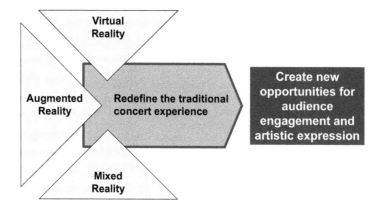

FIGURE 7.5 Example of Role of New Technologies

E. THE ROLE OF IMMERSIVE TECHNOLOGIES IN THE FUTURE OF PERFORMANCES

In recent years, immersive technologies such as virtual reality (VR), augmented reality (AR), and mixed reality (MR) have gained significant traction in various industries, including the arts and entertainment sector. Whilst other forms of performing arts have been receptive to these advancements, the classical music industry is somewhat lagging in embracing and experimenting with such cutting-edge technologies. Still, the application of these technologies in the world of classical music holds tremendous potential for the audience experience and for attracting new, diverse audiences to performances. When orchestras explore innovative ways to integrate immersive technologies into their programming, they redefine the traditional concert experience and create new opportunities for audience enjoyment and artistic expression.

Virtual Reality (VR)

Virtual reality offers a fully immersive, 360-degree experience that transports users into a simulated environment. In the context of performing arts, VR provides a unique perspective on the concert experience, allowing audiences to virtually "sit" amongst the performing artists and experience the performance from the musicians' point of view. This level of immersion offers an unparalleled sense of proximity and intimacy, giving audiences a deeper appreciation of the intricacies of the performance and the individual contributions of each musician.[5] It also bridges the future and the past, offering a contemporary experience of a well-established Western cultural tradition (Garage Staff 2021).

The use of virtual reality also breaks down geographical barriers by offering remote audiences the opportunity to attend concerts from the comfort of their homes. This could be particularly beneficial for reaching audiences in rural or remote areas or those with limited mobility or access to live performances.

BOX 7.3 FUTURE TRENDS START NOW

Well-known examples are the virtual reality experience of the Philharmonia Orchestra (UK) that the audience can access remotely using their own Playstation VR headsets (Davis 2017; Hickling 2016), or the virtual orchestra presented at Dubai Expo 2020 (in 2021) that allows a conductor to lead a virtual ensemble that reacts to their real-time conducting gestures.[6] This cutting-edge system utilises a combination of motion-capture technology, artificial intelligence, and advanced audio processing to create an immersive and interactive experience. The motion-capture technology tracks the conductor's movements and gestures with high precision, while the AI component analyses these inputs and coordinates the musical response. In turn, the advanced audio processing ensures the sound quality of the virtual ensemble remains faithful to that of a live performance. This platform offers a multitude of potential applications, including remote music education, and providing access to world-class orchestras for young conductors who do not have the opportunity to work with such ensembles in person. Additionally, this technology is used for practice and honing conducting skills without the need for a full ensemble. The research project on mathematical modelisation of gestural similarity of conductors (Mannone 2018) is an important step in the development of virtual reality applications.

Last but not least, it could be used to experiment with new artistic creations where the audience is transported to an imaginary world or fly inside parallel universes that illustrate or prolong the music.[7]

Augmented Reality (AR)

Augmented reality superimposes digital information or images onto the user's view of the real world, providing an unprecedented experience that combines both physical and virtual elements. In the performing arts, AR provides audiences with real-time information about the set being performed, such as programme notes, translations of sung texts, or visual representations of the musical themes and motifs.

AR creates interactive experiences, such as inviting audiences to "conduct" the orchestra using their smartphones or other devices. This level of involvement triggers a sense of connection and ownership among audiences, encouraging deeper appreciation and understanding of the music.

Mixed Reality (MR)

Mixed reality combines elements of actual, virtual, and augmented reality, allowing users to interact with virtual objects within their physical environment. This technology offers exciting possibilities for emphasising the visual and sensory aspects of performances. For example, mixed reality creates immersive stage designs, incorporating virtual elements that respond to the music being performed or allowing musicians to "interact" with digital projections and visual effects during the performance.[8]

MR also facilitates innovative collaborations between orchestras and other art forms, such as dance, theatre, or visual arts, by integrating digital elements that bridge the gap between disciplines and create a more holistic artistic experience.

Challenges and Considerations

While the potential applications of immersive technologies in the performing arts are undoubtedly exciting, they also present several challenges and considerations for managers. First and foremost, the cost of developing and implementing these technologies is still significant (if not exorbitant for high-resolution audio and video solutions), and requires securing additional funding or exploring new revenue streams to support their efforts. Additionally, the integration of these technologies necessitates new skill sets and expertise within the organisation, as well as the need to invest in staff training and development.

Moreover, it is crucial to strike a balance between innovative technologies and the integrity and authenticity of the live performance experience. This requires a thoughtful and measured approach to integrating immersive technologies, ensuring that they elevate, rather than detract from, the music itself.

The incorporation of immersive technologies such as VR, AR, and MR into artistic performances presents exciting opportunities for the audience as well as new artistic collaborations and for breaking down barriers to access. Thoughtful integration of these technologies into artistic programming creates innovative and memorable concert experiences that appeal to diverse audiences, ensuring the continued growth and sustainability of the classical music industry.

As orchestras around the world begin to explore the potential of immersive technologies, it is vital to share best practices and learn from each other's experiences. In doing so, the industry collectively navigates the challenges and opportunities presented by these new technologies and harnesses their potential for the benefit of both the art form and its audiences. Remaining open to experimentation and the possibilities offered by VR, AR, and MR allows performing arts to evolve, adapt, and thrive in an ever-changing cultural landscape.

The coming years will undoubtedly see further advances in immersive technologies that will require organisations to remain agile and responsive to these developments in order to stay at the forefront of artistic innovation. Embracing a forward-thinking approach and commitment to the core values of artistic excellence and audience engagement ensures a bright and sustainable future for classical music in the digital age.

F. EXAMPLES OF LEVERAGING TECHNOLOGY AND DIGITAL MEDIA

In today's digital landscape, performing artists and organisations are increasingly utilising a variety of technologies and social media platforms to stay relevant. Leveraging these tools effectively helps not only expand their reach but also enhance the overall experience for their audiences, sponsors, partners,

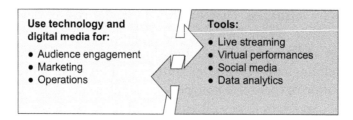

FIGURE 7.6 New Technologies: Scope and Tools

and patrons. This section explores how technology and digital media are used for audience excitement, marketing, and operations, discussing examples of streaming, online performances, social media platforms, and data analytics for improved audience understanding and marketing efforts.

Streaming and Online Performances

The rise of streaming and online performances has opened up new possibilities to connect with audiences. To those listeners who are unable to attend performances in person due to geographical barriers, financial constraints, or time pressure, high-quality streams or recordings of concerts offer an unprecedented chance to remain connected with their passion for classical music or to discover a new form of entertainment without feeling overwhelmed or discouraged. This not only increases accessibility but also provides opportunities to generate additional revenue through ticket sales or donations.

In addition to streaming traditional concerts, the competitive pressure pushes artists to explore innovative performance formats that may (or may not) incorporate immersive technologies such as virtual reality (VR) or augmented reality (AR). These experiences provide audiences with unique, interactive perspectives on the music, enabling them to feel more connected to the performance.

Social Media Platforms for Audience Interaction

Social media platforms have become indispensable tools to promote concerts, release news, and interact with audiences. An active presence on platforms such as Facebook, Twitter, Instagram, TikTok, and YouTube amplifies the opportunities to share captivating content that showcases musicians, provides behind-the-scenes insights, conducts brief interviews, reveals lively anecdotes, and highlights memorable performances.

Social media also facilitates audience interaction, encouraging patrons to share their experiences, ask questions, or debate about the music, programming, or arts and culture. This deepens the audience's understanding of the art form and creates more ownership and investment in the orchestra's life.

Leveraging Data Analytics

Although this section is not exclusively related to the benefits that a sound social media strategy brings, arts and culture institutions also harness the power of technology to better understand their audiences and improve their marketing efforts through data analytics and customer relationship management practices. These tools give an unprecedented ability to collect, organise, and analyse loads of audience data, such as demographics, ticket purchase history, and engagement patterns, and, if linked to social media analytics, these data provide a granular understanding of online attention and behaviour. This valuable information is then used to develop targeted marketing strategies, personalised communications, and tailored programming that resonates with specific audience segments. For example, data intelligence applied to social media posts may extract patterns in the expression of sentiments related to specific events, composers, or genres of music. These statistics inform strategic programming decisions to prioritise activities that best meet the audience's preferences or respond to nascent interest in new forms of art.

Similarly, CRM systems help manage relationships with patrons, donors, and other stakeholders more effectively. Tracking more accurately interactions and communications with individuals provides timely, personalised, and relevant information to feed back a variety of internal decision-making processes on both artistic and business matters.

Overall, technology offers a wealth of opportunities to mesh with audiences, advertise events, sharpen operations, and explore new routes. By leveraging streaming, online (and perhaps virtual) performances, social media platforms, AR, VR, and MR performances, and data analytics, orchestras reach new audiences, deepen connections with existing patrons, and make informed decisions about programming and marketing strategies. Using these tools and continually adapting to the ever-changing digital landscape is crucial to thrive in the 21st century, ensuring the orchestra will remain relevant, accessible, and innovative in its approach to sharing the transformative power of music with the world.

Robotics, AI, and Many More Technologies in a Baton

On 30 June 2023, an event of musical and technological ingenuity occurred when the National Orchestra of Korea, in partnership with the Korea Institute of Industrial Technology, showcased an intriguing blend of human skill and artificial intelligence in a public concert (Arirang News 2023; Dong-hee 2023). The concert was conducted by two entities – maestro Choi Soo-Yeoul, a human conductor *par excellence*,[9] and EveR-6, a robotic orchestra conductor. A brainchild of robotics, mechatronics, machine learning, and AI, EveR-6 offered a glimpse into the possible future of musical orchestration. This novel endeavour is a ground-breaking milestone, demonstrating the rapid advancements and applications of high-tech solutions in an expanding spectrum of human activities, particularly since the public release of Large Language Models in late 2022. The advent of EveR-6 has set a precedent that could redefine the boundaries between art and technology.

BOX 7.4 THE VINYL REVIVAL

It is not within the remit of this book to analyse the vinyl record revival, but its magnitude has reached such levels that it cannot be overlooked, especially as a countertrend in a chapter devoted to the impact of technology on classical music. As highlighted by the Recording Industry Association of America, in the US vinyl sales outstripped CD sales for the first time in 34 years in 2020 (Friedlander and Bass 2023; Biron 2023; Weatherbed 2023; Radde 2023). This remarkable shift underlines the dichotomy between the progression of digital technology and the parallel growth of older, more analogue forms of music consumption.

The *2022 Year-End Music Industry Revenue Report* by the Recording Industry Association of America (RIAA) shows that recorded music revenues in the US have grown for the seventh consecutive year, reaching a record high of $15.9 billion estimated retail value. Streaming services continue to be the biggest driver of growth, with paid subscriptions, ad-supported formats, and new platforms all contributing to the industry's success. In 2022, streaming accounted for 84% of total revenues, with paid subscriptions making up 78% of that figure. Ad-supported streaming grew by 20% and now accounts for 6% of total revenues. Physical sales continued to decline overall, while vinyl records saw an increase in revenue for the sixteenth consecutive year. In 2022, vinyl sales grew by 17%, reaching $1.2 billion in revenue and accounting for 71% of physical format revenues. For the first time since 1987, vinyl albums outsold CDs in units (41 million vs 33 million). However, CD sales fell by 18% to $483 million in 2022.

Key data over time are as follows:

Year	Total Revenue (estimated retail value)	Vinyl Sales Revenue	Vinyl Sales as % of Physical Format Revenues
2018	$9.8 billion	$419 million	n.a.
2019	$11.1 billion	$504 million	n.a.
2020	$12.2 billion	$619 million	n.a.
2021	$15 billion	$1 billion	n.a.
2022	$15.9 billion	$1.2 billion	71

Vinyl sales have been steadily increasing over the past few years and have become a significant portion of physical format revenues. In 2022, vinyl sales accounted for 71% of physical format revenues.

Unfolding against a backdrop dominated by streaming platforms and digital downloads, the resurgence of vinyl is profoundly paradoxical. The antiquated format of the vinyl record, with its physicality and sensory appeal, offers a form of consumption that presents a stark contrast to the fleeting nature of digital music. The tactile ritual of handling a vinyl record, placing it on a turntable, and engaging with the album cover fosters an immersive listening experience unparalleled by its digital counterparts.

The vinyl resurgence can also be viewed as a part of a broader societal push towards "digital detox," a response to digital fatigue and concerns about screen time and data privacy. The analogue vinyl offers an escape from the digital onslaught, a tangible and mindful return to more traditional forms of music consumption. This renewed affection for vinyl extends beyond the realm of nostalgia, signalling a possible shift in our relationship with music. This paradigm shift is particularly salient in the realm of classical music, which has found a renewed platform on vinyl that brings together a multi-century-long musical tradition and an older technology perceived as a form of mechanical tradition from the more recent past. The tactile and immersive experience of vinyl amplifies the richness and depth of this genre, providing a more direct connection between the music and the listener. The sonic warmth of vinyl, in conjunction with its capacity for artwork and liner notes, brings a new layer of appreciation to classical music, making it more accessible to audiences.

Independent record stores have experienced a rejuvenation, paralleling the resurgence of vinyl. These brick-and-mortar establishments have become hubs for vinyl communities, both online and offline. Within these communities, shared passions, knowledge, and the joy of discovering new music are exchanged, enhancing the vinyl experience and fostering a sense of belonging. Such collectives play a pivotal role in sustaining the vinyl revival and could be a driving force in its future growth. Yet, the renaissance of vinyl is not without its challenges. The industry must address environmental sustainability and explore innovative ways to reduce the impact of vinyl production. The focus is on utilising more sustainable materials and energy-efficient manufacturing processes to ensure the viability of vinyl's future.

As we step into the future, the coexistence of the analogue and digital world becomes more intricate. The fusion of digital technology with the vinyl experience is a promising area for exploration. The possibilities are numerous, ranging from augmented reality album covers to apps enhancing the vinyl listening experience. The challenge lies in maintaining a balance that leverages digital technology's benefits while safeguarding the analogue essence of the vinyl experience.

The vinyl record revival, a beacon of resilience and reinvention in the music industry, represents a paradigm shift in music consumption (although minor compared to digital downloads and streams). It underlines the role of physicality and ritual in music (that are also typical of actual orchestral performance), elements that were brought back to life amidst the digital revolution. The implications of this revival are fascinating, (partially) reshaping industry sectors from production to distribution, whilst revitalising independent record stores. Looking ahead, the future of vinyl is intriguingly poised, with digital technology integration, growing vinyl communities, and the need for environmental sustainability. Despite once being considered relics of the past, vinyl records now hold a vibrant role in the soundscape, a testament to the enduring allure of music and the multiple ways we engage with it.

The emergence of digital technology, with its unfathomable promise of accessibility, expanded range of experience and convenience, seemed poised to usurp the legacy of vinyl records. Yet, the physical, tactile allure of vinyl has defied predictions of obsolescence and staged an impressive resurgence. This trend is all the more remarkable in the context of the resurgent popularity of classical music on vinyl, suggesting a niche yet intriguing counterpoint to the prevailing narrative of digital disruption. One could conjecture that vinyl's resurgence can be partly attributed to the "digital detox" phenomenon – a social trend advocating for a reconnection with tangible experiences as an antidote to the pervasiveness of digital technology – or to the higher purchase power of a small community of wealthy aficionados. Vinyl records, in this light, represent an immersive, intentional escape from the relentless screen time, offering a sensory engagement that transcends the mere auditory experience. This is not to underplay the role of nostalgia, but to highlight how vinyl caters to a fundamental desire for meaningful, tactile interactions in an increasingly digitised world. This is particularly evident in the context of classical music. The vinyl format is seen as providing a richer, more nuanced sonic canvas for this genre, enhancing the listener's emotional connection and engagement. The album covers, artwork, and liner notes that accompany vinyl records further enrich this experience, providing immediate context and inviting deeper exploration that often takes place online.

Another aspect of the vinyl revival is its positive impact on independent record stores, which have experienced a marginal renaissance. These establishments are now thriving hubs of vinyl communities, fostering a shared culture of passion, knowledge, and discovery. Such communal experiences further enhance the appeal of vinyl, illustrating how music consumption is not just about the act of listening, but also the shared bonds it fosters. However, the resurgence of vinyl also brings to the fore several challenges, particularly in relation to environmental sustainability. The onus is on the industry to innovate and explore options such as more sustainable materials and energy-efficient production methods.

Looking ahead, the integration of digital technologies with the vinyl experience promises to be a fascinating journey. This could take numerous forms, from augmented reality album covers to apps designed to augment the vinyl listening experience. Striking a balance that capitalises on the benefits of digital technology, without compromising the unique value proposition of vinyl, will be a critical challenge.

In conclusion, the vinyl revival represents a unique narrative of resilience and reinvention. It emphasises the importance of tangible, immersive experiences that engage multiple senses, aspects that digital platforms often failed to emulate so far. Classical music has found a renewed home on vinyl, adding to the depth and richness of the genre. The implications for the music industry are qualitatively significant although still quantitatively limited, influencing sectors from production and distribution to retail. Despite the rise of digital platforms, traditional formats such as vinyl have proven their enduring appeal. As we look ahead, it is clear that vinyl records, once seen as relics of the past, still have a role to play in the industry of music.

Box 7.5 Expanding Perspectives: Review Questions

1   Given the pervasive influence of technology in the classical music industry, how do you envisage management software changing the landscape further in the future? Discuss how automation of administrative tasks supported by generative large language models (such as OpenAI's chatGPT or Google's Bard or Anthropic's Claude) can impact operational efficiency and risk management.

2   Evaluate the importance of social media platforms in the digital age. What potential benefits and challenges does social media engagement bring to performing arts in terms of brand building and fostering a sense of community? How do these benefits and challenges evolve under the influence of artificial intelligence tools on the social media landscape?

3   Digital transformation extends beyond the mere introduction of technology. Discuss the implications, opportunities, and challenges this multi-branch concept presents to orchestras, focusing on how they can leverage technology to enhance audience engagement and improve operational efficiency.

4   Artificial intelligence promises to revolutionise the classical music industry. Discuss in depth the potential applications and impact of AI on composition, performance quality, and accessibility for global audiences. Do you foresee any potential drawbacks or ethical considerations with these applications? In your opinion, which concrete avenues could or should be explored for a fruitful usage of AI in the orchestral ecosystem?

5   With the advent of immersive technologies such as virtual reality (VR) and augmented reality (AR), how do you envision these technologies transforming artistic performances? Delve into the potential for unique,

immersive audience experiences and the challenges these technologies might bring.

6 By reflecting on the examples of organisations that successfully leveraged technology and digital media, how do you think orchestras can further innovate their use of technology? Discuss how these strategies could be refined or expanded to enhance operational efficiency, increase audience engagement, and broaden access to performances in the future.

NOTES

1 A variety of examples of usage or potential usage of AR and VR in arts and culture institutions are available already: Vasileva and Petrova (2019), Camilleri (2020), Kallergis et al. (2020), Choi et al. (2022), Schertenleib et al. (2004), Orman, Price, and Russell (2017). One of the very first real-world usage of artificial intelligence application in the context of a live concert took place in 2015 at the Concertgebouw in Amsterdam (see Arzt et al. 2015), while, very recently, AI is used to develop "a virtual conductor that can generate an emotionally associated interpretation of known music work" (Funk and Eghtebas 2023).

2 Examples of how social media supported cultural institutions' communication strategy are available since the early 2010s (Chaisathan and Satawedin 2017; Gao 2016; Saxton et al. 2012; Blanchard 2013). A recent case study of the Hong Kong Philharmonic Orchestra is available in Deng and Chiu (2023).

3 This, however, does not translate into an immediate monetisation of the recordings, mostly due to the proliferation of recordings on the market, hence the increased competition to catch audiences' attention and money.

4 As already highlighted by Peukert (2019), who looks at this phenomenon from an economic standpoint, digitalisation and internet-enabled platforms, sophisticated yet affordable recording software, and powerful mobile devices, together with automated licensing of user-generated content, have substantially lowered the costs of individual-level cultural participation overall.

5 A recent experiment gave the audience a First Person View (FPV), allowing each person to control their own virtual drone flying amongst the musicians. The position of the virtual drone determines both the video shown on the goggles but also the sound heard by the person ("flying" closer to a section increases the volume of that section compared to other instruments).

6 The concept of conducting a virtual orchestra is, however, not new (Borchers, Samminger, and Mühlhäuser 2001, 2002).

7 In a more technical domain, virtual orchestras are sometimes used to assess (and improve) the acoustics of concert halls (D'Orazio et al. 2020).

8   In the mid-2010s, the company *Opera Italia* started proposing large integrated solutions to operas to "virtualise" the stage by means of a mix of 2D and 3D rendering technologies that would make the transition of set immediate during an opera performance in addition to introducing scenery movement during the performance.

9   Artistic Director of the Busan Philharmonic Orchestra and Principal Guest Conductor of the Korea Chamber Orchestra.

BIBLIOGRAPHY

Albert, Jeff. 2012. "Improvisation as Tool and Intention: Organizational Practices in Laptop Orchestras and Their Effect on Personal Musical Approaches." *Critical Studies in Improvisation/Études Critiques En Improvisation* 8 (1). https://doi.org/10.21083/csieci.v8i1.1558.

Arirang News. 2023. "Conducting Robot EveR-6: Bringing a New Challenge to the Realm of Art." *YouTube*. www.youtube.com/shorts/ZHZEsBoeleI.

Arzt, Andreas, Harald Frostel, Thassilo Gadermaier, Martin Gasser, Maarten Grachten, and Gerhard Widmer. 2015. "Artificial Intelligence in the Concertgebouw." In *Twenty-Fourth International Joint Conference on Artificial Intelligence*. www.academia.edu/download/83618411/Artificial_Intelligence_in_the_Concertge20220409-9058-xc446.pdf.

Bergman, Åsa. 2021. "'Wherever You Are Whenever You Want': Captivating and Encouraging Music Experiences When Symphony Orchestra Performances Are Provided Online." *Open Library of Humanities* 7 (2). https://doi.org/10.16995/olh.4679.

Bibu, Nicolae, Laura Brancu, and Georgiana Alina Teohari. 2018. "Managing a Symphony Orchestra in Times of Change: Behind the Curtains." *Procedia – Social and Behavioral Sciences* 238 (January): 507–516. https://doi.org/10.1016/j.sbspro.2018.04.030.

Biron, Bethany. 2023. "Vinyl Sales Surpassed CDs for the First Time in 35 Years as Records Make 'Remarkable Resurgence'." *Business Insider*, March 9. www.businessinsider.com/vinyl-sales-surpass-cds-first-time-since-1987-record-resurgence-2023-3.

Blanchard, Katharine. 2013. "The Hamilton Philharmonic Orchestra: Building an Online Community." *The McMaster Journal of Communication* 9 (January): 135–170. https://doi.org/10.15173/mjc.v9i0.275.

Borchers, Jan O., Wolfgang Samminger, and Max Mühlhäuser. 2001. "Conducting a Realistic Electronic Orchestra." In *Proceedings of the 14th Annual ACM Symposium on User Interface Software and Technology*. New York: ACM. https://doi.org/10.1145/502348.502376.

Borchers, Jan O., Wolfgang Samminger, and Max Muhlhauser. 2002. "Engineering a Realistic Real-Time Conducting System for the Audio/video Rendering of a Real Orchestra." In *Fourth International Symposium on Multimedia Software Engineering, 2002. Proceedings*, 352–362. ieeexplore.ieee.org. https://doi.org/10.1109/MMSE.2002.1181633.

Camilleri, Vanessa. 2020. "Augmented Reality in Cultural Heritage: Designing for Mobile AR User Experiences." In *Rediscovering Heritage Through Technology: A Collection of Innovative Research Case Studies That Are Reworking the Way We Experience Heritage*, edited by Dylan Seychell and Alexiei Dingli, 215–237. https://doi.org/10.1007/978-3-030-36107-5_11.

Cennamo, Carmelo, Giovanni Battista Dagnino, Alberto Di Minin, and Gianvito Lanzolla. 2020. "Managing Digital Transformation: Scope of Transformation and Modalities of Value Co-Generation and Delivery." *California Management Review* 62 (4): 5–16. https://doi.org/10.1177/0008125620942136.

Chaisathan, P., and P. Satawedin. 2017. "Strategic Communication Management for Symphony Orchestra in the Context of Lanna Culture: A Case Study of the Chiang Mai Youth Philharmonic Band." *FEU Academic Review.* https://so01.tci-thaijo.org/index.php/FEU/article/download/68758/71374/224346.

Choi, Kristine, Garrett Crumb, Richard Li, Raahul Natarrajan, Patrick Tong, Ole Molvig, and Bobby Bodenheimer. 2022. "Experience Orchestra: Manipulating Musical Instruments in VR." In *2022 IEEE Conference on Virtual Reality and 3D User Interfaces Abstracts and Workshops (VRW)*, 918–919. https://doi.org/10.1109/VRW55335.2022.00310.

Davis, Lizzie. 2017. "We Tried Out the Philharmonia Orchestra's New Virtual Reality Experience." *Classic FM.* www.classicfm.com/artists/philharmonia-orchestra/virtual-reality-experience/.

Deng, Suming, and Dickson K. W. Chiu. 2023. "Analyzing the Hong Kong Philharmonic Orchestra's Facebook Community Engagement with the Honeycomb Model." In *Advances in Social Networking and Online Communities*, 31–47. IGI Global. https://doi.org/10.4018/978-1-6684-5190-8.ch003.

Dong-hee, Hwang. 2023. "Robot to Conduct Orchestra for the First Time in Korea." www.koreaherald.com/view.php?ud=20230627000678.

D'Orazio, Dario, Giulia Fratoni, Anna Rovigatti, and Massimo Garai. 2020. "A Virtual Orchestra to Qualify the Acoustics of Historical Opera Houses." *Building Acoustics* 27 (3): 235–252. https://doi.org/10.1177/1351010X20912501.

Edelmann, Noella, Karin Steiner, and Gianluca Misuraca. 2023. "The View from the Inside: A Case Study on the Perceptions of Digital Transformation Phases in Public Administrations." *Digital Government: Research and Practice* 4 (2): 1–18. https://doi.org/10.1145/3589507.

Friedlander, Joshua, and Matthew Bass. 2023. "2022-Year-End Music Industry Revenue Report.pdf." *Recording Industry Association of America.* www.riaa.com/wp-content/uploads/2023/03/2022-Year-End-Music-Industry-Revenue-Report.pdf.

Funk, Marc-Philipp, and Nassim Chloe Eghtebas. 2023. "Can a Virtual Conductor Create Its Own Interpretation of a Music Orchestra?" *arXiv [cs.HC]. arXiv.* https://doi.org/10.48550/arXiv.2304.08434.

Gao, Fangfang. 2016. "Social Media as a Communication Strategy: Content Analysis of Top Nonprofit Foundations' Micro-Blogs in China." *International Journal of Strategic Communication* 10 (4): 255–271. https://doi.org/10.1080/1553118x.2016.1196693.

Garage Staff. 2021. "Symphonies, Operas, and Orchestras in VR." *The Garage.* https://garage.hp.com/us/en/arts-design/orchestra-symphony-opera-VR-performances.html.

Hickling, Alfred. 2016. "You're in the Band: Virtual Reality's Orchestral Future." *The Guardian*, September 29. www.theguardian.com/music/2016/sep/29/virtual-reality-london-philharmonia-orchestra-esa-pekka-salonen-interview.

Jefferson, Ian, Katie Owen, Jim Scott, and Aly Spencer. 2020. "From Transition to Transformation." *McKinsey & Company.* www.mckinsey.com/industries/public-and-social-sector/our-insights/from-transition-to-transformation#/.

Kallergis, Georgios, Marios Christoulakis, Aimilios Diakakis, Marios Ioannidis, Iasonas Paterakis, Nefeli Manoudaki, Marianthi Liapi, and Konstantinos-Alketas Oungrinis. 2020. "Open City Museum: Unveiling the Cultural Heritage of Athens through an – Augmented Reality Based- Time Leap." In *Culture and Computing*, 156–171. https://doi.org/10.1007/978-3-030-50267-6_13.

Kokolek, Natalija, Bozidar Jakovic, and Tamara Curlin. 2019. "Digital Knowledge and Skills – Key Factors for Digital Transformation." In *DAAAM Proceedings*, 0046–0053. DAAAM International Vienna. https://doi.org/10.2507/30th.daaam.proceedings.006.

League of American Orchestras. 2023. "Strategic Framework 2023–2026." *League of American Orchestras*. https://americanorchestras.org/strategic-framework-2023-2026/.

Mannone, Maria. 2018. "Introduction to Gestural Similarity in Music. An Application of Category Theory to the Orchestra." *Journal of Mathematics & Music. Mathematical and Computational Approaches to Music Theory, Analysis, Composition and Performance* 12 (2): 63–87. https://doi.org/10.1080/17459737.2018.1450902.

McKinsey & Co. 2021. "Supporting the Arts: A Portrait of Our Work in the Culture Sector." www.mckinsey.com/about-us/new-at-mckinsey-blog/a-behind-the-scenes-look-at-our-culture-sector-work.

MusicAlly. 2022. "7 Reasons Why AI Music Was Fascinating and Controversial in 2022." https://musically.com/2022/12/14/reasons-ai-music-fascinating-2022/.

Newton, Travis. 2022. *Orchestra Management Handbook: Building Relationships in Turbulent Times*, 1st ed. New York: Oxford University Press.

Ng Kea Chye, Gerald. 2021. "Re-Inventing and Re-Shaping the Symphony Orchestra for Sustainability." In *Wie Wir Leben Wollen. Kompendium Zu Technikfolgen von Digitalisierung, Vernetzung Und Künstlicher Intelligenz*, 113–124. Logos Verlag Berlin. https://doi.org/10.30819/5319.08.

Orman, Evelyn K., Harry E. Price, and Christine R. Russell. 2017. "Feasibility of Using an Augmented Immersive Virtual Reality Learning Environment to Enhance Music Conducting Skills." *Journal of Music Teacher Education* 27 (1): 24–35. https://doi.org/10.1177/1057083717697962.

Parr, Freya. 2020. "The Virtual Orchestras, Choirs and Music Masterclasses Available to Join Online During Lockdown." *Classical Music*. www.classical-music.com/features/articles/how-join-virtual-orchestras-choirs-and-music-masterclasses-online/.

Parviainen, Päivi, Maarit Tihinen, Jukka Kääriäinen, and Susanna Teppola. 2022. "Tackling the Digitalization Challenge: How to Benefit from Digitalization in Practice." *International Journal of Information Systems and Project Management* 5 (1): 63–77. https://doi.org/10.12821/ijispm050104.

Peukert, Christian. 2019. "The Next Wave of Digital Technological Change and the Cultural Industries." *Journal of Cultural Economics* 43 (2): 189–210. https://doi.org/10.1007/s10824-018-9336-2.

Poulios, Ioannis, and Efrosini Kamperou. 2022. "Business Innovation in Orchestra Organizations Supported by Digital Technologies: The Orchestra Mobile Case Study." *Sustainability: Science Practice and Policy* 14 (7): 3715. https://doi.org/10.3390/su14073715.

Radde, Kaitlyn. 2023. "Vinyl Records Outsell CDs for the First Time since 1987." *NPR*, March 10. www.npr.org/2023/03/10/1162568704/vinyl-outsells-cds-first-time-since-1987-records.

Ruby, Daniel. 2023a. "YouTube Statistics 2023: Data for Brands & Creators." www. demandsage.com/youtube-stats/.

Ruby, Daniel. 2023b. "Spotify Stats 2023." www.demandsage.com/spotify-stats/.

Saxton, Gregory D., Chao Guo, I-Hsuan Chiu, and Bo Feng. 2012. "Social Media and the Social Good: How Nonprofits Use Facebook to Communicate with the Public." *arXiv [cs.CY]. arXiv.* http://arxiv.org/abs/1203.5279.

Schertenleib, S., M. Gutierrez, F. Vexo, and D. Thalmann. 2004. "Conducting a Virtual Orchestra." *IEEE Multimedia* 11 (3): 40–49. https://doi.org/10.1109/MMUL.2004.5.

Serdaroglu, Emine. 2020. "Exploring the Use of YouTube by Symphonic Orchestras as an Educational Platform During the Pandemic of Covid-19." *European Journal of Social Sciences Education and Research* 7 (3). https://doi.org/10.26417/770wga72a.

Shaw, Kim. 2020. "Pfizer Uses AI to Create Mozart's New Symphonies." *Campaign Brief Asia.* https://campaignbriefasia.com/2020/12/23/pfizer-uses-ai-to-create-mozarts-new-symphonies-via-f5-shanghai/.

Shevchenko, D., and V. Mihaylov. 2021. "Digital Transformation of the Service Sector." *Scientific Research and Development Economics of the Firm* 10 (3): 41–54. https://doi.org/10.12737/2306-627x-2021-10-3-41-54.

Turner, Ash. 2023. "Number of Apple Music Users & Subscribers." www.bankmycell.com/blog/number-of-apple-music-users.

Van Haaften-Schick, Lauren, and Amy Whitaker. 2022. "From the Artist's Contract to the Blockchain Ledger: New Forms of Artists' Funding Using Equity and Resale Royalties." *Journal of Cultural Economy* 46 (2): 287–315. https://doi.org/10.1007/s10824-022-09445-8.

Vasileva, Sofia, and Tina Petrova. 2019. "Virtual Reality Development and the Socialization of Bulgarian Cultural Heritage." *Journal of International Cooperation and Development* 2 (1): 34–34. https://doi.org/10.36941/jicd-2019-0005.

Weatherbed, Jess. 2023. "Vinyl Overtakes CD Sales for the First Time since 1987." www.theverge.com/2023/3/10/23633605/vinyl-records-surpasses-cd-music-sales-us-riaa.

Whitaker, Amy, and Roman Kräussl. 2020. "Fractional Equity, Blockchain, and the Future of Creative Work." *Management Science* 66 (10): 4594–4611. https://doi.org/10.1287/mnsc.2020.3633.

Wong, Athena Kin-Kam, and Dickson K. W. Chiu. 2023. "Digital Transformation of Museum Conservation Practices: A Value Chain Analysis of Public Museums in Hong Kong." In *Handbook of Research on Digitalization Solutions for Social and Economic Needs,* 226–242. IGI Global. https://doi.org/10.4018/978-1-6684-4102-2.ch010.

Cited content from websites was last accessed on 01 July 2023.

CHAPTER 8

The Ideal Profile of the CEO

As we have underlined more than once in the previous chapters, the role of the CEO is a multidimensional and complex one, requiring a diverse range of skills to navigate a unique set of challenges. Orchestras often face financial constraints stemming from the discrepancy between the widening cost base and the stagnation of revenues; they also confront evolving audience expectations, the need to maintain artistic excellence while exploring innovation without betraying tradition, as well as managing relationships with donors, sponsors, and the broader community. The CEO also seeks for effective coordination between the administrative staff – who are focused on efficiency and effectiveness – and the musicians and artistic teams – who are focused on arts and emotions – to ensure a harmonious yet robust organisation (Ruud 2000). In this context, a critical question emerges: given that the CEO's primary role is to make music performances possible for the audience (Sigurjónsson 2022), should the ideal CEO be a former musician or a skilled business manager with knowledge of the classical music ecosystem? In reality, both types of CEOs are found across various orchestras, and it is not uncommon for a single orchestra to experience leadership from both a manager CEO and a former-musician CEO at different times.

This chapter explores the attributes and properties of each option while considering the broader context of the management team and the ever-changing landscape of the classical music industry.

WHAT YOU WILL LEARN IN THIS CHAPTER

Section	Key Learning Points
A. Essential Qualities and Skills of a CEO	The role of an arts and culture institution's CEO is multifaceted, requiring a combination of qualities and skills to navigate the complexities of managing organisations characterised by a strong

DOI: 10.4324/9781032629636-8

Section	Key Learning Points
	emotional content and a population of highly expressive artists. While the advantages and disadvantages of being a former musician or a skilled business manager are often debated, certain essential traits transcend these categories and broadly contribute to successful management. These include strong leadership skills, effective communication, financial acumen, strategic thinking, adaptability, and a passion for music.
B. Advantages and Disadvantages of a Former Musician as CEO	The debate over whether a former musician or a skilled business manager is better suited to be a CEO is ongoing. On the one hand, former musicians have an intimate understanding of the artistic process and could better relate to musicians on a personal level, they may lack the necessary business acumen required for effective management. They may also struggle with making difficult decisions that impact their relationships with musicians or compromise artistic integrity. On the other hand, skilled business managers have strong financial and strategic thinking skills but may not fully understand the nuances of classical music-making and time-honoured traditions.
C. Advantages and Disadvantages of a Skilled Manager as CEO	While there are advantages to having a former musician as a CEO, there are also advantages to having someone with strong business and organisational managerial skills in this role. A skilled business manager brings valuable business expertise to an organisation that is facing financial constraints stemming from stagnant revenues or rising costs. They can also help balance competing priorities such as maintaining artistic excellence while exploring innovation without betraying tradition. However, some disadvantages include potential difficulty in relating well to artists or understanding the nuances and demands of classical music performances.

A. ESSENTIAL QUALITIES AND SKILLS

The role of an orchestra CEO is multifaceted and multitasking, requiring a combination of qualities and skills to navigate the complexities of managing a cultural organisation. While the advantages and disadvantages of being a former musician or a skilled business manager are often debated, certain essential traits transcend these categories and broadly contribute to successful management. This section discusses the key qualities and skills that a CEO must possess to lead their organisation effectively and nurture growth and innovation while preserving the artistic integrity of the ensemble.

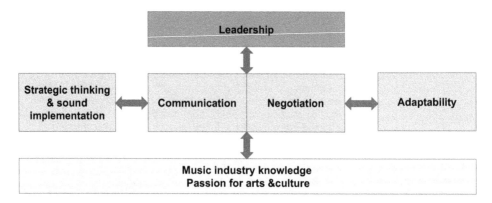

FIGURE 8.1 CEO as a Leader

1 **Leadership:** A strong leader is crucial to the success of any organisation, and arts and culture institutions are no exception. An effective CEO inspires and motivates musicians, staff, and board members alike based on a shared vision and a sense of purpose within the ensemble. This requires a delicate balance of confidence and humility, as well as the ability to listen and empathise with the diverse perspectives and needs of the orchestra community. A successful leader also demonstrates decisiveness and sound judgement in decision-making, guiding the team with clarity and conviction.

2 **Communication:** Effective communication is a pillar of successful management. A CEO must be able to articulate the ensemble's artistic vision and organisational goals clearly and persuasively, both internally and externally. This requires excellent written and verbal communication skills, as well as the ability to tailor messaging to different audiences, from musicians and staff to donors, patrons, and community partners. The CEO must be an active listener too, creating an open and inclusive environment that encourages dialogue and strong relationships with all stakeholders.

3 **Negotiation:** Orchestras often face complex negotiations, whether it be with musicians' unions, venue management, artists' agents, financial institutions, sponsors, or external partners. In-house negotiations are also frequent – for example, it is not always easy to align the finance team that needs to cope with money constraints with the artistic department that swears only by the standards of beauty and harmony. Strong negotiation abilities are essential to navigate these situations, seeking mutually beneficial outcomes that serve the best interests of the ensemble and its stakeholders. This requires a deep understanding of the organisation's needs and priorities, and the ability to

think strategically and creatively. Additionally, an effective negotiator demonstrates patience, persistence, and emotional intelligence, balancing assertiveness with diplomacy and tact.

4   **From Strategic Thinking to Sound Implementation:** In a rapidly shifting and notably fragmented cultural landscape, a CEO must excel as both a strategic thinker and a capable implementer. The ability to anticipate trends and pinpoint opportunities for growth and innovation is crucial, as is the capacity to seamlessly execute devised strategies. Adept strategic thinking encompasses the usual analysis of strengths, weaknesses, opportunities, threats, and other frameworks, followed by the development of a long-term strategic plan that is in harmony with the ensemble's artistic vision and organisational objectives. However, strategic thinking alone is insufficient. A successful CEO must also possess the skills to translate ideas into actionable roadmaps and tangible outcomes. This includes setting priorities, allocating resources judiciously, and closely monitoring progress. In a certain way, CEOs help their organisations remain focused, adaptable, and primed to tackle challenges and opportunities in the classical music world if they maintain a balance between forward-thinking strategy and efficient implementation.

5   **Adaptability:** We have seen several times already that as with any professional organisation, orchestras are subject to constant change, from shifts in audience preferences and funding landscapes to technological advancements and sociopolitical developments. Adaptability and resilience, as well as availability to consider change and respond effectively to new situations, emergencies, or simply seize a chance, are common prerequisites for successful management. This requires a willingness to question assumptions, learn from setbacks, and try innovation while remaining true to the ensemble's core artistic values. In addition, an adaptable leader recommends a culture of agility and searches for continuous improvement, ensuring that the organisation remains responsive and relevant in its dynamic environment and beyond.

While the ideal profile of a CEO varies depending on the specific needs and context of the arts and culture scene, certain essential qualities and skills are universally important for effective management. Leadership, communication, negotiation, strategic thinking, and adaptability are all crucial attributes that contribute to long-term vitality. Cultivating these traits and championing a collaborative environment helps the CEO navigate the complexities of the cultural sector and ensure enduring artistic and organisational growth for the ensemble.

BOX 8.1 LORI ZUPAN AND RICCARDO MUTI: ONE PASSION, TWO APPROACHES

The management of arts and culture institutions, such as orchestras, often sparks debates about whether these institutions are better managed by business-oriented individuals or former musicians. The real-life cases of Lori Zupan at the Ann Arbor Symphony and Riccardo Muti at the Chicago Symphony shed light on these two perspectives.

Lori Zupan served as the business manager of the Ann Arbor Symphony for 35 years. Her tenure was marked by a combination of her love for classical music and expertise in business administration (Coffee 2023). Zupan's work was not confined to the traditional boundaries of a business manager. Over the years, she undertook nearly all of the jobs in the organisation, demonstrating her versatility and commitment. Her comprehensive understanding of the organisation and its history made her a go-to person and the linchpin of the orchestra's continuity. The diverse set of responsibilities she managed was so vast that, upon her retirement late 2022, her role had to be divided among several individuals.

On the other hand, the Chicago Symphony was directed by Riccardo Muti, a renowned conductor with an illustrious career in music. Muti's tenure as the music director began in the 2010–2011 season, and he was declared the music director emeritus for life starting from the next season (Associated Press 2023). His profound musical understanding, shaped by decades of international experience, undoubtedly influenced the orchestra's performances and its artistic direction.

Comparing these two cases, it appears that a business manager like Lori Zupan brings a set of unique advantages to an orchestra. While her passion for classical music was essential, her business expertise and broad skill set were instrumental in handling the diverse administrative and financial tasks necessary for the orchestra's smooth functioning. These skills, often honed through experience in varied roles, allowed her to understand and address the multiple aspects of running an orchestra, from marketing and education to development and financial management.

In contrast, a former musician as an executive director has an in-depth understanding of music and performance but might not have the same breadth of experience in administrative and business-related tasks. The distinct roles and responsibilities necessitate a division of labour between artistic and administrative duties, potentially leading to the need for additional staff or resources.

Thus, while both business managers and former musicians make substantial contributions to the management of orchestras, their impact is likely felt in different areas. The choice between the two depends on the specific needs and circumstances of the orchestra at a given time, making it essential for orchestras to carefully consider these factors when selecting their leadership.

B. ADVANTAGES AND DISADVANTAGES OF A FORMER MUSICIAN

Advantages	Disadvantages
• **Deep understanding of the artistic process**: A former musician has a more profound appreciation of the creative process and the intricacies of performance. This facilitates better communication with musicians and a supportive environment. A specialist CEO has a better understanding of the specific needs of their industry (Gounopoulos and Pham 2018). • **A shared language**: Having a background in music allows the CEO to communicate more effectively with the artistic staff and address their concerns more directly. • **Credibility with the musicians and the public**: A CEO who has been a musician may be more respected by the musicians and artistic staff, as well as the audience, due to their shared passion and experience. • **Sensitivity to artistic needs**: A former musician has a better understanding of the necessary resources and support required for musicians to thrive, ensuring that their needs are prioritised. • **Strong network in the music world:** A former musician is likely to have connections within the industry, which helps in several instances (talent recruitment, collaboration opportunities, etc.).	• **Potential lack of management skills**: A former musician may not have the necessary skills or experience in managing a complex organisation, leading to potential inefficiencies and miscommunication. • **Difficulty in adapting to a new role**: A former musician may struggle to transition from an artistic role to an administrative one, which creates tension and hinders effective decision-making. • **Limited perspective**: A CEO with a background solely in music may lack exposure to broader industry trends and best practices, potentially hindering the ability to adapt and innovate. An expert CEO may lack the exposure to a variety of different industrial backgrounds that nourishes innovation and creative thinking (Custodio, Ferreira, and Matos 2013). • **Risk of favouritism**: A CEO with a strong musical background might display favouritism toward certain musicians or styles, leading to an imbalance in the repertoire or internal conflicts. • **Increased likelihood of managerial conflict** with the artistic director and the conductor regarding authority and artistic vision.

C. ADVANTAGES AND DISADVANTAGES OF A SKILLED BUSINESS MANAGER

Advantages	Disadvantages
• **Strong organisational and strategic skills**: A skilled business manager is likely to have experience in developing strategies, managing resources, and executing plans effectively, which benefits the overall performance. • **Broader industry perspective**: A CEO with a background in management has a broader and more comprehensive understanding of the music industry and its trends, enabling them to identify new opportunities and challenges. • **Transferable skills from other industries**: A manager with experience in various sectors brings fresh ideas and insights, helping the orchestra to view things from a different angle, innovate, and adapt to the changing landscape as long as the new imported perspectives fit the strategic directions (Cheng et al. 2020). • **Business acumen**: A skilled manager is likely to have a strong understanding of business management (financial, HR, marketing and PR, organisation, operations, etc.), ensuring stability and long-term sustainability. • **Ability to build a diverse team**: A CEO with a management background may be more adept at assembling a diverse team with complementary skills, contributing to a more dynamic and effective organisation.	• **Limited artistic understanding**: A CEO without a background in music may struggle to connect with musicians and the artistic staff, potentially creating communication barriers and misunderstandings. • **Perception of being an outsider**: A skilled manager without a music background may face scepticism from musicians and the public, making it harder to establish credibility and trust. They are often perceived as willing to transform everything (Cummings and Knott 2018) for the sole sake of change and leaving their own mark. • **Overemphasis on business aspects**: A CEO who prioritises business management over artistic vision may risk compromising the quality of the performances and its connection with the audience while introducing instability (Karaevli and Zajac 2013) by breaking the balance between artistic and non-artistic components. • **Lack of emotional connection to the art**: A CEO without a musical background might not have the same emotional investment in the artistic programming, execution, and performances, potentially impacting their ability to advocate for its artistic mission.

***

In summary:

	Former Musician CEO	Skilled Manager CEO
Advantages	1 Deep understanding of the artistic process 2 A shared language 3 Credibility with musicians and the public 4 Sensitivity to artistic needs 5 Strong network in the music world	1 Strong organisational and strategic skills 2 Broader industry perspective 3 Transferable skills from other industries 4 Business acumen 5 Ability to build a diverse team

	Former Musician CEO	Skilled Manager CEO
Disadvantages	1 Potential lack of management skills 2 Difficulty in adapting to a new role 3 Limited perspective 4 Risk of favouritism 5 Increased likelihood of managerial conflict with the artistic director and the conductor	1 Limited artistic understanding 2 Perception of being an outsider 3 Overemphasis on business aspects 4 Lack of emotional connection to the art

The role of a CEO is indeed complex and layered, and the ideal profile should encapsulate a balance of artistic vision and sound management practices. When considering the broader context of the management team, it becomes clear that an effective CEO complements, rather than duplicates, the expertise of their artistic counterparts. As the examples of automotive and airline industries demonstrate, CEOs are not expected to be Formula 1 champions, excellent mechanics, plane pilots, or outstanding turbo-reactor engineers in their respective fields. Instead, their primary responsibility is to be an excellent business manager who leads and guides the organisation effectively.

Nowadays, orchestral activities often extend beyond music performances in resident theatres or concert halls. In fact, a variety of special projects and initiatives outside the "domestic walls" are proposed to the community. These include concerts for sponsors, chamber recitals at corporate events, academic lectures, introductory music sessions in kindergarten, community outreach activities, and, last but not least, performances in different cities or countries. Additionally, orchestras may be involved in recording music for movies or TV ads, playing entertaining gigs for well-known consumer brands, creating exciting content for social media, and collaborating with local or international startups to test novel technologies in domains relevant to live music, such as virtual reality concert experiences or innovative music education tools. Some ensembles may even participate in cross-disciplinary projects, fusing music with other forms of art such as dance, visual arts, or theatre. A majority of annual activities might consist of these special projects, which demand an acute sense of project management to be executed successfully. A CEO with a background in management is more likely to possess the necessary project management skills to handle these diverse initiatives, as opposed to a musician CEO who may lack experience in that area; however, this is not a standard rule.

This means prioritising strong management skills and the ability to shape a collaborative environment. A CEO with these qualities brings together the artistic director, conductor, musicians, and other team members to create a harmonious and successful organisation. Focusing on the broader needs, including financial stability, audience engagement, and organisational growth, enables a skilled manager to survive the landmines of the classical music industry.

While a background in music certainly is beneficial in certain situations, it is not an absolute prerequisite for a successful CEO. Instead, a CEO should be an excellent business and organisational leader first and foremost, capable of leveraging the expertise of the artistic director, conductor, and other team members to create a flourishing organisation. When they combine strong business management skills and a leadership attitude with an appreciation for the artistic process and the unique challenges of the classical music industry, CEOs ensure the continued maturing of the orchestra, making the case for prioritising management abilities over musical expertise, especially if the senior management team already comprises artistic profiles.

CASE STUDY 8.1

The Recruitment of a New CEO

The departure of a long-serving CEO leaves an orchestra at a crossroads, creating uncertainty and posing challenges for board members and staff alike. This case study delves into the strategic considerations and recruitment process of a new CEO to ensure a smooth transition and continued success.

IDENTIFYING THE NEEDS

- Assessing the current situation: strengths, weaknesses, opportunities, and threats.
- Determining the necessary skills and qualities for the new CEO.
- Establishing the orchestra's short- and long-term goals.

CREATING A SEARCH COMMITTEE

- Selecting board members, musicians, and staff representatives.
- Defining roles and responsibilities.
- Developing a timeline for the recruitment process.

DEVELOPING A COMPREHENSIVE JOB DESCRIPTION

- Outlining the CEO's key responsibilities and expectations.
- Specifying required qualifications, experience, and skills.
- Highlighting the values and mission.
- Providing a clear overview of the reporting structure.

SOURCING CANDIDATES

- Utilising industry networks and professional contacts.
- Advertising in relevant publications and job boards.
- Hiring a recruitment agency specialised in the arts sector.

SCREENING AND INTERVIEW PROCESS

- Reviewing applications and shortlisting candidates.
- Conducting initial interviews and assessing cultural fit.
- Holding panel interviews with key stakeholders, including board members and musicians.
- Evaluating candidate presentations or proposals.

CANDIDATE ASSESSMENT

- Evaluating candidates based on skills, experience, and organisational fit.
- Considering potential risks and rewards associated with each candidate.
- Seeking external input, such as references and industry insights.

NEGOTIATING TERMS AND FINALISING THE APPOINTMENT

- Extending a formal job offer to the selected candidate.
- Negotiating contract terms, including compensation and benefits.
- Announcing the appointment and introducing the new CEO to the organisation.

The recruitment of a new CEO is a critical decision. The challenge is to identify and recruit a leader who demonstrates the skills, experience, and vision needed to guide the organisation into the future. Key lessons learned from this case study include the importance of understanding the unique needs, involving relevant stakeholders in the recruitment process, and making decisions based on a comprehensive assessment of candidates. Following these principles ensures smooth leadership transitions and continued success under new management.

Box 8.2 Expanding Perspectives: Review Questions

1 Given the multifaceted (and multitasking) role of a CEO, delve into the debate surrounding the ideal qualities and skills required for this position. Discuss the necessity for strong leadership, effective communication, financial acumen, strategic thinking, adaptability, and a passion for music. How do these qualities contribute to successful management? Can they be cultivated, or are they inherent traits?

2 The advantages and disadvantages of a former musician transitioning into the role of a senior manager are a hotly contested topic. Evaluate the pros and cons of this transition, focusing on how a former musician's intimate understanding of the artistic process and ability to relate personally to musicians enhances or detracts from effective management. What challenges could arise when such individuals must make difficult decisions impacting their relationships with musicians or artistic integrity?

3 The role of a skilled business manager as a CEO offers distinct advantages and disadvantages. Analyse the potential benefits and drawbacks associated with a business manager in this role, particularly with respect to bringing business expertise to arts and culture institutions facing growing financial constraints. How can a skilled manager balance competing priorities such as maintaining artistic excellence whilst exploring innovation without betraying tradition? Discuss the potential issues a skilled manager might face in terms of relating to musicians or understanding the nuances of classical music-making.

BIBLIOGRAPHY

Associated Press. 2023. "Riccardo Muti Becomes Chicago Symphony Orchestra's Music Director Emeritus for Life." *WPXI*. www.wpxi.com/entertainment/riccardo-muti/2S5UE3PFYYRZMIWTI6W4RUUUA4/.

Cheng, Teng Yuan, Yue-Qi Li, Yu-En Lin, and Hsiang-Hsuan Chih. 2020. "Does the Fit of Managerial Ability with Firm Strategy Matters on Firm Performance." *Journal of Asian Finance Economics and Business* 7 (4): 9–19. https://doi.org/10.13106/jafeb.2020.vol7.no4.9.

Coffee, Makayla. 2023. "Ann Arbor Symphony Orchestra's Business Manager Retires after 35 Years." www.mlive.com/news/ann-arbor/2023/01/ann-arbor-symphony-orchestras-business-manager-retires-after-35-years.html.

Cummings, Trey, and Anne Marie Knott. 2018. "Outside CEOs and Innovation." *Strategic Management Journal* 39 (8): 2095–2119. https://doi.org/10.1002/smj.2792.

Custodio, Claudia, Miguel A. Ferreira, and Pedro P. Matos. 2013. "Do General Managerial Skills Spur Innovation?" *SSRN Electronic Journal.* Elsevier BV. https://doi.org/10.2139/ssrn.2289701.

Gounopoulos, Dimitrios, and Hang Pham. 2018. "Specialist CEOs and IPO Survival." *Journal of Corporate Finance* 48 (February): 217–243. https://doi.org/10.1016/j.jcorpfin.2017.10.012.

Karaevli, Ayse, and Edward J. Zajac. 2013. "When Do Outsider CEOs Generate Strategic Change? The Enabling Role of Corporate Stability." *The Journal of Management Studies* 50 (7): 1267–1294. https://doi.org/10.1111/joms.12046.

Ruud, Gary. 2000. "The Symphony: Organizational Discourse and the Symbolic Tensions Between Artistic and Business Ideologies." *Journal of Applied Communication Research: JACR* 28 (2): 117–143. https://doi.org/10.1080/00909880009365559.

Sigurjónsson, Njörður. 2022. "Orchestra Leadership." In *Managing the Arts and Culture,* edited by Constance DeVereaux, 1st ed., 240–262. London: Routledge.

Cited content from websites was last accessed on 1 July 2023.

CHAPTER 9

Conclusion

Throughout the course of this book, we have travelled the steep paths of the fascinating world of orchestra management, shedding light on the unique challenges faced by CEOs and managers in a rapidly evolving landscape. The task of managing an orchestra is far from simple, requiring not only a deep understanding of artistic, financial, and operational aspects but also an ability to navigate an unusual organisational structure where key figures, such as the artistic director and conductor, may not report directly to the CEO while the musicians and the artistic department may not even have a background or culture of business efficiency and effectiveness.

Management is, without a doubt, a demanding and intricate profession. The mutating landscape of the music industry, the omnipresent digital age, and the continuous evolution of audience demographics and expectations necessitates that senior managers be adaptable, innovative, forward-thinking, and concrete all at the same time. Operating in this peculiar environment calls for a comprehensive skill set that encompasses artistic vision, financial acumen, operational expertise, and community engagement, among other vital competencies.

There is a legendary anecdote involving the great maestro Arturo Toscanini that underscores the complex and delicate balance required in management. In 1937, Toscanini was approached to conduct the newly formed NBC Symphony Orchestra. He agreed to take the baton, but only under the condition that the ensemble would consist of the finest musicians available. This seemingly straightforward request set in motion a monumental undertaking, as the management at NBC found themselves tasked with assembling an entirely new ensemble from the ground up, grappling with the logistical, financial, and artistic challenges intrinsic to such an endeavour. Toscanini's unwavering artistic standards and commitment to excellence were mirrored by the NBC management's determination to provide the necessary resources and support, ultimately culminating in the creation of a world-class ensemble that

DOI: 10.4324/9781032629636-9

premiered on 25 December 1937.[1] This story – where the line between facts and poetic legend is not clear – not only highlights the importance of synergy between the artistic and business, organisational, strategic, financial, and other components of a management team but also serves as a vivid reminder of the crucial role that managers play in making artistic excellence possible. This lesson remains relevant today, as demonstrated, for example, by the work of Deborah Borda, who served as President and CEO of the Los Angeles Philharmonic (LA Phil) between 2000 and 2017. To elevate LA Phil to a much higher level of excellence, CEO Deborah Borda did not merely bring in a new remarkable conductor or better administrative staff and more efficient operations personnel, but rather improved all the components of the non-artistic and artistic staff, including the musicians, through a comprehensive approach (Los Angeles Philharmonic Orchestra 2016).

As we now look towards the future of management, several emerging trends and challenges come to the forefront. The long-term impact of the Covid-19 pandemic has forced performing arts to adapt and find new ways to reach audiences and generate revenue through virtual performances, streams, and digital platforms. This shift towards digital engagement presents both challenges and opportunities, as they seek to balance the need for innovation and accessibility with the desire to preserve the live concert experience.

Changing demographics also play a significant role in the evolution of management. As society, audiences, and musicians become more diverse, performing arts reflect (or sometimes anticipate) this trend, welcoming inclusivity and engaging with a wider range of communities. This requires rethinking programming, educational initiatives, and outreach efforts, as well as fostering a more inclusive environment within the organisation itself.

The potential influence of globalisation on the classical music industry cannot be ignored. Orchestras that are exposed to a broader range of artistic influences and potential collaborations they would want to explore also face intensified competition for funding, talents, and audiences. In an increasingly interconnected world, managers sometimes struggle to navigate the complexities of international partnerships and cultural exchange while maintaining their artistic identity and integrity. The ability to adapt, innovate, and stay at the forefront of technological advancements is therefore paramount. Senior managers encounter the challenge of traversing the intricate webs woven within their organisation's unique structures, all the while harmonising artistic excellence and sound management practices.

Throughout this book, we have emphasised the pressure on managers to embrace the digital transformation that has permeated every aspect of modern life, including the field of classical music. We have scrutinised the impact of social media platforms, data analytics, and emerging technologies such as artificial intelligence (AI), virtual reality, and augmented reality on the industry. Senior managers who harness these state-of-the-art tools significantly enhance audience engagement and revenue generation while ensuring the continued vitality of classical music in the digital age.

To better equip managers in manoeuvring the challenging terrain of their profession, this book offers an exhaustive framework for understanding the various components of management and a practical toolbox designed to support them in their day-to-day tasks. The inclusion of case studies throughout the book, checklists, templates, and key performance indicators (KPIs) as a complete dedicated chapter enables readers to apply the theoretical knowledge gleaned from the book directly to real-world situations, bridging the chasm between theory and practice.

The diverse range of potential readers for this book includes students embarking upon a career in orchestra management, seasoned managers and CEOs of arts and culture institutions willing to refresh their knowledge and maintain focus on the essential aspects of their field, musicians striving to broaden their understanding of the non-artistic aspects of the profession, board members and stakeholders involved in the governance and oversight of artistic organisations, arts administrators and professionals from other sectors of the creative industries, academics and business school teachers in search of fresh perspectives on key management concepts, and classical music enthusiasts, sponsors, and patrons eager to delve deeper into the behind-the-scenes workings.

The landscape of the arts world presents both formidable challenges and exciting opportunities for those involved in management. The ability to adapt, innovate, and remain on the cutting edge of technological advancements is paramount for today's managers and CEOs. At the same time, they get through the complexities of the unique organisational structure within their orchestras, finding a balance between artistic excellence and sound management practices.

This book seeks to provide readers with a comprehensive understanding of the many facets of management while also supplying them with practical tools and resources to help them confront this dynamic and challenging field. The insights, perspectives, and guidance shared within these pages are intended to ease growth, innovation, and success in the evolving ecosystem of the arts world.

As we close this exploration of orchestra management, let us remember the words of the renowned conductor Leonard Bernstein, who once said, "Music can name the unnameable and communicate the unknowable." Indeed, the ultimate goal of every senior manager and CEO is to create memorable, transformative musical experiences that will endure in the hearts and minds of audiences for generations to come, pushing emotions beyond words. To achieve this noble objective, they remain vigilant, staying on top of the most important things that comprise their profession, and continuously strive for excellence in both artistic and managerial realms.

It is our hope that this book will serve as an invaluable resource, empowering readers to acknowledge and handle the peculiarities of management with confidence, skill, and grace. In doing so, they will not only contribute to the continued vitality and evolution of classical music but also help ensure that the art form remains a cherished and integral part of our global cultural tapestry.

In conclusion, this book aspires to be a guiding light for students, CEOs, and managers tasked with steering the course of orchestras in the turbulent seas of a rapidly changing world. May it equip them with the knowledge, tools, and inspiration needed to face the challenges and seize the abundant opportunities that lie ahead. As they embark on this noble endeavour, let them keep in mind the insightful words of Vincent van Gogh: "Great things are done by a series of small things brought together." And, as CEOs navigate the complex and interconnected components of management while students are still learning them, let them all remember the wisdom of mathematician Isaac Newton: "If I have seen further, it is by standing on the shoulders of giants." By attending to the numerous small yet crucial elements that constitute management and by building on the successes and lessons learned from those who came before, students and managers will not only contribute to the flourishing and evolution of classical music but also ensure that the art form remains a vibrant and treasured thread in the rich tapestry of our global cultural heritage.

NOTE

1 The NBC Symphony Orchestra's first broadcast concert aired on 13 November 1937, directed by maestro Monteux.

BIBLIOGRAPHY

Los Angeles Philharmonic Orchestra. 2016. "Deborah Borda." *LA Phil*. www.laphil.com/musicdb/artists/740/deborah-borda.
    Cited content from websites was last accessed on 01 July 2023.

CHAPTER 10

Key Resources

A. CHECKLISTS FOR CASE STUDIES AND MANAGERS

Orchestra management requires a deep understanding of the artistic, financial, and administrative aspects of the organisation. To be successful in this role, one needs to possess a broad range of skills, including strategic planning, financial management, marketing, fundraising, and human resources management.

In this section, we provide comprehensive checklists designed to guide students and managers through weekly, monthly, quarterly, and annual tasks and milestones, as well as separate checklists that cover specific areas of interest. These checklists encompass key aspects of management and are designed to ensure that senior students and managers stay organised and maintain a strategic focus on the organisation's goals and objectives. With these checklists, we aim to offer a valuable tool to assist students and professionals in understanding how the workload is structured and managed.

These checklists are intended to serve as an **indicative starting point**, and they should be adapted to suit the unique needs and circumstances of each individual organisation or case study. As the classical music industry is continuously evolving, managers need to stay abreast of emerging trends, best practices, and innovative solutions. This flexibility and adaptability enables them to respond effectively to the changing landscape and ensures long-term success and sustainability.

In crafting these checklists, we have drawn inspiration from a vast dataset of general management and orchestra management knowledge and insights. Our objective is to provide a thorough and comprehensive resource that covers the essential aspects of orchestra management while also encouraging whoever will use these resources to think creatively and strategically about their own specific situation.

The time-related checklists are organised into four distinct categories, each focusing on a different time frame: weekly, monthly, quarterly, and annual

DOI: 10.4324/9781032629636-10

tasks and milestones. This structure enables users to prioritise and manage their responsibilities effectively, ensuring that critical tasks are completed in a timely manner and that strategic goals remain at the forefront of their decision-making process.

1 The **weekly checklist** serves as a foundation for the CEO's routine, focusing on essential tasks only such as reviewing upcoming events, meeting with key staff members, monitoring finances, and communicating with board members. This checklist ensures that CEOs maintain a strong grasp on the day-to-day operations while also staying in close contact with their team and stakeholders.

2 The **monthly checklist** builds upon this foundation, encompassing more strategic and long-term tasks such as evaluating financial performance, overseeing human resources management, and preparing board meetings. Incorporating these tasks into their monthly routine allows CEOs to maintain a strategic perspective on their organisation's progress and make necessary adjustments for ongoing success.

3 The **quarterly checklist** delves deeper into the strategic planning process, requiring CEOs to review and update their strategic plan, evaluate marketing and audience development strategies, conduct performance reviews, and run and coordinate the board meetings. This checklist encourages CEOs to take a step back from the day-to-day operations and assess the overall health and direction of their organisation.

4 Finally, the **annual checklist** focuses on key milestones and events that occur throughout the year, such as conducting annual strategic planning retreats, preparing financial statements and reports, and overseeing annual fundraising activities. This checklist serves as a reminder for CEOs to maintain a long-term perspective on their goals and objectives while ensuring that critical annual tasks are completed effectively.

These checklists are designed to provide senior students and managers with a valuable tool that empowers them to maintain a strategic focus on the organisation's success by offering a structured and organised approach to managing tasks and milestones. However, let's repeat that it is essential to remember that these checklists are intended as a starting point, and each student and professional should adapt the checklists to suit their own specific needs and circumstances.

The orchestra industry is a dynamic landscape, and it is vital for CEOs to stay informed, adaptable, and innovative. These checklists are, therefore, a foundation that CEOs are free to leverage to remain proactive and strategic in their decision-making, ultimately leading to greater success and sustainability for their organisation.

While these checklists are a tool for effective management, they do not suffice; managers should invest in their own professional development and growth too. This may involve participating in industry conferences and attending workshops or networking events with fellow professionals. Staying connected to the wider orchestra community and continuously learning from the experiences and insights of others are a guarantee for CEOs to further widen their skill set and knowledge, which ultimately benefits their organisation.

To establish a strong relationship with their staff, board members, musicians, and volunteers should be a primary objective for managers. When they instil a collaborative and supportive work culture, CEOs inspire their team to excel in their roles, leading to a more efficient and successful organisation.

Finally, a strong focus on their audience and stakeholders is a key quality expected from managers. CEOs ensure that their organisation remains relevant and resonates with the community it serves by staying attuned to the needs and preferences of their audience, as well as continuously seeking feedback and input from their stakeholders.

In summary, the checklists provided in this chapter are designed to support students and managers in their journey towards effective and strategic management. CEOs can create a tailored and efficient management system that enables them to navigate the complex world of management with confidence and success by using these checklists as a foundation and adapting them to their unique circumstances. We hope these checklists serve as a valuable resource for students and aspiring and existing professionals as they strive to lead their organisations towards a bright future.

Weekly Checklist

Tasks	Comments
Review Upcoming Events and Concerts	
☐ Confirm rehearsal schedules and logistics	
☐ Review and approve concert programmes and materials	
☐ Ensure venue arrangements are in place	

Tasks	Comments
Meet With Key Staff Members	
☐ Discuss current projects and priorities	
☐ Address any concerns or issues that have arisen	
Review Financials	
☐ Monitor income and expenses	
☐ Review budget-to-actuals and address any discrepancies	
☐ Follow up on outstanding invoices or payments	
☐ Analyse financial trends and projections	
Communicate With Board Members	
☐ Share updates on recent activities and upcoming events	
☐ Address any concerns or requests for information	
Review Marketing and Communication Efforts	
☐ Monitor audience engagement on social media and other channels	
☐ Review upcoming marketing and PR campaigns	
☐ Analyse and report on marketing metrics	
Monitor Ongoing Fundraising Efforts	
☐ Track progress towards fundraising goals	
☐ Touch base with major donors and sponsors	
☐ Identify potential new funding sources	
☐ Prepare grant applications and reports	

Monthly Checklist

Tasks	Comments
Review Strategic Plan Progress	
☐ Assess progress towards short-term and long-term goals	
☐ Identify areas for improvement or adjustment	
☐ Discuss updates with the board and staff	
Evaluate Financial Performance	
☐ Review monthly financial statements	
☐ Compare actual performance to budget	
☐ Make necessary adjustments to financial plans	
Oversee Human Resources Management	
☐ Review staff performance and professional development	
☐ Address any personnel issues or concerns	
☐ Recognise staff achievements and contributions	
Prepare Board Meetings	
☐ Produce comprehensive monthly reports to share with board members	
☐ Overview logistics for the next board meeting	
Review Marketing, Communication, PR	
☐ Review and assess the progress of previous and ongoing campaigns and initiatives	
☐ Plan the coming campaign	
☐ Assess the alignment of the campaign with the strategy	
☐ Collect data and analyse the performance	

Quarterly Checklist

Tasks	Comments
Review and Update Strategic Plan	
☐ Assess progress towards strategic objectives	
☐ Update strategic plan based on new developments or challenges	
Prepare Quarterly Financial Reports	
☐ Compile financial data and analysis	
☐ Present reports to the board and staff	
Evaluate Marketing and Audience Development Strategies	
☐ Review audience engagement data and trends	
☐ Assess the effectiveness of marketing campaigns and initiatives	
☐ Make adjustments to marketing strategies as needed	
Conduct Performance Reviews	
☐ Meet with staff members to discuss performance and goals	
☐ Provide feedback and support for professional growth	
Conduct Board Meetings	
☐ Prepare and distribute meeting materials	
☐ Facilitate discussions on key topics and decisions	
☐ Ensure board members are informed and engaged	

Annual Checklist

The annual checklist for students and managers provides a comprehensive overview of key tasks and milestones to be addressed throughout the year. This checklist helps maintain a strategic focus on long-term goals and priorities, ensuring that the organisation continues to grow, evolve, and thrive. As with the other checklists, this should be seen as a starting point, and students and managers are encouraged to tailor it to their unique requirements.

Tasks	Comments
Strategy and Vision	
☐ Review and update the organisation's strategic plan	
☐ Evaluate progress towards the achievement of long-term goals	
☐ Identify new opportunities for growth, expansion, and collaboration	
☐ Assess the organisation's artistic direction and programming	
☐ Review and fine-tune the organisation's mission, vision, and values	
Financial Management	
☐ Prepare and submit the annual budget and reports	
☐ Review financial performance and trends, making adjustments as needed	
☐ Complete year-end financial reporting and auditing	
☐ Evaluate the effectiveness of fundraising initiatives and identify areas for improvement	
☐ Assess the organisation's financial health and sustainability	
Board and Governance	
☐ Conduct an annual board evaluation and identify areas for improvement	
☐ Review and update board policies and procedures	
☐ Plan and facilitate board retreats, workshops, or training sessions	
☐ Recruit and onboard new board members, if any	
☐ Review and update the board's strategic plan	
Human Resources	
☐ Conduct annual performance evaluations for staff, musicians, and volunteers	

Tasks	Comments
☐ Review and update job descriptions and responsibilities	
☐ Identify and address any skills gaps within the team	
☐ Implement professional development and training opportunities	
☐ Assess and update the organisation's succession plan	

Marketing and Audience Development

☐ Review and evaluate marketing, communication, and PR strategies	
☐ Assess the effectiveness of audience engagement initiatives	
☐ Identify new opportunities for audience development and growth	
☐ Evaluate the organisation's digital presence and online strategies	
☐ Gather and analyse audience feedback and preferences	

Community and Stakeholder Engagement

☐ Cooperate with community partners and stakeholders to assess the orchestra's impact	
☐ Review and update community outreach and education programs	
☐ Identify new opportunities for collaboration and partnership	
☐ Assess the effectiveness of stakeholder communication and strategies	
☐ Evaluate the organisation's social impact and relevance	

Sustainability and Environmental Impact

☐ Review and update the organisation's sustainability plan	
☐ Assess the effectiveness of environmental initiatives and identify areas for improvement	

Tasks	Comments
☐ Work with stakeholders on sustainability issues and concerns	
☐ Monitor and report on the organisation's environmental performance	
☐ Identify opportunities for collaboration on sustainability projects	
Risk Management and Compliance	
☐ Review and update the organisation's risk management plan and the risks register	
☐ Assess the effectiveness of crisis management and contingency planning	
☐ Ensure compliance with legal and regulatory requirements	
☐ Review insurance coverage and make adjustments as needed	
☐ Conduct an annual review of safety and security measures	

An annual checklist is a master guide or a compass to maintain a strategic focus on the key areas of the organisation. This checklist is a starting point, and students and managers should feel empowered to adapt it to suit their unique needs.

Sustainability Checklist

Actions	Comments
1. Set Specific Sustainability Goals and Create an Action Plan ☐ Outline short-term, mid-term, and long-term objectives ☐ Assign responsibilities to specific staff members or departments ☐ Monitor progress regularly and adjust the plan as needed	

Actions	Comments
2. Regularly Track Energy Consumption and Set Reduction Targets ☐ Install energy monitoring systems for electricity, gas, and water usage ☐ Implement a schedule for turning off lights and equipment when not in use ☐ Develop an energy reduction competition among different departments	
3. Opt for Energy-Efficient Equipment and Lighting ☐ Replace traditional bulbs with LED lighting ☐ Upgrade to energy-efficient appliances and equipment when replacements are needed ☐ Install motion sensors for lighting in common areas	
4. Establish a Comprehensive Waste Reduction and Recycling Programme ☐ Provide recycling bins for paper, plastic, glass, and other materials ☐ Implement composting for organic waste in staff areas ☐ Encourage the use of reusable water bottles and coffee cups ☐ Replace disposable items with reusable or biodegradable alternatives	
5. Promote Sustainable Transportation for Musicians, Staff, and Audiences ☐ Offer incentives for using public transport, cycling, or carpooling ☐ Organise group transportation for musicians when travelling to performances ☐ Provide bicycle racks and changing facilities for staff and musicians	
6. Define Sustainable Procurement Policies ☐ Choose suppliers with strong environmental and ethical credentials ☐ Prioritise purchasing locally sourced and eco-friendly products ☐ Incorporate sustainability criteria in vendor selection and contracts	

Actions	Comments
7. Educate Staff, Musicians, and Audiences on Sustainability Initiatives ☐ Organise workshops, seminars, or training sessions on environmental issues ☐ Communicate the sustainability goals and progress through newsletters, social media, and website updates ☐ Encourage audience members to participate in sustainability efforts, such as recycling or using public transport	
8. Implement Sustainable Practices for Touring and Performances ☐ Evaluate the environmental impact of tour transportation and accommodations ☐ Collaborate with venues to ensure waste reduction and recycling efforts ☐ Use digital materials for marketing and communication instead of printed materials	
9. Evaluate the Sustainability of the Repertoire and Materials ☐ Consider the environmental impact of sheet music and opt for digital alternatives when possible ☐ Use eco-friendly materials for instruments, props, and costumes ☐ Collaborate with composers and artists to incorporate environmental themes into performances	
10. Regularly Review and Adjust the Sustainability Plan ☐ Schedule annual sustainability assessments and update the action plan accordingly ☐ Share successes and challenges with the wider community ☐ Continuously look for opportunities to improve and expand sustainability efforts	

Digital and Physical Accessibility Checklist

Actions	Comments
1. Evaluate Current Accessibility Levels ☐ Perform a venue accessibility audit ☐ Assess digital content and platforms for accessibility compliance	
2. Develop an Accessibility Plan ☐ Set short-term, mid-term, and long-term accessibility goals ☐ Involve key stakeholders in the planning process (e.g., staff, volunteers, patrons, and people with disabilities)	
3. Enhance Physical Accessibility ☐ Improve venue entrances, exits, and ramps ☐ Ensure adequate wheelchair seating and companion seating options ☐ Install accessible restrooms and facilities ☐ Offer accessible parking and drop-off areas	
4. Improve Sensory Accessibility ☐ Offer assistive listening devices (e.g., hearing loop systems) ☐ Provide audio description services for visually impaired patrons ☐ Implement sign language interpretation for deaf or hard-of-hearing patrons ☐ Plan sensory-friendly performances with adjusted sound levels and lighting	
5. Enhance Digital Accessibility ☐ Ensure websites and digital content follow Web Content Accessibility Guidelines (WCAG) ☐ Offer alternative formats for digital content (e.g., large print, audio, or Braille) ☐ Incorporate captions and transcripts for video content ☐ Test digital platforms with accessibility tools and users with disabilities	
6. Train Staff and Volunteers on Accessibility Best Practices ☐ Provide regular training on disability awareness and etiquette ☐ Train staff on the use of assistive technologies and devices ☐ Encourage open communication and feedback regarding accessibility improvements	

Actions	Comments
7. Communicate Accessibility Offerings to Patrons ☐ Clearly state accessibility options on the website, marketing materials, and tickets ☐ Develop an accessibility guide for patrons ☐ Ensure staff are knowledgeable about accessibility offerings to assist patrons	
8. Monitor Progress and Gather Feedback ☐ Regularly review accessibility goals and progress ☐ Gather feedback from patrons, staff, and volunteers to identify areas for improvement ☐ Update accessibility plans and practices based on feedback and best practices	

Diversity, Equity, and Inclusion Checklist

Actions	Comments
1. Assess Current Diversity, Equity, and Inclusion (DEI) Levels ☐ Conduct a DEI audit of staff, board, musicians, and volunteers ☐ Evaluate current diversity and inclusion policies and practices	
2. Develop a DEI Strategy ☐ Set short-term, mid-term, and long-term DEI goals ☐ Involve key stakeholders in the planning process (e.g., staff, musicians, board members, and community representatives)	
3. Implement Inclusive Hiring Practices ☐ Use diverse recruitment channels to reach a wider pool of candidates ☐ Implement bias-free screening and interview processes ☐ Offer competitive and equitable compensation packages	

Actions	Comments
4. Support a DEI Organisational Culture ☐ Encourage open dialogue and feed-back about DEI issues ☐ Celebrate cultural and personal differences among staff and musicians ☐ Establish an anti-discrimination and anti-harassment policy	
5. Provide DEI Training ☐ Offer regular training on DEI and unconscious bias ☐ Train leaders to champion DEI initiatives ☐ Provide resources and support for staff and musicians to learn about diverse cultures and experiences	
6. Target Diverse Programming and Collaborations ☐ Showcase works by composers from underrepresented backgrounds ☐ Collaborate with diverse artists, conductors, and soloists ☐ Partner with community organisations to co-create inclusive programs	
7. Increase Outreach and Engagement With Diverse Communities ☐ Develop targeted marketing and communication strategies to reach diverse audiences ☐ Offer accessible and inclusive educational and community programs ☐ Involve diverse community leaders and organisations for mutual support and partnership	
8. Monitor Progress and Gather Feedback ☐ Regularly review DEI goals and progress ☐ Gather feedback from staff, musicians, board members, and the community to identify areas for improvement ☐ Update DEI strategies and practices based on feedback and best practices	

B. USEFUL MANAGEMENT TOOLS

In this section, we offer a range of templates and KPIs designed to assist students and managers in streamlining the orchestral organisations.[1] These resources have been carefully curated as examples and guidelines to help facilitate efficient and effective management.

Every orchestra is unique, and, therefore, the provided tools should be viewed as a starting point. Students and professionals are encouraged to adapt the content, focus, and topics to better align with their individual and organisational needs and requirements or case studies. By customising these resources, they ensure that the management toolbox is most relevant and beneficial to their specific organisation. The aim is to provide a solid foundation upon which aspiring professionals and actual managers could build, ensuring a more targeted and personalised approach to managing their organisations. Tailoring these tools to their specific circumstances fosters a greater sense of ownership and participation, ultimately leading to enhanced performance and a more harmonious and successful organisation.

***

Templates

Fundraising Plan

The scope of this template is to provide a list of the necessary steps to create a comprehensive and actionable strategy for raising funds.

Actions	Comments
1. Fundraising Goals ☐ Define the overall financial target ☐ Break the target down into specific goals (e.g., individual donations, corporate sponsorships, grants, events)	
2. Donor Segmentation and Targeting ☐ Identify and categorise potential donor groups (e.g., individuals, corporations, foundations) ☐ Research and profile key prospects within each group ☐ Determine tailored strategies and messaging for each donor segment	

Actions	Comments

3. Fundraising Strategies and Channels
Select fundraising strategies (e.g., direct mail, online campaigns, events, major gifts)
• *Direct mail*
  ☐ Develop mailing list
  ☐ Create compelling letters and collateral materials
  ☐ Schedule mailings
• *Online campaigns*
  ☐ Develop email list
  ☐ Design email templates and content
  ☐ Schedule email campaigns
• *Events*
  ☐ Determine event format and theme
  ☐ Develop event budget and timeline
  ☐ Secure sponsors, vendors, and venue
• *Major gifts*
  ☐ Identify and research potential major donors
  ☐ Develop solicitation strategies	

4. Donor Stewardship
• *Develop a donor cultivation plan*
  ☐ Schedule regular communication touchpoints (e.g., newsletters, updates, invitations)
  ☐ Plan and execute donor cultivation events
• *Create a donor stewardship plan*
  ☐ Acknowledge and thank donors promptly
  ☐ Provide regular impact reports and updates
  ☐ Implement a donor recognition programme (e.g., naming opportunities, plaques, special events)	

5. Fundraising Team and Responsibilities ☐ Establish a fundraising committee ☐ Assign specific roles and responsibilities to team members ☐ Schedule regular committee meetings to review progress and adjust strategies	
6. Fundraising Calendar ☐ Develop an annual fundraising calendar ☐ Schedule key activities, events, and deadlines ☐ Plan for regular progress check-ins and adjustments	

Actions	Comments
7. Fundraising Budget ☐ Estimate costs for each fundraising strategy and activity ☐ Allocate resources according to priorities and expected return on investment (ROI) ☐ Track expenses and adjust the budget as needed	
8. Performance Metrics and Evaluation ☐ Determine key performance indicators (KPIs) for each fundraising strategy ☐ Establish a system for tracking and reporting on KPIs ☐ Regularly review performance and adjust strategies as needed	

Special Event Marketing Plan

This template aims at easing the definition of a comprehensive and actionable strategy for promoting an event, attracting the right target audience, and achieving the event objectives.

Actions	Comments
1. Event Overview ☐ Define the event's purpose and objectives ☐ Identify the target audience for the event ☐ Establish the event's date, time, and location	
2. Branding and Messaging ☐ Develop an event brand (e.g., logo, theme, tagline) ☐ Create key messages to convey the event's purpose and objectives	

3. Marketing Channels and Strategies
Select marketing channels (e.g., website, social media, email, print)
• *Website*
  ☐ Create an event page with essential information and registration details
  ☐ Publicise the event on the homepage and relevant sections	

Actions	Comments
• *Social media* ☐ Develop a social media posting schedule ☐ Create event-specific graphics and content ☐ Engage with followers and encourage sharing • *Email* ☐ Develop an email campaign schedule ☐ Design email templates and content ☐ Segment email list for targeted messaging • *Print* ☐ Design print materials (e.g., posters, flyers, invitations) ☐ Distribute print materials in strategic locations	
4. Public Relations and Media Outreach ☐ Develop a press release announcing the event ☐ Identify relevant media contacts and outlets ☐ Send a press release and follow up with media contacts	
5. Event Partnerships and Collaborations ☐ Identify potential partners for cross-promotion (e.g., sponsors, local businesses, community organisations) ☐ Develop partnership proposals and agreements ☐ Coordinate joint marketing efforts with partners	
6. Paid Advertising ☐ Determine an advertising budget ☐ Select advertising channels (e.g., online, print, radio) ☐ Develop ad creatives and schedule ad placements	
7. Audience Engagement and Interaction ☐ Plan pre-event activities (e.g., contests, giveaways, Q&As) ☐ Develop event-specific hashtags for social media ☐ Encourage audience interaction during the event (e.g., live-tweeting, photo sharing, polls)	

Actions	Comments
8. Event Registration and Ticketing ☐ Select a ticketing platform ☐ Set up event registration and ticket sales ☐ Inform about ticket availability and pricing through marketing channels	
9. Marketing Calendar ☐ Develop an event marketing timeline ☐ Schedule key marketing activities, deadlines, and milestones ☐ Plan for regular progress check-ins and adjustments	
10. Performance Metrics and Evaluation ☐ Determine key performance indicators (KPIs) for event marketing success ☐ Establish a system for tracking and reporting on KPIs ☐ Regularly review performance and adjust strategies as needed	

Self-Assessment Framework

This "orchestra-oriented" self-assessment framework is a tool that students, managers, and principal musicians could use to evaluate their organisation's (or department's or section's) strengths, weaknesses, opportunities, and threats (SWOT analysis), enabling them to make informed decisions and strategically address areas of concern.

Strengths	Weaknesses
Artistic Quality and Reputation ☐ Evaluate the orchestra's artistic achievements ☐ Assess the quality and reputation of the musicians and conductor ☐ Review recent critical acclaim and awards **Organisational Structure and Management** ☐ Examine the effectiveness of the organisational structure ☐ Evaluate the leadership and management team's skills and experience ☐ Assess the efficiency of communication and decision-making processes	**Artistic Challenges** ☐ Identify areas for artistic improvement or growth ☐ Assess the adequacy of rehearsal and performance facilities ☐ Consider potential challenges in attracting and retaining top talent **Organisational and Management Issues** ☐ Identify inefficiencies or gaps in the organisational structure ☐ Evaluate areas for improvement in leadership and management ☐ Assess potential communication or decision-making issues

Strengths	Weaknesses
Financial Stability ☐ Review the financial health and sustainability ☐ Evaluate the diversity and stability of revenue streams ☐ Assess the effectiveness of fundraising and development strategies	**Financial Concerns** ☐ Identify financial vulnerabilities or areas of concern ☐ Evaluate the effectiveness of current financial management practices ☐ Assess the stability of funding sources and opportunities for growth
Opportunities	**Threats**
Artistic and Programming Opportunities ☐ Identify potential collaborations or partnerships ☐ Explore new or innovative programming ideas ☐ Consider opportunities for international touring or exposure **Organisational and Management Growth** ☐ Evaluate potential improvements to the organisational structure ☐ Assess opportunities for leadership development and training ☐ Identify strategies for communication and decision-making **Financial and Fundraising Opportunities** ☐ Explore new or untapped funding sources ☐ Assess potential growth opportunities in fundraising and development ☐ Evaluate the potential for diversifying revenue streams	**Artistic and Industry Challenges** ☐ Assess potential competition from other orchestras or arts organisations ☐ Identify industry trends or challenges that may impact the orchestra ☐ Evaluate potential threats to the artistic reputation **Organisational and Management Risks** ☐ Identify potential risks or challenges in the organisation's structure ☐ Assess possible leadership or management challenges ☐ Evaluate potential risks related to communication and decision-making **Financial and Economic Threats** ☐ Assess potential economic or financial risks ☐ Evaluate potential threats to funding sources or financial stability ☐ Identify potential financial management concerns or risks

Volunteer Management Plan

This actionable volunteer management plan template helps recruit, train, and manage volunteers while fostering a positive and supportive volunteer culture. Orchestras must maximise the value and contributions of their volunteers, creating a more successful and sustainable organisation by implementing a structured plan instead of approaching volunteer support in an opportunistic or case-by-case manner.

Actions	Comments

Recruitment
• *Define Volunteer Needs*
  ☐ Identify areas where volunteers are more likely to provide effective support
  ☐ Determine the number of volunteers required
  ☐ Develop clear volunteer role descriptions
• *Advertise Volunteer Opportunities*
  ☐ Inform about volunteer opportunities on the website, social media channels, etc.
  ☐ Reach out to local community groups, schools, and universities
  ☐ Utilise volunteer recruitment platforms and networks
• *Volunteer Selection*
  ☐ Develop an application form to gather relevant information
  ☐ Conduct interviews to assess candidates' suitability and interest
  ☐ Check references and complete any necessary background checks	

Training and Onboarding
• *Orientation*
  ☐ Provide a general introduction to the orchestra and its mission
  ☐ Introduce new volunteers to key staff members and other volunteers
  ☐ Offer a tour of the facilities and workspaces
• *Role-specific Training*
  ☐ Offer detailed training for each volunteer role
  ☐ Pair new volunteers with experienced volunteers for mentorship and support
  ☐ Provide written materials and resources for reference
• *Ongoing Support and Development*
  ☐ Schedule regular check-ins with volunteers to address questions or concerns
  ☐ Offer opportunities for additional training and skill development
  ☐ Encourage volunteer feedback and suggestions for improvement	

Actions	Comments

Management and Communication
• *Establish Clear Expectations*
  ☐ Provide guidelines on the policies and procedures
  ☐ Communicate expectations regarding commitment, punctuality, and professionalism
  ☐ Clarify the roles and responsibilities of staff members and volunteers
• *Promote a Positive Volunteer Culture*
  ☐ Encourage open communication and collaboration among volunteers and staff
  ☐ Recognise and celebrate volunteer contributions and achievements
  ☐ Organise social events and gatherings to foster camaraderie
• *Maintain Effective Communication*
  ☐ Establish regular communication channels, such as email updates or newsletters
  ☐ Schedule volunteer meetings to discuss updates and share information
  ☐ Offer opportunities for volunteers to provide feedback and voice concerns	

Evaluation and Retention
• *Volunteer Performance Evaluation*
  ☐ Develop a volunteer performance evaluation process
  ☐ Offer constructive feedback and address any areas of concern
  ☐ Acknowledge and celebrate volunteers' accomplishments and growth
• *Volunteer Retention*
  ☐ Recognise and show appreciation for volunteers' contributions
  ☐ Offer opportunities for volunteers to take on new roles or responsibilities
  ☐ Maintain open communication and address any concerns promptly
• *Offboarding and Succession Planning*
  ☐ Develop a plan for transitioning volunteers out of their roles
  ☐ Conduct exit interviews to gather feedback and insights
  ☐ Plan for succession and replacement of departing volunteers	

Crisis Communication Plan

This customisable crisis communication plan template provides a practical framework for managing internal and external communication during challenging times. Orchestras ensure effective communication and maintain trust and credibility with stakeholders when they follow and adapt these guidelines to their specific needs.

Actions	Comments

Preparation and Planning
• *Identify Potential Crises*
  ☐ Conduct a risk assessment to identify possible crisis scenarios
  ☐ Consider the likelihood and potential impact of each scenario
• *Establish a Crisis Communication Team*
  ☐ Designate key staff members to be part of the team
  ☐ Assign specific roles and responsibilities to each team member
  ☐ Ensure team members are trained and prepared for their roles
• *Develop a Crisis Communication Plan*
  ☐ Create a comprehensive plan, including guidelines for internal and external communication
  ☐ Establish protocols for monitoring, reporting, and escalating crisis
  ☐ Ensure the plan is regularly updated and reviewed	

Crisis Resolution
• *Identify Crisis Causes*
  ☐ Conduct an initial assessment to determine the underlying cause(s) of the crisis
  ☐ Gather relevant information and evidence to support the assessment
• *Hire Internal and External Experts*
  ☐ Identify internal experts to provide guidance on addressing the crisis
  ☐ Consult with external experts if necessary to gather additional insights and recommendations
• *Develop a Crisis Resolution Plan*
  ☐ Define the objectives and strategies for resolving the crisis
  ☐ Outline specific actions and responsibilities for each team member
  ☐ Establish a timeline for implementing the resolution plan	

Actions	Comments
• *Monitor Progress and Adjust the Plan* ☐ Track the implementation of the resolution plan and evaluate its effectiveness ☐ Adjust strategies and actions as needed based on progress and new information ☐ Communicate any changes to the plan with relevant stakeholders	
Internal Communication • *Activate the Crisis Communication Team* ☐ Notify team members and initiate the crisis communication plan ☐ Schedule regular team meetings to monitor and address the situation • *Communicate With Staff and Volunteers* ☐ Provide regular updates on the situation, including any necessary actions or precautions ☐ Address any questions or concerns in a timely and transparent manner ☐ Offer support and resources for staff and volunteers affected by the crisis • *Document and Evaluate the Response* ☐ Keep detailed records of all internal communications and actions taken ☐ Conduct a post-crisis evaluation to identify areas for improvement and learning	
External Communication • *Identify and Prioritise Stakeholders* ☐ Determine the stakeholders most affected by the crisis ☐ Prioritise communication with these stakeholders based on their level of impact • *Develop Key Messages and Talking Points* ☐ Draft clear and concise messages to convey the essential information ☐ Ensure messages are consistent, accurate, and empathetic ☐ Update messages as needed to reflect new information or developments • *Choose Appropriate Communication Channels* ☐ Select the most effective channels for reaching each stakeholder group (e.g., email, social media, press releases) ☐ Ensure all channels are monitored and updated regularly • *Engage With Media and the Public* ☐ Designate a spokesperson to represent the orchestra during the crisis ☐ Prepare the spokesperson with key messages and talking points ☐ Monitor media coverage and respond to inquiries promptly and professionally	

Actions	Comments
• *Post-Crisis Communication* ☐ Provide updates and follow-up information as the situation resolves ☐ Communicate any changes or actions taken to prevent future crises ☐ Express gratitude for the support and understanding of stakeholders	

Annual Artistic Programming

This template for Annual Artistic Programming includes quarterly evaluation and follow-up sections to ensure a comprehensive and dynamic approach to artistic programming.

Annual Planning	
Actions	*Comments*
Define Artistic Vision and Goals ☐ Review and refine the artistic vision and mission ☐ Set specific artistic goals for the upcoming year ☐ Align goals with the strategic plan and audience development strategy	
Identify Themes and Special Events ☐ Brainstorm potential themes or focus areas for the programming ☐ Consider incorporating special events, anniversaries, or commemorations ☐ Align themes and events with the artistic vision and goals	
Develop Programme Line-up ☐ Select repertoire, guest artists, and collaborators ☐ Ensure diversity and balance in programming ☐ Consider audience preferences, community engagement, and educational opportunities	
Establish Performance Schedule ☐ Determine the number and timing of concerts and events ☐ Coordinate with venue availability and other scheduling considerations ☐ Finalise dates and times for all performances	

Monitoring and Follow-up

Actions	Comments

First Quarter
• *Review Annual Plan*
  ☐ Assess progress towards artistic goals
  ☐ Identify any necessary adjustments to the programming or schedule
  ☐ Address any challenges or opportunities that have emerged	

• *Monitor Audience*
  ☐ Analyse ticket sales, attendance, and audience feedback
  ☐ Evaluate the effectiveness of marketing and promotional efforts
  ☐ Adjust strategies as needed to maximise audience engagement
• *Prepare for Upcoming Performances*
  ☐ Confirm repertoire, guest artists, and production details
  ☐ Coordinate rehearsal schedules and logistics
  ☐ Update marketing and communication materials	

Second Quarter
• *Mid-Year Review*
  ☐ Assess progress towards artistic goals and make adjustments as needed
  ☐ Evaluate the success of completed performances and events
  ☐ Identify opportunities for improvement or new initiatives
• *Monitor Audience*
  ☐ Continue analysing ticket sales, attendance, and audience feedback
  ☐ Refine marketing strategies based on performance to date
  ☐ Connect with the community to gather input and build relationships
• *Prepare for Upcoming Performances*
  ☐ Finalise details for the remaining performances in the year
  ☐ Ensure all production elements are on track and on budget
  ☐ Update marketing and communication materials	

Actions	Comments

Third Quarter
• *Review Annual Plan*
  ☐ Assess progress towards artistic goals and identify any remaining challenges or opportunities
  ☐ Begin planning for the following year's programming
  ☐ Evaluate the effectiveness of the artistic programming overall
• *Monitor Audience*
  ☐ Analyse end-of-year ticket sales, attendance, and audience feedback
  ☐ Assess the impact of community engagement and educational efforts
  ☐ Determine areas for improvement in audience development	

• *Wrap-up and Evaluation*
  ☐ Gather feedback from musicians, staff, and stakeholders on the artistic programming
  ☐ Conduct a comprehensive evaluation of the year's artistic achievements
  ☐ Identify lessons learned and best practices to inform future programming	

Fourth Quarter
• *Year-end Evaluation and Pre-planning*
  ☐ Reflect on the accomplishments and challenges of the past year's programming
  ☐ Assess the overall success and impact of the artistic programming
  ☐ Begin preliminary planning for the following year, incorporating lessons learned and new opportunities	

Stakeholder Analysis

A sound stakeholder analysis is a crucial step in the strategic planning and decision-making process. It enables the students and managers to identify and understand the key stakeholders who influence or are affected by the organisation's activities, goals, and objectives. Evaluating the needs, expectations, and interests of each stakeholder group allows the managers to develop targeted solutions, proposals, and communication strategies, fostering positive relationships and the business performance.

This stakeholder analysis template is designed to guide the students and managers through the process of identifying and prioritising the stakeholders, as well as mapping their interests, influence, and potential impact. Students and managers should feel free to use this template as a starting point and adapt it to better suit their specific needs and requirements.

Identify Stakeholders

Students and managers should begin by listing all relevant stakeholders, including individuals, groups, and organisations that may have an interest in or be affected by the activities. Examples of stakeholders include:

- Musicians
- Staff
- Board members
- Audience members
- Donors and sponsors
- Partner organisations
- Local community
- Media outlets
- Government agencies and regulators

Categorise Stakeholders

Group the stakeholders into categories based on their relationship to the organisation. Examples of categories might be:

- Internal stakeholders: Musicians, staff, board members
- External stakeholders: Audience members, donors and sponsors, partner organisations
- Community stakeholders: Local community, media outlets, government agencies

Prioritise Stakeholders

Assess the importance of each stakeholder group by considering their level of influence and interest in the orchestra. Prioritise stakeholders by placing them into a matrix based on their:

- Level of interest: How invested is the stakeholder in the activities and success?

- Level of influence: How much power does the stakeholder have to affect the performance and decision-making?

Map Stakeholder Interests and Expectations

For each stakeholder group, identify their key interests, needs, and expectations. Consider the following:

- What are their main concerns or priorities related to the orchestra?
- What do they expect from the organisation?
- How might their interests align or conflict with the goals and objectives?

Assess Stakeholder Impact

Evaluate the potential impact each stakeholder group may have on the business or artistic performance and decision-making. Consider the following:

- How does the stakeholder positively or negatively affect the organisation?
- What opportunities or challenges do they present?
- How important is their support or approval for the success?

Develop Stakeholder Strategies

Based on the analysis, the students or managers develop targeted strategies for each stakeholder group. The following are to be considered:

- What type of engagement is most appropriate for each stakeholder (e.g., consultation, collaboration, information sharing)?
- How can the manager address their needs and expectations while also achieving the orchestra's goals?
- What communication channels and methods are most effective for each stakeholder group?

Upon completion of this stakeholder analysis, students and managers will have gained valuable insights into the relationships, interests, and expectations of your key stakeholders. This information will enable them to create more effective strategies for communication and collaboration, ultimately enhancing the performance.

7-S Framework

The 7-S Framework is a management model developed by McKinsey & Company that focuses on seven internal elements of an organisation that must be aligned for it to be successful. While the framework was not specifically designed for the classical music industry, it can easily be applied to it. Here is a version focused specifically on the orchestra business and industry, with suggestions for what the CEO should focus on for each element.

1 **Strategy**: Developing a clear and compelling strategy is a priority for the CEO. They focus on identifying the orchestra's unique value proposition, target audience, and revenue streams. This includes decisions about what repertoire to perform, which venues to play in, and how to work with audiences.

2 **Structure**: Designing an organisational structure that supports the goals and objectives is a priority for the CEO. They focus on creating a structure that allows for efficient decision-making, effective delegation of responsibilities, and productive relationships with external partners and stakeholders.

3 **Systems**: Implementing efficient and effective systems and processes to support the organisation's operations is a priority for the CEO. They focus on developing and implementing systems for financial management, concert production, marketing and PR, and audience engagement that work together seamlessly.

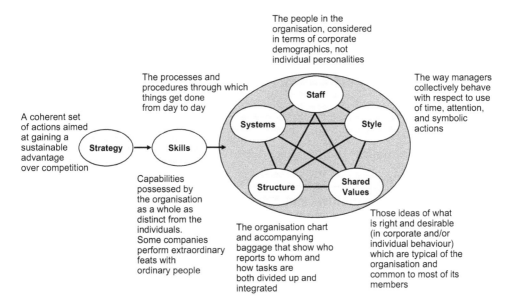

FIGURE 10.1 The 7-S Framework

4 **Staff**: Recruiting and retaining top talent is a priority for the CEO. They focus on creating a positive work environment, providing competitive compensation and benefits, and offering career development opportunities to musicians and administrative staff.

5 **Skills**: Ensuring that musicians and staff have the technical and artistic skills required to deliver high-quality performances is a priority for the CEO. They focus on providing ongoing training and professional development opportunities, as well as performance evaluations to identify areas for improvement.

6 **Style**: Contributing to a positive and collaborative organisational culture is a priority for the CEO. They focus on open communication, effective conflict resolution, and collaborative decision-making to support creativity, innovation, and excellence.

7 **Shared Values**: Identifying and promoting shared values that guide the organisation's decision-making and behaviours is a priority for the CEO. They focus on values related to artistic excellence, community engagement, diversity and inclusion, and financial sustainability. By aligning these values with the goals and operations, the CEO creates a strong and resilient organisation that weathers any challenges that come its way.

The CEO focuses on developing a clear and compelling strategy, designing an effective organisational structure, implementing efficient and effective systems and processes, recruiting and retaining top talent, providing ongoing training and professional development opportunities, championing a positive organisational culture, and shared values that support the organisation's decision-making and behaviour.

Examples of Key Performance Indicators (KPIs)

KPIs for CEO

Financial Performance:

- Revenue growth: Assess the CEO's ability to drive revenue growth through effective business strategies and efficient operations.
- Profit margin: Evaluate the CEO's success in maintaining a healthy profit margin by controlling costs and maximising revenue.
- Financial sustainability: Measure the CEO's effectiveness in ensuring long-term financial stability.
- Contractors and providers: Determine financial sustainability and cost optimisation of contracts with external service providers.

Strategy and Vision:

- Strategic planning: Evaluate the CEO's ability to develop and implement a clear and compelling strategic vision.
- Organisational alignment: Assess the CEO's success in aligning the organisation's various departments and functions with the overall strategic vision.
- Adaptability: Measure the CEO's effectiveness in responding to changes in the industry and adapting the organisation's strategy accordingly.

Governance and Board Relations:

- Board engagement: Evaluate the CEO's ability to effectively work with the board, keeping them informed and involved in key decisions.
- Board satisfaction: Assess the level of satisfaction among board members with the CEO's leadership, communication, and strategic direction.
- Compliance: Measure the CEO's success in ensuring compliance with all relevant laws, regulations, and governance standards.

Team Leadership and Management:

- Employee satisfaction: Evaluate the CEO's ability to maintain a high level of employee satisfaction and morale within the organisation.
- Talent development: Assess the CEO's success in fostering a culture of professional development and growth for employees.
- Organisational culture: Measure the CEO's effectiveness in establishing a positive, inclusive, and collaborative organisational culture.
- Sustainability: Assess the impact of measures taken to promote sustainability in several areas.

Stakeholder Relationships:

- Community engagement: Monitor the number of outreach and educational events organised.
- Community impact: Measure the impact on the community through surveys or direct feedback.
- Accessibility: Monitor the availability of accessible seating, parking, and accommodations for patrons with disabilities.
- Partnership development: Measure the CEO's effectiveness in establishing and nurturing strategic partnerships with other organisations.

Donor and Sponsor Management:

• Donor retention rate: Assess the percentage of recurring donors.
• Sponsorship acquisition: Track the number of new sponsorships secured.
• Donor and sponsor satisfaction: Gauge satisfaction levels through regular surveys or feedback.

Artistic Excellence:

• Artistic quality: Evaluate the CEO's ability to ensure the highest artistic standards are maintained across the concerts and events.
• Audience satisfaction: Assess the CEO's success in delivering exciting and relevant programming that resonates with audiences.
• Educational and community impact: Measure the CEO's effectiveness in overseeing the educational and community outreach programmes.
• Diversity, equity, and inclusivity: Ensure the music performed includes a variety of music traditions and cultures. Similarly, ensure the composers as well as the guest artists and conductors are selected against transparent criteria of diversity, equity, and inclusivity. Quantify wherever possible, and report regularly.

Innovation, New Technologies, and Digital Content Production:

• Technological innovation: Evaluate the CEO's ability to identify and integrate new technologies and digital tools into the operations and concerts.
• Digital content strategy: Assess the CEO's success in developing and executing a robust digital content strategy, including streaming, recordings, and social media content.
• Digital audience growth: Measure the CEO's effectiveness in growing the digital audience through innovative online initiatives.
• Digital revenue streams: Evaluate the CEO's ability to develop and exploit new digital revenue streams, such as online ticket sales, digital subscriptions, and licensing agreements.
• Continuous improvement: Assess the CEO's commitment to embracing innovation, staying abreast of industry trends, and continuously improving the digital offerings.

Staff and Human Resources:

• Overall staff satisfaction: Gauge employee satisfaction levels through regular surveys.

- Staff turnover rate: Monitor the number of employees leaving the organisation.
- Staff performance: Assess the performance of employees based on annual evaluations or other performance metrics.
- Diversity, equity, and inclusivity: Monitor the evolution of diversity, equity, and inclusivity in the staff overall.

Marketing and Communications:

- Brand awareness: Monitor the level of public recognition and familiarity with the brand.
- Media coverage: Track the amount of media coverage the organisation receives.
- Digital presence: Assess the growth and quality of the online presence, including website traffic and social media.

Risk Management:

- Risk identification: Regularly identify potential risks and vulnerabilities within the organisation.
- Risk mitigation: Monitor the implementation of risk mitigation strategies and their effectiveness.
- Crisis response: Evaluate the effectiveness of the CEO's leadership during challenging situations or crises.

KPIs for Finance Department

Financial Health:

- Current ratio: Assess the organisation's ability to pay short-term liabilities using its short-term assets.
- Debt-to-equity ratio: Monitor the ratio of the organisation's total liabilities to its equity, indicating financial leverage.
- Operating cash flow: Measure cash generated from core operations.

Budgeting and Financial Planning:

- Budget variance: Compare actual financial results with the budgeted amounts to assess financial performance.
- Budget preparation time: Track the time taken to prepare, review, and finalise the annual budget.

- Financial forecasting accuracy: Measure the accuracy of financial forecasts by comparing them to actual results.

Financial Reporting and Compliance:

- Timely financial reporting: Monitor the timeliness of financial reports submitted to the board and other stakeholders.
- Audit findings: Assess the number and severity of audit findings, including internal and external audits.
- Regulatory compliance: Track the organisation's adherence to financial and legal regulations.

Cost Management and Efficiency:

- Cost reduction: Measure the percentage reduction in costs compared to the previous period.
- Programme cost efficiency: Assess the cost-effectiveness of individual programmes or events.
- Overhead ratio: Calculate the proportion of total expenses allocated to overhead costs, such as administration and fundraising.
- Contractors and providers: Determine the financial sustainability and cost optimisation of contracts with external service providers.

Revenue Diversification and Sustainability:

- Revenue diversification: Measure the variety of revenue sources, such as ticket sales, donations, sponsorships, and grants.
- Earned revenue ratio: Calculate the proportion of total revenue generated from earned sources, such as ticket sales and merchandise.
- Unrestricted funds ratio: Assess the percentage of unrestricted funds in relation to total revenue, indicating financial flexibility.

Investment Management:

- Investment performance: Track the returns on the organisation's investments, such as endowments or other financial assets.
- Investment risk: Monitor the risk profile of the investment portfolio.
- Asset allocation: Assess the diversification of investment assets across various classes, such as stocks, bonds, and cash equivalents.

Grant and Fundraising Management:

- Grant success rate: Measure the percentage of grant applications that result in funding.
- Fundraising efficiency: Calculate the funds raised per pound spent on fundraising efforts.
- Fund utilisation: Assess the percentage of granted funds used for their intended purpose.

Financial Systems and Processes:

- Automation rate: Monitor the percentage of financial processes that are automated.
- System integration: Assess the integration of financial systems with other organisational systems, such as CRM or ticketing platforms.
- Financial process improvement: Track the implementation of process improvements and their impact on efficiency and effectiveness.

KPIs for Artistic Director

The same KPIs apply whether the artistic director is a single individual devoted to that role or a committee of section principals.

Artistic Vision and Programming:

- Programme diversity: Assess the variety of musical genres, composers, and artists represented in the concerts and events.
- Audience engagement: Measure the response to artistic initiatives in diverse audience segments.
- Innovation: Track the implementation of innovative programming, such as multimedia performances, collaborations, or premieres of new works.
- Diversity, equity, and inclusivity: Ensure the music performed includes a variety of music traditions and cultures. Similarly, ensure the composers as well as the guest artists and conductors are selected against transparent criteria of diversity, equity, and inclusivity. Quantify wherever possible, and report regularly.

Artistic Quality:

- Performance quality: Evaluate the artistic performance standards, considering factors such as musicianship, ensemble cohesion, and overall artistic expression.

- Guest artist satisfaction: Measure the satisfaction of guest artists, conductors, and composers with their collaboration experience.
- Artistic awards and recognition: Track the number of awards, nominations, or positive reviews received by the orchestra and its musicians.

Musician Development and Support:

- Audition success rate: Monitor the percentage of successful auditions and the quality of musicians attracted.
- Musician satisfaction: Assess the overall satisfaction of musicians with their working environment, artistic direction, and professional development opportunities.
- Musician turnover rate: Measure the rate of leaving musicians, indicating the level of job satisfaction and stability.

Education and Community Outreach:

- Educational programme reach: Evaluate the number of participants in educational initiatives, such as workshops, masterclasses, or school concerts.
- Community engagement: Measure the success of programmes and collaborations aimed at community involvement and support.
- Impact assessment: Assess the impact of educational and community outreach efforts on participants using qualitative and quantitative indicators.

Collaboration and Partnership Development:

- Number of partnerships: Track the number of artistic partnerships and collaborations established with other organisations, such as ensembles, choirs, or arts institutions.
- Partnership satisfaction: Measure the satisfaction of partner organisations with their collaboration experience.
- Co-production success: Evaluate the success of co-produced projects in terms of artistic quality, audience engagement, and financial outcomes.
- Diversity, equity, and inclusion: Assess the level of diversity, equity, and inclusion using quantitative and qualitative variables. Take corrective actions when needed. Promote diversity, equity, and inclusion always.

Artistic Budget Management:

- Artistic budget variance: Compare actual artistic expenses with budgeted amounts to assess financial performance.
- Cost-effectiveness: Assess the cost-effectiveness of artistic initiatives, considering factors such as audience reach, artistic quality, and community impact.
- Return on investment: Measure the financial return on investment for artistic projects, including ticket sales, fundraising, and sponsorship revenue.

Stakeholder Communication and Relationship Management:

- Internal communication: Evaluate the effectiveness of communication with musicians, staff, and other key stakeholders.
- External communication: Assess the quality and impact of artistic communication with audiences, donors, sponsors, and the wider community.
- Relationship building: Monitor the success of relationship-building efforts with external stakeholders, such as guest artists, partner organisations, and funding bodies.

KPIs for Conductor

Artistic Leadership and Performance Quality:

- Ensemble cohesion: Evaluate the conductor's ability to create a unified sound and strong ensemble playing.
- Interpretation: Assess the conductor's skill in interpreting a diverse range of musical styles and repertoire.
- Artistic expression: Measure the conductor's effectiveness in drawing out the emotional and expressive qualities of the music.

Rehearsal and Preparation:

- Rehearsal efficiency: Evaluate the conductor's ability to use rehearsal time effectively, balancing technical and artistic development.
- Musician preparation: Assess the conductor's skill in preparing musicians for performances, including communication of artistic expectations and technical requirements.

- Adaptability: Measure the conductor's ability to adapt to unexpected challenges or changes, such as last-minute programme alterations or guest artist substitutions.

Musician Development and Support:

- Musician motivation: Evaluate the conductor's ability to inspire and motivate musicians to achieve their best performance.
- Professional development: Assess the conductor's commitment to supporting the professional growth of musicians, such as providing feedback or offering opportunities for solo performances.
- Communication and rapport: Measure the conductor's effectiveness in building strong working relationships with musicians and a positive and collaborative rehearsal environment.
- Diversity, equity, and inclusion: Track actions taken to promote and implement measures aiming at a better diversity, equity, and inclusion at every stage of the artistic and leadership workstreams.

Audience Development:

- Audience connection: Evaluate the conductor's ability to link with audiences, both during performances and through pre-concert talks or other initiatives.
- Programme accessibility: Assess the conductor's skill in creating programmes that appeal to a broad range of audience segments, including first-time concertgoers and experienced listeners.
- Audience feedback: Measure audience satisfaction with the conductor's performances using qualitative and quantitative indicators such as surveys, focus groups, or social media analysis.

Collaboration and Partnership Development:

- Collaborative skills: Evaluate the conductor's ability to work effectively with guest artists, conductors, and other collaborators.
- Partnership development: Assess the conductor's commitment to building relationships with other arts organisations, educational institutions, or community groups.
- Interdisciplinary collaboration: Measure the conductor's success in developing and executing interdisciplinary projects, such as collaborations with dance companies, theatre groups, or visual artists.

Education and Community Outreach:

- Educational leadership: Evaluate the conductor's ability to lead educational initiatives, such as workshops, masterclasses, or school concerts.
- Community engagement: Assess the conductor's commitment to community involvement and support through performances, collaborations, or other outreach efforts.
- Impact assessment: Measure the impact of the conductor's educational and community outreach efforts on participants using qualitative and quantitative indicators.

Stakeholder Communication and Relationship Management:

- Internal communication: Evaluate the conductor's effectiveness in communicating with musicians, staff, and other key stakeholders.
- External communication: Assess the conductor's skill in representing the orchestra to the public, media, donors, sponsors, and the wider community.
- Relationship building: Measure the conductor's success in building and maintaining strong relationships with external stakeholders, such as guest artists, partner organisations, and funding bodies.

KPIs for Operations Department

Concert and Event Production:

- Event execution: Evaluate the department's ability to deliver smooth, well-organised concerts and events that meet or exceed artistic and audience expectations.
- Production efficiency: Assess the team's effectiveness in managing production schedules, adhering to budgets, and meeting deadlines.
- Technical proficiency: Measure the department's success in addressing technical requirements, such as stage set-up, lighting, and sound production.

Venue and Facilities Management:

- Venue maintenance: Evaluate the department's ability to maintain clean, safe, and well-maintained performance and rehearsal spaces.
- Facility utilisation: Assess the effectiveness of the department in maximising venue usage, optimising scheduling, and minimising downtime.

- Compliance: Measure the department's success in ensuring that all facilities meet relevant health, safety, and accessibility regulations.

Logistics and Tour Management:

- Tour planning: Evaluate the department's ability to plan and execute successful tours, both domestically and internationally, within budget and time constraints.
- Travel and accommodation: Assess the team's effectiveness in managing travel, accommodation, and logistical arrangements for musicians, staff, and equipment.
- Incident management: Measure the department's ability to proactively identify and address potential risks and respond effectively to unforeseen challenges during tours.

Equipment and Inventory Management:

- Instrument care and maintenance: Evaluate the department's ability to maintain and manage the instruments, ensuring they are in optimal condition for performances.
- Inventory management: Assess the team's effectiveness in managing inventory of sheet music, supplies, and equipment, ensuring availability when needed and minimising waste.
- Equipment procurement: Measure the department's success in sourcing and procuring equipment and supplies in a cost-effective and timely manner.

Staff Management and Development:

- Staff recruitment and retention: Evaluate the department's ability to hire and retain high-quality operations staff.
- Training and development: Assess the effectiveness of the department in providing training and professional development opportunities for staff members.
- Team communication and collaboration: Measure the department's success in fostering a positive, collaborative working environment and facilitating clear communication among team members.
- Diversity, equity, and inclusion: Track actions taken to promote and implement measures aiming at a better diversity, equity, and inclusion at every stage of the operations.

Budget Management and Financial Reporting:

- Budget adherence: Evaluate the department's ability to manage operations budgets, ensuring accurate tracking and reporting of expenses.
- Cost control: Assess the team's effectiveness in identifying and implementing cost-saving measures without compromising the quality of operations.
- Financial transparency: Measure the department's success in providing clear, accurate, and timely financial reporting to stakeholders.

Sustainability and Environmental Impact:

- Resource management: Evaluate the department's ability to minimise waste and reduce the environmental impact of operations.
- Sustainable practices: Assess the team's effectiveness in implementing sustainable practices, such as energy efficiency measures or environmentally friendly procurement.
- Environmental reporting: Measure the department's success in tracking and reporting on environmental performance and sustainability initiatives.

KPIs for Human Resources Department

Recruitment and Retention:

- Talent acquisition: Evaluate the department's ability to hire and onboard high-quality candidates for open positions within the organisation.
- Employee retention: Assess the effectiveness of HR in maintaining a low staff turnover rate, employee satisfaction, and a positive work environment.
- Succession planning: Measure the department's success in identifying and developing potential leaders within the organisation, ensuring continuity and stability.

Training and Development:

- Professional development opportunities: Evaluate the department's ability to provide employees with access to relevant training, workshops, and courses.
- Skill development: Assess the effectiveness of HR in identifying skill gaps and developing plans to address them through targeted training and development initiatives.

- Performance evaluation: Measure the department's success in implementing regular performance reviews, setting clear objectives, and providing constructive feedback.

Employee Relations:

- Employee satisfaction: Evaluate the department's ability to maintain high levels of employee satisfaction through surveys, feedback mechanisms, and proactive initiatives.
- Conflict resolution: Assess the effectiveness of HR in addressing and resolving workplace conflicts, grievances, and issues in a timely and fair manner.
- Team building and communication: Measure the department's success in promoting a culture of collaboration and open communication throughout the organisation.

Compensation and Benefits:

- Market competitiveness: Evaluate the department's ability to ensure that compensation packages remain competitive within the industry, attracting and retaining top talent.
- Benefits administration: Assess the effectiveness of HR in managing and communicating employee benefits, including health insurance, retirement plans, and other perks.
- Payroll management: Measure the department's success in ensuring accurate and timely payroll processing, including compliance with tax and legal regulations.

Diversity, Equity, and Inclusion:

- Workforce diversity: Evaluate the department's ability to diversify the workforce, ensuring representation across age, gender, ethnicity, and other demographics.
- Inclusive policies and practices: Assess the effectiveness of HR in implementing equity and inclusion policies, such as flexible working arrangements and anti-discrimination rules.
- Equity: Track breaches of equity between staff categories, and propose corrective policies or measures. Assess implementation of existing measures and report on a regular basis.

- Awareness and training: Measure the department's success in raising awareness of diversity, equity, and inclusion issues and providing training on unconscious bias and cultural sensitivity.

Compliance and Risk Management:

- Legal compliance: Evaluate the department's ability to ensure that the organisation remains compliant with employment laws and regulations.
- Health and safety: Assess the effectiveness of HR in managing workplace health and safety, implementing policies and procedures, and addressing potential risks.
- Data protection and privacy: Measure the department's success in safeguarding employee data, complying with data protection regulations, and maintaining confidentiality.

HR Metrics and Reporting:

- HR analytics: Evaluate the department's ability to track and analyse key HR metrics, such as time-to-hire, cost-per-hire, and employee turnover.
- Reporting: Assess the effectiveness of HR in providing regular, accurate, and comprehensive reports on workforce data to inform decision-making.
- Continuous improvement: Measure the department's success in using data-driven insights to identify areas for improvement and implement targeted HR initiatives.

KPIs for Marketing, Communication and PR Department

Marketing Strategy and Planning:

- Annual marketing plan: Evaluate the department's ability to develop and implement a comprehensive marketing plan aligned with the organisation's objectives.
- Target audience segmentation: Assess the effectiveness of the department in identifying and targeting key audience segments.
- Market research: Measure the department's success in conducting market research to inform marketing strategies and understand audience preferences.
- Diversity, equity, and inclusion: Track actions taken to promote and implement measures aiming at a better diversity, equity, and inclusion at every stage of the marketing, PR, and communication work.

Branding and Identity:

- Brand awareness: Evaluate the department's ability to increase brand awareness through marketing initiatives and PR efforts.
- Brand consistency: Assess the effectiveness of the department in maintaining a consistent brand identity across all marketing channels and materials.
- Brand reputation: Measure the department's success in managing and enhancing the organisation's reputation through proactive PR and crisis management.

Digital Marketing and Social Media:

- Website performance: Evaluate the department's ability to maintain an appealing and user-friendly website, including monitoring key metrics such as traffic, bounce rate, and conversion rates.
- Social media: Assess the effectiveness of the department in managing social media channels, increasing followers, and driving engagement.
- Email marketing: Measure the department's success in implementing targeted email campaigns, tracking open rates, click-through rates, and conversions.

Advertising and Promotion:

- Campaign effectiveness: Evaluate the department's ability to develop and execute effective advertising campaigns across various channels, including print, digital, and outdoor advertising.
- Promotional materials: Assess the quality and effectiveness of materials produced by the department, ensuring consistency and adherence to brand guidelines.
- Return on advertising spend (ROAS): Measure the department's success in achieving a positive return on investment for advertising campaigns.

Public Relations and Media Relations:

- Media coverage: Evaluate the department's ability to secure positive media coverage, including print, broadcast, and online outlets.
- Press releases: Assess the effectiveness of the department in crafting and distributing thrilling press releases that generate media interest.
- Media relationships: Measure the department's success in building and maintaining strong relationships with key media contacts.

Sponsorship and Partnerships:

* Sponsorship acquisition: Evaluate the department's ability to identify and secure sponsorships from relevant companies and organisations.
* Partnership development: Assess the effectiveness of the department in establishing and maintaining mutually beneficial partnerships with other organisations and stakeholders.
* Sponsorship activation: Measure the department's success in leveraging sponsorships and partnerships to maximise exposure and benefits for both parties.

Event Promotion and Community Engagement:

* Event promotion: Evaluate the department's ability to effectively market events, including concerts, workshops, and community programmes.
* Attendance targets: Assess the effectiveness of the department in achieving attendance targets for events and maintaining healthy ticket sales revenue.
* Community engagement: Measure the department's success in involving the local community, raising awareness of the organisation's offerings, and forging a sense of ownership and pride.

Analytics and Reporting:

* Marketing performance metrics: Evaluate the department's ability to track and analyse key marketing performance indicators, such as customer acquisition cost, return on marketing investment, and customer lifetime value.
* Reporting: Assess the effectiveness of the department in providing regular, accurate, and comprehensive reports on marketing performance to inform decision-making.
* Continuous improvement: Measure the department's success in using data-driven insights to identify areas for improvement and implement targeted marketing initiatives.
* Diversity, equity, and inclusion: Measure and report the key criteria of diversity, equity, and inclusivity in promoting the orchestra.

Any Other Relevant and Cross-Departmental KPIs

Cross-Functional Projects and Initiatives:

* Number of successful cross-functional projects: Measure the quantity and quality of projects that involve collaboration between multiple departments.
* Cross-departmental knowledge sharing: Assess the frequency and effectiveness of cross-departmental training sessions, workshops, or meetings.
* Interdepartmental synergies: Evaluate the extent to which departments work together to streamline processes, share resources, and identify areas for improvement.

Organisational Culture and Employee Engagement:

* Employee satisfaction: Monitor the overall satisfaction of employees across all departments using regular surveys and feedback mechanisms.
* Employee retention: Measure the success of the organisation in retaining talent across all departments, with a focus on long-term employee commitment.
* Cross-departmental social events: Assess the frequency and impact of social events that create connections and rapport among employees from different departments.

Organisational Reputation and Brand Recognition:

* Public perception: Evaluate how the orchestra is perceived by the community, considering factors like brand awareness, reputation, and public opinion.
* Media coverage: Measure the success of the organisation in generating positive media coverage that encompasses multiple departments and their achievements.
* Community partnerships: Assess the quantity and quality of partnerships with other community organisations, businesses, or institutions, reflecting the commitment to collaboration and community impact.

Audience Development and Patron Experience:

* Cross-departmental audience engagement: Evaluate how various departments contribute to audience development initiatives and collaborate to enhance the patron experience.
* Patron satisfaction: Measure the overall satisfaction of patrons, considering aspects such as venue accessibility, programme variety, and customer service, which involve multiple departments.

- New audience acquisition: Assess the success of cross-departmental efforts to attract new audience segments and broaden the reach.

Innovation and Adaptability:

- Cross-departmental innovation: Evaluate the organisation's capacity to embrace change and adopt innovative solutions across all departments.
- Response to external challenges: Measure the resilience and adaptability when facing unexpected challenges, such as changes in funding, audience preferences, or global events.
- Continuous improvement: Assess the organisation's commitment to ongoing learning and improvement, with a focus on cross-departmental collaboration and shared growth.

Diversity, Equity, and Inclusivity:

- Diversity in orchestra composition: Measure the representation of individuals from diverse backgrounds and underrepresented groups, including musicians, conductors, and other artistic personnel, admin staff, and management team.
- Diverse and inclusive programming: Evaluate the diversity and inclusivity of programming by assessing the repertoire choices and composers palette that reflect a range of musical styles, cultures, historical periods, and people.
- Outreach and education initiatives: Measure the impact and reach of the outreach and educational programs aimed at engaging diverse communities and groups, particularly those with limited access to classical music.

NOTE

1 We refer here to common operations-related KPIs. For peak performance indicators of orchestra, see Marotto, Roos, and Victor (2007).

BIBLIOGRAPHY

Marotto, Mark, Johan Roos, and Bart Victor. 2007. "Collective Virtuosity in Organizations: A Study of Peak Performance in an Orchestra." *The Journal of Management Studies* 44 (3): 388–413. https://doi.org/10.1111/j.1467-6486.2007.00682.x.

About the Author

Salvino A. Salvaggio holds a PhD in social sciences and has more than 30 years of experience in innovation-intensive industries and organisations. He currently works as a Consultant to the Qatar Foundation.

Salvino's diverse background includes positions at Accenture, McKinsey & Co, Ooredoo, and Qatar Foundation, as well as serving on several boards over time. In addition, he has taught at multiple universities and launched his own tech startups. A published author and recipient of an international literary prize, Salvino was appointed Knight Commander by the President of the Italian Republic in 2007.

Index

For Product Safety Concerns and Information please contact our EU
representative GPSR@taylorandfrancis.com
Taylor & Francis Verlag GmbH, Kaufingerstraße 24, 80331 München, Germany

www.ingramcontent.com/pod-product-compliance
Ingram Content Group UK Ltd.
Pitfield, Milton Keynes, MK11 3LW, UK
UKHW051946210425
457613UK00037B/355